Improvisation and Music Education

This book offers compelling new perspectives on the revolutionary potential of improvisation pedagogy. Bringing together contributions from leading musicians, scholars, and teachers from around the world, the volume articulates how improvisation can breathe new life into old curricula; how it can help teachers and students to communicate more effectively; how it can break down damaging ideological boundaries between classrooms and communities; and how it can help students become more thoughtful, engaged, and activist global citizens. In the last two decades, a growing number of music educators, music education researchers, musicologists, cultural theorists, creative practitioners, and ethnomusicologists have suggested that a greater emphasis on improvisation in music performance, history, and theory classes offers enormous potential for pedagogical enrichment. This book will help educators realize that potential by exploring improvisation along a variety of trajectories. Essays offer readers both theoretical explorations of improvisation and music education from a wide array of vantage points, and practical explanations of how the theory can be implemented in real situations in communities and classrooms. It will therefore be of interest to teachers and students in numerous modes of pedagogy and fields of study, as well as students and faculty in the academic fields of music education, jazz studies, ethnomusicology, musicology, cultural studies, and popular culture studies.

Ajay Heble is Director of the International Institute for Critical Studies in Improvisation, and Professor of English in the School of English and Theatre Studies at the University of Guelph. He is the author or editor of several books, and the founder and Artistic Director of the Guelph Jazz Festival.

Mark Laver is an Assistant Professor of Music at Grinnell College, where he teaches classes on jazz and popular music. His work has been published in *Popular Music and Society, Popular Music, Black Music Research Journal,* and *Critical Studies in Improvisation.* Laver is also a busy saxophonist who has performed with Lee Konitz, William Parker, and Dong-Won Kim, among many other leading international artists.

Routledge Studies in Music Education

Improvisation and Music Education

Beyond the Classroom

Edited by Ajay Heble
and Mark Laver

Routledge
Taylor & Francis Group

NEW YORK AND LONDON

First published 2016
by Routledge
711 Third Avenue, New York, NY 10017

and by Routledge
2 Park Square, Milton Park, Abingdon, Oxon OX14 4RN

Routledge is an imprint of the Taylor & Francis Group, an informa business

Library of Congress Cataloging-in-Publication Data

Names: Heble, Ajay, 1961– editor. | Laver, Mark, editor.
Title: Improvisation and music education: beyond the classroom / edited by Ajay Heble and Mark Laver.
Other titles: Routledge studies in music education; 3.
Description: New York; London: Routledge, 2016.
Series: Routledge studies in music education; 3 | Includes bibliographical references and index.
Identifiers: LCCN 2016003817
Subjects: LCSH: Improvisation (Music) | Music—Instruction and study.
Classification: LCC MT68 .I47 2016 | DDC 781.3/6071—dc23
LC record available at http://lccn.loc.gov/2016003817

ISBN: 978-1-138-83016-5 (hbk)
ISBN: 978-1-315-73739-3 (ebk)

Typeset in Sabon
by codeMantra

For our parents—our first and most cherished teachers: Sushila Heble and the memory of Dr. Madhav Heble; Margaret Laver and Thomas Laver.

Contents

SECTION II
Histories, Institutions, Practices

SECTION III
Improvisation and Community-Engaged Pedagogy

List of Examples, Figures, and Tables

Examples

Figures

Table

Acknowledgments

This book has its origins in a three-day conference in Guelph, Ontario, Canada, in May 2013, on Improvisation Pedagogy and Community Impact organized by Mark Laver during his postdoctoral fellowship with the Improvisation, Community, and Social Practice (ICASP) project. Many of the chapters in this book are revised and expanded versions of presentations from that conference. We want to acknowledge everyone who participated in and contributed to the success of that event. We particularly wish to thank the Social Sciences and Humanities Research Council of Canada (SSHRC) for supporting the conference, and, indeed, for its commitment to and generous funding of both the ICASP project and the recently formed International Institute for Critical Studies in Improvisation (IICSI). SSHRC's support for our work on improvisation has made many amazing things possible.

We are grateful to all our contributors for allowing us to publish their work in this book and to the anonymous reviewers for the press who provided helpful feedback and suggestions. Thanks to Liz Levine, Andrew Weckenmann, and Nancy Chen at Routledge for their editorial guidance and support.

Special thanks to the incredible team at the International Institute for Critical Studies in Improvisation. Rachel Collins has been a mainstay of this project, and she has contributed in so many ways during our preparation of the manuscript—from formatting and standardizing the chapters and bibliographies, to corresponding with contributors, to preparing our index, to keeping us on track and on schedule. We also want to thank Kim Thorne and Elizabeth Jackson for their tremendous and ongoing support. We can't say enough about what a pleasure it is to be able to work with such dedicated, resourceful, and generous staff. Their can-do attitude has created a climate of genuine intellectual excitement out of which this project has emerged.

Much gratitude also to the Office of the Vice President (Research) at the University of Guelph, and especially to Kevin Hall and John Livernois for their kind and generous support.

An earlier version of Ajay Heble's interview with Jane Bunnett appeared on the Improvisation, Community, and Social Practice (ICASP) website (http://www.improvcommunity.ca), and in the limited-edition book, *Things*

That You Hope a Human Being Will Be: 2011 Improviser-in-Residence Jane Bunnett, edited by Ajay Heble and Alissa Firth-Eagland. We'd like to acknowledge the original publishers, ICASP and the Musagetes Foundation. The version that appears here includes an expanded preface.

Thanks to Tanya Darisi, Christine Duncan, Alissa Firth-Eagland, Kyra Gaunt, Rich Marsella, Michelle Kisliuk, Daniel Kruger, Eric Schnell, Kimber Sider, Joe Sorbara, Paul Steinbeck, Scott Thomson, Shawn van Sluys, and Ellen Waterman.

Finally, and most importantly, we are enormously grateful to our families, especially our partners, Sheila and Erin, and our children, Maya, Kiran, and Nora, whose love, support, friendship, and encouragement continue to sustain us in all our endeavors, academic and otherwise. We wish to dedicate this book to our parents—Sushila Heble and the memory of Dr. Madhav Heble and Margaret Laver and Thomas Laver. As our most cherished teachers and mentors, they have gifted us with the freedom to explore, encouraged us with the spirit of discovery, guided us with their generosity, and inspired us with their example.

1 Introduction

Improvisation and Music Education: Beyond the Classroom

Ajay Heble and Mark Laver

What does it mean to teach improvisation? Can the skills required to participate in a mode of music making that, at least in its most provocative historical instances, has sought to accent and embody real-time creative decision making, risk taking, interaction, adaptation, surprise, and responsiveness be effectively conveyed in a classroom or in a university? Is improvisation a practice that is best understood as being "learned but not taught," as Patricia Shehan Campbell asks, "or can it be facilitated by a teacher?"[1] And what happens when improvisation gets institutionalized in an academic setting? Does it run the risk of losing what many see as its critical and creative edge, its transformational capacity, the very force of its out-of-tuneness? In his important essay, "Teaching Improvised Music: An Ethnographic Memoir," George Lewis suggests, indeed, that "a good way to start a heated debate among experienced improvisors is to pose the question of whether improvisation 'can be taught'—a question which, as often as not, refers to the kind of pedagogy associated with schools."[2] Lewis continues: "As the study of improvisative modes of musicality, regardless of tradition, has begun to assume a greater role in the music departments of a number of major institutions of higher learning, it is to be expected that the nature, necessity, and eventual function of such pedagogy would be scrutinized—and eventually contested—from a variety of standpoints, both inside and outside the academy."[3]

Improvisation and Music Education: Beyond the Classroom seeks to intervene in such debates by offering compelling new perspectives on the revolutionary potential of improvisation pedagogy. Bringing together contributions from leading musicians, scholars, and teachers, the book shows us how improvisation can breathe new life into old curricula; how it can help teachers and students to communicate more effectively; how it can break down damaging ideological boundaries between classrooms and communities; and how it can help students become more thoughtful, engaged, and activist global citizens.

Improvisation has long been an uncomfortable subject for music educators. In a curricular and pedagogical paradigm that often hinges primarily on music notation—a paradigm where performance classes have historically emphasized reading and writing music, and history classes so often characterize music history as an evolving sequence of notated musical texts—improvisation has often been disparaged, devalued, and treated as an afterthought, if not entirely ignored. In the last two decades, however, a growing number of music educators, music education researchers, musicologists, cultural theorists, creative practitioners, and ethnomusicologists have suggested that a greater emphasis on improvisation in music performance, history, and theory classes, as well as within the context of broader community settings, offers enormous potential for pedagogical enrichment along a number of trajectories.

First, as a curricular focus, as Gabriel Solis suggests, improvisation offers a "way out" of the ossified logocentric canons and hierarchies that have long structured music education.[4] When we conceive of "musical works" not as fixed texts but as improvisatory musical processes and continuities that are forever in flux—if we heed Christopher Small's call to reconceive of music as a lived process that is radically contingent upon the real world experiences of the participants[5]—we can begin to imagine new critically reflexive possibilities for music theory and historiography that deconstruct the hegemony of "great composers" and their "great works."

Second, as a pedagogical method, improvisation invites educators to "deterritorialize the classroom."[6] Following the scholarship-cum-advocacy of critical pedagogues like Paulo Freire and bell hooks, improvisation as a pedagogical heuristic demands that music teachers recognize the intrinsic dynamism and fluidity of knowledge, and calls on teachers to conceive of their work as a critical dialogue with their students rather than a simple transfer (or what Freire famously termed "banking") of a fixed pool of information.[7]

Finally, improvisation can teach a critical acuity and an ethic of deep empathy toward alternative voices that has the potential to empower students, help them develop greater socio-critical awareness, and inculcate a sense of human empathy and obligation. Indeed, many pedagogues engaging with improvisatory methodologies search for ways to bring learning outside of the classroom by developing applied research projects that bring students (as well as educators) into contact with marginalized and aggrieved communities. For these teachers and scholars, improvisational pedagogies demand engagement with communities outside of the traditional sites of institutionalized education.

Recognizing its potential to enrich music education, a rapidly growing number of state and provincial governments across the U.S. and Canada have made improvisation a mandatory part of elementary and high school music curricula, particularly since the mid-1990s. However, according to numerous anecdotal reports from music educators, many teachers continue to neglect improvisation in their classrooms. This neglect appears to be the result of three principal factors. First, relatively few teachers have engaged seriously with improvisation themselves in the course of their own training, and are consequently inadequately equipped to teach their students how to improvise. Second, there is a real paucity of methodological literature that addresses improvisation in music education; hence, even those teachers who are driven to incorporate improvisation into their curricula in a meaningful way have only limited resources upon which they can draw. Third, many teachers remain skeptical of improvisation both as a curricular focus and as a pedagogical heuristic in large part because little work has been done to evaluate the impact of improvisation in the classroom.

Improvisation and Music Education: Beyond the Classroom is designed to address these three lacunae by offering readers both theoretical explorations of improvisation and music education from a wide array of vantage points, and practical explanations of how the theory can be implemented in real situations in communities and classrooms. The book opens with "Teaching Improvisation," a section that addresses the challenges and rewards of introducing improvisation-oriented performance classes in a variety of institutional contexts. From empowering students to take charge of their own learning, to offering students ways to cope with social and performance anxiety, to more effectively integrating theory with practice, authors David Ake, Jesse Stewart, Kathryn Ladano, Chris Stover, Howard Spring, and Gabriel Solis detail their approaches to teaching improvisation—and to improvisational teaching.

Section two, "Histories, Institutions, Practices," focuses more specifically on the challenges and rewards involved in introducing improvisation as a key curricular theme in a variety of institutional contexts, particularly the category of institution that is of greatest interest to many of our readers, college and university music departments. Chapters by Parmela Attariwala, Peter Schubert and Max Guido, Vincent P. Benitez, Scott Currie, Tanya Kalmanovitch, and William Parker remind us of long-neglected improvisatory traditions within the Western Art Music canon, show us how to use improvisation to train students to compose and perform a wide range of musical genres and idioms in a conservatory setting, interrogate established canons and methods, and describe how an improvisational pedagogy forces us to tear down the structural and epistemological divisions between the institutional music subdisciplines of performance, theory, composition, musicology, and ethnomusicology.

The third and final section, "Improvisation and Community Engaged Pedagogy," features essays and stories from David Dove, Matt Swanson and Patricia Shehan Campbell, Ajay Heble and Jane Bunnett, Mark Laver, Mark V. Campbell, and George Lipsitz—musicians, scholars, and educators who have worked to bring improvisation outside of the traditional academic milieux by establishing (or collaborating with) accessible improvisation-based music programs in underserved communities, by working with children and adults with special needs, and by breaking boundaries between pedagogy and performance, classroom and community. Collectively, these authors call for practice-based methods that offer students visceral experiences of theoretical concepts, outward-looking approaches that take students out of the academy and into direct contact with community teachers and vernacular knowledges, and a pedagogy of discomfort that refuses to allow students, teachers, or administrators to settle into customary habits, easy biases, or familiar hierarchies. They destabilize the conventional understanding of "outreach" as a unidirectional flow of knowledge from the inside of an academic institution to the outside, positing instead a dialogical engagement that coheres around reciprocal exchanges of teaching and learning.

Improvisation in Context

Improvisation and Music Education: Beyond the Classroom builds on work associated with two large-scale research initiatives (Improvisation, Community, and Social Practice, and the International Institute for Critical Studies in Improvisation), and brings to the pages of this book some contributions that initially emerged during a three-day summit in Guelph, Ontario, Canada, on Pedagogy and Community Impact. This event, held in May 2013 under the auspices of the Improvisation, Community, and Social Practice project, brought together performers, educators, and researchers who have sought to incorporate improvisation into the content and method of their teaching practices in order to compare strategies and experiences.

It's worth noting that, over the course of the last decade or so, and in no small measure as a result of the two large-scale research initiatives noted above—initiatives that have resulted in a peer-reviewed journal, annual conferences across multiple sites, a book series, the training, mentoring, and placement of graduate students and postdoctoral fellows—we've seen the emergence of critical studies in improvisation as a new interdisciplinary field of academic inquiry. We've also seen how growing interest in this field has sparked a transformed understanding of the artistic, social, and pedagogical implications of improvisational practices. In many respects, the growing recognition of this new field bears striking similarities to the growth of another recently emergent and adjacent field, performance studies. In the introduction to their edited collection *Teaching Performance Studies*, Nathan Stucky and Cynthia Wimmer point out that "over the past three decades, the record of transformations [with regard to performance studies] can be seen in scholarly and artistic conferences, public performances, university classrooms, the actions of tenure and promotion committees, and the archive of print and electronic material."[8] They note that performance studies "has achieved standing in scholarly organizations; its presence is evidenced in scholarly publications and performances, and it increasingly can be seen in the curricula of colleges and universities both in the United States and abroad."[9] Something similar, we would argue, can now be said about critical studies in improvisation.

Indeed, the links between the two fields—performance studies and critical studies in improvisation—may run deeper, as Linda Park-Fuller implies in her chapter, "Improvising Disciplines: Performance Studies and Theatre," in the *Teaching Performance Studies* volume. Taking up the ways in which the field of performance studies is "shifting, transforming, metamorphosing—in my hands, in my mind, in its relationship to my department, my university, and the world,"[10] Park-Fuller uses the metaphor of improvisation "to discuss pedagogic aspects of our work at the disciplinary level ... at the local level ... and at the most essential level of classes and activities."[11] Exploring "performance studies as a postmodern, improvisational discipline, as an institutional course of study, and as a teaching philosophy, subject, and tool," she argues for a notion of performance studies "as an improvisational *method* of pedagogy—a method of thought, a method of building curriculum, academic decision making, and teaching/learning, and most of all, a method of service."[12] Her claim is that "the concept of improvisation provides one way of imagining our work [in performance studies] as liberating yet accountable, active and interactive, inclusive yet distinguishing, artistic, and political. Its positive connotations of inspiration, collaboration, spontaneity, freedom-in-structure, and creation-through-performance are ... compelling to me as a way to explain 'what' it is that I do and teach and love."[13]

Another productive area of overlap, as evidenced in many of the chapters in this volume, occurs with the theory and practice of critical pedagogy. Indeed, the legacy of work in critical pedagogy has significantly informed how many of the authors in this volume operate in the classroom as well as how we think about the relationship between classrooms and communities. Drawing on the influential work of Paulo Freire, Henry Giroux, bell hooks, and others, critical pedagogy, as a field (and as a social movement), has opened up vital questions around what, how, and why we teach. Giroux, for instance, has encouraged us to think about pedagogy not just in terms of the transmission of knowledge within classrooms, but more broadly as "the complicated processes by which knowledge is produced, skills are learned meaningfully, identities are shaped, desires are mobilized, and critical dialogue becomes a central form of public interaction."[14] In this context, as Heble and Waterman have previously suggested in their editorial to the special issue on improvisation and pedagogy of the journal *Critical Studies in Improvisation/Études critiques en improvisation*, some key questions arise: to what extent (and in what ways) might improvisational musical practices be understood as vital (and publically resonant) pedagogical acts? in what ways might they generate new forms of knowledge, new understandings of identity and community, and new imaginative possibilities?

These questions are particularly pertinent when considering the important role that communities of autodidactic pedagogies have played, for instance, in jazz history. In influential musicians' organizations such as the Association for the Advancement of Creative Musicians (AACM), Black Artists Group (BAG), and the Union of God's Musicians and Artists Ascension, as George Lewis, Ronald Radano, and others have noted, the creation of new forms of improvised music making has often been connected with the revitalization of U.S. communities of color in the face of social and economic degradation. Writing about the role that collaborative improvisation has played in the AACM, Lewis draws on notions of critical pedagogy to focus on how collaborative organizations created by cultural practitioners of African descent have promulgated new perceptions, understandings, and forms of artistic and social practice.[15] In the contexts of these autodidactic communities of practice, suggests Lewis, improvisation becomes "a kind of pedagogical relation, in which we listen to know where we are and where the others are; where ideas and information are communicated from each to the other; where one learns about the other through hearing what the other has to play; and where one learns about oneself through listening to the responses from the other that seem somehow to be related to you."[16]

In their essay on the role of improvisation in music teacher education, "Improvisation as an Informal Learning Process," Panagiotis Kanellopoulos and Ruth Wright are also explicit in articulating links between improvisational practice and the aims of critical pedagogy. "Awareness," they write, "has grown during the last 30 years that important learning occurs in situations other than the classroom."[17] Kanellopoulos and Wright situate this kind of informal (beyond the classroom) learning within the context of critical pedagogies that "have long sought to develop a model in which learning and teaching exist in a dialogic relationship."[18] They argue, indeed, that "immersion in improvisation as a core element in music teacher education"[19] has much in common with the aims of critical pedagogy. Recalling Freire's critique of the banking concept of pedagogy in favor of a dialogic model of learning, they suggest, moreover, that "learning to set the rules through interaction and not through reference to some universal musical norm is what improvisation might offer to education, and this is one way in which music education might be linked to emancipation."[20] For Kanellopoulos and Wright, improvisation becomes "a way of placing musical imagination at the centre of the educational process, and to proceed to modes of musical practice that address issues of being and thinking together, thus becoming a form of socio-musical and thus political practice."[21]

For Lewis and for Kanellopoulos and Wright, as for Freire, hooks, Giroux, and other foundational critical pedagogues, rules, structures, and norms (whether social or musical; whether in classrooms or communities) aren't abstract or fixed; they emerge organically through dialogical interaction. By the same token, according to much of the scholarship that has come out of the field of music education in the last several decades, improvisation is commonly understood to *precede* formal and procedural norms, both musically and cognitively.[22] For Maud Hickey, "improvisation is a *disposition* to be encouraged, facilitated and modeled in our classrooms," alongside—but distinct from—other technical musical skills that must be more methodically "taught."[23] Writing in this volume, Matt Swanson and Patricia Shehan Campbell suggest that children are "improvisational natives," for whom the impulse to improvise is a natural part of play. In fact, they go a step further, arguing that institutionalized music education has historically had an antagonistic, oppressive relationship to improvisation: "Ironically, it is the formal institutions of music education that begin to erode these impulses in favor of more rigid and sequential approaches to music making, to the point that students at the tertiary level have often lost sight of the creative, playful propensities that they had known as children."

The broad consensus in the literature suggests that teaching improvisation demands an improvisatory pedagogical approach that, according to Keith Sawyer, draws from "the collaborative and emergent nature of effective classroom practice."[24] For Maud Hickey, an improvisatory disposition must be "enabled" and "nurtured";[25] because it is immanent and fundamental, it cannot be constructed through a set of routine procedures. Teaching practice must constitute a dialogical, nonhierarchical engagement with a collective of diverse learners. For community music scholar and improvisation advocate Lee Higgins, this means that teaching is closer to "facilitating": "facilitation is concerned with encouraging open dialogue among different individuals with differing perspectives. Exploration of diverse assumptions and options is often one of the significant aims."[26] For David Dove, writing in this volume, it means a "curriculumless sound"—an approach to teaching that is radically contingent upon the needs of the learners in dialogue with the priorities of the teacher.

Both teaching improvisation and improvisational pedagogy thus reflect what Daniel Fischlin, Ajay Heble, and George Lipsitz have termed an "ethics of cocreation" that underlies and permeates improvisation: "Improvisation is an important social, musical, and ethical practice for understanding and generating the potential forms of cocreation—deeply relational, profoundly contingent—without which our collective relation to each other and to all things would be unthinkable."[27] In other words, teaching and learning improvisation is coterminous with—and inextricable from—a cocreative ethic. As teachers, as learners, and as improvisers, everyone involved in an improvisatory scenario must be deeply attentive to one another and to the shared process in which they collectively are engaged. Think again of George Lewis's suggestion that improvisation is a "pedagogical relation, in which we listen to know where we are and where the others are." Moreover, this kind of attentiveness—which is contiguous to empathy—is not merely theoretical or abstract; it is *both* theoretical *and* embodied. As Michelle Kisliuk and Kelly Gross have written,

> First-hand, embodied experience that students have with music and dance can facilitate an understanding, or at least an awareness, of both macro- and micropolitics. In learning to dance and sing in new ways, one becomes vitally aware of issues of self and other, and of 'here' and 'there,' challenging the distancing that takes place in much disembodied scholarship. Direct involvement in a process of musical creation engenders a kind of self-awareness that leads to activity instead of abstraction.[28]

Despite this enormous optimism that pervades the writing on improvisation and education, equally pervasive in that existing literature is a curious defensiveness about the legitimacy of improvisation as a subject and as a method. By the same token, virtually every scholar and practitioner of improvisation has pointed to an overall paucity of literature on the subject. Writing in *Music Educators Journal* in 1996, Paul Goldstaub lamented, "Certainly the time has come for every institution that trains music teachers to take an active role in developing programs that promote and teach improvisation. Sadly, very few schools are doing this."[29] Patricia Shehan Campbell and Lee Higgins echoed Goldstaub fourteen years later in the preamble to their book, *Free to be Musical: Group Improvisation in Music,* writing, "We have observed many more words than actual practices in the placement of improvisation within the process of a truly musical education."[30] Clearly, there is a pressing need for further work that considers improvisation across theory and practice, across genre, in classrooms and beyond.

Improvisation Inside and Out

Where there is continued skepticism toward—and defensiveness of—improvisation, it commonly derives from the slippery quality of the term itself. As a word that cuts across musical genres, time periods, geographical regions, modes of performative expression, even across the presumed distinction between art and everyday life, improvisation is sometimes perceived to lack a solid core: a clear, quantifiable essence that can be taught according to consistent, easily evaluated procedures that are directed toward the achievement of a singular learning outcome. As Bruno Nettl notes in his "Preface" to the edited collection *Musical Improvisation: Art, Education, and Society,* "the things that we call improvisation encompass a vast network of practices, with various artistic, political, social, and educational values."[31] With the breadth and diversity of the chapters that follow, in some respects *Improvisation and Music Education: Beyond the Classroom* does little to pin improvisation down. On the contrary, the authors use improvisation to pivot between a multiplicity of themes, places, and learners: from seventeenth-century figured bass to the twenty-first-century avant-garde; from undergraduate classrooms in Kitchener, Ontario, and Urbana-Champaign, Illinois, to a public housing project in inner city Houston; and from autistic children, to recent teenaged immigrants, to senior citizens. Rather than posing a problem, we argue that the "slipperiness" of improvisation makes it a highly malleable subject that can dramatically enrich virtually any educative scenario.

Mindful of the virtually limitless potential areas of inquiry afforded by the kind of early foray into an emergent field that *Improvisation and Music Education: Beyond the Classroom* represents, we have chosen to focus specifically on music, lest that productive, "slippery" quality of improvisation slide into something more inchoate. While we have chosen to retain music as our principal concern, however, we hope that this book will help stimulate a conversation that moves boldly across disciplinary boundaries. Evidently the groundwork for such a conversation has already begun to emerge through the ongoing work of a number of creative, provocative scholars, such as actor and theatre scholar Keith Johnstone, sociologist George Lipsitz (the author of the final chapter in this collection), Bob Ostertag, legal scholar Sara Ramshaw, psychologist and creativity theorist Keith Sawyer, performance studies scholars Nathan Stucky and Cynthia Wimmer, and American literature scholar Rob Wallace.[32]

While we have chosen to anchor our discussions in music, per se, that does not mean that we have narrowly targeted this examination at a particular genre. Evidently, as numerous authors in this volume suggest, when improvisation appears as a subject of inquiry in postsecondary education, it often does so in jazz studies. Certainly, jazz scholars and educators have offered numerous points of entry in their inquiries into the history and practice of jazz improvisation; but improvisation offers still richer potential when it isn't conceptually tethered to a single genre. Indeed, this "problem of genre" (as Gabriel Solis terms it in his chapter in this volume)—the widespread understanding that improvisation is the exclusive domain of jazz (and occasionally organ) curricula—threatens to constrain the possibilities for the broad impact of improvisation across music study, limiting opportunities for non-jazz students, in Solis's words, to "expand their creative agency."

If, as Fabian Holt suggests, "genre is not only 'in the music,' but also in the minds and bodies of particular groups of people,"[33] educators must move away from teaching music as if it were "pure, rational, and autonomous," and toward a model that better integrates theory, practice, and everyday life. Such a model would not only more richly contextualize musical practice, but, according to recent research in learning and cognition, would make a student's learning experience more impactful and enduring. David Borgo has described the "theory of distributed cognition":

> In place of the Cartesian view that envisioned "mind" as separate from and dominant over "body" (I think, therefore I am), the theory of distributed cognition upholds the embodied view that mind is *in* the body and the body is *in* the mind, and further maintains that mind extends *beyond* the physical body.[34]

For both Solis and Scott Currie, improvisation offers an opportunity to address the "problem of genre" by moving between improvisational musical practices, as well as between the many global regions from which those practices have emerged. As Solis observes, "Improvisation, understood broadly, is a part of virtually every musical tradition, from the big classical traditions of Europe, Africa, and Asia to the little musical communities established by school children around the world with a minimum of adult input." For Currie, a similarly far-reaching curricular agenda has productively engaged with a number of ossified institutional structures and conventions at his home institution, the University of Minnesota, including "Euro-American focused curricula, strict disciplinary specializations, academic/applied (theory/practice) divisions, town-vs.-gown boundaries, and text-centered pedagogical paradigms."

Just as educators such as Solis and Currie seek to challenge the "problem of genre" by extending the geographic scope of postsecondary improvisation studies, others like Vincent P. Benitez, Massimiliano Guido, and Peter Schubert extend the historical scope by making improvisation a central element of their classes on European music theory from the sixteenth through nineteenth centuries. As these authors elaborate, the integration of improvisation into a music theory curriculum derives from a more honest and accurate account of historical performance practices. To quote from Schubert and Guido in their co-authored chapter, "for the long period we are focused on (1500–1800), improvisation was either prior to, or co-existed with, composition: choirboys often grew up to become composers, and Kapellmeisters and virtuoso instrumentalists both improvised and composed." Moreover, as Benitez notes, it offers a "dynamic" set of tools for engaging students with music theory, and optimally helps students more effectively bridge practice and what Schubert and Guido call "paper theory."

The catholicity of these endeavors finds a precedent in the Contemporary Improvisation program established by Gunther Schuller at the New England Conservatory (NEC) in 1972, as detailed by Tanya Kalmanovitch in her chapter. At NEC, improvisation afforded a means to pursue Schuller's "vast and quixotic project" of developing a conservatory that would admit "all of the world's musical languages." For Kalmanovitch, as for Schuller, this ambitious project was designed to benefit musicians as both "creative agents" (recalling Solis's phrase) and as working professionals. These interrelated priorities appear again in Parmela Attariwala's chapter, an ethnographic overview of the place of improvisation in conservatory-style music institutions in Canada. According to Attariwala's primary interlocutors, bass clarinetist Lori Freedman and cellist Matt Brubeck, "reclaiming the ability to create without the aid of notation—a once-integral skill for performers of the Western classical tradition—holds not only numerous pedagogical and pragmatic benefits for students of composed Western music, but also allows them to collaborate and create with musicians from non-notated traditions on a direct, non-mediated level." In other words, in a music industry where stable work is increasingly scarce, improvisation represents a crucial skill—or, to recall Maud Hickey's figuration, a crucial *disposition*—upon which twenty-first-century musicians will likely rely as entrepreneurial freelancers in an unpredictable, precarious marketplace. As Currie notes, "careers in music demand broader international perspectives and greater professional responsiveness to diverse contexts than ever."

This attentiveness to what practicing musicians say and do pervades the book but is especially in evidence in chapters by ethnomusicologist Howard

Spring, bassist William Parker, and pianist and musicologist David Ake. Spring critiques what he perceives to be a general failure in the field of ethnomusicology to scaffold pedagogies of improvisation on the aural and kinetic practices of actual improvisers. He describes his gen-ed world music classes at the University of Guelph, where he gets students with widely variegated levels of musical experience to actively participate in music making, engaging directly with the underlying principles that structure improvisation for improvisers in different idioms from around the world. William Parker, meanwhile, reminds us to anchor theories of pedagogy in the language and logic of practice, observing that the term "improvisation" itself was not operative in the community that taught him how to "come on and play."

By the same token, in the chapter that opens the book, David Ake considers "the problem of genre" from a similar perspective. Responding to trumpeter and blogger Nicholas Payton's recent online commentaries (with titles such as "Jazz is Dead," "Here Lies Jazz [1916–1959]," and "I Don't Play Jazz"), Ake reflects on the ethics of teaching classes on "jazz" history and practice, when so many central figures in the genre—from Payton to Duke Ellington to Miles Davis to Max Roach—have explicitly, emphatically rejected "jazz" as a descriptor of their music. Ake decries historical and music-analytical approaches that insulate musical sound from the messy contingencies of musical life, methods that artificially construct jazz as something that is apolitical and timeless—"pure, rational, and autonomous." In answer to Ake's call for historically engaged analysis, Chris Stover makes a case for "analytic identity as a *multiplicity*" in his jazz theory classes at The New School, pursuing an approach to analysis in his classes that refuses to "dislocate [...] understanding from our own experience, including the ways in which our experience is itself historically and culturally situated."

In his chapter, Jesse Stewart describes how he strives to ensure that his classrooms—both at Carleton University in Ottawa, Ontario, and at Discovery University, a program run by the Ottawa Mission offering "free university-level classes, taught by university professors, to adults experiencing poverty or other forms of economic distress"—embrace the kind of messiness and contingency that Ake and Stover advocate. By combining performance, reading, and discussion, Stewart helps guide diverse groups of students through a learning paradigm that is equal parts musical and social. To borrow the phraseology from Patricia Shehan Campbell's aforementioned 2009 essay, "Learning to Improvise Music, Improvising to Learn Music," Stewart's students are engaged in both "learning to improvise music" and "improvising music to learn"—that is, "through the process of making music up, people learn whatever can be learned of self and others and of the world beyond music."[35]

Other chapters in the volume similarly address this dialectic. For Kathryn Ladano's students at Wilfrid Laurier University in Waterloo, Ontario, practicing free improvisation can mean learning to manage social and performance anxiety. For the students who worked with Mark V. Campbell during his community outreach project with Immigrant Family Services in Guelph, Ontario, *Control This,* improvising with the MPC digital music controller meant finding their expressive voices as adolescents in a new country. For Campbell himself, it meant critically reflecting on the roles of expertise, virtuosity, and gender in his own pedagogical praxis. For Matt Swanson and Patricia Shehan Campbell, it means helping their students reconnect with creative impulses from childhood that have been suppressed by years of rigid institutionalized music education.

Significantly, in all of these cases, the "learning of the self" that Campbell articulated in her 2009 essay is imbricated with "learning of [...] others and the world beyond music."[36] As Ladano writes, even an affliction like performance anxiety that manifests as an individual problem finds a poten-tial therapeutic solution in the collective: "free improvisation can become a means of integrating individuals—even those (perhaps especially those) who may be isolated or alienated by performance anxiety—into the collective, making the community a potential space for empowerment and healing." The "empowerment and healing" of individuals is largely coterminous with the fomentation of diverse, vibrant, supportive communities.

In Houston, Texas, David Dove works with a team of improvisers under the auspices of Nameless Sound, an organization that he founded in 2001. Nameless Sound artists offer workshops in venues ranging from public housing projects to schools to shelters for women and families in the city, striving to enrich the community through improvised art. In Guelph, Ontario, the Improviser-in-Residence project engages in a similar kind of outreach, bringing internationally renowned improvisers to that city, where they collaborate with university students, children with special needs, adults suffering from various forms of trauma, and a variety of other groups, facil-itating creativity and expression among those members of the community who often have the most to say but are often the least likely to be heard. In his contribution to the volume, Ajay Heble presents an interview he con-ducted with Jane Bunnett, the iconic Canadian saxophonist and composer and first Improviser-in-Residence. Meanwhile, Mark Laver offers a com-mentary on his participation in *The Share,* a project organized by 2012 Improvisers-In-Residence Scott Thomson and Susanna Hood that posed a compelling rejoinder to the rapid encroachment of neoliberal management strategy at the host institution, the University of Guelph. Finally, in New Orleans, Louisiana, George Lipsitz describes the inspiring work undertaken by the Students at the Center program that works in aggrieved neighbor-hoods to transform young people from "objects of power into powerful subjects," from "spectators into witnesses," and from "bystanders [into] upstanders."

In short, if, as we suggested at the outset, improvisation is a little out of tune with the mainstream of music institutions, perhaps it is precisely its tenuous, outsider, dissonant status that affords it its transformational capac-ity. If improvisation does chafe within secondary or tertiary music curricula, it is well positioned to serve as an agitator, to fruitfully discomfit the more comfortably, uncritically ensconced elements of those curricula, to destabilize old, unquestioned methods, and to instill in students a vital capacity for critical thought, for creative agency, for empathy, and for justice.

Notes

1. Campbell, "Learning to Improvise Music."
2. Lewis, "Teaching Improvised Music," 79.
3. Ibid.
4. Solis, "Introduction."
5. Small, *Musicking*.
6. Heble and Waterman, "Sounds of Hope."
7. Freire, *Pedagogy*.
8. Stucky and Wimmer, "Introduction," 1.
9. Ibid., 13.
10. Park-Fuller, "Improvising Disciplines," 205.
11. Ibid.
12. Ibid., 208–9.
13. Ibid., 215.
14. Giroux, "Foreword," xi.
15. Lewis, "Collaborative Improvisation," 42.
16. Ibid., 46.
17. Kanellopoulos and Wright, "Improvisation as an Informal Learning Process," 133.
18. Ibid., 136.
19. Ibid.
20. Ibid., 144.
21. Ibid., 150.
22. See, for instance, Kratus, "A Developmental Approach"; Goldstaub, "Opening the Door"; and Brophy, "Developing Improvisation."
23. Hickey, "Can Improvisation be 'Taught'?," 287.
24. Sawyer, "What Makes Good Teachers?," 2.
25. Hickey, "Can Improvisation be 'Taught'?," 286.
26. Higgins, "The Creative Music Workshop," 330.
27. Fischlin, Heble, and Lipsitz, *Fierce Urgency*, xii.
28. Kisliuk and Gross, "What's the 'It'?," 250.
29. Goldstaub, "Opening the Door," 51.
30. Higgins and Campbell, *Free to Be Musical*, 2.
31. Nettl, "Preface," xi.
32. See, for instance, Johnstone's *Impro: Improvisation and the Theater*; Lipsitz's recently co-authored work, *The Fierce Urgency of Now: Improvisation, Rights, and the Ethics of Cocreation*; Ostertag's *Creative Life: Music, Politics, People, and Machines*; Sara Ramshaw's *Justice as Improvisation: The Law of the Extempore*; Sawyer's various works on creativity, especially *Group Creativity: Music, Theater, Collaboration* and *Explaining Creativity: The Science of Human Innovation*; Nathan Stucky and Cynthia Wimmer's edited volume, *Teaching Performance Studies*; and Wallace's *Improvisation and the Making of American*

Literary Modernism. See also Rebecca Caines and Ajay Heble, eds., *The Improvisation Studies Reader: Spontaneous Acts,* an anthology that explicitly cuts across disciplinary boundaries and that draws on music, theatre, dance, film, performance studies, literature, philosophy, and sociology.

33. Holt, *Genre in Popular Music,* 2.
34. Borgo, "Free Jazz," 72.
35. Campbell, "Learning to Improvise Music," 120.
36. Ibid.

Works Cited

Borgo, David. "Free Jazz in the Classroom: An Ecological Approach to Music Education." *Jazz Perspectives* 1, (May 2007): 61–88.

Brophy, Timothy S. "Developing Improvisation in General Music Classes." *Music Educators Journal* 88, (July 2001): 34–53.

Caines, Rebecca, and Ajay Heble, eds. *The Improvisation Studies Reader: Spontaneous Acts.* New York: Routledge, 2014.

Campbell, Patricia Shehan. "Learning to Improvise Music, Improvising to Learn Music." *Musical Improvisation: Art, Education, and Society,* edited by Gabriel Solis and Bruno Nettl, 119–42. Urbana: University of Illinois Press, 2009.

Fischlin, Daniel, Ajay Heble, and George Lipsitz. *The Fierce Urgency of Now: Improvisation, Rights, and the Ethics of Cocreation.* Durham, NC: Duke University Press, 2013.

Freire, Paulo. *Pedagogy of the Oppressed.* Thirtieth Anniversary Edition. Trans. Myra Bergman Ramos. New York: Continuum, 2008.

Giroux, Henry A. "Foreword. Contending Zones and Public Spaces." In *Zones of Contention: Essays on Art, Institutions, Gender, and Anxiety,* edited by Carol Becker, ix–xii. Albany: State University of New York Press, 1996.

Goldstaub, Paul. "Opening the Door to Classroom Improvisation." *Music Educators Journal* 82, (March 1996): 45–51.

Heble, Ajay, and Ellen Waterman. "Sounds of Hope, Sounds of Change: Improvisation, Pedagogy, Social Justice." *Critical Studies in Improvisation/Études critiques en improvisation* 3, no. 2 (2008).

Hickey, Maud. "Can Improvisation Be 'Taught'?: A Call for Free Improvisation in Our Schools." *International Journal of Music Education* 27, (November 2009): 285–99.

Higgins, Lee. "The Creative Music Workshop: Event, Facilitation, Gift." *International Journal of Music Education* 27, (October 2008): 326–38.

Higgins, Lee, and Patricia Shehan Campbell. *Free to Be Musical: Group Improvisation in Music.* Lanham, MD: Rowman & Littlefield, 2010.

Holt, Fabian. *Genre in Popular Music.* Chicago: University of Chicago Press, 2007.

hooks, bell. *Teaching to Transgress: Education as the Practice of Freedom.* New York: Routledge, 1994.

Johnstone, Keith. *Impro: Improvisation and the Theater.* London: Faber and Faber, 1979.

Kanellopoulos, Panagiotis, and Ruth Wright. "Improvisation as an Informal Learning Process: Implications for Teacher Education." In *Future Prospects for Music Education: Corroborating Informal Learning Pedagogy,* edited by Sidsel Karlsen and Lauri Väkevä, 129–57. Newcastle Upon Tyne, UK: Cambridge Scholars, 2012.

Kisliuk, Michelle, and Kelly Gross. "What's the 'It' That We Learn to Perform?: Teaching BaAka Music and Dance." In *Performing Ethnomusicology: Teaching and Representation in World Music Ensembles*, edited by Ted Solís, 249–60. Los Angeles: University of California Press, 2004.

Kratus, John. "A Developmental Approach to Teaching Music Improvisation." *International Journal of Music Education* 26, (November 1995): 27–38.

Lewis, George E. "Collaborative Improvisation as Critical Pedagogy." *Nka: Journal of Contemporary African Art* 34, (Spring 2014): 41–47.

———. "Teaching Improvised Music: An Ethnographic Memoir." In *Arcana: Musicians on Music*, edited by John Zorn, 78–109. New York, NY: Granary Books/Hips Road, 2000.

Nettl, Bruno. "Preface." In *Musical Improvisation: Art, Education, and Society*, edited by Gabriel Solis and Bruno Nettl, ix–xv. Urbana and Chicago: University of Illinois Press, 2009.

Ostertag, Bob. *Creative Life: Music, Politics, People, and Machines*. Urbana: University of Illinois Press, 2009.

Park-Fuller, Linda M. "Improvising Disciplines: Performance Studies and Theatre." In *Teaching Performance Studies*, edited by Nathan Stucky and Cynthia Wimmer, 205–18. Carbondale: Southern Illinois University Press, 2002.

Radano, Ronald M. "Jazzin' the Classics: The AACM's Challenge to Mainstream Aesthetics." *Black Music Research Journal* 12, no. 1 (1992): 79–95.

Ramshaw, Sara. *Justice as Improvisation: The Law of the Extempore*. New York: Routledge, 2013.

Sawyer, R. Keith. *Explaining Creativity: The Science of Human Innovation*. New York: Oxford University Press, 2012.

———. *Group Creativity: Music, Theater, Collaboration*. Mahwah, NJ: Lawrence Erlbaum Associates, 2003.

———. "What Makes Good Teachers Great? The Artful Balance of Structure and Improvisation." In *Structure and Improvisation in Creative Teaching*, edited by R. Keith Sawyer, 1–25. New York: Cambridge University Press, 2011.

Small, Christopher. *Musicking: The Meanings of Performing and Listening*. Middletown, CT: Wesleyan University Press, 1998.

Solis, Gabriel. "Introduction." In *Musical Improvisation: Art, Education, and Society*, edited by Gabriel Solis and Bruno Nettl, 1–17. Urbana: University of Illinois Press, 2009.

Stucky, Nathan, and Cynthia Wimmer. "Introduction: The Power of Transformation in Performance Studies Pedagogy." In *Teaching Performance Studies*, edited by Nathan Stucky and Cynthia Wimmer, 1–29. Carbondale: Southern Illinois University Press, 2002.

Wallace, Rob. *Improvisation and the Making of American Literary Modernism*. London: Bloomsbury, 2010.

Section I
Teaching Improvisation

2 On the Ethics of Teaching "Jazz" (and "America's Classical Music," and "BAM," and "Improvisational Music," and …)[1]

David Ake

As the rather convoluted chapter title suggests, this essay focuses on issues of ethics, pedagogy, and improvisation. Yet, unlike some of the other authors in this collection, I will not directly address how learning and applying improvisational concepts may be "politically and materially pertinent to envisioning and sounding alternative ways of knowing and being in the world," one of the primary goals of Improvisation, Community, and Social Practice (ICASP), the Canada-based research project that sponsored the publication of this book.[2] Rather, I want to turn the camera around, so to speak, to look at some of the ethical issues involved when we teach the practice and history of musical improvisation, or one corner of the music-improvisation world, at any rate, namely jazz.

I focus on jazz here because it remains the most widely taught improvisationally based music genre in North America's schools. Even given recent efforts to include various "world musics" in curricula, jazz is the only improvisationally based genre available for formal study in many institutions. (When college music students say they are taking an "improv class," 95% of the time, they mean *jazz* improv.) Not coincidentally, and despite its early ignominious reputation, jazz now ranks on these shores behind only European classical music in its level of cultural prestige and institutional support, a situation that merits celebration but also reflection on how and why we now teach and value jazz as we do. It also suggests important questions, ethical and otherwise, about why certain music genres are taught in colleges while others remain ignored (a query that falls outside the scope of this particular chapter but that other authors explore in this collection). For all of these reasons, any discussion of pedagogy and improvisation must attend to jazz.

Before jumping in, I should declare a few things about my own positions vis-à-vis this subject. To start, I count myself among those for whom the idea of a "jazz community" or a "jazz tradition" still makes sense, even as some of us explore and question how such a community or tradition might be created, bounded, and maintained.[3] And, along with my work as a musicologist and musician, I am a longtime jazz educator, having spent a significant portion of my academic career teaching lessons and small ensembles, as well as history classes on jazz and popular music, at the University of Nevada,

Reno (UNR), before moving to positions at Case Western Reserve University and, most recently, the University of Miami. Moreover, while this chapter may most directly concern my fellow jazz educators and scholars, I intend and hope that it will be meaningful and applicable to anyone interested in how we learn, teach, and value music, improvisational and otherwise. This is not primarily a critique or endorsement of any particular method of pedagogy. Rather, in the broadest sense, it is about making decisions—sometimes difficult ones—on how we should share our visions of music with others. It is also about identity, about recognizing and respecting the differences and similarities between oneself and others.

Jazz Is Dead (Again/Still) … or Not

I start with some thoughts by and about the African American trumpeter Nicholas Payton. Payton was born in New Orleans, in 1973, and garnered widespread recognition, even in his late teens, as one of the so-called Young Lions, performing and touring with such established stars as Elvin Jones and Joe Henderson. In 1997, he earned a Grammy Award for his recording with a fellow trumpeter, the legendary Doc Cheatham, who was 91 at the time.

Here are excerpts from blogs Payton posted on his official website between November 2011 and October 2014, when I am writing this:

- Jazz is Dead
- Here lies Jazz (1916–1959)
- I don't play jazz
- I don't let others define who I am
- I am a postmodern New Orleans musician
- I am Nicholas Payton and I play Black American Music [BAM]
- BAM's primary mission is to strip itself away from the derogatory j-word ["jazz"]
- [BAM]: Created by blacks for everyone[4]

These and other blog entries by Payton have struck a sensitive nerve among a fair number of his readers, leading some to deride him as "angry," "divisive," "racist," and even "the Charlie Sheen of jazz." This heightened response is due in part to the global reach of the Internet and the nearly instantaneous rate at which information (and misinformation) can travel around the blogosphere. Just as important to understanding the impassioned retorts, though, is jazz's aforementioned rise in respectability over the past half century, its much cultivated—and largely deserved—reputation as a bastion of interracial harmony, and the fact that Nicholas Payton enjoys (or once enjoyed) a large following of people who consider themselves to be *jazz* fans.

Included among those followers was a handful of my music students at UNR. Shortly after Payton posted his first blogs about BAM, a white student majoring in that school's Program in Jazz and Improvisational Music pulled me aside in the hallway. Holding back tears, he asked me, "If jazz is dead or if it's BAM, what am I doing here?" This student's distressed state reminded me just how deeply our notions of self, purpose, and belonging are embedded in the way we label things, activities, and people. At stake for that student was not only all of the time, energy, and resources he had invested in developing the skills and knowledge required of a "jazz musician," but also, and more consequently, his very sense of who he was as a person: was he now, or must he now become, or could he *ever* become a creator of Black American Music? How I responded to that student's existential crisis—and his reaction to Payton's blogs amounted to nothing short of that—will come out over the course of this chapter.

We could spend an entire book unpacking and debating the merits, fallacies, contradictions, chutzpa, and humor of Payton's blogs, let alone the arguments and counterarguments they inspired. As I only have a limited word count here, however, I want to draw your attention to just a few aspects of this debate.

First, while some of Payton's blog entries have struck certain readers as inflammatory, curious, even absurd, a dispassionate appraisal of those entries reveals the charges of race baiting against Payton to be largely unfounded. He makes a number of clear, well-reasoned, and nonessentialistic arguments about history, music, culture, and identity. He states repeatedly that he does not envision BAM—Black American Music—as a domain reserved or owned exclusively by one ethnic group. Of course, race matters to Nicholas Payton. Race has always mattered to anyone attentive to how musics originating in black communities have been rejected, respected, emulated, or appropriated by folks from other communites. As an African American artist himself, Payton has a particularly vested interest in this history. His preferred designations of Black American Music or BAM serve as effective reminders of the ethnic and geographical origins of a slew of musics, including a great deal of jazz—or what he sometimes calls "the j-word"—even as he acknowledges room for all of us (which came as a relief to that deeply distressed UNR student, once I pointed that out to him).

The second aspect of these blogs that I want to address concerns jazz's supposed demise. Nicholas Payton may not wish to identify himself with the j-word, but he is mistaken when he proclaims the death of that genre. Yes, jazz serves as a marketing category, as he derisively informs us in his blogs. But it is much more than that. Countless people worldwide embrace and embody jazz, proudly and in their own ways. Just check out all of the active musicians who came of age in the 1940s and '50s, that is to say, before the time when Payton claims jazz perished. More than a few of those artists are still playing inspired music. (As I write this, Jimmy Cobb, Roy Haynes, Ahmad Jamal, Lee Konitz, Sonny Rollins, and Randy Weston are going strong well into their eighties.) Or consider the dozens of supremely creative musicians who emerged more recently, and who continue to perform and compose compelling work under the jazz umbrella. Also, we should not forget all of the listeners who follow and identify with those musicians and the music they make. Jazz is alive and well to all of these individuals and in all of these ways. (And my UNR student was very happy to be assured on that front, too.)

Yet even if we disagree with Payton's stance on jazz's vitality, we need to acknowledge and consider further his efforts toward self-identification and his abhorrence of the jazz category, as they point to some of those issues of ethics and pedagogy promised at the outset. Namely, assuming that neither "jazz" nor "jazz education" are going away any time soon, how should we educators reconcile Payton's self-professed antipathy to the jazz label with our vision of the jazz genre, a vision that would presumably include Payton and his music?

Certainly, the easiest way for instructors to get around this particular dilemma is simply to make no mention of Nicholas Payton in any of our classes. So he played with Doc Cheatham, Elvin Jones, and Joe Henderson. So what? He's crazy. If he wants nothing to do with our seemingly irresistable impulse to trace an ongoing lineage of great New Orleans *jazz* trumpeters, so be it. We still have Terence Blanchard, who played in Art Blakey's Jazz Messengers. Better yet, we have Wynton Marsalis, who, as founder and director of Jazz at Lincoln Center, has never shrunk from serving as the genre's standard bearer.

The problem is, of course, that Nicholas Payton is hardly the first musician to distance him- or herself from the jazz designation. Duke Ellington, Miles Davis, and Max Roach represent only three of the best-known figures to have done so publicly, even as jazz educators routinely laud these musicians as some of the preeminent representatives of the genre. In this sense, the questions I posed above take on a much broader and more consequential character.

One solution to this larger dilemma is to avoid names altogether and concentrate solely on the notes. Now, I stated at the outset that this chapter isn't about any specific pedagogical method. I just want to point out that one *could* teach an entire course on jazz improvisation without invoking the names or sounds of any historical personages. One would need merely to draw up, discuss, and play from graphs that depict chord symbols with lists of associated pitch classes (perhaps organized as scales or modes). Once a student has memorized these correlations—and testing knowledge of them would be fairly straightforward—that student could be judged capable of playing "correctly" over pretty much any given form or harmonic progression, and earn an A for the course, without ever hearing the music of, or even the name, Miles Davis, let alone Nicholas Payton. Hence, teachers and students of jazz improvisation would not be burdened by troublesome matters of race or nationality (or gender, or sexuality, or class). There would be no need to worry about potentially confusing terms like black music or BAM. It would all be just jazz—pure, rational, and autonomous.

I am exaggerating, of course. But mentioning this as one possible approach to learning jazz improvisation is hardly as far fetched as some might think. In fact, we have a name for it; we call it chord-scale theory. And, more generally, it's called music theory. Now, I do not wish to raise the ire of any music theorists who may be reading this. No doubt, we *can* learn a great deal by looking at form, rhythm, and other musical nuts and bolts. Studying harmonic progressions in jazz, for example, helps us to recognize similarities and differences among compositions and also enhances our awareness and appreciation of the range and complexity of problems that improvisers face when going about their business. Yet while it can be very handy for educators and students to isolate certain musical data, we should take heed not to conceive of music as a *thing* that can be fully grasped and explained by pulling it apart, analyzing it, piece by piece, like anatomy students do to corpses. (If it were possible to comprehend jazz's full range and meanings in this way, Nick Payton might have a legitimate point about the death of this genre.)

Rather, we should bear in mind and emphasize to our students Christopher Small's concept of musicking, music as a verb, an *activity*, or set of activities, engaged in by and for people.[5] With this in mind, we gain a more holistic and accurate notion of jazz when we use music theory only as a means to explore larger questions of *why* certain like-minded groups of human beings, from certain eras or places, have understood, responded to, identified with, or rejected certain ways of making music. By bringing questions like these into our classrooms, students not only learn about different ways of creating and interpreting jazz, but also begin to grasp how they and their work might fit into one or more of these communities. Indeed, they learn, perhaps for the first time, that there are multiple jazz communities, a point to which I will return.

Musicology, Jazz, and Postmodernism

As many of you are no doubt aware, my somewhat sardonic critique of music theory is hardly new. It betrays my own schooling, at the University of California, Los Angeles (UCLA) during the mid-1990s, in what some still call the "new musicology," which itself grew out of the culture clashes of the 1960s and '70s, when academicians began questioning the assumptions on which their disciplines—and everything else—were founded. It should come as no surprise, then, that academic jazz studies and musicology's then-nascent postmodernist bent emerged at roughly the same time. After all, one of postmodernism's primary goals was to deconstruct narratives of presumed hierarchies. In musicology, this has meant primarily the narrative that would place European classical music over, well, everything else. Jazz offered an ideal alternative genre for scholars, in that many felt it had been long overlooked or undervalued, due, in no small part, to implicit or explicit racial bias.

In a somewhat ironic twist, just as some scholars (and journalists, fans, musicians, and even politicians) were working toward and celebrating jazz's rise up the ladder of prestige, others—myself among them, I guess—were setting their sights on jazz's own canons and supposed hierarchies. Callous as this may seem after the long struggle to garner widespread recognition for jazz as a significant cultural contribution by African American musicians, our efforts to challenge these canons were driven by a desire for even greater openness in and beyond the genre. That spirit certainly lay at the heart of the criticisms of what many of us perceived to be the too-narrow view of jazz espoused by the likes of Stanley Crouch and Wynton Marsalis, as well as the efforts of those same so-called neoclasssicists to elevate jazz at the expense of other genres, including soul, funk, hip hop, and other Black American Music idioms. Jazz as welcoming, malleable, diverse, a music that plays well with others: this was the account we postmodernists espoused (and still espouse).

Many of us have brought this point of view to our teaching, as well as our publications. Thanks to the work of such scholars as Sherrie Tucker, Loren Kajikawa, and Chris Washburne, jazz students can now consider themselves to be part of a history that includes the likes of the Prairie View Co-eds, Jon Jang, and Ray Barretto, as well as Bird, Monk, and Trane.[6] Meanwhile, scholars from a host of disciplines have shown that jazz thrives in virtually all regions of the globe, their accounts serving as important reminders (or initial revelations) to those who have tended to consider jazz a purely (North) American artform.[7] We have also been proud of the inroads we have made to expand understandings of jazz in the applied areas of lessons, ensembles, and composition/arranging classes, as a greater variety of names, ethnicities, sounds, grooves, and instruments now appear as jazz at school concerts, recitals, and festivals.

This expansiveness even seems to have spread beyond educational institutions. We watch, pleased and amazed, as the twenty-something bassist and singer Esperanza Spalding—a postmodern jazzwoman if there ever was one—tours with the likes of Joe Lovano, Geri Allen, and McCoy Tyner; records with Jack DeJohnette, Terri Lyne Carrington, and also Nicholas Payton (on a release bearing the disconcerting title *Bitches*); becomes the first woman ever to win Jazz Artist of the Year in the *Down-Beat* Reader's Poll; plays at the 2009 Nobel Peace Prize Concert in Oslo; and wins the 2011 Grammy Award for Best New Artist—not Best New *Jazz* Artist, mind you, but Best New Artist, period, over teen hearthrob Justin Bieber—all in the course of only two years! Huzzah for jazz's postmodernists, right? And then along comes Nick Payton, who calls himself a postmodern trumpeter ... and *not jazz*!

What I have come to realize since my students brought Payton's blogs to my attention is that so much of my own work as a scholar and teacher has focused on encouraging readers, students, and colleagues to accept the broadest view of jazz possible, that I might have given short shrift to figures like Payton and others who demonstrably do not wish to be called jazz. Not that I have completely sidestepped this issue, but I have found it all too easy to explain away hiccups in the jazz story I would wish to tell. I never viewed this as an *ethical* issue until now, because these discussions generally involved musicians from an ever-more-remote past who had been accepted and revered as jazz legends long before I came to the music.

For example, I have explained Duke Ellington's preference for calling his work "swing," or "beyond category," or "the music of my people" as a logical reaction against Paul Whiteman's syrupy reign as the King of Jazz in the 1920s and '30s. Although as John Howland, Jeffrey Magee, Elijah Wald, and others have shown, our current binary correlations of sweet jazz with white communities and hot jazz with black communities do not capture the complex sonic and social realities of the prewar era.[8] (Did you know, for instance, that Guy Lombardo and His Royal Canadians—among the sweetest of the sweet bands—held the attendance record at Harlem's Savoy Ballroom in 1930?)[9]

Then there's Max Roach. I require my students to read Roach's "What 'Jazz' Means to Me," a blistering indictment, first published in *the Black Scholar*, in 1972, in which he writes, "The term 'jazz' has come to mean the abuse and exploitation of black musicians; it has come to mean cultural prejudice and condescension ... and that is why I am presently writing a book, *I Hate Jazz*. [Jazz is] not my name and it means my oppression as a man and musician."[10]

I do not believe Roach ever published that book. Even so, his proposed title—*I Hate Jazz*—leaves little room for doubt on his position. Yet, I have even found a narrative to explain away Roach's renunciation of the jazz label by noting that many bop-era musicians wanted to be seen as artists, rather than "mere" entertainers, and that Roach's critique is passé now because today's top jazz musicians typically *do* receive greater respect and play under better conditions than those from earlier eras. And I can counter Roach's rebuke of higher education, "Nobody has ever bestowed a doctorate upon musicians like Charlie Parker or Duke Ellington," because that's simply not true anymore. Oscar Peterson, David Baker, Wayne Shorter, Ornette Coleman, and Herbie Hancock represent just some of the musicians to have earned such accolades.[11]

Similarly, I have explained to my students how Miles Davis's rejection of the jazz label coincided with his move toward fusion in the late 1960s, assuring them that jazz people are now enlightened enough to embrace the straight-eighth grooves and electric instruments of Davis's later works. (Well, we postmodernist folks count fusion as jazz, at any rate, even if those moldy-fig neoclassicists do not.)

In such ways, and from the safe distance that passing decades afford us, we can comfortably assure our students (and ourselves) that conditions have changed: Ellington's early twentieth-century notion of swing is now what we call jazz; Max Roach's insistence that he and his cohort deserve greater appreciation and remuneration has largely been fulfilled; and jazz is broad enough stylistically to include Miles Davis's funk-based grooves. So don't worry about what these guys said in the past; everything's fine. They are all securely jazz now.

Again, though, we are left with the antijazz rhetoric of Nick Payton, who is not only of our own day, but who has also enjoyed a great deal of success creating what many of us would consider to be mainstream jazz fare. What do we do with a musician who can swing and improvise with the best of them, yet states, "I do not play jazz," and "I do not let others define who I am"? Do we, as educators, not owe Nicholas Payton and like-minded musicians the right to define themselves, regardless of how we see them?

To be honest, I have gone back on forth on this question and have even sought guidance from the ethics policies of a number of learned societies, where I found a few relevant directives. For instance, the American Musicological Society states that teachers have a responsibility "to present different interpretations of subject material in a fair and balanced way," while the Society for Ethnomusicology notes, "Ethnomusicologists accept the necessity of preparing students ... to understand the social, cultural, political, economic, and legal realities of the communities in which they plan to work."[12]

After weighing this and other input, I asked myself once more: *Would* it be more ethically valid for me fully to accept and respect Nicholas Payton's claim that he plays postmodern New Orleans music or BAM—*not jazz*— and so, presumably, to exclude him and his work from my jazz curricula? Or should I continue as I have to include names of and works by individuals like Payton, Ellington, Roach, Davis, and others who have openly disavowed the jazz designation? My answers, for now at least, are No and No. That is to say, no, despite Payton's exhortations, I will not exclude him or any of the others who reject the jazz designation. At that same time, no, I cannot continue as I have to avoid, explain away, or sidestep this matter.

In the first place, while I recognize that I—a white American—am consciously violating the efforts toward self-agency and self-definition by Nicholas Payton—a black American—and so conjuring all manner of troubling historical precedents and memories, I must balance Payton's personal position with the practical reality that jazz will remain a viable category for countless people and institutions for the foreseeable future. And I must balance Payton's assertions with the fact that he was a member of Elvin Jones's *Jazz Machine*, and that, to this day, Payton continues to garner much of his professional reputation and livelihood through interviews in publications such as *JazzTimes* and *Jazziz,* and that his appearances since he began the BAM blogs include the Istanbul Jazz Festival, Chicago's Jazz Showcase, Birdland (which bills itself as the Jazz Corner of the World), and dozens of similarly named venues. Historical memory matters here, too. The truth is, Nicholas Payton cannot simply wish jazz away. Indeed, through the very act of proclaiming the death of jazz or referring to it as "the j-word" or "so-called jazz," he reinscribes himself into and revivifies the very jazz narrative he seeks to eradicate.

Beyond the specific case of Nick Payton, no single person or group of people owns or can control jazz history. Once a musical performance, or any cultural activity, is thrown out into the world, its fate—how people will embrace or reject it, reuse it to their own purposes—is largely out of the hands of those who created it. And the same holds true for the public personas and identities of the individuals who enacted that performance. What is more, Payton does not (and cannot possibly) speak for all African American musicians on this (or any other) issue. Art Blakey (Jazz Messengers), Ornette Coleman (*Shape of Jazz to Come, Free Jazz*), and Wynton Marsalis (Jazz at Lincoln Center) are only a few of the many black players who have adopted the term *jazz* in their own ways and for their own purposes. And on a purely gut level, I cannot believe that it would be more ethically valid for us to configure a jazz curriculum that included only those musicians who willingly operated under the jazz label. Would we really prefer a jazz story that included Whiteman but not Ellington? Blakey but not Roach? Ornette but not Archie Shepp? Wynton but not Miles? The answer in each case, of course, is no. All of these musicians belong here, because all of them have played significant roles in shaping how jazz looks, sounds, and is understood by millions of people around the world.

To be sure, we should heed Nicholas Payton when he implores us to remember and celebrate the immensely deep, lasting, and ongoing contributions from black American musicians and communities. But it is also important to recognize that jazz incorporates or represents the sounds and people of Argentina, Australia, Brazil, Cuba, India, Japan, Norway, Poland, and other regions. It is urban … and suburban and rural. It can be politically radical or apolitical or staunchly conservative. For some it is deeply spiritual; for others it remains the Devil's music. It has a swing feel or it doesn't. It uses blues inflections, or it doesn't. It features a great deal of improvisation, or some, or none. It is all of these things and more. (Though it is not infinite, as demonstrated by the existence of carefully guarded boundaries separating jazz from other genres.)

Spaghetti

For many reasons, it has been all too easy to treat jazz—to imagine it, to value it, and so to teach it—as if it referred to a single, if ever-changing, object, concept, or activity. One of our primary jobs as educators, I think, is to show people and help them make sense of all of these simultaneous and often competing, even contradictory, visions of the music. Lately, I have been looking for a better way to convey to my students these complexities. For now, I'm going with the spaghetti metaphor.

In English, at least, *spaghetti* is a singular word that refers to multiple strands. Like *spaghetti*, *jazz*, too, is a singular word that refers to an agglomeration. We could think of each strand as a single jazz narrative, imagining itself as the Truth. Some of these strands are wound tightly around other strands. Some strands lie around the bowl's edges, seemingly disconnected from everything else. Or maybe we could imagine "jazz" as the bowl that holds all of those strands in one place. Either way, the editors of the *New Orleans Times Picayune* weren't entirely wrong in 1918, when they decried jazz's social impact, just as Billy Taylor wasn't wholly mistaken when he hailed jazz as "America's Classical Music."[13] Neither of these positions is entirely wrong, but neither of them is entirely correct. Each represents just one way of understanding the music. Now, I don't want to carry this food metaphor too far, lest we begin to imagine jazz the way some have, as a "gumbo," made of disparate elements brought together to create one tasty dish.[14] Jazz isn't all tasty. Some of its strands are bland. Some are downright toxic: racist, sexist, or homophobic. Jazz, like spaghetti, is tangled and messy.

So, yes, jazz educators have every right to include Nicholas Payton and similarly jazz-averse artists in our curricula. That said, we also have the responsibility to give full voice to the ambivalences and criticisms those musicians voice. We should highlight, not bury, the strands that would denounce jazz. We should encourage our students to ponder *why* certain musicians, even highly successful ones, would choose to avoid or reject the jazz label. In this way, students learn that jazz isn't all good; it fights with itself; it even tries to destroy parts of itself at times.[15] All of this goes to show us that it remains very much alive. And once teachers introduce their students to the jazz spaghetti bowl, or whatever metaphor they want to use, they also have the duty to ask those students to consider which jazz strand or strands they would embrace or embody, and which they would oppose. Teachers even have the obligation to ask their students—particularly those who may wish to pursue music as a career—if climbing into this messy bowl is really what they want to do. After all, jazz is not for everyone.

"Jazz" (Not "BAM," Not "Improvisational Music," Not …)

Despite certain overlapping practices and sounds, "BAM" can never entirely replace "jazz" as a genre designation. Neither can "improvisational music," nor any other term. There can be no exact synonym or replacement for any of these because each of them carries its own array of understandings (and misunderstandings), meanings, and values. Indeed, aside from "music," no single word in the English language has been entrusted to represent as many sounds, identities, practices, and ideas over the past century as "jazz." Some people may believe we have asked too much of that word, that it now carries so many meanings as to become practically meaningless. And yet millions of listeners, musicians, publications, and institutions do continue to find it useful. For this reason, we educators should draw attention, in as many classes and settings as possible, to the word's failings, and remind everyone of its critics. We should show our students how and why the definitions, boundaries, perceptions, values, purposes, and sounds of jazz have been questioned and challenged. But then we should also remind them just how resilient and broad and inclusive this word, and the musics and peoples it has come to represent, continues to be. Above all, we should let them know that none of these matters is settled, that questions remain, and that individuals answer these questions themselves, whether they know it or not, whenever they study, create, talk about, and teach jazz.

Notes

1. This chapter is adapted from a keynote address I delivered at the Guelph Jazz Festival Colloquium, in September 2012. The theme of that colloquium was *Pedagogy & Praxis: Improvisation as Social Justice and Social Responsibility*. I thank Ajay Heble and the Colloquium's organizers for the invitation to speak at that event and to contribute this chapter to their collection.
2. Heble, "About ICASP."
3. See, for example, Ake, Garrett, and Goldmark, *Jazz/Not Jazz*; DeVeaux, "Constructing the Jazz Tradition"; Prouty, *Knowing Jazz*.
4. Payton, "Archive," http://nicholaspayton.wordpress.com/.
5. Small, *Musicking*.
6. Tucker, *Swing Shift*; Kajikawa, "The Sound of Struggle"; Washburne, "Latin Jazz."
7. To take just a few examples, see Atkins, *Jazz Planet*; Cerchiari, Cugny, and Kerschbaumer, *Eurojazzland*; Heffley, *Northern Sun, Southern Moon*; Feld, *Jazz Cosmopolitanism in Accra*; McKay, *Circular Breathing*; and Shand, *Jazz: The Australian Accent*.
8. Howland, *Ellington Uptown*; Magee, *The Uncrowned King of Swing*; Wald, "Louis Armstrong."
9. Wald, "Louis Armstrong," 37.
10. Roach, "What 'Jazz' Means to ME," 267.
11. Ibid., 268. Truth be told, and despite Roach's claim, Ellington *did* receive three honorary doctorates—from Washington University, Morgan State University, and Yale University—in 1967, a full five years before Roach published his article.
12. American Musicological Society, "Guidelines for Ethical Conduct"; The Society for Ethnomusicology, "Position Statement on Ethics."
13. "Jass and Jassism"; Taylor, "Jazz: America's Classical Music."
14. See Burns, "Gumbo: Beginnings to 1917."
15. See Pat Metheny's outraged response to a Kenny G recording, http://www.jazzoasis.com/methenyonkennyg.htm.

Works Cited

Ake, David, Charles Hiroshi Garrett, and Daniel Goldmark, eds. *Jazz/Not Jazz: The Music and Its Boundaries*. Berkeley: University of California Press, 2012.

American Musiciological Society. "Guidelines for Ethical Conduct." American Musicological Society website. Accessed October 14, 2014. http://www.ams-net.org/administration/ethics.php.

Atkins, E. Taylor, ed. *Jazz Planet*. Oxford: University Press of Mississippi, 2012.

Burns, Ken. "Gumbo: Beginnings to 1917." In *Jazz: A Film by Ken Burns*. Arlington, VA: 2001. DVD.

Cerchiari, Luca, Laurent Cugny, and Franz Kerschbaumer, eds. *Eurojazzland: Jazz and European Sources, Dynamics, and Contexts*. Boston: Northeastern University Press, 2012.

DeVeaux, Scott. "Constructing the Jazz Tradition: Jazz Historiography." *Black American Literature Forum* 25, no. 3 (Autumn, 1991): 525–60.

Feld, Steven. *Jazz Cosmopolitanism in Accra: Five Musical Years in Ghana*. Durham, NC: Duke University Press, 2012.

Heble, Ajay. "About ICASP." Improvisation, Community, and Social Practice website. Accessed October 7, 2014. http://www.improvcommunity.ca/about.

Heffley, Mike. *Northern Sun, Southern Moon: Europe's Reinvention of Jazz*. New Haven, CT: Yale University Press, 2005.

Howland, John. *Ellington Uptown: Duke Ellington, James P. Johnson, and the Birth of Concert Jazz*. Ann Arbor: University of Michigan Press, 2009.

"Jass and Jassism." In *Keeping Time: Readings in Jazz History* (2nd ed.), edited by Robert Walser, 7–8. New York: Oxford University Press, 2015. Originally published in *The Times Picayune*, June 20, 1918.

Kajikawa, Loren. "The Sound of Struggle: Black Revolutionary Nationalism and Asian American Jazz." In *Jazz/Not Jazz: The Music and Its Boundaries*, edited by David Ake, Charles Hiroshi Garrett, and Daniel Goldmark, 190–216. Berkeley: University of California Press, 2012.

Magee, Jeffrey. *The Uncrowned King of Swing: Fletcher Henderson and Big Band Jazz*. New York: Oxford University Press, 2008.

McKay, George. *Circular Breathing: The Cultural Politics of Jazz in Britain*. Durham, NC: Duke University Press, 2005.

Metheny, Pat. "Pat Metheny on Kenny G." *JazzOasis.com*. Accessed November 12, 2014. http://www.jazzoasis.com/methenyonkennyg.htm.

Payton, Nicholas. "Archive." Nicholas Payton website. Accessed October 15, 2014. http://nicholaspayton.wordpress.com/.

Prouty, Ken. *Knowing Jazz: Community, Pedagogy, and Canon in the Information Age*. Oxford: University Press of Mississippi, 2012.

Roach, Max. "Beyond Categories." In *Keeping Time: Readings in Jazz History* (2nd ed.), edited by Robert Walser, 305–10. New York: Oxford University Press, 2015. First published as "What 'Jazz' Means to ME." *The Black Scholar* (Summer 1972): 3–6.

Shand, John. *Jazz: The Australian Accent*. New South Wales: University of New South Wales Press, 2008.

Small, Christopher. *Musicking: The Meanings of Performing and Listening*. Hanover, NH: Wesleyan University Press, 1998.

Society for Ethnomusicology. "Position Statement on Ethics." The Society for Ethnomusicology website. Accessed October 14, 2014. http://www.ethnomusicology.org/?page=EthicsStatement.

Taylor, William "Billy." "Jazz: America's Classical Music." In *Keeping Time: Readings in Jazz History* (2nd ed.), edited by Robert Walser, 285–89. New York: Oxford University Press, 2015.

Tucker, Sherrie. *Swing Shift: "All-Girl" Bands of the 1940s*. Durham, NC: Duke University Press, 2000.

Wald, Elijah. "Louis Armstrong Loves Guy Lombardo." In *Jazz/Not Jazz: The Music and Its Boundaries*, edited by David Ake, Charles Hiroshi Garrett, and Daniel Goldmark, 31–48. Berkeley: University of California Press, 2012.

Washburne, Christopher. "Latin Jazz, Afro-Latin Jazz, Afri-Cuban Jazz, Cubop, Carribean Jazz, Jazz Latin, or Just … Jazz.: The Politics of Locating an Intercultural Msuic." In *Jazz/Not Jazz: The Music and Its Boundaries*, edited by David Ake, Charles Hiroshi Garrett, and Daniel Goldmark, 89–110. Berkeley: University of California Press, 2012.

3 Improvisation Pedagogy in Theory and Practice

Jesse Stewart

This chapter examines musical improvisation's capacity to foster a sense of community both inside the university classroom and out, focusing in particular on three improvisation-related pedagogical initiatives that I have been involved with over the past few years: (1) the facilitation of a university music ensemble dedicated to improvisatory modes of music making; (2) the directorship of a third-year university music course titled "Improvisation in Theory and Practice"; and (3) the facilitation of a similar course for musicians and nonmusicians alike outside of a traditional university environment. I will discuss some of the things that I have learned through these experiences in the hopes that they might be of use to other educators who are interested in incorporating improvisation into their own pedagogical endeavors.

Shortly after I began teaching at Carleton University in Ottawa, Canada, it came to my attention that the music program's Contemporary Music Ensemble did not have a director. I volunteered to serve as an interim facilitator for the group, a position that I occupied from 2009 to 2011. All musicians were welcome to join the group without an audition. As a result, we had several nonmusic students, graduate students, and community members in the ensemble, although the majority of the ensemble consisted of undergraduate music students. The total number of participants hovered between fifteen and twenty-five during my two-year tenure with the ensemble. Because of the eclectic nature and unusual instrumentation in the group, our musical activities tended to gravitate toward the performance of indeterminate works and various forms of musical improvisation. Each semester, we would work on one large project that we would present at the end of term. One semester, we created an improvised sound track to the 1927 silent film *Metropolis*. Another term we performed Terry Riley's famous minimalist composition *In C*. We also focused on the work of Pauline Oliveros, concentrating in particular on her series of pieces known as *Sonic Meditations*. The group had the good fortune of working directly with Pauline Oliveros during a residency that she conducted at Carleton that year.

The Contemporary Music Ensemble also performed Cornelius Cardew's massive graphic score titled *Treatise*. The score consists of 193 pages of lines, symbols, and shapes that are meant to be interpreted musically. The ensemble worked together over twelve weeks to come up with a strategy for interpreting the score. I ended up creating a simple animated version of the score in which a vertical blue line traversed each page from left to right at different speeds depending on the amount of visual information on the page. The ensemble interpreted the symbols musically when the blue line passed over them. During the performance—which was over two hours in duration—both the members of the ensemble and the audience were seated facing a screen upon which the animated score was projected, allowing the audience to see and hear how we interpreted the piece.

The ensemble also spent a considerable amount of time improvising without reference to particular indeterminate compositions. Sometimes I—or other members of the group—would conduct an improvisation using hand signals inspired by various people including Butch Morris, Walter Thompson, and Dave Clark. I encouraged everyone to take turns conducting the ensemble, and at times we had multiple conductors offering input simultaneously.

Sometimes, when we worked without a conductor, I would suggest a particular parameter or set of parameters that would structure our improvisations. Often these suggestions were aimed at limiting the number of musicians improvising at any one time in an effort to ensure that everyone would be able to hear one another. I also encouraged ensemble members to bring their own ideas and suggestions for group improv activities.

We worked on a simple dialogical model wherein we would improvise and then we would discuss what happened in the improvisation. In our discussions, I tried to steer us away from critical or evaluative comments about the improvisation and more toward description and analysis. I would ask questions like, "What just happened?" "What did you hear?" "What couldn't you hear?" "What patterns of musical interaction did you feel a part of or not feel a part of and why?" "Did you feel supported musically? Why or why not?" We would also talk about different musical roles that we assumed during an improvisation as well as the social implications of those roles.

This dialogic process generated some interesting discussion and some of the most valuable learning experiences for me and I think for other members of the ensemble. On one occasion, a female flutist in the ensemble (whom I will call Shirley) started to assume a leadership role within the music, soloing atop the musical ground being created by the other members of the ensemble. Within a few seconds, another flutist in the group, a young man, started to solo at a much louder dynamic level than Shirley, who promptly stopped playing. This was perhaps the most blatant example of a pattern that I have witnessed many times, namely, male band members silencing female members of the group within the context of so-called free improvisation. When the piece finished, my first inclination was to ask, "What were you doing? Shirley was trying to solo." But instead, I asked the group, as I normally did, "What just happened?" In response, Shirley talked about what she had tried to do musically, and how her musical ideas were quashed when the other flutist started soloing over top of her. She told him how his musical actions made her feel. The other flutist was clearly embarrassed. He apologized and explained that he didn't know he had done that, let alone that his musical actions could carry the kind of impact that they had had on his female coperformer. From that moment on, his playing—and that of much of the rest of the ensemble—was more respectful of all the different voices within the group. Because of that incident, everyone seemed to take to heart the idea that the musical decisions that we make in an improvisatory context have an impact that goes well beyond the sound of the music, and we therefore need to make ethical and responsible decisions when improvising.

I am quite certain part of the reason that the incident had such an impact on him (and on the group as a whole) was that Shirley confronted him directly. In retrospect, I think my decision to not intervene, but instead to create a space for Shirley and others to comment, was the right decision pedagogically. That was a valuable lesson for me: as in musical improvisation, when we improvise pedagogically, sometimes laying out and letting someone else take the lead is the most appropriate and effective decision we can make.

Based in part on my experiences with the group, I ended up mounting a course titled "Improvisation in Theory and Practice," which I taught at Carleton University for the first time in the winter of 2013. The course outline states: "This course will examine musical improvisation as both a theoretical practice and a practical theory. In addition to weekly discussion seminars that focus on selected texts drawn from the emergent field of improvisation studies, the class will engage in experiential forms of learning by actively improvising in a weekly performance-oriented seminar." The assigned textbooks in the course were Derek Bailey's *Improvisation: Its Nature and Practice in Music* and Daniel Fischlin and Ajay Heble's edited anthology *The Other Side of Nowhere: Jazz, Improvisation, and Communities in Dialogue*. On Tuesday afternoons, we discussed readings from these books as well as some additional readings drawn from the online journal *Critical Studies in Improvisation*. We focused on a variety of issues related to improvisation including history/historiography, genre, race, gender, sexuality, and pedagogy, critically examining the ways in which these issues have intersected with improvisatory musical practices historically.

On Thursday afternoons, the seventeen members of the class improvised with one another, working on a similar dialogical model to the one associated with the Contemporary Music Ensemble: we would improvise (often within a loose set of parameters suggested by me or other members of the group), and then we would talk about our improvisations. Although the structure of the course seemingly separated the theory component (Tuesdays) and the practical component (Thursdays), I went to great lengths to emphasize that everything we were doing was both theory and practice—whether we were improvising with one another musically or discussing scholarly writing about improvisation.

Students came to the class from a wide variety of musical backgrounds; some had experience improvising within particular musical genres such as jazz and rock. Other students who were steeped in the classical tradition claimed to have no experience with musical improvisation. I suggested otherwise based on the fact that in every mode of music making involving human musicians—even notated and highly prescriptive forms of music—performers routinely make decisions in the course of performance: decisions in response to the acoustics of the room, to the sound or action of a particular instrument, and so on.

Given the diverse musical backgrounds of the students in the course, I suggested that we focus on free improvisation or what I prefer to think of as "pan-idiomatic improvisation." To quote from the course outline again:

> The Thursday afternoon performance seminars will focus primarily on so called "free" improvisation—what Derek Bailey has called "non-idiomatic" improvisation; that is, improvised music that does not try to represent a particular musical genre in a sustained way. Instead, we will be free to draw on musical techniques and signifiers derived from virtually *any* musical tradition, incorporating them into the music that we create collaboratively in the moment of performance. In this regard, it is perhaps more accurate to think of our musical activities as constituting a form of "pan-idiomatic" free improvisation rather than "non-idiomatic." Focusing on such modes of musical interaction will provide opportunities for participants to hone their listening skills and expand their musical vocabularies, two transferrable skills that are of obvious value in any musical context.

We recorded all of our improvising sessions, and I made an MP3 of each session available to the members of the class in order to provide opportunities for them to reflect on, and critically engage with, their own playing and that of the class as a whole. Audio recordings cannot really capture the complexities of an improvisatory music performance, offering instead a kind of sonic snapshot of a multilayered experience. Nonetheless, listening to recordings of our own improvisations can be a very powerful learning tool—they can draw attention to both individual and group musical habits that might be so deeply ingrained that they go unnoticed in the course of performance. In my view, such ingrained musical habits are often hegemonic in the Gramscian sense: they are taken for granted but are nonetheless ideologically coded.

Grading and evaluation in the course revolved around the following:

1 Participation in class discussions/reading response questions
2 An improv journal in which students reflected on course content including assigned readings, class discussions, group improvisations, and the recordings of our Thursday afternoon performance seminars

3 A short research essay that asked students to research the history of their own instrument in relation to improvisatory modes of music making
4 A long essay (and proposal) that could be on any topic related to musical improvisation
5 A presentation of an idea for the final group performance
6 The final group performance itself

In my view, if a person really wants to absorb the language of any mode of music making, it is important that he or she listens to—and learns from—the history/histories of that music. As a means to that end, I began most classes with some listening. I also included a recommended listening list on the course outline that included YouTube links to recordings by many improvisers including Derek Bailey, Anthony Braxton, William Parker, Milford Graves, Fred Anderson, Kidd Jordan, Hamid Drake, AMM, Cecil Taylor, Tony Oxley, Alexander Von Schlippenbach, Evan Parker, the Globe Unity Orchestra, Instant Composers Pool, Peter Brötzmann, George Lewis, Fred Frith, John Zorn, Muhal Richard Abrams, Roscoe Mitchell, Pauline Oliveros, Irene Schweizer, Joëlle Léandre, Maggie Nicols, Bill Dixon, the Art Ensemble of Chicago, Phil Minton, Butch Morris, Wadada Leo Smith, and others. Unfortunately, I do not know the extent to which members of the class actually listened to the recordings. One thing I will do differently the next time I offer the course will be to add a listening test to further encourage students to listen to recordings by accomplished improvisers outside of class time.

At a few points throughout the semester, students voiced dissatisfaction about the assigned readings in the course and our discussions thereof. On numerous occasions, students voiced questions like, "Why can't we just improvise? Why do we have to spend so much time reading about it?"[1] A number of students questioned the emphasis that some of the readings placed on power dynamics within improvisatory modes of music making, and the emphasis on difference along lines of gender, race, sexuality, and the like. On numerous occasions in our class discussions and in the students' improv journals, I heard or read statements like, "Sexism and racism are things of the past. They aren't an issue for our generation. So why do we have to keep talking about them?" One of the effects of statements like this, when they were voiced in class, was to discourage class members who found themselves in minoritized positions to voice their own experiences of discrimination on the bandstand, in the classroom, or in society in general. Several women in the class expressed discomfort with the masculinist tone of some of the things that were said in class, but they generally did so privately within the context of their journals. In some cases, they went on to indicate that they chose to remain silent in class because they didn't want to gain a negative reputation among their male classmates, thereby running the risk of being further ostracized or otherwise punished for speaking out.

I exerted as much critical pressure as possible on masculinist attitudes within the class and on pronouncements concerning the irrelevance of race, class, and gender to the study and performance of improvised music. In response to the suggestion that racism was a thing of the past, I drew attention to the institutional frameworks that have surrounded cultural production and music education historically and the overwhelmingly disproportionate amount of support that modes of music making that have emerged out of European and European-American communities have received when compared to jazz and other forms of improvisatory musics to have emanated primarily out of the African Diaspora. Drawing on George Lewis's important work (1996), we talked about the problematic—and patently false—racialized taxonomies of improvised music that continue to circulate in many discourses surrounding contemporary music. I also drew attention to the fact that our class—which consisted overwhelmingly of white university students—was not in the best position to make pronouncements concerning the supposed end of racism, classism, or sexism. This led to an intense, and I think generative, discussion of privilege—white privilege, male privilege, class privilege, and the like. We discussed some of the ways in which privileges of various kinds play out inside the academy, on the bandstand, and in the wider public sphere.

These conversations were not easy or comfortable. But I regarded them then—as I do now—as being fundamentally important to both the aims of the class and to the study and performance of musical improvisation. These sorts of power dynamics continue to exist, shaping both cultural production and knowledge production. We do not do ourselves—or our students—any favors by turning a blind eye to them or pretending they don't exist. In some ways, a class on improvisation, particularly a class on "pan-idiomatic" improvisation, is uniquely positioned to foster discussions about the negotiation of differences, musical and otherwise, and the cultural politics of music making. But it is important that the discussion doesn't end there. Indeed, I hope that educators working in all facets of the music curriculum—including both performance and musicology courses with more canonized institutional and intellectual histories—find opportunities to have these sorts of conversations with their students.

I took some comfort in something that one student wrote in his journal in response to some of the discussions we were having in class. He began by saying, "It is kind of upsetting how many readings we do are focused on inequality," thereby echoing statements that several of his classmates had made. But then he went on to state:

> The passages from this week about gender and improvisation were pretty hard-hitting. I found that as much as I wanted to disagree with the idea that these injustices are present in our daily lives as musicians, I simply couldn't. Prior to this class I've been in group situations where collaborative musical improvisation was taking place between a

mixed gendered group and as I look back I can recall times where the female participants were being ignored in certain ways and not given the opportunity to lead the jam. I've seen male musicians interrupt contributions of their female peers. I've even seen certain musicians of the male variety give hostile looks towards a female musician who is trying to add something different into the sonic mix. When I realized that these issues of gender that we've been discussing in class are very real, it gave me a really terrible feeling. I hope I've never subconsciously contributed to this injustice, but from now on I will certainly be more careful to consider everyone in an improvisatory musical setting before picking up my instrument.

I was pleased to read this statement, which I believe was sincere. Interestingly, I heard a corresponding change in this student's playing around the time that he voiced these ideas. To my ears, he became a better improviser. He listened more attentively; he found ways to support his bandmates musically to a greater extent, even if that meant laying out when his first instinct was to play.

I'd like to discuss one other aspect of the course that I thought yielded interesting results, namely, the group project. Toward the end of the semester, the class was divided into five groups consisting of four students each. Each group was asked to come up with a proposal for a final public performance of improvised music that would include every member of the class and present a public concert of improvised music. Each group presented its proposal to the entire class, and then the class as a whole discussed which project they would pursue. They ended up combining ideas from several groups to come up with a new idea: a performance titled "Sounds in Space" that featured a series of planet-inspired improvisatory performances that would take place in multiple rooms in Carleton University's music department. The idea was to create an environment in which the audience would have to circulate between and among the different rooms, in effect improvising their own pathways through the space and through the music.

In the Saturn-themed room, the class created a prepared piano installation, with which visitors could interact. In addition to preparations to the piano itself, the members of the class created a series of chimes that were activated by pressing on the keys of the prepared piano. Five pianists in the class took turns doing solo and duo piano improvisations in the rooms labeled Mercury and Uranus. In the Earth room, a student in the class who was also doing an independent project with me in new media built an eight-foot-tall, three-dimensional plywood tree. A series of small speakers hung from the tree's branches played recordings that she had made of four generations of her family members discussing their Indian ancestry and family history.

The class decided that the windowless room in the center of the music floor should be the sun, around which all the planet-themed rooms would orbit. This room featured improvised performances by various ad hoc group-ings of musicians as well as chalk drawings done in real time in response to the music. Interestingly, the visual artists who created the murals and, in fact, quite a few of the musicians who ended up performing, weren't actually members of the class. A few of them weren't even music students but were friends of class members or others who heard about the performance and decided to participate. To my mind, this affirmed improvised music's potential to foster inclusivity and a sense of community.

One of the most elaborate aspects of the performance was the Mars-themed room. At the time, I happened to have a portable twenty-foot geo-desic dome that I was planning to use in an art installation the following summer. When the class found out about the dome, they asked if they could borrow it for the performance. We ended up setting it up inside the larg-est space in the music department. At fifteen-feet tall, the dome was just touching the ceiling. The audience was seated inside the dome, while the musicians were arranged outside the dome's walls. The class created a short video using found footage of recent space missions to Mars and images of the Martian landscape taken by the Mars Rover. This video was projected onto the sides of the white dome along with red-colored lights that were visible to both the performers and the audience. The members of the class created an improvised musical soundtrack to accompany the video.

The "Sounds in Space" performance was highly ambitious. The members of the class all seemed to feel a considerable amount of investment in the project, which generated a strong sense of community among performers and audience members alike. I think the high level of investment and sense of community in this project stemmed largely from the fact that the project was the class's idea. In what amounted to a kind of improvisatory peda-gogy, I established some loose parameters surrounding the assignment, and I helped to facilitate some of the brainstorming and logistics related to the project. But mostly I tried not to get in the way of the students' creativity.

In the fall of 2014, I had an opportunity to offer the "Improvisation in Theory and Practice" course again, this time through a program called "Discovery University" that was inspired by the Clemente Course in the Humanities developed by Earl Shorris in New York City in the mid-1990s. Run by the Ottawa Mission, Discovery University offers free university-level classes, taught by university professors, to adults experiencing poverty or other forms of economic distress. There are no tuition fees. Likewise, text-books and transportation to and from class are provided free of charge.

In the months before the class began, the Ottawa Mission advertised the course, emphasizing that no prior musical training was required. Prospective students applied to be in the class, providing a rationale for why they want to participate. We decided to limit the course enrollment to fifteen: as most improvisers know, when the number of improvising musicians in a given ensemble increases, the capacity for group cohesiveness and listening gener-ally decreases, particularly in the case of inexperienced improvisers. In my experience, this is often true for discussion seminars as well. Even an enroll-ment of fifteen poses musical and pedagogical challenges.

The Discovery University class was structured in much the same way as the previous edition of the course: classes alternated between discussion seminars and performance seminars. In addition to our Friday afternoon classes, the students participated in weekly small-group discussion sessions on Wednesday evenings that were facilitated by a number of volunteers. These discussion sessions provided opportunities for further analysis of, and reflection on, our Friday class discussions, the assigned readings, and recordings of the improvised music we made together. They also provided an opportunity for members of the class to share concerns and ideas about the course with their discussion group facilitators who relayed the informa-tion to me.

We began the term by looking at the etymological origins of the term "improvise," which comes from *improvisus*, the Latin word for "not seen beforehand." With that definition in mind, I emphasized the fact that we are all improvisers; we all respond to unanticipated actions and events on a daily basis. Framing our activities in this way helped to demystify musical improvisation for some of the participants, especially those without prior musical training.

We often discussed the social implications of musical improvisation. I emphasized that part of the aim of the course was to create as inclusive an environment for music making as possible. I suggested that within free improvisation, there are no wrong notes; there are only different choices that we can make as improvisers. I also emphasized our shared responsibility to one another and to the music that we created together: we need to be mindful of our musical choices and their effects on our coperformers and on the sound of the music as a whole. We also examined the power dynamics in improvised music, including the music we made together in class. I was encouraged by something that one of the students wrote at the end of the semester: "This particular course, Music and Improv, has affected a change in my outlook re[garding] inclusiveness and individual voice. I must learn more. It fits in with my commitment to democracy. [...] I thought music was not for me although I am creative in writing and arts/crafts. Also in survival. I love sound and now I am exploring music even more."

One of the pedagogical challenges in the course was how to foster a climate of trust and mutual respect, a challenge that all educators face when introducing improvisation into a class full of people who don't know each other. Compounding this challenge in the context of the Discovery University course was the fact that several students in the class experienced anxiety conditions and/or other mental health issues. This prompted me to reexam-ine certain assumptions that I had held about ways of fostering a sense of community and trust inside a classroom. For example, in virtually every other improvisation-focused pedagogical situation with which I have been involved, I have always suggested that the class set up in the round so that all members of the class can see and hear one another. In addition to creating a sense of collegiality and community within a class and/or ensemble, this circular model of socio-musical space has the added benefit of facilitating visual cues among all members of the group. However, within the Discovery University class, several students found the circular seating arrangement uncomfortable because it reminded them of group therapy sessions, an unpleasant association. When this was brought to my attention, I suggested that we try to imagine that we were gathered around a campfire, and the fire would be the music we would make together. We also explored a variety of other seating arrangements.

During our first class meeting, one member of the class who indicated that he lives with an anxiety condition suggested that we begin our performance-oriented classes with some sort of meditation in order to calm our nerves and create an environment that would be conducive to mindfulness and creative expression. In response, I introduced the class to Pauline Oliveros' *Sonic Meditations*. We began with *Sonic Improvisation VIII*: "Environmental Dialogue," which asks performers to begin by observing their own breathing. "As you become aware of sounds from the environment," the score reads, "gradually begin to reinforce the pitch of the sound source. Reinforce either vocally, mentally or with an instrument. If you lose touch with the source, wait quietly for another."[2] This piece seemed to focus our listening, heightening our awareness of all of the sounds around us. It also provided an opportunity for us to discuss the importance of active listening within any improvisatory setting.

At our next performance seminar, I suggested that we begin with *Sonic Meditation* X, which consists of the following instruction:

> Sit in a circle with your eyes closed. Begin by observing your own breathing. Gradually form a mental image of one person who is sitting in the circle. Sing a long tone to that person. Then sing the pitch that person is singing. Change your mental image to another person and repeat until you have contacted every person in the circle one or more times.[3]

As soon as I had read the score's instructions, one member of the class quietly left the room and did not return for the remainder of the class. He later explained to me that he has schizoaffective disorder, one of the results of which is that he has what he described as "trust issues": the thought of closing his eyes in a room full of strangers seated in a circle—and then singing a tone to each of them—was overwhelmingly stressful for him. In response, I assured him that we would not do any more exercises that required us to close our eyes.

From that point on, I tried a variety of other approaches at the outset of class to focus our attention and put class members at ease. One of the most successful strategies was to begin with conducted improvisations; it seemed as though the members of the class appreciated the structure that a conducted improvisation offered. It also enabled me to change things quickly if it became clear that some members of the class were uncomfortable with a particular musical situation. One of the most useful conducting gestures I used was to hold up my hands and rapidly switch from palms facing forward to palms facing backward. We used this gesture to signal that all performers currently sounding should stop, and all performers not sounding should begin playing. In addition to allowing us to change the pattern of musical interaction quickly, this hand signal introduced abrupt changes in the texture of the music that were often quite interesting musically.

There were several significant differences between the Discovery University class and the previous edition of the course. For one thing, the Discovery University class was considerably more diverse in terms of race, gender, culture, level of musical ability, and physical ability/disability. On numerous occasions, we discussed the ways in which improvisation—musical and otherwise—can help us negotiate our differences without minimizing or erasing those differences but rather exploring and celebrating them. I encouraged class members to draw on their own musical and cultural backgrounds in the music we made together. One week, a member of the class sang a First Nations chant that the rest of the class supported with improvised percussive and vocal accompaniment. Another week, a member of the class brought in a Vietnamese children's rhyme that she remembered from her childhood. I encouraged her to use it as the basis for a vocal improvisation that would provide a starting point for a group improvisation. As she recited the poem, she switched between Vietnamese and English, experimenting vocally and adding animal sounds and other vocal sounds in response to the text. The rest of the class supported her musically, responding to the sounds that she made both vocally and instrumentally. To my ears, this was one of the most interesting improvisations that we created together. The class agreed that we would include the nursery rhyme in our end-of-term performance.

Unlike a traditional university course, there were no written assignments or grades in the class (or in any Discovery University course for that matter). At first, I worried that the absence of a method of evaluation might discourage students from doing the assigned readings. However, I found the opposite to be true: all of the students in the course came to class fully prepared and engaged. It became clear that the vast majority of the students genuinely wanted to be there; they wanted to learn and make music with one another.

Another significant difference between the two versions of the course was the fact that many of the musicians in the Discovery University class had little or no prior musical training. Because of this, I encouraged the students in the class to use their voices as musical instruments if they felt so inclined, and to bring in a variety of found objects that we would explore as musical instruments. Among the items brought in by members of the class were a cheese grater, cookie tins, cat toys, tin cans, a pitch pipe, bells, recorders, and rummage-sale ukuleles. I too brought in a variety of instruments for the members of the class to explore including shakers, bells, rattles, waterphone, and other percussive odds and ends.

I also brought in some higher-tech instruments including an instrument known as the "reactable," a virtual modular synthesizer and digital sampler in the form of an interactive illuminated table. By placing and manipulating blocks on the reactable surface, performers can control different parameters of pre-recorded sounds in an intuitive way. In addition to the reactable, I provided several iPads equipped with the "Adaptive Use Musical Instrument" or AUMI software, which uses an iPad's built-in webcam to track movements, translating those movements into user-selected sounds. The AUMI helped put all of the musicians in the course on more equal footing: no one can really be better at improvising with the AUMI than anyone else.

At one point, one member of the class used his umbrella to trigger a response from the AUMI software. This act immediately struck me as a beautiful performative gesture that had the added advantage of being more easily detectable by the iPad's webcam than some smaller movements. It occurred to me that an umbrella might be an interesting metaphor for some of the issues that we were discussing in the course and that some class members dealt with in the context of their own lives: an umbrella is both a symbol of protection/shelter and inclusiveness. Furthermore, the radial arms of an umbrella can be seen as a symbol of the considerable diversity within the class and the sense of community that developed among the participants, while the central supporting shaft represented our individual identities. In this view, the fabric that forms the protective outer layer of an umbrella could be seen to symbolize the improvisatory music that we made together, which was supported by the class at both individual and collective levels. As one class member put it, "We were dependent on one another while at the same time we were independent as each of us was doing our own thing, playing whatever we wanted for as long as we wanted." We discussed these ideas in class and agreed that *Umbrella*s would be the title of our end-of-term performance. Our course also happened to coincide with the so-called "Umbrella Revolution" in Hong Kong, a movement with which many members of the class stood in solidarity.

The class was fortunate to have been invited to perform on December 1, 2014, at the National Arts Centre 4th Stage, a 180-seat cabaret-style performance venue inside one of Canada's pre-eminent concert halls. We worked out a loose structure for the performance within which improvisation took place. We began with a spoken introduction, delivered by me, that explained that the performance was the culmination of a semester-long course offered through the Discovery University program. The other members of the class were seated inconspicuously throughout the audience. While I was speaking, the other performers began tapping rounded stones together, creating a sonic texture reminiscent of the sound of rainfall. In my reading, the fact that the other members of the ensemble were hidden at the outset of the performance signified the fact that those who are economically disadvantaged are often rendered invisible by mainstream society and dominant discourses. The class's sonic interruption of my opening monologue posed a symbolic challenge to such discourses, creating a space for their voices to be heard in the improvisatory, community-affirming music that followed.

The sound of the tapped stones gradually increased in density and volume until the sound of thunder was added. At that point, I opened a colorful umbrella on stage, and the performers seated in the audience responded by opening umbrellas of their own. I then moved to an AUMI-equipped iPad and used the movements of my umbrella to trigger woodblock samples reminiscent of the sound of the tapped stones. One by one, other members of the class came to the stage, triggering additional sounds from three more iPads running the AUMI software. I then moved to the drum set, playing drums with my umbrella. The rest of the class gradually made their way to the stage adding improvised piano, electric guitar, recorder, waterphone, and various percussion sounds to the mix.

At one point during the performance, we incorporated our voices, using the constituent phonemes in the word "umbrella" as our lexicon of improvisatory vocal sounds. I used the reactable to add pre-recorded samples of the word "umbrella" spoken by the members of the class in four different languages. I layered these samples on top of the vocal sounds being supplied by the class and on top of one another, speeding some up, slowing others down, and adding various delays and reverb effects in an attempt to reconstitute the sound of rain once again, this time using speech sounds. We continued to improvise atop this texture, eventually incorporating the Vietnamese nursery rhyme that one class member had introduced to us several weeks before. In an improvisatory vocal style that traversed the entire continuum between speech and song, she delivered one line of the poem at a time in English and/or Vietnamese, incorporating a wide variety of extended vocal techniques. She introduced one innovative vocal technique that we had not seen her (or anyone else for that matter) use before: at one point she picked up a plastic water-filled cup and blew into the straw while humming, placing her cordless vocal mic against the bottom of the cup. This created a very interesting sonic texture that seemed to heighten the rest of the ensemble's— and audience's—attention to her vocals.

Toward the end of the piece, I introduced a recursive drum groove atop of which the electric guitarist played an improvised solo. This seemed to have a cohesive effect on the rest of the ensemble and the music we created together. One member of the group summarized:

> I could feel something different in our playing. We started to relax and enjoy ourselves and you could feel the rhythm of the music. I looked across the stage and we were all playing in sync. I was moving to the beat and felt completely at ease. This went on for several minutes and was not rehearsed. I don't remember this happening at any of the practices or at the dress rehearsal. ... It was a great feeling of combined success.

I too felt that the *Umbrellas* performance and the Discovery University "Improvisation in Theory and Practice" course as a whole represented a combined success. In the past, I have tended to shy away from discussing my own work as an educator. The main reason is that I would not want to inadvertently objectify the students with whom I have had the good fortune of collaborating or their work. But I also recognize that it is important for educators, musicians, students, researchers, and other cultural workers who are committed to musical improvisation to share our experiences and our ideas with one another in forums such as this. By doing so, we can learn from one another and work together to develop and implement pedagogies of improvisation both inside the classroom and out.

Notes

1. In his excellent essay "Teaching Improvised Music: An Ethnographic Memoir" (which was part of the required reading for the "Improvisation in Theory and Practice" course), George Lewis discusses a similar response from some of the students in an improvisation class that he taught at the University of California, San Diego.
2. Oliveros, *Sonic Meditations*, VIII.
3. Ibid., X.

Works Cited

Bailey, Derek. *Improvisation: Its Nature and Practice in Music.* Cambridge, MA: Da Capo Press, 1992.

Fischlin, Daniel, and Ajay Heble, eds. *The Other Side of Nowhere: Jazz, Improvisation, and Communities in Dialogue.* Middletown, CT: Wesleyan University Press, 2004.

Lewis, George. "Improvised Music after 1950: Afrological and Eurological Perspectives." *Black Music Research Journal* 16, no. 1 (Spring 1996): 91–122.

———. "Teaching Improvised Music: An Ethnographic Memoir." In *Arcana: Musicians on Music*, edited by John Zorn, 78–109. New York: Granary Books, 2000.

Oliveros, Pauline. *Sonic Meditations.* Sharon, VT: Smith Publications, 1971.

4 Free Improvisation and Performance Anxiety in Musicians

Kathryn Ladano

Introduction

Various types of anxiety affect people in different situations and at different points in their lives. For musicians, performance anxiety can have potentially devastating effects on professional careers. It can negatively affect both the ability to present musical skills to the public and the overall enjoyment of being a musician. This type of anxiety is quite prevalent and has affected many musicians at one time or another, to varying degrees of severity. Despite its prevalence, few musicians know how to alleviate their anxiety beyond prescription medication such as beta-blockers.

Although somewhat resistant to definition, performance anxiety exists in many different forms, both in our daily lives and in the performing arts. In music, it is generally acknowledged to feature the experience of apprehension and/or impairment of musical skills in public. The symptoms are wide ranging and can affect individuals very differently, making the disorder more difficult to classify. Performance anxiety is particularly prevalent among music students at the postsecondary level, yet there are few resources available or systems in place to help them work through it.

Several recent studies show promise that the practice of free improvisation among musicians with performance anxiety may help alleviate symptoms. Not only do these studies show that practicing improvisation can reduce anxiety, they have also shown that free improvisation, in particular, can help musicians recover the joy experienced in making music, which may have been lost due to anxiety. Recent work by music therapists has also shown that the practice of improvisation holds benefits that go beyond performance anxiety, helping musicians to engage in more creative forms of music making where the pressure of playing wrong notes is eliminated. This process opens the door for musicians to create their own personal art, shifting their focus internally, potentially helping to unlock and deal with repressed emotions in a positive way.

Through the examination of specific studies conducted on improvisation and anxiety, research on improvisation pedagogy, my experiences as a teacher of improvisation, and my recent interviews with students and professors of improvisation, this chapter will explore the ways in which the practice of free improvisation can benefit individuals with performance anxiety, and how these benefits may extend to help young musicians in particular, to work through a variety of anxieties and pressures. It will also explore the ways in which incorporating free improvisation practice into music education could benefit young musicians, providing them with new ways of dealing with the stresses of university life. By turning to free improvisation as a means of coping with performance anxiety, we might begin to shift the discursive and psychic axes of anxiety from the individual to the collective. Evidently, performance anxiety manifests as a profoundly individual problem: those afflicted feel unable to perform *as individuals* in front of *groups*. In a carefully cultivated pedagogical or performative space, however, free improvisation can become a means of integrating individuals—even those (perhaps especially those) who may be isolated or alienated by performance anxiety—into the collective, making the community a potential space for empowerment and healing.

What Is Performance Anxiety?

One of the most common forms of anxiety experienced by professional, amateur, and student musicians is performance anxiety. Although descriptions of the disorder can vary, one of the most widely used definitions, provided by psychologist Paul G. Salmon, describes it as follows:

> The experience of persisting, distressful apprehension and/or actual impairment of performance skills in a public context, to a degree unwarranted given the individual's musical aptitude, training, and level of preparation.[1]

In the fifth edition of the *Diagnostic and Statistical Manual of Mental Disorders (DSM-V)*, released in 2013, performance anxiety is considered to be a subset of social phobia and is defined as follows:

> A persistent fear of one or more social or performance situations in which the person is exposed to unfamiliar people or to possible scrutiny by others. The individual fears that he or she will act in a way (or show anxiety symptoms) that will be embarrassing and humiliating.[2]

Although performance anxiety definitions can be quite broad as they can encompass many different types of similar fears, the definition of music performance anxiety was elaborated in 2001 by psychology professor Andrew Steptoe, who suggests that it has four distinct components:

1 Affect or feeling (the primary component), resulting in feelings of anxiety, tension, dread, panic, etc.
2 Problems of cognition, resulting in loss of concentration, memory, failure, or the misreading of a musical score.

3 Behavioral reactions such as failure of technique, or trembling.
4 Physiological reactions such as breathing disturbances, salivation, heart-rate increase, etc.[3]

Steptoe's definition is useful because it differentiates music performance anxiety from more general definitions of stage fright and focuses on the most common symptoms experienced. Steptoe has also acknowledged that this kind of anxiety can build gradually over time in anticipation of a performance.

The causes of performance anxiety are usually not known by those experiencing it. Research has suggested numerous potential causes: musical or technical deficiencies, cognitive or emotional problems, career stress, or post-traumatic experiences.[4] It is often a complex problem in musicians, with potentially complex solutions. Treatments are numerous but often include cognitive therapy, drugs, psychotherapy, and meditation. Unfortunately, most music students are unable to receive help dealing with this kind of anxiety, which is extremely prevalent, particularly in postsecondary music programs, where there is considerable pressure to perform perfectly in order to ensure high marks in performance courses. Students who do end up seeking help to deal with their anxieties usually must do so outside of their respective programs via the treatment options listed above.

Treatments such as medication and psychotherapy are certainly helpful, but music therapist Cheryl Dileo has argued that because musicians respond to music differently than nonmusicians, the most viable approach to treating anxiety in musicians is through the use of music itself.[5] Recent research has taken this approach, specifically using the practice of free improvisation as a treatment for performance anxiety. Because this practice can be conducted with relative ease within any music program, perhaps it offers a viable solution to performance anxiety, making it more readily available to pressured students. Additionally, this type of practice holds pedagogical benefits that extend beyond performance anxiety. I will discuss these in more detail in the section Free Improvisation and Education.

What Is Free Improvisation?

Improvisation is the most common of all types of musical expression. It exists in every culture and would have been the very first type of performance, practiced before any music was notated or memorized. In fact, all we do in music and art is improvised at one point or another. Composers improvise their musical creations before transforming them into compositions; Arnold Schoenberg—whose scores are famous for their exhaustive level of composition, musical instruction, and detail—defined composition as a "slowed down improvisation."[6] Many classically trained musicians today find improvisation to be outside of their comfort zone, whereas musicians in earlier times, such as the Medieval, Baroque, and Classical eras, were expected to be able to improvise.[7] For example, in the Baroque era, musicians improvised based on a figured bass pattern, and in the Classical era, cadences/cadenzas and ornamentations were often improvised. Beethoven was renowned as a skilled improviser before achieving recognition as a composer.[8] Improvisation was common and played a very important role during the height of Western art music in the seventeenth and eighteenth centuries. Today, improvisation exists, but artists within the classical tradition often painstakingly preserve compositions such as orchestral works, striving to recreate them as authentically as possible without placing much emphasis on individual creativity. By the nineteenth century, the rise of conservatories and the concert hall gradually put an end to the majority of concert improvisation, placing a greater emphasis on specialization and note-for-note playing of musical scores.[9] At the end of the eighteenth century, music conservatories rose in prominence with the primary purpose of preserving musical standards through standardized instruction.[10]

Like performance anxiety, free improvisation has also been resistant to definition. Simply put, free improvisation tends to lack any specific rules, relying more on aural cues and individual expression, rather than fitting into a specific harmonic, rhythmic, or formal framework. Derek Bailey quite accurately describes it as being "the most widely practiced of all musical activities and the least acknowledged and understood."[11] Researcher Jared Burrows discusses free improvisation in a very simple way, implying that it is perhaps best defined in open terms with minimal restrictions: "Freely improvised music is a music in which there are no preconceived systems for melody, harmony, or rhythm. In this kind of music making, musicians simply begin playing when they choose and stop when they are finished."[12]

In his book, *Free Play*, violist and author Stephen Nachmanovitch focuses on the inner sources of improvisation and how he feels this type of expression can result in the pure joy of creating art. Nachmanovitch is no stranger to this type of activity, having spent years cultivating a musical practice where improvisation has been marginalized. In the book, he discusses his first, very personal experiences practicing free improvisation. He describes such an experience as follows:

> I had found a freedom that was both exhilarating and exciting. Looking into the moment of improvisation, I was uncovering patterns related to every kind of creativity; uncovering clues as well to living a life that is self-creating, self-organizing, and authentic. I came to see improvisation as a master key to creativity.[13]

Researchers and music therapists are beginning to discover that experiences such as this are not unique, and that the practice of free improvisation may hold great benefits for musicians with performance anxiety, and potentially other anxieties as well, offering a valuable creative outlet where one need not worry about playing a wrong note. This liberation from mistakes is key in assessing the value of freely improvised music and is likely the main reason why it has been seen to reduce anxiety. When musicians no longer need to fear playing incorrect notes or getting lost, they can concentrate on different aspects of music, allowing them to look inward and think more creatively about what they are producing. This type of musical exploration is still far too uncommon in our educational system. If it were practiced more regularly as part of standard musical training, it is possible that performance anxiety could be addressed more effectively. At the very least, the incorporation of free improvisation practice would allow individuals to work together as a collective in an encouraging environment where students are free from judgment, as opposed to a more traditional masterclass environment where "mistakes" are pointed out and students engage in a continual search for perfection.

Free Improvisation As Therapy for Performance Anxiety

Several studies from the past 25 years have shown evidence that the practice of free improvisation can benefit musicians suffering from performance anxiety. Music therapist Louise Montello conducted the first two studies of this kind in 1989, and with the assistance of Coons and Kantor in 1990. Montello's 1990 study involved a twelve-week music therapy intervention for freelance professional musicians experiencing performance anxiety. It featured three components: musical improvisation, three performances in front of an audience, and awareness techniques such as verbal processing of anxiety responses.[14] The results of this study showed that the participants became "significantly more confident as performers and less anxious" than the control subjects used.[15] Montello's 1989 study also showed group improvisation to be an effective means of treating performance anxiety. In her therapy sessions, she found that her subjects became more accepting, less judgmental, and more musically expressive as they were able to take the focus off themselves during performance and express their music to an audience in ways that made them feel less self-conscious.[16]

Music therapist Youngshin Kim also conducted two separate studies on free improvisation and performance anxiety. In his 2005 study, he examined the combined effects of musical improvisation and desensitizing techniques on reducing performance anxiety in female college pianists. The results of this study showed that a combined treatment of improvisation and desensitization was effective at reducing anxiety, and the majority of subjects felt that improvisation "played an important role not only in reducing their subjective anxiety, but also in recovering the joy of music making."[17] His second study in 2008 used two different approaches to treating performance anxiety: improvisation-assisted desensitization, and music-assisted progressive muscle relaxation and imagery. The results showed both treatments as effective in improving anxiety in the subjects, with no difference in effectiveness of one treatment over the other. Although Kim's results are intriguing and show promise that the practice of free improvisation may hold benefits for musicians with anxiety, it would be interesting to know if his results varied according to gender or instrument type.

The most recent study on free improvisation and performance anxiety was conducted by Robert Allen and published in 2010. Allen's study compared performance anxiety symptoms in students performing a free improvisation versus a repertory piece and used a gender-balanced sample of 36 piano students ranging in age from seven to eighteen years. The objectives of this study were to examine the relationship of students' levels of anxiety to free improvisation and repertory pieces in a performance, and to examine the effectiveness of free improvisation as a treatment for the reduction of performance anxiety.[18] The students were assigned to three separate groups, and those in the treatment group received six weekly individual sessions observed by a researcher in which they developed a free improvisation. All of the students in these sessions were taught basic devices that could be used to develop their ideas, such as scales, harmony, and rhythmic elements. The results of Allen's study showed free improvisation to be an "effective treatment for significantly reducing anxiety during the public performance of a musical work."[19] Allen's research found anxiety levels to be significantly higher for repertory pieces; following the study, the majority of students in all age groups agreed to the statement: "Improvising makes me feel better about performing in front of people."[20] Although these results are promising, there are clear limitations to Allen's study. Like Kim, Allen focused entirely on piano students, so the effect of free improvisation on anxiety levels in musicians of different instruments is still unclear. His study also did not incorporate group improvisation, so the differences of practicing free improvisation in a group or solo setting, if any, are also unclear. Very little research of this kind has been conducted in the context of group improvisation, which is something that needs to be addressed in order more fully to understand the impact free improvisation practice may have on individuals with performance anxiety, or other types of anxieties.

Music therapist Dorita Berger has found some success using improvisation as a therapy tool for clients experiencing anxiety. She has suggested that "Music improvisation therapy … is the most direct therapeutic intervention to address the problems of the musical being as a person and as a musician."[21] Her work, indeed, has gone beyond performance anxiety to help musicians suffering from a variety of different mental and emotional issues. She has found that through the act of improvisation, unconscious and often repressed feelings emerge. She describes one such experience with a professional violist: "In working improvisationally, E.M. heard the sounds and sensed bodily impulses created by the sounds of his repressed anger. Exploring these musically not only helped him find relief and possible resolution but also self confidence in his creative abilities to make music without needing to be technically perfect."[22] This experience is significant because the violist was able to effectively use improvisation not only to gain confidence in performance settings, but also to work through emotional issues such as his repressed anger.

Evidence to support free improvisation as a viable treatment for performance anxiety (and potentially other anxieties) certainly exists, but these studies are still relatively new, not overly abundant, and feature many limitations. However, my own observations and personal experiences support the conclusions of these studies. I currently work as a professional improvising musician and as a professor of improvisation at Wilfrid Laurier University where I direct the Improvisation Concerts Ensemble and teach private studio lessons in improvisation. This work has put me in regular contact with many university students who major in a variety of different instruments and are enrolled in all years of study; many of them struggle with various types of anxieties and personal problems on a daily basis. It has also allowed me to think about and work through my own anxieties through my performance work. As a musician heavily affected by performance anxiety myself, I have found over the years that free improvisation helped reduce my levels of anxiety both before and during performances. For example, when performing recitals of composed music, I always begin each performance with a short freely improvised piece, and this significantly reduces my anxiety, making the rest of my program much more comfortable for me to get through. In addition to performance anxiety, I suffer from social anxiety disorder (or social phobia). This makes social encounters of all kinds, particularly with individuals whom I do not know intimately, extremely difficult and anxiety inducing. I have found that free improvisation in group settings has helped me greatly in this respect. What I am unable to communicate with words in a social setting, I am able to communicate musically through my instrument with confidence; I am also able to release most of the anxiety that has built up inside of me through creative expression. This allows for a very powerful catharsis that I experience fairly regularly as a professional improviser. These experiences can also allow me to form connections with individuals that I simply would not be able to form otherwise, letting meaningful friendships develop when my anxieties would normally stand in the way. Because of these experiences, I believe that the studies on performance anxiety previously discussed have missed a crucial element in that none conducted clinical trials in the context of group improvisation.

My own practice of free improvisation has helped me to reduce anxiety, and my observations in the classroom have shown that this practice clearly works for others as well. Many of my students experience performance anxiety but are also under a considerable amount of pressure because of personal issues and school pressures such as juries, examinations, recitals, ensemble performances, and papers. These stresses are painfully obvious, as students entering the classroom begin to appear more lifeless as the term and the year go on. Allowing students the freedom to improvise and try to express some of these stresses always alters the mood in class in a positive way. I am always very careful to create an accepting, nonjudgmental environment in my class (something that I will discuss in more detail in the next section), where students can explore their musical ideas and interact with others, without worrying about playing wrong notes or losing marks for not playing perfectly. I find this is the ideal atmosphere for students to relax and use their improvisations as a means of expressing their thoughts and feelings, and if they feel comfortable, using it to unleash and work through various anxieties and stresses. Some of my students have performed solos in class in which they appeared to be using the opportunity as a platform to express deep-rooted hurt and pain. These incidents can be incredibly moving to witness, but it is the student's demeanor after these performances that is the most remarkable; students often light up, implying that the experience acted as a sort of release, helping them feel better about different stresses in their lives. Even if this release is only temporary, I believe it to be very important because even a small reprieve from stressed thoughts and feelings can be beneficial, and certainly new outlets for individuals to release these types of feelings can only be positive. More specific examples and discussion of these kinds of experiences in the classroom and why this type of work could benefit music education in general will be discussed in the following section.

Free Improvisation and Education

How prevalent would performance anxiety be if musicians were exposed to free improvisation as a part of their core musical training? The answer to this question is naturally something that we can only speculate on. Research certainly suggests that practicing free improvisation can help both student and adult musicians in a variety of deep and meaningful ways, ways that seem to be lacking in our traditional system of music education. In her book, *Musical Improvisation for Children,* author Alice Kay Kanack believes that when learning and practicing improvisation, an environment free from judgment is essential to allow young students to more fully express themselves. This in turn can aid in a student's self-expression and the development of confidence and a strong sense of self. Kanack notes that for children practicing improvisation, particularly in a group setting, the most important element of a successful creative experience is having fun. A fun, pressure-free environment allows young students to relax, release their inhibitions, and enjoy a free creative exploration while fostering positive relationships with others.[23] My own experiences with students older than those described by Kanack support this idea. In postsecondary education, however, most classes do not conform to the type of environment described by Kanack as the focus is on grades and credits. Teachers of improvisation must find ways of creating a safe, accepting environment while also being mindful of the fact that grades must be given at the end of the year. For many teachers, including myself, the focus for grades tends to shift to attendance, participation, mental presence, and effort, over more traditional types of assessment such as performance quality or examinations.

Over the past year, I conducted a series of interviews with students and teachers of improvisation at the postsecondary level. The individuals interviewed came from a variety of backgrounds and educational institutions, but all were either currently working or currently being educated in a North American postsecondary institution. The individuals interviewed varied widely in terms of experience and notoriety and included some of my own students, music therapists, free improvisers, jazz improvisers, classically trained musicians, and world-renowned improvisers and authors on the subject, such as Pauline Oliveros. During each of my interviews, the connection between free improvisation and anxiety was discussed, revealing that many students in particular found the practice of free improvisation in the context of their university classes helped them in a number of different, but meaningful ways.

Some of the comments that indicated that free improvisation practice helped the students interviewed were as follows:

- "Improvising gets emotions out, similar to a stress relief."[24]
- "If anything, [my improvisation class] gives me a release. Not having to play the exact right note at any given time is a *very* refreshing change of pace."[25]
- "Whether it is done alone or in groups, and whether it be free or more structurally formulated (like through jazz), I find it to be very meditative. It allows me to escape the anxious state I regularly find myself in. While any form of improvisation will allow me to enter this meditative state, I find the ethereal textures that free improvisation allows for and its loose format intensifies the meditation and further encourages the absolution of those anxieties."[26]
- "I was feeling really, really anxious, and then I improvised and then it calmed me down and gave me some perspective, and through the course of improvising I came to a central peace."[27]
- "Taking safe risks throughout the course increased my confidence and courage muscles by about 10 times."[28]

Although most responses were very positive, some students expressed either negative or indifferent comments regarding free improvisation practice and its potential use as a therapy for anxiety. One student stated that practicing free improvisation helped with her anxieties, but not in a classroom setting. She experienced release from her anxieties only when she was alone and at home with no one listening. "The catharsis I have experienced through that has been quite helpful. Sometimes it is profound, sometimes (although rarely) bringing tears of release, and sometimes it is just a pleasant pick-me-up."[29] Although this comment is primarily positive, the benefits of practicing free improvisation in a classroom setting are largely nonexistent for this particular student. Another student stated that while improvisation has helped him work through anxieties, "prolonged improvisation however, tires the mind and the emotions, causing a greater burden or negative affect to the player."[30] Perhaps there is a limit to how much this type of practice should or could be applied to anxiety release. This is an interesting aspect of using improvisation therapy that was not addressed in any of the studies discussed earlier. It appears to be a relatively unique problem since no other participants interviewed mentioned concern about prolonged improvisation.

In an ideal educational environment, the type of creative musical environment discussed by Kanack would be accessible to students through all ages and levels of development. Most of the teachers of improvisation I interviewed echoed Kanack's ideas and successfully applied them to their classes at the postsecondary level. One teacher interviewed described her optimal class environment as follows:

> An optimal environment for teaching improvisation is making the time to create a musical and emotional space where students can begin to trust and feel safe enough to explore and to take risks. I draw a student's attention to her/his strengths and growth as an improviser because we don't acknowledge (authentically) nearly enough in a University system that focuses so much on achievement and perfection.[31]

As this individual convincingly states, our traditional systems of education focus strongly on faultlessness. This type of emphasis may result in the formation of musical barriers in young musicians, potentially allowing anxieties to thrive. As environments free from judgment (real or perceived) seem to become scarcer as children age, perhaps the implementation of free improvisation throughout one's education could act as a counter to this. Most young adults feel very much judged, often trying to "fit in" or avoid standing out as abnormal. If more of these students were given an opportunity to express themselves in an environment where judgment was not tolerated and expressing their different musical personalities was encouraged, it could be extremely beneficial to those who do not feel that they can truly act as themselves, suffering from anxieties as a result.

Although music curricula are changing and more teachers try to incorporate at least some use of improvisation, most current undergraduate students still lack the experience of learning and practicing improvisation, unless they are specifically registered in a course that teaches or incorporates it. From my own experiences teaching improvisation to undergraduates, it is clear that those with no prior experience can find this type of work very daunting at first,[32] particularly if there are other students in the class who are already strong improvisers. I believe part of the reason for this is that these students must regularly complete successful auditions and juries in order to be successful in their programs. They are used to an environment in which playing correct notes is good, and playing incorrect ones is bad. When these students improvise for the first time, it can be difficult for them to accept the idea that their own musical ideas are valid and can inspire others in the class.

Initially, these students can sometimes have difficulty accepting or believing that improvisation is not part of an exclusive club, but rather is available to all of us. The "stronger" students in the class do not in fact have any secret knowledge that the newcomers lack. Certainly, in my own early experiences in improvisation, I regularly told others and myself that improvisation was something I would never be able to do. I too believed that it was some kind of magical ability that some people had and others did not, and there was no way to change this. Today, conversations with music students and other nonimprovising professionals lead me to believe that many musicians and students still share these kinds of thoughts. "I can't improvise" is a phrase I still hear all too often. Although I try to eliminate these kinds of thoughts in my students over time, many other students decide not to study improvisation simply because they believe they lack the ability to do so.

The natural question then arises: How can music teachers instill the belief in their students that one's own musical ideas, created through improvisation, are valid? Is this type of creativity something that can be expressed at any age or level of musical development and in any style of music education? Renowned improviser and educator Pauline Oliveros believes that natural creativity exists in all of us. She describes the process of opening up her students and workshop participants in the following way:

> The important thing for me is facilitating a community of creative interest. Creativity is inborn—a birthright that is often suppressed by social imperatives. I try in my classes to open the ages so that the creative spirit of the students can flourish. I do this through listening and encouraging listening, sharing and discussion ... facilitating a listening, caring and sharing environment is an invitation to creative work.[33]

Oliveros highlights the dialectical relationship between individuals and collectives within an improvisative space—be they classrooms or communities inside or outside of academic institutions. Creativity is "inborn"—creativity is (in her reading) an individualized phenomenon—but it is articulated principally in and through social formations. If creativity can be "suppressed by social imperatives," then it can (and for Oliveros, must) equally be facilitated through alternative social and community actions.

Improvisation in education is a relatively new subject of research, and I have only scratched the surface of it here. There is much to suggest that free improvisation practice could benefit learners in meaningful ways if it were part of the standard curriculum for music students. The practice of free improvisation in a safe, accepting environment where students can express their deepest feelings and creative thoughts can only benefit young musicians facing the various anxieties and challenges that come with youth. For young adults who feel isolated and unable or unwilling to express their thoughts and feelings to others, perhaps free improvisation can offer them a different type of communication, where negative thoughts can become raw musical expression rather than aggressive acts of physical hurt or violence.

Conclusion

Research conducted using free improvisation as a treatment for performance anxiety shows very promising results. Even though there are some limitations to these studies such as small sample sizes, lack of diversity in instruments used, and in some cases the sampling of only one gender, all of these studies have shown overwhelmingly positive results with the majority of subjects. This research also shows indications that the benefits of practicing free improvisation likely extend far beyond aiding performance anxiety. For example, the overwhelming sense of freedom and joy experienced in creating a musical work in the moment was well documented in Allen's subject interviews.[34] This result is thought provoking and suggests that incorporating improvisation into music education may not only help students deal with their anxieties, but also provide a valuable and gratifying outlet for creative freedom, something that most students in performance programs at universities are not getting.

Although performance anxiety is quite prevalent in young musicians, its causes are often overlooked. One must wonder if it is our musical culture's strong emphasis on note-for-note reproductions of classical compositions, reinforced by conservatories and university music faculties, that leads or contributes to performance anxiety in young musicians. This type of environment has little tolerance for incorrect notes or rhythms, placing a very high degree of pressure on musicians. This pressure could be at least partially alleviated by courses or ensembles that allow for greater creative freedom, and it is unfortunate that most students dealing with performance anxiety have few places to turn for help within their programs.

In my own experiences as the codirector of the Improvisation Concerts Ensemble at Wilfrid Laurier University, I have found that classically trained students find free improvisation to be very therapeutic and liberating in most cases. Students (especially those from the classical tradition) often initially find this type of performance to be intimidating, but once they are able to engage in its process, expressing themselves and their unique musical personalities, the results are overwhelmingly positive. I believe that part of the reason for this is that the emphasis changes from playing correct notes to creating unique musical pieces that can express one's innermost thoughts, feelings, and emotions. There appears to be a very personal creative process that unfolds during the creation of an improvisation that can affect individuals in very different and potentially powerful ways. The fact that very few music institutions incorporate improvisation into their curricula is what I believe to be a great disservice to music students, because it appears to hold great benefits for both their musical and emotional well-being. If free improvisation practice is a viable solution to helping young musicians with various anxieties, as it appears to be, we should be working to make it a more widely available practice for all ages and skill levels.

Notes

1. Kenny, *Psychology of Music Performance Anxiety*, 48.
2. American Psychiatric Association, *DSM-5*, n.p.
3. Ibid., 49.
4. Kim, "Combined Treatment," 17.
5. Ibid., 17.
6. Nachmanovitch, *Free Play*, 6.
7. Nettl et al., "Improvisation."
8. Ibid., 7.
9. Ibid., 8.
10. Taruskin, "Chapter 5 Virtuosos."
11. Ibid., ix.
12. Burrows, "Resonances," 74.
13. Ibid., 6.
14. Kenny, *Psychology of Music Performance Anxiety*, 195.
15. Ibid., 195.
16. Berger, *Toward the Zen of Performance*, 26.
17. Kim, "Combined Treatment," 23.
18. Allen, "Free Improvisation and Performance Anxiety," 220.
19. Ibid., vi.
20. Ibid., 101.
21. Berger, *Toward the Zen of Performance*, 19.
22. Ibid., 7.
23. Ibid., 42.
24. Interview with student improviser, December 15, 2014.
25. Interview with student improviser, February 14, 2015.
26. Interview with student improviser, March 16, 2015.
27. Interview with student improviser, March 3, 2015.
28. Interview with student improviser, March 9, 2015.
29. Interview with student improviser, January 5, 2015.
30. Interview with student improviser, December 15, 2014.
31. Interview with improvisation teacher, February 27, 2015.
32. I find that students new to improvisation are quick to get over their initial fears, once they are able to accept the idea that anything they create is acceptable.
33. Oliveros, *Deep Listening*, 57.
34. Allen, "Free Improvisation and Performance Anxiety," 153.

Works Cited

Allen, Robert G., Jr. "Free Improvisation and Performance Anxiety Among Piano Students." PhD diss., Boston University, 2010. ProQuest (305184799).

American Psychiatric Association. *Diagnostic and Statistical Manual of Mental Disorders: DSM-4*. 4th ed., text rev. Washington, DC: American Psychiatric Association, 2000. http://dsm.psychiatryonline.org.ezproxy.library.yorku.ca/book.aspx?bookid=22.

American Psychiatric Association. *Diagnostic and Statistical Manual of Mental Disorders: DSM-5*. 5th ed., text rev. Arlington, VA: American Psychiatric Association, 2013. http://dsm.psychiatryonline.org.ezproxy.library.yorku.ca/book.aspx?bookid=556.

Berger, Dorita S. *Toward the Zen of Performance: Music Improvisation Therapy for the Development of Self-Confidence in the Performer*. Saint Louis, MO: MMB Music, 1999.

Burrows, J. "Resonances: Exploring Improvisation and Its Implications for Music Education." PhD diss., Simon Fraser University, 2004.

Kanack, Alice Kay. *Musical Improvisation for Children*. Miami: Warner Brothers Publications, 1998.

Kenny, Dianna T. *The Psychology of Music Performance Anxiety*. Oxford: Oxford University Press, 2011.

Kim, Youngshin. "Combined Treatment of Improvisation and Desensitization to Alleviate Music Performance Anxiety in Female College Pianists: A Pilot Study." *Medical Problems of Performing Artists* 20, no. 1 (2005): 17–24.

———. "The Effect of Improvisation-Assisted Desensitization, and Music-Assisted Progressive Muscle Relaxation and Imagery on Reducing Pianists' Music Performance Anxiety." *Journal of Music Therapy* 45, no. 2 (2008): 165–91.

Nachmanovitch, Stephen. *Free Play: Improvisation in Life and Art*. New York: Penguin Putnam, 1990.

Nettl, Bruno, Rob C. Wegman, Imogene Horsley, Michael Collins, Stewart A. Carter, Greer Garden, Robert E. Seletsky, et al. "Improvisation." *Grove Music Online, Oxford Music Online*. Oxford: Oxford University Press, 2001.

Oliveros, Pauline. *Deep Listening: A Composer's Sound Practice*. New York: iUniverse, 2005.

Taruskin, Richard. "Chapter 5 Virtuosos." *The Oxford History of Western Music: Music in the Nineteenth Century*. New York: Oxford University Press, n.d. Accessed April 23, 2013. http://www.oxfordwesternmusic.com/view/Volume3/actrade-9780195384833-chapter-005.xml.

5   Analysis, Improvisation, and Openness

Chris Stover

1

A discussion unfolded recently on a friend's Facebook page, stemming from a post in which that friend invited the community's thoughts about the functional identity of the chord three bars from the end of Chopin's well-known *Prelude in E minor*, op. 28 no. 4. This chord is spelled as a C major triad over a bass B♭, emerging out of a larger context of E minor (albeit a rather chromatically charged E minor), and pointing toward the composition's final, key-affirming cadence that begins after a pause in the next bar. Over the course of the next two hours or so some twenty musicians weighed in with opinions, some thoughtful, some sarcastic; some well-thought-out, some quickly and understandably dashed-off (it's Facebook after all); some well-versed in mid-nineteenth century harmonic idioms and some coming to it as outsiders. All of the musicians that contributed belong to an extended community, variably linked via numerous professional and personal networks, not least by their shared e-friendship with the original poster.

2

When engaging a new piece of music from an analytic perspective, I often ask my music theory students: "When is a melodic note unequivocally a chord tone, when it is an upper extension, when is it part of a chord-scale, and when is it an expressive non-chord tone?" I do this not to steer them toward some reified idea of a "correct" answer (nor should I think of myself as qualified to make such a determination), but to open a creative space for the consideration of analytic identity as a *multiplicity*, as a response to the prompt "yes, and?", as always, essentially, *n + 1*. Looming through this discussion is an open question of what this or that interpretation means for the analytic identity of the musical object or gesture, which always, and I'd argue necessarily, includes what we might *do* with that information from a productive standpoint.[1]

3

Like many, I've become fascinated with that particular subgenre of cooking show where contestants are given a highly proscribed array of ingredients and a task to accomplish with them under severe time restraints. As a cooking enthusiast I am moved by the creative ways in which contestants work within their constraints to produce what seem from the other side of the screen to be rather remarkable culinary works. These shows have been cited as exemplary examples of improvisation in action, reinforcing how Gary Peters[2] begins his query into the nature of improvisation via the "scrapyard challenge" of British television. As a scholar of improvisational interaction, I am drawn to questions like "how much of this activity is truly improvisatory, and how much of it draws upon a repertoire of learned behaviors?", which invites deeper and more fundamental questions about the nature of improvisation. But I am also curious about the decisively noninteractive aspects of the improvisatory act in these shows, as well as their radical judgmental thrust, which seem to me to be antithetical to the nature of improvisational performance, especially if we take the tenets and goals of improvisational interaction to be some variant on those offered by Berk and Trieber[3]: trust, acceptance, attentive listening, spontaneity, storytelling, and nonverbal communication.[4] I will unpack these below but for now offer that the negative competitive thrust of this genre of cooking show pushes to the foreground issues of the aims, means, and limits of improvisational performativity in a way that will become positive when resituated in the open space of an improvisationally oriented classroom.

A key point of philosopher Hans-Georg Gadamer's study of meaning is that we can't dislocate our understanding from our own experience, including the ways in which our experience is itself historically and culturally situated. A conventional approach to critical thinking asks us to challenge our preconceptions in order to locate the ways in which they bias our thinking, or bracket them in pursuit of alternative perspectives and knowledge bases and trajectories. For Gadamer, rather than denying that we have prejudices, or trying to bracket them (a futile endeavor at any rate), we are encouraged to interrogate them, to understand them, and to make them transparent, and by doing so continue to bring them to bear on the object under scrutiny. Object and conceptual frame come into conversation in this way, and through their dialogue one develops a greater understanding of both. There is a circularity here that has gone by many names in philosophical circles but most important for this project is the acknowledgment of its circularity as well as its open-endedness—there is potentially no end to the inquiry into something's essence, which is to say its meaning.[5]

For Gadamer, meaning is constituted through the ongoingness of experience, through the act of discovery, through action and activity. This way of thinking through meaning dovetails very well into some recent trends in progressive educational practice, including the "flipped classroom," the continuing investigation into the efficacy of thinking in terms of "multiple intelligences" or "learning styles," and the various efforts to introduce an improvisational orientation to the teaching/learning experience. All of these foreground creative interaction and the openness of improvisational experience, which will be demonstrated below through a consideration of analysis as an improvisational act, including reading the analytic act as a way to open a horizon of productive improvisational possibilities as jazz musicians engage their material. In other words, a direct line will be drawn between an improvisational attitude toward analysis and the way that analysis can be channeled toward enriching the improvisatory aspects of making music.

There are two themes to consider here that will prove to be relevant to this project. First is an acceptance of and engagement with the types of opennesses suggested above—a consideration of multiple intelligences, a range of learning styles, and so on. Second is the way in which Gadamer asks us, again, not to bracket the prejudices of our prior experience and the lenses provided by the singularities of our knowledge accumulations, but to use the experience of looking through those lenses to see what useful information is brought to bear on the observed object or process, and to use the act of creative observation to turn the analytic lens back on ourselves and consider what sorts of useful information are suppressed through some particular reading. By thinking creatively about the intersection between these two themes, we can start to define how an open, creative, improvisational engagement can unfold. There are no wrong answers, but *no* answer should be greeted uncritically. Both of these themes inform a beginning point for considering the profusion of possibilities offered by the flipped-classroom model, the creative consideration and acknowledgment of multiple intelligences, and the engagement of multiple learning styles in pursuit of a plural reading of analytic identity in the music theory classroom.

If we dig deeper into the Facebook exchange that opens this chapter, we can begin to witness the playing out of these themes. Approximately twenty musicians weighed in with thoughts around the original poster's question, which had to do with the functional identity of the third bar from the end of Chopin's *Prelude in E minor*, op. 28 no. 4, shown in Example 5.1.[6]

Many of the responses suggested that the chord in that measure, a C Major triad with B♭ in the bass, articulates a "German Augmented Sixth" chord, with several posters noting that the B♭ should (1) technically have been spelled as A♯, and (2) be located in an upper voice to form an augmented sixth above the C. This reading invited a second question regarding chord inversion: Can an augmented sixth chord still function as such if the augmented sixth interval is inverted to become a diminished third below the putative root of the chord?[7] One respondent also asked if this inversion is common or even allowable, prompting the response, "if I recall, there were (are?) theorists who … were emphatic that German sixth chords

Example 5.1 Frédéric Chopin, *Prelude in E minor*, op. 28 no. 4, last five bars. The chord that serves as the subject of the Facebook exchange is highlighted with an arrow.

could not be inverted if they were to be labeled as German sixth chords," to which another poster responded, "since this clearly functions as a Ger+6 and occurs in an inversion, those theorists would be wrong."[8]

Although a hasty theoretical reading might accept an inverted, misspelled augmented sixth chord as analytically adequate and move on, it is in the alternative narratives that we start to find a ground to explore the richness and openness of analytic identity. In the Facebook exchange, these included

1 Alternative harmonic readings ("V7 of N[eapolitan]"—this poster did then submit that this might be a stretch; "chromatic sub for IVm7—Amin7 with A raised to a B♭")
2 Readings filtered through jazz practice ("tritone sub of V/V")
3 Even more site-specific jazz practice ("In Berklee-harmony-speak, it's a subV7/V. Put a perforated arrow on that bitch and call it a day")
4 Considerations of voice-leading behaviors ("The voice leading goes from C to B♭ in the bass, thus the necessity for the "inverted" +6"; "The 4th bar from the end is a 6/4 prolongation of the move toward the +6 chord (sorry, getting Schenkerian here ...)—the A in the 5th bar from the end should move up to A♭ for the intensification, but gets displaced an octave into the bass voice. So the 5th bar from the end is a VI chord, about to become V of III, but then gets diverted via Chopin's crazy descending counterpoint to end up as the +6, but not until two bars (and much voice leading) later ...")

This is a multiplicity of functional interpretations, each filtered through the history of experience, fields of knowledge, discursive felicities, and analytic needs and wants of the various contributors. Various responsive streams spun out of each node (including a sarcastic "too bad for me I don't speak Berklee" and a sensible "there are a few ways to describe it ... but it sure makes sense hearing it"), further complexifying the interactive improvisational nature of the analytic project.

The point of thinking in terms of multiplicity is not just that there is more than one "correct" answer—this should be apparent for any sensitive, nondogmatic analyst. Rather, it is to actively engage the openness of the question as an opportunity for expressive, interactive dialogue. There are multiple correct answers but also likely some "wrong" ones. A "wrong" answer reveals interesting questions about perspectives and conceptual frames, and in the open space of a multiplicity, there is ample room for carefully considering the factors that condition one's perspective and how that perspective might be modified by being made transparent and open to careful interrogation, but also what useful information that perspective brings to the emerging understanding of the observed object.

Some of the "wrong" answers in the Facebook exchange were offered humorously.[9] For example, one poster wrote, "the function is to create the unexpected. It causes you to sit up a little in anticipation." While at first blush this response doesn't seem very analytically helpful, it actually contains some highly useful information that should be taken seriously. For one, it questions the word "function," which music theorists tend to assume refers to harmonic function (in tonal music, at least; at any rate syntactic function)—how that harmonic object is behaving in the context of the global or local key. But that is not how most people use the word *function*, which more generally refers to some thing's purpose for being there.[10] For another, it allows us to back-form a consideration of harmonic function based on the desired expressive outcome of the musical event—in this poster's mind to introduce something unexpected that focuses the listener's attention in some particular way.

Another "wrong" answer, "I think it's some cool music and then they had to explain why it works," opens up a provocative space to question the relationship between theory and practice, in this case interrogating the conventional wisdom among some practitioners that theory necessarily follows practice. Theory and practice are not exclusive performative spaces, nor is the act of theorizing a reductive *a posteriori* description of practice. Rather, the two exist in a dialogic relationship, informing and abetting one another in an ongoing dialectic flux. This is evident through even a quick consideration of the history of the interpenetration between, say, compositional practice and theory—viz. composer-theorists from Heinrich Christoph Koch to Arnold Schoenberg to George Russell to Anthony Braxton—and the countless ways in which the theorized reification of a compositional idea engendered further, previously unthought-of compositional trajectories. This is what Gadamer means when he asks us to bring the object and the conceptual frame into dialogue. I would like to radicalize the relation between theory and practice even further to define a ground where these are, essentially, mutually enriching perspectives within the same performative space—therefore *not* a dialectic, but a *rhizomatic* space where every node is linked unproblematically to every other node.[11] This is what I take home from a discussion like this Facebook exchange, and it speaks to the value of an open, improvisationally driven dialogue. Can we imagine a network that links *all* of the analytic perspectives offered (and more) to explain the function, behavior, and context of that C-major-over-B♭ chord, in pursuit of a truly plural reading that transcends methodology and idiom, considering each from the perspective of the poster that offered it (and also, as Gadamer would insist, inverting each to consider how it explains aspects of the offerer's perspective), and thinking carefully through what value each brings to the always-emerging plural identity of musical passage?

For another example, consider the second chord of Billy Strayhorn and Duke Ellington's "Take the A Train," shown in Example 5.2.[12] This chord could be construed in a number of ways, including but not limited to

1   V7(♯11) of V, or a secondary dominant chord (tonicizing V, or making V a temporary tonic)
2   V7(♭5) of V, a subtly distinct reading of (1) that we will revisit below
3   A "II dominant" chord; that is, a predominant functioning chord built on scale degree 2 ($\hat{2}$)
4   A product of voice leading, namely the G—G♯—A strand articulated in the melody as the first bar progresses to bar 5 (see Example 5.4)
5   A whole-tone structure, which may or may not have sonic implications for the listener that signify train sounds (which Ellington evoked frequently in his music)
6   An "unexpected chord" that causes the listener "to sit up a little"[13]

Example 5.2 Billy Strayhorn and Duke Ellington, "Take the A Train," first eight bars.

A secondary dominant (V of V) reading is slightly problematic because of where it goes next: many theoretical narratives would read the move from bars 3–4 to bar 5 as a denial of an expressive trajectory; that is, we tend to expect a less structurally dissonant chord to build to a chromatic intensification before resolving. This difficulty is ameliorated somewhat if we consider the ii–V of bars 5–6 as a single syntactic unit with its own internal motion. In this reading V of V progresses to ii–V as a composite unit, which is itself construed as a composing-out of dominant function. In other words, as Example 5.3 illustrates, the D7 chord can be read as tonicizing a *V-complex* (with Dm7 folded into G7 as a voice-leading prolongation), which then progresses to tonic as expected. Among the things that this reading does is allow us to rethink the D7 chord as a predominant chord, and therefore part of the fundamental harmonic structure of the song rather than as a nearer-to-surface chromatic intensification of diatonic harmony.[14] This, then, supports the undertheorized possibility that the syntactic structure of jazz harmony and melody is *essentially* chromatic, unlike conventional analytic discourse around earlier tonal music, which regards chromaticism as nearer-to-surface level embellishments of fundamental diatonic motions.[15]

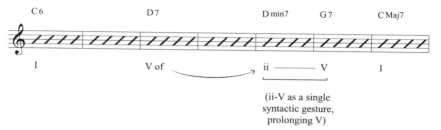

Example 5.3 D7 tonicizing a prolonged ii–V complex.

The question of whether bar 3 should be notated as D7(#11) or D7(b5) is a further point of consideration, and further extends our open reading. Like most music notation, lead sheet chord symbols operate as signs, signifying a proscribed range of performed actions that interpret those signs as sonic information with some kind of semantic meaning. For the improvising jazz musician, there are distinctive performative possibilities (and foreclosures) that each of these signs suggests.[16]

Readings (4), (5), and (6) further enrich our horizon of possibilities. By focusing, for example, on the melodic G# as a voice-leading action linking G to A, we locate it as a subordinate chromatic prolongation in a hierarchically prior diatonic context. This creates an interesting (but, from a productive perspective, compelling) aporia: the G# as a structural chord tone (a constituent part of the chromatic predominant chord) that is *also* melodically transient. We should also pay attention to the motivic implications of the G—G#—A figure as it points toward the faster melodic activity of bar 6. As Example 5.4 shows, there are three chromatic strands that could be described as stemming directly from the opening figure, all ornamenting functional chord tones.

Not only does this reading emphasize the tight motivic connections that unfold through "A Train's" melody, it suggests fruitful possibilities for the improvising musician in terms of developing motivic ideas that communicate with the original tune on multiple levels. Likewise, the fifth and sixth readings offer lines of flight away from the typical purview of the music theory classroom. As many commentators have noted, music theory tends to foreground the more easily inscribable aspects of musical texture and process: notes, melodies, and chords.[17] But thinking in terms of train sounds, or simply unusual sounds that draw one's attention in some particular direction, can open compelling spaces for inquiry into further possibilities.[18] This is

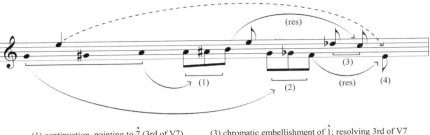

(1) continuation, pointing to $\hat{7}$ (3rd of V7) (3) chromatic embellishment of $\hat{1}$; resolving 3rd of V7

(2) inversion, pointing to $\hat{4}$ (7th of V7) (4) octave-displaced $\hat{3}$ resolves 7th of V7

Example 5.4 Four realizations of voice-leading implications of opening "A Train" gesture.

true of all of the readings suggested, of course. And we could imagine other creative readings that reveal further aspects of the music's essence that we might desire to channel in different productive ways. The point here is, again, not to choose between readings to make a clear determination about which is (even provisionally or strategically) best, but to consider the possibility that all of these readings are "correct" in useful ways, and then to consider how they might be brought into dialogue with one another.

On Multiple Intelligences and Pluralities of "Learning Styles"

Berk and Trieber describe six principles of improvisation: trust, acceptance, attentive listening, spontaneity, storytelling, and nonverbal communication.[19] Through these principles they foreground several secondary goals, like brainstorming in pursuit of innovative solutions and the suspension of critical judgment. I am particularly interested in one of the ways that Berk and Trieber characterize "acceptance": "players must be willing to accept a new idea in order to explore its possibilities—not just say 'yes', but have an attitude of 'yes, and ...'"[20] Players are encouraged to accept an offer, build on it, and use it to discover new ideas.[21] This is a hallmark of what performing jazz musicians say they privilege as well. I also find "storytelling" to be a compelling notion. Exemplary performers are often said to, and young jazz musicians are asked to, "tell a story" through their improvisational utterances, but with little further detail about what it means to tell a story through nonverbal codes (not to mention how one—performer or listener—will know whether a story has been successfully told). Through the collective improvisational space of a classroom that celebrates and encourages the performativity of analysis (where *performance* and *narrative* are more or less exchangeable, and where *narrative* is a form of *storytelling* that engenders *meaning* on some level, and where meaning is defined as being fluid, multiple, and always emergent), all analytic action amounts to a form of storytelling and comes together to form an ongoing analytic narrative.

In our Facebook scenario above, several of these principles were clearly in play. There was a mutual trust engendered by the collegial respect of the participants; again, all were professional musicians on friendly terms, and even points of disagreement were made respectfully (if sometimes jocularly). Conflicting perspectives were accepted and challenged, and in a few cases opinions were changed on the basis of a well-argued post. It was clear that posters were reading the posts to which they were responding carefully: the online-discussion version of attentive listening. All of this was highly spontaneous; the entire discussion took place over less than two hours, and remained narrowly focused on the question at hand. And again I'd argue that there was a great deal of storytelling involved, if one believes that the analytic act—any analytic act—is a performance that tells a story about the analyzed object and our relationship to it.

Among the many values that Berk and Trieber suggest that an improvisational orientation brings to the classroom is the idea that through improvisation many types of intelligences can be reached. Howard Gardner's conception of multiple intelligences is well known in educational theory, as are the critical opinions of a number of significant detractors.[22] Gardner's categorization of intelligences has taken a few forms since its inception, but Berk and Trieber offer nine intelligences: verbal/linguistic, visual/spatial, bodily/kinesthetic, interpersonal, intrapersonal, quantitative/analytical, musical/rhythmic, naturalistic, and environmental.[23] Any learner has access to all of these in various degrees, and Gardner's theory suggests that every learner has a tendency toward some bundle of them. Berk and Trieber suggest that a teaching/learning scenario be constituted such that "four to six of students' intelligences are tapped instead of just one or two,"[24] building, therefore, on strengths rather than weaknesses. Improvisation, focused through the basic principles outlined above, is conceived here as an ideal practice for reaching those intelligences.

For Berk and Trieber, an improvisational orientation is unscripted, spontaneous, intuitive, and interactive. It is actively engaged in the co-creation of ideas, without the foreclosure of an authoritative presence determining what constitutes right or wrong. In the classroom, this means that students get to determine actions and solutions. The teacher here is a prompter, or facilitator (and probably sometimes a referee)—jazz musicians might draw comparisons to a leadership style like that of Miles Davis, who would encourage and nudge the members of his band to seek out underexplored trajectories within the context of the songs they were playing (though Davis, one might argue, was not always the most disinterested prompter!). Berk and Trieber want to harness improvisation in the service of deep learning, following James Rhem's four criteria: motivational context, learner activity, interaction with others, and a well-structured knowledge base. If these are indeed the best conduits for deep learning, then it seems that an improvisational space is ideal for exploring how those contexts can be engendered and those activities carried out.[25]

Berk and Trieber explore how to invoke improvisational actions to engage particular intelligences, learning styles, and technological fluencies of millennials, or what they refer to as "Web Geners." In particular, they emphasize a tendency toward visual learning and a drive toward experiential, hands-on learning. It is important to note, however, that the fact that different learning styles exist, and that multiple intelligences are found across a body of learners, is not unique to a digitally native generation. Howard Gardner's seminal work, after all, was published in 1983, and David Robotham refers to studies as far back as the late 1960s.[26] The primary difference is that the notion of multiple intelligences, and how they work, how they interpenetrate, and how they might be engaged in cooperative/collaborative/improvisational settings has worked its way into aspects of public discourse.

Turning back to improvisation in the classroom, we might consider improvisation, as Berk and Trieber do, as a form of problem solving. The power of improvisation is in its attention-to-present, in the fact that it is always intended toward being in the moment. "The point of concentration requires close attention to the problem rather than to the individuals who are addressing the problem."[27] This is an interesting phenomenological stance: of course it is still the individuals who are attenuated to the problem, but in an open interpretive space their attention is directed toward the transcendental nature of the problem, toward the possibly that there might be ever-new information that informs its ever-emergent identity.

On Music Theory As an Open Discursive Space

In both the Chopin and Ellington examples above, a specific problem—the analytic identity of a very small passage of music—was offered, along with an invitation to think of that problem in open terms, suggesting that a determinate analytic identity is not the goal, but that through repeated, sensitive engagement we develop an ever-richer understanding of the passage and the way it locates within the complex network of relationships that define its context. A recurring theme has been the interdependent relationship between theory and practice, and it is to this point that I would like to turn briefly in order to explicate what it means for both the analytic project generally and for the discipline of music theory as it continues to interrogate its own relationship to musical practice.

Recent pedagogical theory considers a theoretical framework as a scaffold: a frame that is crucial to the construction of an edifice but that is ultimately irreducible to that edifice and, in the end, necessarily discardable.[28] Music theorist Christopher Hasty challenges the scaffold model, suggesting an alternative relationship between theoretical (or pedagogical) frameworks and the practical applications that they intend. In Hasty's entreaty, theory and practice are not only intimately intertwined, they each provide a fluid ground for the others' reinscription and reinterpretation. Rather than being a fixed methodological framework, theory is constantly in motion (and *essentially* so), and likewise practice constantly engages the query that theory offers it:

> The success and efficiency of scaffolding devices is always open to criticism and to efforts toward improvement. What is taught and how it is taught are, of course, crucial ingredients for musical culture. Music theory can be empowering or alienating, socially inclusive or exclusive, relatively creative or sterile. Like any teaching, it will value and foster certain human potentials over others and thus, to some extent, shape the initiate. For this reason, music theory is always an ethical question. If, more than a set of devices, music theory is a thinking about music communication, then it is an opportunity to think about ethical issues such as power, inclusivity, and creativity. In such an opening, music theory and pedagogy would be understood as overlapping or continuous disciplines. The question of time or passage is a way forward.[29]

Hasty urges us to resist thinking of the signs used by music theory (and the concepts those signs represent) as fixed, and instead to focus on their creative potential. In doing so he stresses the *ongoing-ness* of their value for practice, as well as their essential mutability. Ultimately, he poses a compelling foil to the *just-forget-about-that-and-play* mantra so pervasive in the jazz world (and elsewhere), challenging the very notion that scaffolding is a tool for learning that is discarded once the learning is done: "once the work is done, once learning is complete, the heuristic device becomes superfluous and can fall away." But "to say such symbols fall away is to say that they have lost their mobility, their ability to keep up with growing, their ability to change knowing by being productive in ever new ways." This suggests that the theoretical project (an "edifice of learning") is "an end or a static ideal." Instead Hasty suggests that, if we want to keep the building/scaffold metaphor, we should "think of a building or structure in experiential, temporal terms, ... as a dwelling or an environment to be lived in, a place to make a life that is always entering into new contexts or situations."[30] This is a particularly compelling thought, because it resonates with the music-as-lived-experience way that jazz musicians frequently characterize their practice, and brings music-theoretical discourse into that practice. "If the language that is used in the making and learning of music is viewed as a sort of environment, then it likewise need not be seen either as something other than music or as something absolute, fixed, unchanged," rather, that language, as the musical processes it claims to signify, is "something we live in and in living shape to our ends."[31]

All of this, then, resonates with the aspects of the relation between theory and practice that I am attempting to develop in this essay. The way that I wish to develop this relation is through improvisation, and in order to do it, I want again to conflate the general notion of thinking improvisationally with the more focused practice of teaching improvisation, using one more focused case study as my ground. My case study involves two brief moments in Antônio Carlos Jobim and Newton Mendonça's iconic bossa nova song "Desafinado," creating an open, improvisational interrogative space. This space also involves a conscious attempt to engage most of Gardner's multiple intelligences, which, we'll find, points to a number of fruitful alternative readings that enrich the always-emerging analytic identity of the musical passages under scrutiny.

Plural Identity in "Desafinado"

"Desafinado," first recorded by João Gilberto in 1958, and perhaps best known in the U.S. through Gilberto's 1964 collaboration with jazz saxophonist Stan Getz, provides a compelling entry point for studying the interaction of harmony, melody, and lyrics. The opening phrase is shown in Example 5.5.

Example 5.5 Antônio Carlos Jobim, "Desafinado," opening phrase.

The first moment of ambiguity in "Desafinado" is the first point of harmonic change in measure 3, which, coincidentally, is the same chord as the commensurate moment in "Take the A Train." Like "A Train," a dominant seventh chord built on $\hat{2}$ supports a chromatic melodic move: in "A Train" it was the melodic ascent to $\sharp\hat{5}$; in "Desafinado" the melody moves to $\flat\hat{6}$, the flat fifth of the chord. Both Jobim and subsequent editors are careful to represent this note as $\flat\hat{6}$, whereas the same pitch class is notated as $\sharp\hat{5}$ in the previous measure, as a lower neighbor to $\hat{6}$.[32] It's also important to note that various chromatic notes in "Desafinado" support textual meaning; the various "wrong" or "out of tune" notes draw the listener's attention to problems that the narrator is explaining, as in:

> *Se você disser que eu desafino amor*
> *saiba que isto em mim provoca imensa dor*
>
> If you tell me that I'm out of tune, my love,
> You should know that it produces a great pain,[33]

with a provocative parallelism between "amor" ("love") and "dor" ("pain") as each locates the out-of-tune note. Although this opening line is worth a chapter of its own, I would like to focus on the moment that immediately follows, first scrutinizing it on its own and then comparing it with the commensurate point in the second phrase of the song. Example 5.6 shows these two excerpts: starting in measures 9 and 25, respectively.

Example 5.6 Two consequent phrases in "Desafinado."

What does an open, improvisationally driven analytic inquiry reveal about these two passages? First, it demonstrates the inherently multiple identity of harmonic function. The Gmin7 chord that begins the phrase is an unproblematic ii in the home key of F major, and everything that has happened up to this point validates this reading. When we reach measure 10, however, we must retroactively consider the functional identity of what is now the immediate-past event. Gmin7 → A7 form a compound syntactic event, iv to V in D minor. But the expected D minor tonic arrival turns out to be D major (which is then transformed via chromatic voice leading to a dominant-functioning D7, eventually pointing us back to the home key at the next phrase-beginning). There are thus at least three coexisting functional readings of the Gmin7 chord: ii in the home key (suggesting a V to follow); iv as a diatonic predominant chord in D minor (the relative minor of F major); and iv as a chromatic predominant chord in D major (borrowed from D major's parallel minor key). Each of these readings is the result of a different *temporal* perspective; therefore, a plural reading emerges as time passes, through an open and playful consideration of what harmonic function can mean in different contexts.[34] This is abetted by the interplay of consonance and dissonance in the melody. The appoggiatura in measure 9 is repeated a step lower in measure 10, possibly leading the listener to expect a melodic sequence. This sequence is denied, however, when the melody instead leaps down to a dissonant D♯; ♯11 of the chord and reminiscent of the main motivic gesture from the previous phrase. As in the previous phrase, the lower neighbor D♯ is recast two bars later as E♭, reflecting the main lyrical theme of the song.

All of this activity acquires further significance sixteen measures later, in the commensurate part of the second "A" section. Here Gmin7 moves to A7, and this time to Dmin7—an expected tonic outcome of the iv–V syntactic object. This Dmin7, though, has a dual identity of its own, because as we progress to measure 28 it gives way to an E7 chord, effecting another iv–V that in turn resolves to AMaj7, eliding into what we would expect, given the tendencies of songs in this genre, to be the bridge of the song.[35] This AMaj7 might validate the earlier, unexpected DMaj7—at any rate it provides a highly salient parallel to the earlier progression. Furthermore, the denied sequence-expectation in measures 9–10 is fulfilled in the corresponding next phrase, and extends to one further appoggiatura upon the arrival of the Dmin7 chord in measure 27.

There are other creative readings that we can consider in pursuit of an analytic multiplicity. A strong case can be made, for example, for the plural analysis above engendering the truncated phrase structure that introduces the "B" section four bars early: the A major arrival (and new phrase-beginning), a logical outcome of the major/minor interplay, and the multiple tonic interpretations of the D major/minor arrivals that began in the movement toward measure 11. We should also be aware of how our expectations, based on prior experiences of these types of harmonic motions, are fulfilled or denied as the music progresses, again focusing on how later actions engender reconsiderations of early harmonic identities.[36]

The analysis thus far touches on musical intelligence (in numerous ways, not limited to careful considerations of harmonic and melodic function and the expressive roles of consonance and dissonance), quantitative/analytic intelligence (as traditional "problem solving"), verbal and linguistic intelligence (both from the perspective of how to talk about analytic identity and through considerations of the lyrics themselves), and possibly intrapersonal intelligence—what Berk and Trieber also describe as emotional intelligence—considering what effects various readings have on an emerging conception of musical meaning. What if we deliberately focus on other intelligences to see what new analytic information emerges? This is exactly what we did in October 2014 at The New School, in an open, improvisational inquiry into the essence of "Desafinado," with our only stipulation going in being the assumption that there is always something new to discover. We listened to the two recordings mentioned above, I read the lyrics in Portuguese and then in English translation, and we worked from the Chediak score with three editorial amendments.[37] Through the act of open, collective analytic engagement, we circled around many of the above points, and stimulating debate ensued about their interpenetration and the possibility of multiple correct readings. The discussion made a particularly compelling turn when I asked the class to use some of Gardner's intelligence categories as *prompts*; to consider the implications of thinking consciously from, say, a bodily/kinesthetic or interpersonal or environmental perspective. One result of this was that several students who don't tend to speak in an open discussion joined in with compelling suggestions, as if once freed from the constraints of sanctioned theoretical orthodoxy, they were finally comfortable talking about aspects of the music that were interesting to them as listeners or performers. For example, a bodily/kinesthetic perspective suggested a number of fruitful points, such as

1 The idea of notes *grabbing* our attention in a particularly literal way
2 Feelings of discomfort ("oh, that's not what I wanted there …")
3 The fact that the "wrong" notes always resolve, lending a hopeful undercurrent to the narrative

And there were more points, including further inquiry into the relationship between music and text, especially the way in which the "out of tune" notes in the first phrase support the keywords "love," "pain," "yours," and "me" ("amor," "dor," "seu," "me").[38]

Further bundles of intelligences were invoked when one student remarked on the juxtaposition between on one hand the syncopated nature of the melody, the strikingly unexpected notes and intervals, and the constant newness of the harmonic motion, and on the other hand the smooth, intimate nature of João Gilberto's vocal delivery (not to mention Stan Getz's lyrical improvisation, which never strays far from the melody). This took the conversation into a closer consideration of Mendonça's lyrics:

> *Só privilegiados têm ouvido igual ao seu*
> *Eu possuo apenas o que Deus me deu*

> Only the privileged have ears like yours,
> I have only what God has given me.

And then,

> *Eu mesmo mentindo devo argumentar*
> *Que isto é bossa nova, que isto muito natural …*

> Even if I am lying, I argue
> that this is bossa nova, that this is very natural …

One student described how "even though some things are not what you would expect, that some chords are a little weird, you expect that it's going to repeat itself. But it *keeps* throwing you off. Maybe that's what he's going for, maybe that's the context of the song—the singer is saying, well I can't hear it that well but that's my song." Another student continued with the theme of vocal delivery and how Gilberto's performance style brings out the hopeful undercurrent to the lyrics.[39] Just as the ever-new and often shocking ebbs and flows of harmonic motion are tempered by an underlying tonal logic that only becomes evident as more musical information is revealed (that is, through the act of hearing and interpreting those harmonic motions), the autocritical nature of the text is tempered by a delivery that reinforces the playfulness of its self-deprecation. Nowhere is this more evident than in the second "A" section where the ongoing performance is described as "antimusical"—one student noted the irony of referring to one of the most well-known songs by one of the most important Brazilian composers as "anti-music."

An environmental perspective, likewise, prompted a compelling discussion about the situation under which each recording was made (in Rio de Janeiro and New York City, respectively, with Brazilian musicians versus a mix of Brazilian and U.S. musicians, etc.), and eventually led to a very interesting comparison of the keys of the two performances. While the score of "Desafinado" is invariably given in F, Gilberto's first recording is in E, while the collaboration with Getz is in E♭. A student with perfect pitch made this observation, but many students agreed that there was a palpable sonic difference between the two.[40]

We completed our initial group investigation by inverting the goals of our analysis to consider analytic implications in productive terms: what improvising musicians can *do* with this information, from the perspective of an open interpretive field. Two vocalists in turn interpreted the song (in English), and a saxophone player, a trumpet player, and a piano player each played an improvised solo, all with a rhythm section from the class. We discussed the thought process of each participant, with a focus on how they navigated harmonic spaces, melodic shapes, dissonance/consonance relations, textual meanings, and large-scale formal design. The most significant theme that emerged was how each improviser was thinking about how the melody of the tune located within the harmony, which, it seemed to all involved, refocused each solo away from a harmony (or chord-scale)-first orientation toward one that attempted to bring out salient melodic features. Although the longer-term effect of our analytic inquiry on various improvisatory decisions is yet to be determined (and at any rate is a topic for a paper in itself), it was clear to all that there was an effect, which amounted to reversing the experiential lens to consider what this or that analytic frame reflected back on the analyst-*cum*-interpreter.

We have only begun to explore the possibilities that an improvisational perspective affords for the analytic act, but the results so far have been highly compelling. The open, no-wrong-answers, interactive environment that we nurtured contributed to a great deal of trust; indeed all of Berk and Trieber's tenets and goals of improvisational interaction—trust, acceptance, attentive listening, spontaneity, storytelling, and nonverbal communication—were foregrounded in various ways. We engaged the analytic act from the perspective of a number of intelligences, and in doing so considered not only how different types of intelligences brought out different features of the music, but how by using those intelligences as prompts we could strategically orient ourselves to consider previously un-thought-of viewpoints. Finally, following Gadamer's entreaty, we enlisted the productive component of our project to deliberately turn the analytic inquiry back on ourselves, to consider what different hermeneutic perspectives mean for the improvising performing musician and that musician's relationship to the performed material. Although the focus of this study has been on the value of analysis for thinking through improvisational acts in jazz settings, as the opening Chopin example suggests, an improvisational attitude can inform a close engagement with any number of musical genres. Furthermore, an improvisational attitude in the theory classroom can translate to an improvisational attitude toward the interpretation of any music being analyzed; as Bruce Ellis Benson has described compellingly, any performance of a classical "work" (for example) is necessarily an improvisational act.[41] A creative, plural analytic reading of that work can engender a dogma-free engagement with its essence (or bundle of essences), and open a horizon of interpretive possibilities, enriching a work's expressive potential and how that potential might be realized in performance. This way of thinking in turn intensifies the connection between theory and practice, locating the former as an important, creative way of gaining access to the latter in increasingly nuanced expressive ways.

Notes

1. See Stover, "Analysis as Multiplicity," for a detailed explication of this process.
2. Peters, *philosophy of Improvisation*, 16–18.
3. Berk and Trieber, "Whose Classroom," 31–32.
4. I find the vitriol of the show's judges distasteful and entirely inappropriate, even if many would argue that it makes for good television.
5. For example, philosopher Martin Heidegger refers to this process as the *hermeneutic circle* (the continuous return to the object in terms of newly acquired information or perspective, with "information" projecting from the object to the observer and perspective the other way around, both in continuous, conscious, intentional modification), while Edmund Husserl refers to the dialogue between the *transcendental* nature of the object (there is always something outside of the known that remains to be discovered) and the intentionality of the observer (who is always projecting her or his own history of experiences and referential perspectives onto the object). Husserl's transcendence here is exactly the open-endedness alluded to above. Gadamer's pursuit of meaning also interprets the name *hermeneutics*, and he extends the ways in which Heidegger constitutes identity through relationships in a world to consider issues of intersubjective and historically located meaning. See Heidegger, *Being and Time*; Husserl, *Ideas*; Gadamer, *Truth and Method*.
6. A complete transcript of the exchange (with posters' names stricken, and a few small editorial amendments to fix obvious typos and to protect the posters' anonymity) can be found at http://www.morezero.com/chopin_fb_exchange.pdf.
7. I say "putative root" because in many contemporary music-theoretical narratives the bass note of an augmented sixth chord (♭6) is not necessarily considered to be a root, since they are introduced more commonly as chromatic intensifications of first-inversion subdominant chords (iv6). Walter Piston's popular textbook chases an alternative narrative that stacks notes in thirds by letter name (resulting in a sometimes rather extraordinarily complicated figured bass notation); the German augmented sixth chord Ab-C-Eb-F♯ (spelled from the bass up) is construed as an F♯ chord with a diminished third, diminished fifth, and diminished seventh above the root—in the key of C minor (its native habitat), ♯IV7/5/3. Regarding inversions of augmented sixth chords, Steve Laitz offers the term "diminished third chord" to describe the musical situations where ♯4 is in the bass, below ♭6, and provides several examples from nineteenth-century literature where the chord appears in this context.
8. See note 7 above: I should clarify that no reputable theorists are making this claim.

9. Or they were occasionally offered with a touch of disdain for the nature of the question or of the debate: this, unfortunately, is a too-frequent sidebar when some musicians encounter what they feel to be the irrelevance of theoretical inquiry; a position toward which it should be incumbent on the more analytically curious to continue to proselytize.

10. We might explore further uses of the word *function*, such as its modern use to describe a party or similar social event—the analytical ramifications of this usage are intriguing.

11. This is frequently referred to as "integrated learning" in educational theory (see Larson, "Integrated Music Learning" for a particularly good and germane example). The value of thinking in terms of rhizomes (a concept that Gilles Deleuze and Félix Guattari introduced to critical discourse) is that in addition to linking all nodes in an integrated system, it reaches out to other new nodes, always in the process of imagining new spaces and new connections. A complex integrated system is closed by definition (even though Larson tries to skirt this conception by leaving one node blank in his graphic example), but a rhizome is *essentially* open.

12. Many other songs begin with this harmonic progression: to cite just a few that jazz musicians commonly interpret, McHugh and Fields's "Exactly Like You," João Gilberto's "O pato," and, as we'll see below, Antônio Carlos Jobim and Newton Mendonça's "Desafinado."

13. This list extrapolates from an open, interactive analytic project in my Theory 2B class at The New School from February 2014—the class was not recorded, so I am working from my hastily sketched notes that immediately followed the exchange. I have reworded construal (6) for rhetorical purposes, to bring it into conversation with the like-themed response from the Facebook exchange above. (The original response was something along the lines of "Strayhorn thought it sounded cool.")

14. In his paper "Jazz Harmony, Transformations, and ii–V Space," Michael McClimon offers a useful transformational model for what he calls "ii–V space" that has relevance to this way of thinking through jazz syntax.

15. For a summary of the contemporary debate about what constitutes background-level syntax in jazz, see McFarland, "Schenker and the Tonal Jazz Repertory."

16. These include scale choices and expressive decisions about what kinds of melodic/harmonic relations to pursue.

17. In other words, these are the aspects of musical fabric that are least problematically represented in musical notation. See Ake, "Learning Jazz, Teaching Jazz" and Borgo, *Sync or Swarm*, 171–72 for two thoughtful critiques.

18. Joya Sherill's lyrics here implore that "you must take the A Train"; is it a coincidence that the G♯ occurs on the word "train"?

19. Berk and Trieber, "Whose Classroom?," 31–32. I have omitted their seventh principle, "warm-ups," only because I (and, I believe, the authors) think of warm-ups as more of a technique to develop the first six than a principle in itself.

20. Berk and Trieber, "Whose Classroom?," 32.

21. And that "yes, and …" suggests the kind of openness or multiplicity (and, and, and …) that I am staking out here—the *n + 1* of Deleuze's pluralized difference-as-identity.

22. See Gardner, *Multiple Intelligences* and *Frames of Mind*, among his many works on the subject. In addition to Berk and Trieber ("Whose Classroom?"),

Marks-Tarlow (*Creativity Inside Out*) foregrounds the utility of improvisational spaces for engaging multiple intelligences across a diverse group of students. Among Gardner's detractors, Sternberg ("How Much Gall?") and Waterhouse ("Multiple Intelligences") challenge, respectively, the notion of multiple intelligences on the ground that it uncritically conflates intelligence with learning styles or aptitudes, and that it has no empirical backing in cognition studies. Gardner is never shy to debate his detractors, arguing at one point that he is "much more interested in matters of interpersonal intelligence that examine directly how a person works with a group of peers than in paper-and-pencil measures that involve selecting the correcting answer" (*Multiple Intelligences*, xix). While I take these criticisms seriously, I find value in the notion that through a consideration of multiple intelligences we can consider further ways to engage the (analytic, etc.) problem at hand, and that through those actions can invert the improvisational trajectory to find useful ways to access different intelligences and to communicate with different learning styles. I also appreciate Gardner's ongoing efforts not only to refine and redefine his categories of intelligences, but to rethink the borders between them and to question the nonpermeabilities of those borders.

23. Berk and Trieber, "Whose Classroom?," 36.
24. Ibid.
25. The relation between improvisation and deep learning is amplified when we read more carefully how Berk and Trieber unpack Rhem's four criteria. They offer evidence of how improvisation satisfies all four criteria, in turn:

> (1) motivational context, the intrinsic desire to know, make choices, and take ownership and responsibility for seeking a solution or making the right decision quickly; (2) learner activity, the experiential, inductive discovery in collaboration with other team members to synthesize, problem solve, or create knowledge; (3) interaction with others, with the spontaneity, intuition, quick thinking, brainstorming, trust-building, risk-taking, role-playing, and rapid decision making of improvisational dynamics; and (4) a well-structured knowledge base, where content is reshaped, synthesized, critiqued, and even created to demonstrate understanding and comprehension as well as analytical and evaluative skills. ("Whose Classroom?," 38)

> This narrative is in the context of the role improvisation has played in business and management training (which is far outside the bounds of the present essay), but translates easily to the classroom.

26. Gardener, *Frames of Mind*, 83; Robotham, "Aspects of Learning."
27. Berk and Trieber, "Whose Classroom?," 29.
28. This is the viewpoint of many practitioner-teachers: how many of us have, after internalizing a complex theoretical concept (perhaps in the theory classroom), been admonished to "now just forget about all of that and play!"? For an alternate account (but that of course enriches the current narrative) of the value that scaffolding offers for thinking through music theory pedagogy in improvisational terms, see Michaelsen, "Improvising to Learn."
29. Hasty, "Learning in Time," 4–5.
30. Hasty, "Learning in Time," 8. I can't let this suggestion go by without noting its close affinity with Heidegger's very definition of ontology, beginning with relations, dwelling, environment, contexts, attention, care, and more, and from there constituting the objects that occupy the relation-nodes.

31. Hasty, "Learning in Time," 8.
32. That is, in "Desafinado," the C♯ lower neighbor in measure 2 is transformed into a D♭ in measure 3. Almir Chediak's edition (*Songbook Tom Jobim, Vol. 3*), the Brazilian fake book *Aquarela Brasileira* (Cançado, *Aquarela Brasileira*), and *The New Real Book* by Chuck Sher all spell the arrival note in measure 3 as D♭. It is worth noting that in Paulo Jobim's arrangement for the *Cancioneiro Jobim* it is spelled as C♯ (and the chord as G7(♯11)), but the piano voicing avoids the fifth of the chord (D). Sher's *New Real Book* version has a number of "incorrect" chords, if we take the Jobim edition to designate any kind of *urtext*, but its editors freely admit that many songs in the many volumes of the *New Real Book* synthesize common (or iconic) jazz practice, in essence problematizing the very notion of text (which is why "incorrect" is in scare quotes in the previous sentence).
33. All translations are by the author.
34. Some further contextual possibilities include D minor's dual identity as a new tonic and as vi in the home key of F, and whether A7 is the point at which our perception changes or whether iv–V should be considered as a single syntactic unit (as in the ii–V above), the identity of which is bound up in the temporal constitution of the Gmin7 chord (that is, its qualitative change through time is an essential part of its identity—this is a somewhat simplified Deleuzian reading).
35. While this is a topic for another paper, it is worth noting briefly that the end of the second "A" section has given editors and musicians alike no end of trouble; c.f. the convoluted barlines of various "fake book" editions of the song. I don't find this section to be particularly contentious; indeed, one of my goals for the current analysis is to disambiguate this section, and demonstrate that not only are the phrase boundaries clear, but that they are the logical results of earlier projections in the music.

    For those unfamiliar with the song, "Desafinado" is cast in the extended form, A-A'-B-C-A'-D; sixteen, twelve, twelve, eight, twelve, and eight bars respectively. Its overall tonal arch begins in F major, moves to A major for the "B" section, to C major for the "C" section, and then back to F. A motivic parallelism links the "B" and "C" sections, and the "D" section serves as a tag or coda.
36. For example, the Gmin7 in measure 9, ii in the home key, leads an enculturated listener to expect a V chord (C7) to follow. C7 does not materialize, but another dominant functioning chord does, so our surprise is tempered somewhat by the fact that Gmin7 to A7 is still a "legal" harmonic action according to how we expect tonal motions to behave.
37. The editorial amendments were in measure 14 where an E in the melody should be D♭, and measure 39, where a Bmin7(♭5) should be Bmin7 (and the melodic F♮ a dissonant upper neighbor), and in measure 40, where in both Gilberto recordings an V7 chord in the local key is played. None of these edits directly affected the passages under consideration. I also suppressed a few chord extensions in the score (except to the extent that they represent inner-voice melodic motions) and added bar numbers. We added double bars to indicate phrase and section boundaries as a group aural project; I did not share the formal map from footnote 35 until after we had let the music communicate that part of its essence to us through multiple listenings.
38. By closely considering the relation between text and melody in this way, we also reinforce what Steve Larson, in "Integrated Music Learning," describes as

an integrated system for knowledge acquisition. In advocating for an integrated model, Larson asserts that "anytime we combine two ways of knowing a musical relationship, each of those ways of knowing is strengthened." Larson's work has been highly influential on my own thoughts about bringing an improvisational attitude into the analytic act, not least because of the compelling way that he articulates the value of incorporating improvisational techniques into the music theory classroom, including a pedagogical justification that flows from the reasons that we require music-theory courses of *all* music students and *only* of music students. The best reason is that we believe it teaches skills that will support their music-making, music-teaching, and music-learning pursuits. And such theoretical ideas (or rather, such musicianship skills) are really only useful in those activities if they can be accessed in real time ... Knowing facts about music ... is only useful if those facts can be brought to bear as quickly as the musical situation ... requires. Improvisation not only requires that those skills be accessible, but also *makes* them available (Larson, "Integrated Music Learning").

39. Compare this to the earlier student's suggestion that the eventual resolution of the "out of tune" notes also led a hopeful subtext to the song.
40. The student with perfect pitch described the E Major version as "mysterious" and the E♭ version as "smooth and shiny," suggesting that it was being made "user friendly" for a U.S. audience.
41. Benson, *The Improvisation of Musical Dialogue.*

Works Cited

Ake, David. "Learning Jazz, Teaching Jazz." In *The Cambridge Companion to Jazz*, edited by Mervyn Cooke and David Horn, 255–69. Cambridge: Cambridge University Press, 2002.

Benson, Bruce Ellis. *The Improvisation of Musical Dialogue: A Phenomenology of Music*. Cambridge: Cambridge University Press, 2003.

Berk, Ronald A. and Rosalind H. Trieber. "Whose Classroom is it, Anyway? Improvisation as a Teaching Tool." *Journal on Excellence in College Teaching* 20, no. 3 (2009): 29–60.

Borgo, David. *Sync or Swarm: Improvising Music in a Complex Age*. London: Continuum, 2005.

Cançado, Beth, ed. *Aquarela Brasileira: Letras de 312 músicas populares brasileiras e internacionais cifradas para violão*. Brasilia: Editora Corte Ltda, 1995.

Chediak, Almir, ed. *Songbook Tom Jobim, Vol. 3*. Rio de Janeiro: Luminar editor, 1999.

Covington, Kate. "Improvisation in the Aural Curriculum: An Imperative." *College Music Symposium* 37 (1997). http://symposium.music.org/index.php?option=com_k2&view=item&id=2135:improvisation-in-the-aural-curriculum-an-imperative&Itemid=146.

Deleuze, Gilles. *Difference and Repetition*. Translated by Paul Patton. New York: Columbia University Press, 1994.

Gadamer, Hans-Georg. *Truth and Method*. Revised translation by Joel Weinsheimer and Donald G. Mitchell. New York: Continuum, 2004.

Gardner, Howard. *Frames of Mind: The Theory of Multiple Intelligences*. Tenth Anniversary Edition. New York: Basic Books, 2011.

———. *Multiple Intelligences: The Theory in Practice.* New York: Basic Books, 1993.

Hasty, Christopher. "Learning in Time." *Visions of Research in Music Education* 20 (2012). http://www-usr.rider.edu/~vrme/v20n1/visions/Hasty%20Bamberger.pdf.

Heidegger, Martin. *Being and Time.* Translated by Joan Stambaugh. Albany: State University of New York Press, 2010.

Husserl, Edmund. *Ideas: General Introduction to Pure Phenomenology.* Translated by W.R. Boyce Gibson. New York: Routledge, 2012.

Jobim, Antônio Carlos. *Cancioneiro Jobim: Obras completas.* Rio de Janeiro: Casa da palavra, 2001.

Laitz, Steven G. *The Complete Musician: An Integrated Approach to Tonal Theory, Analysis, and Listening.* 3rd ed. New York: Oxford University Press, 2011.

Larson, Steve. "'Integrated Music Learning' and Improvisation: Teaching Musicianship and Theory Through Menus, Maps, and Models." *College Music Symposium* 35 (1995). http://symposium.music.org/index.php?option=com_k2&view=item&id=2116:integrated-music-learning-and-improvisation-teaching-musicianship-and-theory-through-menus-maps-and-models&Itemid=146.

Marks-Tarlow, Terry. *Creativity Inside Out: Learning through Multiple Intelligences.* Reading, MA: Addison-Wesley, 1995.

McClimon, Michael. "Jazz Harmony, Transformations, and ii–V Space." Unpublished paper presented at the Society for Music Theory National Conference, Milwaukee, WI, 2014.

McFarland, Mark. "Schenker and the Tonal Jazz Repertory: A Response to Martin." *Music Theory Online* 18, no. 3 (2012). http://www.mtosmt.org/issues/mto.12.18.3/mto.12.18.3.mcfarland.html.

Michaelsen, Garrett. "Improvising to Learn/Learning to Improvise: Designing Scaffolded Group Improvisations for the Music Theory Classroom." In *Engaging Students: Essays in Music Pedagogy, Vol. 2.* Online publication, 2014. www.flipcamp.org/engagingstudents2/essays/michaelsen.html.

Peters, Gary. *The Philosophy of Improvisation.* Chicago: University of Chicago Press, 2009.

Piston, Walter. *Harmony.* 5th ed. Revised by Mark DeVoto. New York: Norton, 1987.

Rhem, James. "Close-up: Going Deep." *The National Teaching & Learning Forum* 5, no. 1 (1995): 4.

Robotham, David. "Aspects of Learning Style Theory in Higher Education Teaching." *The Geography Discipline Network.* Online publication, 1999. http:// www2.glos.ac.uk/GDN/ discuss/kolb2.htm.

Sher, Chuck, ed. *The New Real Book.* Petaluma, CA: Sher Music Co, 1988.

Sternberg, Robert. "How much Gall is Too Much Gall? Review of *Frames of Mind: The Theory of Multiple Intelligences.*" *Contemporary Education Review* 2, no. 3 (1983): 215–224.

Stover, Chris. "Analysis as Multiplicity." *Journal of Music Theory Pedagogy* 27 (2013): 111–140.

Waterhouse, Lynn. "Multiple Intelligences, the Mozart Effect, and Emotional Intelligence: A Critical Review." *Educational Psychologist* 41, no. 4 (2006): 207–225.

6 Embodied Action Frameworks
Teaching Multicultural Ear Training

Howard Spring

The Problem

If you have never played hockey you probably would find it difficult to appreciate the underlying tactics and strategies of the game as much as somebody who has played hockey from early childhood on. The sensorimotor skills and cognitive ability of the experienced hockey player acquired through years of playing afford an understanding of the underlying principles of a hockey game that is rarely available to a non- or inexperienced player. The practical knowledge of the experienced player allows for a richer understanding of, and appreciation for, the game. It also provides a way for players to make decisions in the moment—that is to improvise—in ways that are coordinated with, and make sense to, the other players.

Similarly, if you've never played improvised music in a band, you probably wouldn't be as readily aware of the shared set of underlying musical assumptions, expectations, and practices that resonate among the performers and that guide the musical decisions being made in the moment. It would be difficult to hear the music in the same way as an experienced musician whose practical knowledge provides a set of understandings that link the continuous musical decisions and responses made during the course of an improvised performance to the underlying organizational frameworks that coordinate that performance.

In the setting of an introductory ethnomusicology class, we often find an analogous situation. Like the inexperienced hockey player or novice improvising musician, music and nonmusic students are asked to engage with something with which they have had little or no acquaintance. What then is the best way to teach these students to understand what they are hearing, to make aural sense of it? By teaching students to perform some of the underlying frameworks that inform musicians' improvisations, we provide them with a way to inhabit the music they are listening to in a way that is closer to the musicians' experience.

Unfortunately, underlying musical grammars and frameworks are seldom given sufficient emphasis in world music and ethnomusicology classrooms; certainly, the various textbooks and their accompanying musical examples that I've used over the last twenty-five years in introductory ethnomusicology classes, although helpful, have been limited in this regard. I have always felt less than satisfied in the way they discussed musical examples and the suggestions they made to facilitate students' aural understanding. It is not that textbooks don't address some of the underlying frameworks of improvised performance, but they do so in an abstract way.

What does it mean to inhabit the music in a way that is similar to the musicians' experience? Cultural anthropologists and ethnomusicologists can offer some insight into the answer to this question. They distinguish two perspectives in analyzing a culture: the emic and etic. In general, the emic perspective tries to answer questions about how community members make meaning, respond to rules of behavior, think about, perceive, imagine, categorize, and explain the world. The etic perspective shifts the focus from local observations, categories, explanations, and interpretations to the analytic and comparative frameworks and concepts projected on the culture by the researcher.[1] Emic and etic perspectives are not dichotomous. They are mutually influencing, graded, porous, and complementary. One can change one's perspective over time through experience and, to some degree, choice.

In the past, the etic standpoint claimed a universal validity in keeping with its function of comparative study. That is, the original goal of the etic approach was to apply purportedly universal categories to various cultures for the purposes of cross-cultural comparison. But nobody is outside a culture. Those not taking an emic point of view bring their own culture-specific concepts and values to bear on any culture that they are not familiar with.

In the classroom context, students bring their own perspectives, whether conscious or unconscious, to the learning of new musical material. These perspectives don't necessarily disappear because a new framework is learned. The relationship between the new framework and the previous one depends on many personal, social, and cultural factors that inform the kind of prior knowledge and the robustness of this knowledge that students bring to the learning situation. For example, students already familiar with counting pulses and cycles of pulses in Western music due to access to Western musical training would have a different experience learning to keep tala from those students who did not have the opportunity to acquire this skill. On the other hand, a student who has aurally learned African American–based improvised musics in an informal setting might make more sense out of the idea of improvisation in a rhythmically cyclic context than a student whose music training focused on music reading skills.

Even though the details of the nature of mutual influences between the emic and etic viewpoints will vary with the background of each student, they probably all involve the dialectical processes of accommodation and assimilation. Assimilation means that perceptions of the outside world are internalized and transformed to better fit the inner mental structures already in place. Accommodation means that mental structures are transformed to better fit the external evidence of the world.[2]

Usually "emic" and "etic" have been applied in ethnomusicology in the context of studying what has been considered non-Western music—the emic being the "native" point of view and the "etic" being the researcher's (usually Western) point of view. For the purpose of this discussion, however, I base the distinction between the viewpoint ("hearpoint"?) of the musician and that of the nonmusician respectively, regardless of culture, although these can and often do overlap. Because this is different from the common meaning of emic and etic, I will use the terms *musemic* to designate the musician's perspective and *musetic* for the nonmusician's perspective.

From the musemic point of view then, we can ask: How do musicians *think* about what they are doing? How do they perceive their musical practice? How do musicians make *aural sense* of what they are doing? What are the skills required by musicians who play a particular music? What kinds of knowledge are needed to perform? And perhaps most importantly for the purpose of this discussion: How do *improvising* musicians make aural sense of what they are doing? These kinds of questions and their answers are underrepresented in most introductory ethnomusicology textbooks. Most take the descriptive musetic point of view in contrast to the musemic performative one.

I am not arguing that the musetic approach found in introductory ethnomusicology textbooks is not a valuable one; just that it is not the only one. It leaves out an important consideration, and it is this hitherto underrepresented perspective that I want to focus on here with the intent of helping to restore the balance between the musemic and the musetic in the teaching of aural skills in ethnomusicology, especially those of improvised musics. By learning about some of the underlying performative knowledge that musicians need to know in order to improvise, students can deepen their aural and conceptual understanding in ways that are usually not available to them using typical textbook approaches.

Surveying the Field: Textbooks and the Musemic Perspective

To get a sense of what is routinely going on in ethnomusicology and world music survey classrooms, let us consider a handful of the most widely used postsecondary textbooks. Kay Kaufman Shelemay's book, *Soundscapes: Exploring Music in a Changing World*, now in its third edition, contains many opportunities for students to hear music in different ways, but rarely do these opportunities grow out of the musician's perspective. There are over eighty musical examples, each with a listening guide that provides basic information, musical highlights, timings, text transliterations and translations, descriptive commentary providing a minute-by minute account of the music, as well as summaries and descriptions of the overall structure. There is also a substantial section devoted to listening to various aspects of music (timbre, instruments, etc.). Interactive Listening Guides at the publisher's website highlight musical events as they occur in real time. And there are a number of other kinds of useful listening exercises. Of these eighty-plus examples, however, only ten invite students to actively make music.[3] Moreover, only four examples ask the student to perform in the style being discussed: two are from Indonesia (*Kecak* [251] and *Kotekun* [112]), one from Ethiopia (chant [341]), and, finally, only one applied to an improvised music: a piece from South India [135]. In this case the student is asked to clap *Adi Tala* while listening to the recording. It is only this last example that takes a clear musemic perspective—in this case, by inviting students to engage with the tala framework that is critical to understanding rhythm and meter in South (and North) Indian music.

Michael Bakan's book, *World Music: Traditions and Transformations*, also contains many listening examples with accompanying listening exercises. Bakan devotes a number of chapters to "How Music Works." Each of these is devoted to a different musical category: rhythm, pitch chords and harmony, dynamics, timbre, instruments, texture, and form. These are illustrated by recorded and online examples. There are also "Musical Guided Tours" and "Guided Listening Experiences" that are made up of text-based descriptions, discussions, and summaries. In some cases, students are asked to perform some of these examples. In this case, as in the Shelemay book, the Kecak[4] is used, as is the Fontomfrom African drum ensemble.[5] The most recent instructor's manual also provides instructive and interesting listening activities. Throughout the text and instructor's manual, however, Bakan rarely requires students to learn and apply performative knowledge from the musician's point of view. Of the over one hundred musical examples, there are only five that encourage students to engage from something resembling a musemic perspective: Kecak in chapter 5, keeping Tala in chapter 8, African rhythms in chapter 10, some Latin American music rhythmic patterns in chapter 11, and rhythms of various Egyptian genres in chapter 12. And significantly, although some of these ask students to play or sing aspects of the music (e.g., Zaar rhythms in chapter 12), they don't require students to perform in sync with the recorded performance, a crucial component of the approach I describe below.

What's more, while the Shelemay and Bakan books engage with musemic frameworks in a severely limited way, of the textbooks that I have encountered, they are the only ones to do so at all. Other top-selling texts like Bruno Nettl's *Excursions in World Music* and Jeff Todd Titon's *Worlds of Music: An Introduction to the Music of the World's Peoples* rely almost exclusively on a textual play-by-play approach: they offer students a musical road map to help direct and focus their listening, but in so doing they keep the terms of engagement strictly passive and silent. Students interact with the sounds that they hear exclusively as outsiders. It should be noted, by way of contrast, that all of these textbooks do an excellent job of thoroughly situating musical sound in cultural context, inviting students to adopt a meta-analytical approach to conceptualizing the large-scale relationships between sounds, sound-makers, and contexts. Nevertheless, if teachers of ethnomusicology are motivated to foster any degree of intercultural understanding among their students, the exclusively (or primarily) analytical approach offered by

Shelemay, Bakan, Nettl, and Titon falls dramatically short, precisely because none of these texts offers any opportunity for *active* intercultural *engagement*. The barriers between self and other, insider and outsider, emic and etic, remain more or less firmly in place.

Embodied Action Frameworks

By learning to perform underlying frameworks that inform improvisation, students can begin to encounter the music in a more authentic way, coming closer to a "real-life" experience of the music. Furthermore, students can begin to actualize the answers to some of the musemic questions noted above—how do musicians think? how do they make aural sense of their music? etc.—through their performances. By "actualizing the answers" through performance, I mean teaching students to assimilate through bodily, musically synchronous performance activities, the underlying forms of musical organization and knowledge that musicians use in order to produce their music: to teach them what I call *embodied action frameworks* (EAFs).

Using EAFs to teach students to aurally understand improvised music harnesses bodily responses to music as well as intellectual ones and engages students in real-time musical activity that exploits, at least in part, the knowledge of musicians. The key here is not only to teach students to hear the sounds that musicians make, but to teach them to perform the formative principles that guide the improvised patterning of these sounds. Of course, it takes many years of practice and education in one form or another to gain expert knowledge of any music, but my goal here is not to make my students into experts. Rather it is to introduce students to some of the practical musical frameworks through performance so that students will perceive the musical materials that inform the sounds that are immediately apparent. Care should be taken in making this clear to students. Once they realize the considerable degree of knowledge and skill required even at an introductory level, they often find a new respect for the makers of improvised music.

There is a long history of ethnomusicologists learning musical practices and theoretical knowledge in the field from carriers of musical traditions through formal and informal instruction and musical participation.[6] A goal in using EAFs is to enhance listening by bringing this kind of approach into the classroom—for both specialist and nonspecialist students. It should be noted that making aural sense of music is more than just understanding and being able to perform with some degree of "insider" knowledge. It also means, as ethnomusicologist Judith Becker points out, listening that is appropriate to the situation, a person, a culture, a genre, or a style. This kind of contextualization is crucial to multicultural ear training. Without denying its importance, I am focusing on the sonic dimension of ear training because it is central to this wider notion of listening as defined by Becker and is not as thoroughly discussed as are contextual matters in the pedagogical literature.

Becker also points out that our perceptions seem natural, seemingly not informed by where and when we are. However, we all listen in a certain way, with certain implicit expectations and associated meanings that are contingent on the synchronic and diachronic contexts in which we are listening. This unconscious tendency to hear in culturally and historically dependent ways is akin to sociologist Pierre Bourdieu's concept of *habitus*. In the context of hearing music, Becker calls this the *habitus of listening*. In some ways the task of teaching EAFs is to alter the habitus of listening in our students.[7]

In his essay "Speech, Music, and Speech about Music," Charles Seeger distinguishes between "speech knowledge of music" and "music knowledge of music."[8] One important aspect of music knowledge of music is gained through the embodied practice of performance. By embodied I not only mean that we use our bodies to create music. I mean that music is the result of the body's perceptual and motor capacities intermingled with cognitive activities. This contrasts with the cognitivist brain-centered approach, which emphasizes the manipulation of symbols through rules and processes.[9] Sensori-motor capacities, historically and culturally situated, are at least as important as the processes of conceptualization, reflection, and analysis, which characterize much ethnomusicology pedagogy. As musicologist and musician Vijay Iyer argues, hearing music "is structured by the body and its situatedness in its environment."[10]

Embodiment involves a strong connection between perception and motor activity.[11] Teachers can take advantage of these sensorimotor couplings by teaching students to perform, not just understand at the abstract passive level, the musical underpinnings of the music they are trying to grasp, those same underpinnings that the musicians themselves use to organize what they do. Students make aural sense of their musical perception by exploiting the close relationship between their senses and action. Further, they should be able to perform underlying musical frameworks synchronically with a performance of the music, either recorded or live. By learning how to perform them with the proviso of accurately doing so while they are listening to a performance, they gain "music knowledge of the music."

Recent research in neurobiology strongly suggests reasons why the EAF approach is effective. The discovery of a mirror neuron system in the primate brain has radical implications for evidence of the embodied nature of music cognition. I must note that the most compelling experiments on mirror neurons have been done with macaque monkeys. Neuroimaging experiments done with humans have been less conclusive, so care must be taken in drawing hard and fast conclusions. Nevertheless, the research has been highly suggestive.[12]

The existence of a mirror neuron system can be seen as a neuroanatomical concomitant to the embodied action notion of musical perception. That is, when we hear music, our brain is activated as if we were performing the same action. This corporeal mirroring results in the hearer and the producer of music co-experiencing the same act. In short, the neural system has a resonance mechanism (more on resonance later). This resonance mechanism, which is unconscious and automatic, in essence mirrors one agent to another allowing the listener to represent the actions of another using the same neural system as used to execute those actions in the first place. In a way, mirror neurons establish a link between individuals via a simulation mechanism, whereby one uses the same neural resources to represent and understand the actions of others (such as music making) as one's own. The goal of using EAFs is to create this link.

Neuroscientists Itvan Molnar-Sakacs and Katie Overy propose such a system that, according to them, allows

> an individual to understand the meaning and intention of a communicative signal by evoking a representation of that signal in the perceiver's own brain. … The experience of music thus involves the perception of purposeful, intentional and organized sequences of motor acts as the cause of temporarily synchronous auditory information. Thus, according to the simulation of mechanisms implemented by the human mirror neuron system, a similar or equivalent motor network is engaged by someone listening to singing/drumming as the motor network engaged by the actual singer/drummer … this allows for co-representation of the musical experience, emerging out of the shared and temporally synchronous recruitment of similar neural mechanisms in the sender and the perceiver of the musical message.[13]

Frameworks

By "framework" I mean the underlying armature referred to in the last section. Frameworks inform individual instances of performance. One advantage of understanding the framework of musical practice in an embodied active way is that it helps students make sense of a music they hear no matter the particular example they are listening to.

Framework, the way I'm using it here, is something like the sociopsychological category of "schema"—that is, culturally constructed mental structures that organize how we see, interpret, and act in the world.[14] All human beings organize categories, rules, actions, and knowledge, which they use to interpret and act on the world. In a way, schemas are like filters in that they help us structure the mass of sensory information that we encounter in our dealings with our environment. But schemas are not rigid. New information is processed according to how it fits into these organizational frameworks, and at the same time, schemas can be altered to conform to the new information.

Schemas can be used not only to interpret but to predict. Recalling our hockey illustration that started this chapter, Wayne Gretzky is said to have claimed that to be a great hockey player, one must not only be aware of where the puck is, but where the puck is going to be. Likewise, to be a competent musician and, I argue, a competent listener, one must not only be aware of where one is in the music but also know the underlying structure well enough to anticipate where the music is probably going to be.

Whether improvising in an ensemble setting or solo, musicians need to track the musical course of a performance in accordance with prevailing socio-cultural and musical constraints informed by conceptual and practical frameworks. For music that is not primarily improvised, some kind of notation often provides this musical tracking and guidance function. In primarily improvised musics, which often have minimal notation or none at all, learned and shared underlying schemas/structural performance frameworks provide the tracking and guidance functions making musical coordination and prediction among musicians and listeners possible.

Research[15] has shown that listeners can implicitly internalize the schema of musical production with which they grew up so that they can predict the probable course of the music, or at least be annoyed, interested, or amused when the rules that govern the style are broken or bent in unexpected ways. But, what about learning to hear music from another culture? This requires explicit learning. Learning the basic underlying structure of performance for a particular kind of music is central to our perceiving it as not just a sequence of random sounds. In short, to grasp where the music is, where it is probably going to be, when it deviates from where we expect it to be, when and how relationships shift between the guiding frameworks and the immediately heard, is one way to make sense of music. Learning to perform frameworks provides the means for achieving this level of listening.

The idea of a framework that tracks and guides improvisational practice may seem to fly in the face of the relative unpredictability often attributed to improvisation in comparison to notated musics. Improvised musics usually exhibit a greater degree of variation from performance to performance than notated music. This seems to suggest that for performing and listening to improvised music, a different kind of competence is required than is needed for performing and listening to notated music. But the difference between composed and improvised music is a matter of degree rather than of kind. Not every performance of, say, Beethoven's fifth symphony sounds the same; not every performance of John Coltrane improvising on "My Favorite Things" is completely different. They both exhibit variations from performance to performance reflecting in-the-moment decisions informed by various kinds of musical preparation including the internalization of tracking and guiding frameworks. Improvisation allows for more variability in those decisions than does composed music perhaps, but both composed and improvised musics are limited by musical as well as socio-cultural constraints. Improvised music is constrained by frameworks that limit the possible variation of the music in patterned ways, resulting in a kind of controlled unpredictability.

Frameworks, from the point of view of the embodied nature of learning, can be considered as action schemas. Students learn to perform underlying organizational and rule-bound practices that are applicable to a range of specific instances of the framework. By internalizing these frameworks through embodied actions, students make aural sense of the immanent features of a musical performance that are guided by these underlying frameworks.

New information is processed according to how it fits into these organizational frameworks or, on the psychological level, schema. Information that does not fit into them cannot be comprehended without some kind of accommodation on the part of the schema or assimilation of the information. One way to look at learning is that the learner actively builds and revises schema in light of new information and understandings. The more developed the schema in kind, relations, and number, the more expert one becomes. The role of teaching underlying musical frameworks is that it develops students' musical schema, thus allowing them to accommodate to, and assimilate new music such as they would hear in an ethnomusicology class.

The following are a few examples. Frameworks may be explicit. In India ragas are frameworks for making melodies, providing hierarchies of note choices, typical ornaments, phrases, and the like for both composed and improvised music. Tala, the given patterns of finger counts, claps, and waves that track the location of where the music is in the rhythmic cycle of a piece and guide the performer in terms of possible variation, is a framework for organizing improvised rhythmic practice. "Keeping tala" is a good example of an embodied framework that informs melodic and rhythmic improvised variations.

Frameworks can also be implicit. Jazz guitarist Charlie Christian used five or six underlying melodic frameworks in his improvisation, varying them constantly depending on the musical context, resulting in a strong sense of stylistic consistency while at same time providing creative variety. Hearing Christian's solos with the performance knowledge of these few underlying melodic and rhythmic frameworks in our ears and memories through learning to sing them helps us understand how Christian organized his improvised solos and the kinds of factors he responded to in doing so.[16]

Resonance

The ability to perform underlying musical frameworks in sync with an improvised musical performance is analogous to the action of sympathetic resonance. Much of the general literature on pedagogy focuses on understanding through reflection. As valuable as this is, it is only part of the story in the context of teaching students to aurally grasp music with which they are not familiar. Understanding through resonance is the other part of this story and is accomplished through the teaching of EAFs.

Musicologist Veit Erlmann in his book *Reason and Resonance: A History of Modern Aurality* describes reflection as deliberative and coolly detached.[17] One who reflects "searches for the truth by completely withdrawing from the world and whose intellect seems to be akin to a mirror."[18] Reflection is like a mirror, says Erlmann, in that "it reflects light waves without its own substance becoming affected, the mind mimetically represents the outside world while at the same time remaining separate from it."[19] In contrast, resonance calls up the image of the string that vibrates synchronously with another vibrating string. Resonance involves the conjunction of subject and object in contrast to reflection's distancing. Reflection usually requires separation and autonomy; resonance works through sympathy. In some ways, resonance represents the "the collapse of the boundary between perceiver and perceived."[20] This reminds us of the same kind of porous boundaries implied by the action of mirror neurons—and of the potential for reciprocity between emic and etic perspectives.

Erlmann goes on to talk about the history and connections between "reason" and "resonance" and shows how they are not as opposed as we might think at first. Nevertheless, here I am interested in how we can use the idea of resonance by itself as a useful approach to the teaching of multicultural hearing.

One of the major differences between reflection and resonance is that reflection occurs after the fact, whereas resonance occurs simultaneously with the action. To "resonate" with music, literally to re-sound, a student performs the underlying musical frameworks in real time synchronously with the music that he or she is listening to, which is, after all, what musicians are required to do. This is different from listening for and being able to identify immediately apparent features or from using analytic listening to mark different parameters of the music, both of which are valuable and common in the ethnomusicological pedagogy literature. But learning to "play along" meaningfully requires a different kind of knowledge—one that is closer to a musician's experience of the music.

In order for resonance to occur, there have to be shared frequencies between two bodies. In order to make aural sense from the musemic point of view, there have to be shared performative frameworks among performer/listeners. By learning EAFs, existing cognitive and behavioral structures/schemas/frameworks assimilate new material which is in turn accommodated, the details of which will be different for each student, but not completely different. The resulting musical behaviors and ideas from both accommodation and assimilation will be similar enough to allow for synchronized performance practices.

Participatory approaches used in learning to make sense of music, of which EAF is one, are not new and have been suggested by many teachers and educational researchers. Some ethnomusicology textbooks and their associated instructor's manuals do some of what I am calling EAFs, but they comprise a surprisingly small component of the overall material, as discussed above. Passive and reflective listening practices, and analytic approaches, characterize most of the literature. Although these are all valuable, teaching with EAFs, with their focus on sympathetic resonance, adds a powerful tool to these approaches, one that makes the musician's practical knowledge, the "musical knowledge of music," an explicit and central part of multicultural ear training.

Further, the EAF approach highlights another aspect of music making that is often missed in more traditional approaches: the making of music as a social process. That is, in contrast to, say, the common standard textbook approach of listening while following along on a chart that points out aspects of the music as the recording goes forward, EAF training requires students to take on different roles, as they would in an actual music ensemble, or different roles at different times, thus learning their place in the framework, their responsibilities to the music and their fellow musicians, and the importance of their mutually influencing musical interactions. To resonate with the music, they must resonate with each other.

EAFs in the Classroom

I've tested the efficacy of the EAF approach in my introductory ethnomusicology classes. During a twelve-week semester, I covered six musical areas all with improvisation as an important musical practice. Every two weeks I gave the class a listening test. Every two weeks I alternated teaching methods between the textbook approach and the EAF approach. The next time I taught the course I reversed the musical areas to which these approaches were applied. In both cases the EAF approach resulted in higher listening test scores.

I admit that so far my testing is not very rigorous. Even though the students were not aware of what I was doing, there were many other factors I did not control for. Nevertheless, the results were quite consistent—consistent enough to suggest more rigorous testing be done in the future.

When I used the EAF approach in my classes, there was initially some resistance. I think the resistance I encounter from students occurs because it questions assumptions about who can and who cannot competently engage with music. To judge from the informal responses of both music and non-music students near the beginning of the term, the latter assume that they are incapable of hearing music on the level that I am suggesting here. For the former, listening as a basis for intellectual discourse is suspect. Students are more likely to believe written evidence than aural evidence. This is true of Western academic culture in general: it has a bias in favor of literacy as opposed to aurality. We are more likely to trust statements about music that are based on the notated score of a particular piece of music than on a recording of that music. This does not apply just to Western art music. Notated transcriptions of improvised music, such as a jazz solo, carry more weight than aural sources in the academic discourse of jazz. We are less willing or less confident to form an argument, come to a conclusion, or make a judgment based solely on aural evidence.[21] This widespread wariness, at least in my experience, of the legitimacy of aural sources makes it less likely that students will rely on their ears, to trust their ability to make compelling insights about music, especially improvised music, using the aural dimension, to believe that they can trust their own ability to hear in an authoritative way that is comparable to the trust they have in reading a book or article. In using the EAF approach, the hope is to disabuse students of this idea.

Introducing students to musicians' tools that sharpen their aural abilities, thereby strengthening their trust in them, does more than help students make aural sense of improvised music and interrogate traditional attitudes about their musical capabilities. It also gives them a glimpse into the demanding skills and sophisticated knowledge required to improvise. It is no accident that improvised musics have been, until recently, pretty well neglected in Western academic music studies, even though many, if not most, major Western composers were skilled improvisers, and most of the world's musics include improvisational practices.[22] Improvisation has typically been characterized as mysterious, undisciplined, unplanned, unteachable, unknowable, "natural," a matter of instinct without reference to history or culture rather than a practice that requires discipline, knowledge, study, cultural and historical awareness, and practice. In the words of improviser Derek Bailey, "improvisation enjoys the curious distinction of being both the most widely practiced of all musical activities and the least acknowledged and understood."[23]

The 1998 introduction to one of the few book-length studies devoted to musical improvisation up to that time is called, "An Art Neglected in Scholarship."[24] The author of the introduction (and one of the book's editors), ethnomusicologist Bruno Nettl accounts for this neglect by citing the lack of technology that would allow for the study of improvised musics and, perhaps more troubling, embedded attitudes of musicology reflecting broader social ideas and values. The attitudes are typical of the "Western middle class culture towards societies in which improvisation is significant … [societies] whose arts may be appreciated but are not to be taken very seriously …",[25] attitudes that "connect improvisation as a musical practice but even more as a concept, with a kind of third world music … associated mainly with the cultural outsiders."[26]

Although much has changed in this regard due to the growth of ethnomusicology and developments in audio and video recording technology, I find a residue of these attitudes in my classes. By introducing students through appropriate EAFs to the highly evolved physical and intellectual skills required to improvise, we help undercut the notion that improvised music, associated with "others," is somehow less than Western "serious" composed music, and it undermines the racial and ethnic chauvinism that often goes along with this attitude. To be sure, the connection between the way in which we teach students to hear improvised musics and ideas about aurality and social/ethnic/"racial" hierarchies needs more research. Understanding this connection becomes more important as the study of improvisation becomes progressively more central in music curricula.

Notes

1. For a discussion of the various issues in this regard, see Kubik, "Emics and Etics."
2. I am taking these terms from the work of learning theorist Jean Piaget (1896–1980) whose research on childhood learning became highly influential. Even though he concentrated on children's learning, his ideas are highly suggestive for learning in general.
3. These ten examples appear in "Try It Out" sidebars scattered throughout the book.
4. Bakan, *World Music*, 98.
5. Ibid., 192.
6. For a summary of work done by ethnomusicologists on teaching and learning and its place in the discipline of ethnomusicology, see Tim Rice, "The Ethnomusicology of Music Learning and Teaching."
7. Becker, "Exploring the Habitus of Listening," 420.
8. Seeger, "Speech, Music, and Speech about Music," 16.
9. Andy Clark, *Supersizing the Mind*, 4.
10. Iyer, "Embodied Mind," 388.
11. For an overview of the literature, see Simone Schutz-Bosbach and Wolfgang Prinz, "Perceptual Resonance." For a nonspecialist discussion of these relationships and the research literature on this topic, see Robert J. Zatorre, Joyce L. Chen, and Virginia B. Penhune, "When the Brain Plays Music."
12. For a good summary of recent literature on mirror neurons see J. M. Kilner and R. N. Lemon, *What We Currently Know about Mirror Neurons*.
13. Molnar-Szakacs and Overy, "Music and Mirror Neurons," 235–236.
14. The history of this idea in the sense that I am using it here originates with Kant and is elaborated by Bartlett and Piaget. For a short history of this term, see McVee, Dunsmore, and Gavelek, "Scheme Theory Revisited." The term was first applied to music by Leonard Meyer and then by Gjerdingen and others. See Vasili Byros, "Meyer's Anvil."
15. Berkowitz, *The Improvising Mind*, 114–18.
16. Spring, "The Use of Formulas."
17. Erlmann, *Reason and Resonance*, 9–10.
18. Ibid.
19. Ibid.
20. Ibid.
21. Academic music journals require notated transcriptions of improvised music as evidence for claims made about it. Even today, with broad access to sonic evidence, this is still the case.
22. Bailey, Improvisation, ix.
23. Ibid.
24. Nettl, "Introduction: An Art Neglected in Scholarship."
25. Nettl, "Introduction," 6.
26. Ibid., 7.

Works Cited

Bailey, Derek. *Improvisation: Its Nature and Practice in Music*. New York: Da Capo Press, 1992.

Bakan, Michael B. *World Music: Traditions and Transformations*. 2nd ed. Boston: McGraw-Hill, 2012.

Becker, Judith. "Exploring the Habitus of Listening: Anthropological Perspectives." In *Handbook of Music and Emotion: Theory, Research, and Applications*, edited by Patrick N. Juslin and John A. Sloboda, 127–58. Oxford: Oxford University Press, 2010.

Berkowitz, Aaron L. *The Improvising Mind: Cognition and Creativity in the Music Moment*. New York: Oxford University Press, 2010.

Byros, Viasili. "Meyer's Anvil: Revisiting the Schema Concept." *Music Analysis* 31, no. 3 (October 2012): 273–346.

Clark, Andy. *Supersizing the Mind: Embodiment, Action, and Cognitive Extension*. Oxford: Oxford University Press, 2011.

Erlmann, Veit. *Reason and Resonance: A History of Modern Aurality*. New York: Zone Books, 2010.

Iyer, Vijay. "Embodied Mind, Situated Cognition, and Expressive Microtiming in African American Music." *Music Perception* 19, no. 3 (Spring 2002): 387–414.

Kaufman Shelemay, Kay. *Soundscapes: Exploring Music in a Changing World*. 3rd ed. New York: W. W. Norton and Company, 2015.

Kilner, J. M., and R. N. Lemon. "What We Know Currently about Mirror Neurons." *Current Biology* 23, no. 23 (December 2013): 1052–62.

Kubik, Gerhard. "Emics and Etics Re-Examined, Part 1: Emics and Etics: Theoretical Considerations." *African Music* 7, no. 3 (1996): 3–10.

McVee, Mary B., Kailonnie Dunsmore, and James R. Gavelek. "Schema Theory Revisited." *Review of Educational Research* 75, no. 4 (Winter 2005): 531–66.

Molnar-Szakacs, Istvan, and Katie Overy. "Music and Mirror Neurons: From Motion to 'E'motion." *Social Cognitive and Affective Neuroscience* 1, no. 3 (2006): 235–41.

Nettl, Bruno, Timothy Rommen, Charles Capwell, Isabel K. F. Wong, Thomas Turino, Philip V. Bohlman, and Byron Dueck. *Excursions in World Music*. 6th ed. Boston: Pearson, 2012.

———. "Introduction: An Art Neglected in Scholarship." In *In the Course of Performance: Studies in the World of Musical Improvisation*, edited by Bruno Nettl and Melinda Russell, 1–26. Chicago: University of Chicago Press, 1998.

Rice, Tim. "The Ethnomusicology of Music Learning and Teaching." *College Music Symposium* 43 (2003): 65–85.

Schutz-Bobach, Simone, and Wolfgang Prinz. "Perceptual Resonance: Action-Induced Modulation of Perception." *Trends in Cognitive Science* 11, no. 8 (August 2007): 349–55.

Seeger, Charles. "Speech, Music, and Speech about Music." In *Studies in Musicology, 1935–1975*, 16–30. Berkeley: University of California Press, 1977.

Spring, Howard. "The Use of Formulas in the Improvisations of Charlie Christian." *Jazzforschung/Jazz Research* 22 (1990): 11–51.

Titon, Jeff Todd, ed. *Worlds of Music: An Introduction to the Music of the World's Peoples*. 5th ed. Belmont, CA: Schirmer Cengage Learning, 2009.

Zatorre, Robert J., Joyce L. Chen, and Virginia B. Penhume. "When the Brain Plays Music: Auditory-Motor Interactions in Music Perception and Production." *Nature Reviews Neuroscience* 8 (July 2007): 547–558.

7 From Jazz Pedagogy to Improvisation Pedagogy
Solving the Problem of Genre in Beginning Improvisation Training

Gabriel Solis

Although improvisation does not have the taboo or invisible status in the academy today that Bruno Nettl described in 1974,[1] it still remains marginal to a significant extent. That is, it is limited more or less to three situations: jazz curricula, early music ensembles, and in certain cases, New Music ensembles. Of these, the jazz improvisation course—often taught in a graded two- or four-semester sequence, and seldom taken by students who do not major in jazz—is usually the only place where improvisation is the subject of extended, formal pedagogy. Even organists, whose performance practice includes improvisation of some kinds, do not always get formal training in improvisation. Pedagogical approaches vary, but usually organ improvisation training is embedded in private lessons and is somewhat haphazard. As a consequence, most students majoring in music at a tertiary level do not have any experience with improvisation in their training. In meetings of departmental curriculum committees, my colleagues do not always share my concern that this diminishes those students' opportunity to become fully educated, fully capable musicians. Nonetheless, the College Music Society's *Taskforce on the Undergraduate Music Major* (TF-UMM) articulated an increased emphasis on improvisation as part of educating music majors in the twenty-first century as a central goal.

Motivated by my experiences teaching improvisation to music education students, I suggest here that the TF-UMM's goal, though laudable, may be limited by what I call "the problem of genre"—the fact that most improvisation pedagogy is oriented to producing idiomatic players of specific genres, mostly post-bop style jazz.[2] This is a problem, as I see it, because idiomatic training in jazz is primarily useful to students who wish to play jazz; the skills involved in improvising bop-style melodic lines over chord changes in a swing rhythmic language are not obviously transferrable to other musical settings. I would go further, in fact: this narrow band of skill training is not without merit, of course, but its narrowness runs counter to the goals of incorporating improvisation more broadly into tertiary-level music education, and of thereby expanding their creative agency. In the most simple sense, this is because those students who do not (and do not wish to) play jazz will not pursue jazz improvisation training beyond a basic level; but in a more important sense, as I will elaborate later in this chapter, the most compelling reasons for teaching improvisation to students who do not play jazz are actually undermined by a decontextualized focus on teaching basic jazz competencies. Solving this problem of genre requires an understanding of improvisation as a term describing a range of potentially quite distinct creative practices in a variety of world traditions and historical styles. And it requires a pedagogical model designed with that procedural multiplicity in mind. As my argument in this chapter unfolds, I suggest that ultimately this approach is not intended to produce what Derek Bailey called "non-idiomatic" improvisers,[3] but rather to produce creative musicians who understand their own genres self-reflectively and metacritically. That is significant because such knowledge—which I think of as a kind of ethnomusicological learning—can help them develop as performers and teachers into what I would call "agents of musical creativity" in any genre.

Improvisation, understood broadly, is a part of virtually every musical tradition, from the big classical traditions of Europe, Africa, and Asia to the little musical communities established by schoolchildren around the world with a minimum of adult input. From the alternative rock band practicing in a suburban North American garage to the sitarist working through ragas with a guru in North India, and from the *gendèr* player complementing the lines of a *dhalang* in a Central Javanese shadow puppet play to an Ewe drummer adding a *kloboto* part to a performance of *Agbekor* on stage or in a village in Ghana, musicians constantly make music that affords opportunities to enact creative decisions in the act of performance. That said, though each tradition may have explicit teaching methods, this aspect, the art of making creative decisions *ad libitum*, is not always the subject of formal pedagogy.

My approach to improvisation teaching and learning in the contemporary Western academy recognizes and celebrates the desire to integrate improvisation into music pedagogies and to build pedagogies for improvisation. Moreover, it aims to bring together two frames of reference that I think are crucial to thinking through the problem of genre I address here: ethnomusicology and pedagogical theory. I begin with some brief notes from the ethnographic context in which my ideas about improvisation pedagogy have developed and a discussion of two short pedagogical examples I have used in the past and reflections on them. This leads to some discussion of relevant insights by scholars working in improvisation and pedagogy that inform my ideas both about what a meta-generic improvisation pedagogy might do and why it is crucial to the goal of educating all student musicians to be agents of their own creativity. Finally, I put the theories and my experience in dialogue to try to elucidate the stakes of moving beyond jazz as the principal model of improvisation in contemporary Western music pedagogies.

Briefly, I would point to two writers whose work is particularly relevant to my thoughts on this subject: Patricia Shehan Campbell and David Borgo.[4] Campbell's article, "Learning to Improvise Music, Improvising to

Learn Music," from a volume I edited with Bruno Nettl offers a three-part framework to describe the value of improvisation for music education.[5] They are "learning to improvise music" (developing the skills that allow musicians to perform in styles that use improvisation); "improvising to learn music" (acquiring basic musical skills, including musicianship, theoretical understanding, and so forth, through improvisational musical activity); and "improvising music to learn" (nurturing humane, humanistic values through the practices of musical improvisation). What is important here is that learning to improvise music, to become a jazz soloist, for instance, is only one of three possible goals. It is an important one for some musicians, but for many it is not. Those who teach improvisation will no doubt have had experiences in the classroom where all of these three processes were activated at once, but my impression is that often one or another rises to focal awareness in a given session. As I see it, a nearly exclusive emphasis on learning to improvise music in improvisation courses as they are commonly taught today may crowd out the other two goals; and yet for most students (perhaps even those who ultimately wish to become jazz musicians), the other two goals are more critical to lifelong creativity.

Borgo, in the article "Free Jazz in the Classroom," argues for improvisation in all levels of music education based on a theory of knowledge as "embodied," "situated," and "distributed."[6] The idea of improvisation as an embodied and situated knowledge is relatively easy to make sense of: its embodiment is something it shares with all musical knowledge—it requires muscle memory and aural response (there is a reason David Sudnow titled his account of learning to improvise *Ways of the Hand*); and it is a knowledge that resides in practice. We learn to improvise in specific settings, with specific people, and so on, and all of that specificity is part of our knowledge of improvisation. The two can be separated into content and context, but that separation is artificial at some level. The idea that knowledge is distributed (in his words, "knowledge as action rather than artifact exists not only in the mind of the individual, but rather as something shared between individuals in a physical and social setting") is harder to grasp, but it also offers the most radical possibilities.[7] The point is that my knowledge resides in some measure in you, my interlocutor. This is ontologically tough to deal with, because it undermines the idea of the coherent subject, but it is good to think with. In the context of improvisation pedagogy, it requires us to think about the ways our music making as a kind of praxis requires others to become complete. One way this manifests might be in rhythmic entrainment, where creating "good time" is definitively not a matter of each musician in a performance individually maintaining a strong internal metronome sense, but rather a matter of each musician being sensitive and responsive to the others' sense of time.[8] Borgo's work suggests a more extensive vision of distribution, though, that sees all domains of musical improvisation as subject to this kind of intersubjectivity. This is important to my larger argument about improvisation pedagogy because it underwrites the collectivity of my approach. This is tangential in some ways to the problem of genre in the abstract, but not necessarily in practice. The common model of beginning jazz improvisation pedagogy (as critiqued by Ake and others) is oriented toward mastery of a body of abstract information and its deployment in playing solos. This is generally enriched with embodied, situated, and distributed experiences in combos particularly, but those are largely only part of the jazz curriculum, as documented by Murphy.[9] Other students, however, often do not have those more enriched experiences. A model of improvisation pedagogy that helps students work creatively regardless of genre specialization would expand this sense of distribution and make their experiences easier to integrate into other aspects of their musical lives.

Ethnographic Context

My thinking about improvisation pedagogy has been significantly affected by two qualitatively rich experiential contexts. The first is through working in a large North American school of music that has built a jazz program over the course of slightly more than a decade, and in which I have been directly involved as both educator and administrator; the second is through teaching an improvisation pedagogy course for my own university's Masters of Music Education program and for the University of Melbourne Masters of Music Studies curriculum. The first context has principally given me a perspective on why I think moving past a fundamental focus on jazz genre competencies is such an important goal for most student musicians. The second has given me some, admittedly anecdotal, ideas about what is possible with non-jazz students and what the stakes and outcomes of an improvisation pedagogy that builds on students' own genre competencies might be.

The consensus among jazz-focused graduate students and faculty with whom I work and whom I interviewed for this project is that the improvisation class as they imagine it for jazz students is not about developing a sense of aesthetics so much as it is about providing a toolbox for idiomatic playing. Faculty, in particular, thought of the improvisation course as linked and interlaced with a suite of other courses—history, theory, composition, arranging, and analysis—and with private lessons, small group playing, and for most, some kind of large ensemble. The implication is that while the improvisation class does not provide much opportunity, itself, for reflection on "why" questions, instead focusing on "how" questions, the full jazz curriculum is meant to put "what," "why," and "how" questions in dialogue with one another. Some students I interviewed had mixed feelings about the extent to which it actually did so, expressing concern that institutional structures can lead to an overemphasis on technique ("how," that is) in curricular experiences. In a sense, the attitudes reflected by this particular academic jazz community mirror almost exactly the critiques of and apologies for jazz pedagogy found in the literature on the topic from the last decade.[10]

One of the most revealing conversations I had about this came in a discussion of David Ake's and Ken Prouty's work with a graduate jazz guitar student. He agreed that in a general way, university programs restrict individual student musicians' creativity, and he drew an example from his own experience. He said he feels that while electric guitars are capable of a nearly infinite array of timbres, students everywhere are essentially required to play on a narrow-bodied semiacoustic with the tone knob turned all the way down, producing a dark, hollow tone. I suggested that instructors' desire for a certain tone quality in specific settings could be handled as a conversation, a learning opportunity to think about the contextuality of aesthetics, and he agreed. And yet, in the next breath, he acknowledged that as a teacher he gets better results with a more authoritarian, less Socratic approach.[11] This contradiction is likely familiar to readers who have experience teaching music of any kind, not only jazz improvisation; I suggest that like much of the conflict chronicled in Ake, Prouty, and John Murphy's works, it is at least partly explained by the shifting relationships that are enabled as students progress. It is certainly easier, and perhaps more appropriate, to engage in dialogues about aesthetics with advanced students than with beginners.

To the extent that the notion of aesthetics and technique developing in tandem through a suite of courses does work, in any case, it only does so for jazz students. Non-jazz students who take an improvisation course but not the rest of the curriculum are left only with bits of jazz technique and very little in the way of useful aesthetic, experiential, musical knowledge. In conversations I have had with such students, I note that they find it difficult to apply what they learn in the class to their regular musical pursuits.

The music teachers I worked with in Melbourne in 2010 and in a similar course at the University of Illinois show a related problem. In a course titled "Improvisation Pedagogy in World Musical Cultures," I have worked with graduate students who had a range of professional experience, from primary and secondary classroom and ensemble music instruction to private violin teaching, and from music education policy to teaching introductory musicianship in a pop music conservatory. These students share a desire to incorporate improvisatory practices into methods for teaching music that is largely non-jazz. Many of them have expressed being intimidated by the concept of improvisation, tying it fairly firmly and unilaterally to modern jazz, and to high levels of technical skill and genre competency (that is, both knowing what to play in a modern jazz context and knowing how to play it). The students in the classes all have developed a very high level of musical skill and considerable musical knowledge—the kind of experiential knowledge that may or may not be accessible to them in metacritical, discursive forms, but that is the basis on which they make interpretive musical decisions in repertoire they know all the time, and through which they learn to play new repertoire idiomatically.

I structured the class around discussions of formal and informal pedagogies for improvisation from specific traditions drawn from my experiences as a performer—jazz, Baroque Western classical music, Ewe percussion ensembles, *capoeira*, and Javanese gamelan—and worked on developing pedagogical exercises for their own idiosyncratic teaching situations.

Exercises

I want briefly to present two exercises that I use in this class in order to think about what they teach and how they serve the goals described in this paper: developing critical reflection and agency in teaching and learning musical creativity.

The first exercise is extremely simple, requiring only a bare minimum of technical skill and no specific genre competence, and is something I have adapted from my colleague in music education, Matthew Thibeault.[12] In a nutshell, two people sit at a single piano. One plays a one-octave, ascending C-major scale in half notes. The other plays a two-octave, ascending C-major scale in any rhythmic configuration, provided this part ends in time with the first part. After completing that, they trade parts. Next, one player continues to play a one-octave, ascending C-major scale while the other plays a line that rises from one C to a C two octaves above, in any rhythmic configuration, but adding any kind of stepwise movement up or down. (This is actually a little tricky—most people want to add leaps as well at this juncture.) Again they trade parts. The third portion adds leaps to the variable part. After each part the players are given an opportunity to reflect on the experience. Whenever I have taught this, the students have reflected on the musical aspects of what each other had done—for instance, recognizing and thinking about one another's use of motives and patterns, about moments of consonance and dissonance, and so on—but they also regularly focus on the social, interpersonal lessons of the activity. They describe it as intimate, vulnerable, anxiety producing, and a source of satisfaction. The one playing the fixed role particularly is free to listen to the other, and the players routinely find themselves—even though their part is predetermined—feeling that they are part of a creative process, playing an important role, and quietly enjoying giving support and encouragement to their partners. In their reflections after the whole exercise, students have described this as an experience that opens their ears to musical process in a way that they do not normally experience in daily music making. Although it is possible to do the same exercise on any instruments, the physical experience of sitting at the piano together, watching one another's hands, and feeling a kind of bodily proximity, seems to be important. I note that when I have taught this, none of the participants knew each other before this opening exercise, and it has served as a focal point of conversation throughout the course as they got to know each other musically. The idea, in fact, of knowing "who you are" musically is among the most fundamentally remarked aspects of the whole experience for student-musicians.

The C-major scale exercise is in many ways not what my students imagine, going into this course, when they think of "improvisation." It is not technically challenging, it is not particularly musically interesting, though they do bring their particular musicalities to the activity, and perhaps most importantly, nearly every aspect of the exercise is governed by rules. This last point, as readers of this volume will know, is in fact common to most actual musical improvisation, but the point is that it contravenes students' imagined senses of what improvisation is.

The other exercise I want to describe is one that I've programmed at the very end of the class in one instance, and toward the middle in others. It does, indeed, engage students in something much more like what they think of as "improvisation" in the first place. This is an exercise in collective, "free" improvisation. I have them read Borgo's article "Free Jazz in the Classroom" the night before, but I set up no specific parameters in advance, except to ask them to think about the range of activities we have engaged in and readings we have discussed prior to this, and to try to listen as much as play. Unsurprisingly, on the first go-around the participants tend to play as much as they possibly can, and largely the same things over and over. On reflection, my students in 2012 particularly thought the music they made felt monochromatic and claustrophobic. This was absolutely new territory for all but one of them, and it felt both taboo and hard to manage. We did a number of further stints of playing, punctuated by critical reflection, and gradually the students developed ways of signaling a desire to guide the music in one way or another (largely physical gestures); slowly each individual started to play less and use silence as well as sound as a way of giving shape to the experience; and very slowly they made forays into less "safe" musical sounds. Avant garde–sounding approaches to rhythm, dissonance treatment, and so on were *not* the point of the exercise, but it was interesting to hear the students talk about their uses of sounds that did not "go" easily with the things others were playing.

In both of these exercises, as well as in the others I have explored with my classes, the question of what was being taught and learned was crucial to the students. My most recent class found it useful to bracket off the notion of improvisation to some degree, precisely because the exercises often did not fit their preconceptions. They discussed at some length the question of how much variability was available to them, and the ways in which they felt they were actively creating form or elaborating a precomposed form, in place of discussing the idea of improvisation, as such. Were they improvising? Were they composing in real time? Were they interpreting instructions that served as a "model," in Nettl's terms?[13] Any or all of these might have been accurate ways to describe their playing, but they resisted such language because it did not seem relevant to the questions about creative musicality in the moment of playing. This discursive shift was useful, as part of a praxis-based pedagogy, I believe, in part because it opened up a set of topics for conversation that are implicit, but difficult to talk about explicitly within a framework in which "improvisation" and "composition" are the principal categories of analysis—even if they are seen as points on a continuum.

Perhaps the most important payoff of this exercise is that it gives the musicians a perspective on their own musical languages. By playing responsively, and by knowing that others are listening and responding to them, students report a significant sense of objectification of their own sound worlds. They become aware of how they sound to others as bearers of musical genre, and hopefully take the chance to use that knowledge to inform their playing—both in the moment, and afterward. In a sense, to me, this is a beautiful example of praxis ethnomusicology—theory in action. The student-teachers are learning musical skills, but far more importantly, they are learning about themselves as encultured, social musical subjects. Playing creatively together was, itself, a form of auto-ethnomusicological investigation. It is also a case in which I believe Campbell's three kinds of learning (learning to improvise music, improvising to learn music, and improvising music to learn) are fused into a single activity.

Theories of Improvisation, Theories of Pedagogy

My experiences in these two contexts find considerable resonance in more general educational theories, particularly those of John Dewey and Paulo Freire,[14] as well as their interpretation in the work of music educationalists such as Campbell and Borgo.[15] The key element of this scholarship, as I see it, is the development of agency and critical reflection as both process and outcome in education. Dewey's work, written for the most part between 1897 and 1916, stressed the possibility and value of a dialogic, processual model of teaching and learning. It is hard *not* to hear the concerns of socially engaged improvising musician-teachers prefigured in his work. He did not, so far as I know, speak specifically about improvisation, but his work, especially *Democracy and Education* (1916), is suffused with a logical chain that connects creative communication to social and intellectual development; social and intellectual development to personal agency; and agency to freedom and democracy. The following is worth quoting at length:

> Not only is social life identical with communication, but all communication (and hence all genuine social life) is educative. To be a recipient of a communication is to have an enlarged and changed experience. ... The experience has to be formulated in order to be communicated. The formulate requires getting outside of it, seeing it as another would see it, considering what points of contact it has with the life of another so that it may be got into such form that he can appreciate its meaning. Except in dealing with commonplaces and catch phrases one has to assimilate, imaginatively, something of another's experience in order to tell him intelligently of one's own experience. All communication is like art. It may be fairly said, therefore, that any social arrangement

that remains vitally social, or vitally shared, is educative to those who participate in it. Only when it becomes cast in a mold and runs in a routine way does it lose its educative power.[16]

Freire, whose work is best known from the *Pedagogy of the Oppressed* (1970), shares with Dewey a dialogic ideal in pedagogy and a goal of using co-creativity and critical reflection to educate for democracy. His work is more explicitly revolutionary than Dewey's, and couched in the terms of Marxist class struggle, rather than American Pragmatism, but the two work together remarkably well, particularly in conceptualizing why improvisation (or, perhaps better, experimental co-creation) should be part of any music education, and in articulating an intersocial, communicative, processual pedagogy for improvisation.

I note that there is an extensive literature—or perhaps better two literatures—on jazz improvisation pedagogy, one practical and one critical, but relatively speaking, less on improvisation pedagogy outside of jazz. Readers of this volume may be familiar with both of the jazz literatures, but it is worth noting a couple of aspects that may have gone unremarked in the past. The first has to do with the practical literature. Here I'm thinking of the work by Jerry Coker, David Baker, Jamey Aebersold, and others, largely developed as instructional material to support secondary- and tertiary-level jazz instruction.[17] These are fairly resolutely task-oriented, tending to have more or less one purpose: helping student musicians realize the goal of idiomatically playing bebop or post-bop melodies over standard jazz chord changes. To the extent that they offer aesthetic, philosophical ideas or instruction, they do so only in marginal zones—introductions, for the most part. That said, it is worth noting that *they do* usually include such marginalia, and moreover, they are not generally intended as stand-alone improvisation pedagogies; these books are clearly meant to be used as resources to supplement an interactive, human-to-human, apprenticeship-like model of education. Coker, for instance, says a person should learn to improvise because "there is creative interplay between all members of the group, which is an enviable trait for any field of human endeavor."[18]

The critical literature produced largely by musicologist-performers who have experience teaching (and studying) in collegiate jazz programs tends to take jazz improvisation pedagogy to task not because of its laser-like focus on developing idiomatic knowledge, but because they see it failing to develop critical jazz competencies. Ake's study of mainstream jazz educators' reception of Coltrane via the so-called Coltrane Matrix (that is, the "Giant Steps" changes and their implications for post-bop chord-scale extensions) is emblematic.[19] He argues that with the improvisation class's common use of chord-scale theory and emphasis on "note choice" over things like rhythmic conception, "jazz pedagogy remains decidedly classically based."[20] Ken Prouty has argued similarly that the improvisation course fails to teach improvisation broadly (or in some sense even narrowly).[21] It is worth pointing out that John Murphy, in his apology for jazz improvisation pedagogy, does not disagree with Ake's (and Prouty's) basic analysis of this limitation of the jazz improvisation class, so much as he argues that the other, less formal, more apprenticeship-like elements of institutional jazz education are important and had been overlooked in recent scholarship—an argument that I think has merit.[22]

My purpose in developing an improvisation pedagogy course that is not focused on jazz is that it can draw students more fully into questions about the process of music making at the same time as it hones idiomatically meaningful skills. The knowledge students develop over the course of this class is, as Borgo puts it, "capability-in-action," rather than "stored artifacts."[23] Because of this, it brings students relatively quickly from seeing themselves as nonimprovisers to seeing themselves as improvisers. Moreover, my experience suggests that it speeds up the process of making them comfortable not only as improvisers, but as music teachers who are able to see opportunities for improvisation in their own students' lives and build improvisation into their curricula, whether they work in primary, secondary, or tertiary levels. It would not be impossible to achieve similar goals using a more narrowly genre-based jazz improvisation model, I believe, as, indeed, many teachers do; but such a model gives up its lessons most easily, and in many cases only to those students who are already committed to contemporary "mainstream" jazz performance. I am inclined to look for an improvisation pedagogy that solves this problem of genre and integrates improvisational thinking into the experiences of more students. It is significant, I believe, that the College Music Society TF-UMM agrees.

Conclusion

I do not propose that every student at my institution or any other should take an improvisation class because I think they should all become jazz musicians, avant gardists, or even because I think they should all engage in what they, themselves, would conceptualize as improvised performance. I would, I suppose, be delighted if some of them did, but I think there's a more important lesson in the experiences I've had with a kind of improvisation pedagogy that sees mainstream modern jazz as only one among many possible approaches to improvisation. The point is the opposite of what Freire would call the "banking" model of education—where students may be filled up with genre competencies determined in advance.[24] Genre competencies, of course, are important building blocks to aesthetically and socio-musically rewarding experiences in performance; but it is my experience that improvisation pedagogy, when its basic orientation is not to teaching a single set of genre markers, can give students profoundly important opportunities to develop as creative agents with a deeper, more reflective knowledge of their preexisting genre competence. This has consequences well beyond the development of the ability to play a specific kind of music—jazz, for instance. In fact, it may not lead to improvisational performance in public, at all. Rather, the key is that I think the lessons encapsulated in the exercises I have explored with students—learning to be socially connected, to experience musical intimacy with others and invest in a collaborative creative practice, and learning to hear yourself "from the outside," so to speak—are pedagogically critical, even when they are only part of the practice regimes of the students, and not deployed in performance contexts, or when they are used only in participatory, nonpresentational music contexts. Significantly, when engaged in deeply, they give students a base upon which to exercise creative agency, and make them better musicians. They can be important elements of any kind of music making, inform creativity at any level, from what we might think of as "interpretation" to what we might call "free improvisation," "composition," and a range of activities in between. My contention is that at an even larger level, they are lessons that ultimately play a role in making music education into education for freedom and democracy.

Notes

1. Nettl, "Thoughts on Improvisation."
2. A number of other scholars have critiqued jazz pedagogy for its exclusive focus on the types of modern jazz that have come to be known as "mainstream," notably David Ake and Ken Prouty.
3. Bailey, *Improvisation*, xi.
4. Campbell, "Learning to Improvise Music"; Borgo, "Free Jazz in the Classroom."
5. Campbell, "Learning to Improvise Music," 120–21.
6. Borgo, "Free Jazz in the Classroom," 62.
7. Ibid.
8. Clayton, Sager, and Will, "In Time with the Music"; de Wilde, *Monk*.
9. Murphy, "Beyond the Improvisation Class."
10. Ake, *Jazz Cultures*; Ake, *Jazz Matters*; Murphy, "Beyond the Improvisation Class"; Prouty, *Knowing Jazz*; Prouty, "The 'Finite' Art."
11. Personal communication, 2014.
12. Thibeault, "The Power of Limits."
13. Nettl, "Thoughts on Improvisation."
14. Dewey, *Democracy and Education*; Freire, *Pedagogy of the Oppressed*.
15. Campbell, "Learning to Improvise"; Borgo, "Free Jazz in the Classroom."
16. Dewey, *Democracy and Education*, 8–9.
17. Coker, *Jerry Coker's Complete Method*; Baker, *Jazz Improvisation*; Aebersold, *Nothin' but the Blues*.
18. Coker, *Jerry Coker's Complete Method*, 4.
19. Ake, *Jazz Cultures*.
20. Ibid., 116.
21. Prouty, *Knowing Jazz*; Prouty, "The 'Finite' Art."
22. Murphy, "Beyond the Improvisation Class."
23. Borgo, "Free Jazz in the Classroom," 61–62.
24. Freire, *Pedagogy of the Oppressed*.

Works Cited

Aebersold, Jamey. *Nothin' but the Blues: Jazz and Rock*. New Albany, IN: Jamey Aebersold, 1971.

Ake, David. *Jazz Cultures*. Berkeley: University of California Press, 2002.

———. *Jazz Matters: Sound, Place, and Time since Bebop*. Berkeley: University of California Press, 2010.

Bailey, Derek. *Improvisation: Its Nature and Practice in Music*. New York: Da Capo Press, 1992.

Baker, David. *Jazz Improvisation: A Comprehensive Method of Study for All Players*. Rev. ed. Bloomington, IN: Frangipani Press, 1983.

Borgo, David. "Free Jazz in the Classroom: An Ecological Approach to Music Education." *Jazz Perspectives* 1, no. 1 (2007): 61–88.

Campbell, Patricia Shehan. "Learning to Improvise Music; Improvising to Learn Music." In *Musical Improvisation: Art, Education, and Society*, edited by Gabriel Solis and Bruno Nettl, 119–42. Urbana: University of Illinois Press, 2009.

Clayton, Martin, Rebecca Sager, and Udo Will. "In Time with the Music: The Concept of Entrainment and Its Significance for Ethnomusicology." *European Seminar in Ethnomusicology Counterpoint* 1 (2004).

Coker, Jerry. *Jerry Coker's Complete Method for Improvisation for All Instruments*. Rev. ed. Van Nuys, CA: Alfred Music Publishing, 1997.

Dewey, John. *Democracy and Education: An Introduction to the Philosophy of Education*. New York: Macmillan, 1916.

de Wilde, Laurent. *Monk*. Paris: Gallimard, 1997.

Freire, Paulo. *Pedagogy of the Oppressed*, trans. Myra Bergman Ramos. New York: Continuum, 1970.

Murphy, John. "Beyond the Improvisation Class: Learning to Improvise in a University Jazz Studies Program." In *Musical Improvisation: Art, Education, and Society*, edited by Gabriel Solis and Bruno Nettl, 171–84. Urbana: University of Illinois Press, 2009.

Nettl, Bruno. "Thoughts on Improvisation." *Musical Quarterly* 60, no. 1 (1974): 1–19.

Prouty, Ken. "The 'Finite' Art of Improvisation: Pedagogy and Power in Jazz Education." *Critical Studies in Improvisation/Études critiques en improvisation* 4, no. 1 (2008).

———. *Knowing Jazz: Community, Pedagogy, and Canon in the Information Age*. Jackson: University of Mississippi Press, 2012.

Sudnow, David. *Ways of the Hand: The Organization of Improvised Conduct*. Cambridge, MA: MIT Press, 1993.

Thibeault, Matthew. "The Power of Limits and the Pleasure of Games: An Easy and Fun Piano Duo Improvisation." *General Music Today* 25, no. 3 (2012): 50–53.

Section II

Histories, Institutions, Practices

8 Time to Change the Curriculum
Revaluing Improvisation in Twenty-First-Century Canada

Parmela Attariwala

For many students of Western classical (art) music performance, the prospect of improvising can be terrifying. The fear and inability to create music without notation means that Western classical performers continue to be separated from performers of non-notated musical traditions who do not require a composer to function as interlocutor in the process of expressing and creating works—works both within and across musical traditions. Yet, reclaiming the ability to create without the aid of notation—a once-integral skill for performers of the Western classical tradition—not only holds numerous pedagogical and pragmatic benefits for students of composed Western music, but also allows them to collaborate and create with musicians from non-notated traditions on a direct, unmediated level.

> *My own forays into creating music—composing, improvising within structure and freely improvising—occurred gradually, beginning in my teenage years. Although I undertook musical training firmly within the tradition of Western classical violin performance aimed toward accurate replication of the printed page, I had teachers who had inherited a degree of structural literacy about Western classical music that included elements of improvisation. They encouraged me to create my own cadenzas. My family, meanwhile, put me in situations that required musical collaboration with musicians who shared my ethnocultural—but not musical—heritage. Thus, I was motivated to create music (while also acquiring the skills to re-create it).*
>
> *Over the past two decades I have been deeply involved in creative improvisation: as a workshop participant, performer, coach, curator, and advocate. The voices I present below represent a cross section of colleagues who, with the exception of two world music performer-creators, are Western classically trained performers who believe that developing improvisatory abilities—creating sound without the use of notation—is an important skill for today's institutionally trained musicians to develop. It not only benefits interpretive elements of Western classical music performance, but has pragmatic financial benefits, and high social value in a world that is becoming increasingly diverse musically and culturally.*

The West and the Rest: Valuing Composition, Devaluing Improvisation

In the introduction to *In the Course of Performance*, Bruno Nettl lists eight "positions" scholars have maintained on improvisation, including the claim that it is "a kind of music making that sets apart the musical cultures outside the Western art music establishment."[1] Meanwhile, Laudan Nooshin suggests that colonialist power dynamics have contributed to an "othering" of improvisatory musics in musicological literature[2]:

> It was also perhaps no coincidence that the very period when Europe was consolidating its colonial power was also the time that improvisation started to become devalued in favor of the solidity, permanence and strength represented by the great, notated, nineteenth-century masterworks.[3]

Although Nooshin's focus is on non-Western musics (Iranian classical music, specifically), the dynamic of othering non-notated musics has had negative consequences for all types of improvisatory musical traditions (including the place of improvisation within the Western classical music tradition). Moreover, the preeminent position given by scholars to composed music minimizes the role improvisation has had in the evolution of the Western classical music tradition, effectively negating improvisation as an aspect of the Western classical performer's craft. If one attributes improvisation at all to the creative side of music making, the attribution belongs solely to the composer.

Early music specialist Bruce Haynes provides a useful summary of the function of improvisation in the pre-Romantic era and the abrupt shift toward fixed composition based upon notions from Classical antiquity:

> [The] separation between composing and performing hasn't always existed. Before the rise of Romanticism, improvisation and composition were normal activities for any musician. In a time when new pieces were in constant demand, being a composer was nothing special, just part of the process of producing music ... [Musicians] had to know how to make up music on the spot.[4]

Haynes describes baroque notation as a "thin" form of notation: writing that gives performers space to ornament, embellish, and shape the music according to their own taste and circumstances. Thus, he characterizes the baroque musician as "a combination of an improvising jazzman and a reading Classical player."[5]

The creative license and dexterity that typified the baroque musicians' craft disappeared toward the end of the eighteenth century in tandem with the mental and material changes that accompanied the Industrial and French revolutions. Haynes notes that the shift occurred swiftly, citing as a contributing factor "major change[s] in the designs and techniques of every kind of musical instrument at the beginning of the Romantic period. ... [It] was a rupture with the past that took place in less than two generations."[6]

Compositionally, the post-Baroque era composers—attempting to create a "classical" music—began composing music intended to be self-contained and complete. Their works were to be "autonomous" to the circumstance of performance[7]: untaintable by improvisatory skills of the performer. Thus, the score as a product and physical entity represented a work of art and the composer—not the performer—the true bearer of the creative craft. Most importantly to our discussion, the Western art (classical) music composer from the classical era onward reduced the performer's role to that of merely putting into sound the carefully crafted details the composer had set on the page.

The notion of the composer as genius and the composition as the art of civilized Europeans also influenced European encounters with non-European cultures. Moreover, as Christine Battersby notes, the European concept of genius is also a gendered one, wherein the genius is always a male, and often a male who exhibited feminine traits.[8] Foremost among the genius' feminine traits is the ability to "create"—to give birth to—the artwork, the score, the play, the poem: an ability nevertheless predicated upon a masculine virility, a "male sexuality made sublime."[9]

With particular relevance to the othering of improvisatory musical forms by those upholding the Western classical music tradition, Battersby notes,

> It was genius that was evoked to explain the difference between civilized man and both animals and savages. It was genius that was supposed to make the "Art" (with a capital "A") that European civilization produced different from the "crafts" (with a small "c") produced by primitives and other lesser human types. It was genius that made Poetry different from verse ... Music more than mere tune, harmony and rhythm. Genius was the bedrock of European culture.[10]

Thus, orientalists contributed to the devaluing of improvisation and improvisatory musical traditions (regardless of whether those traditions emanated from within Europe) by attributing notation—the textual proof of the true artist's labor—with the Western classical music's superiority as a musical form.

Revaluing Improvisation

In the latter half of the twentieth century, though, scholars—ethnomusicologists and cultural critics in particular—have begun to erode Western classical music's position as the pinnacle of musical expression. Nooshin points out that improvisation and improvisatory musical traditions "have started to become revalued at a time which represented a particular kind of challenge to the existing order in Europe and North America."[11] The rapid decolonization of non-European territories at the end of the Second World War, followed by postcolonial reimaginings of indigenous nationhood, subsequently resulted in an awareness of and investment in local cultural identities.

Globally, international organizations such as the United Nations Educational Scientific and Cultural Organization (UNESCO) and its signatory countries protect cultures and cultural artifacts that are (or have been) at risk of being dominated or subsumed by other cultures. This, in combination with the ease of international travel and migration, means that—especially in Europe and North America—non-Western and non-classical musical traditions now share performance space with the Western classical musical establishment.[12] Moreover, in a country like Canada, where most noncommercial artists and arts organizations receive public arts funding, funders have been under increasing pressure (from the governments that provide their allocation) to reconcile the substantial sums of grant funding that goes to Western classical organizations and performers with the demographic reality that these organizations and musicians no longer represent a dominant cultural value for the majority of citizens served by the public funders.

Reevaluating Musical Culture in Multicultural Canada

Until the mid-1990s, musicians working in forms other than non-Western classical in Canada received little to no funding from public arts funders, which have been primary sources of funding for noncommercial Canadian artists and presenters since the creation of the Canada Council for the Arts (Canada Council) in 1957.[13] This artistic exclusion began to change with the institution of multiculturalism into law by the 1988 Multiculturalism Act. Within the act, one finds directives charging all governmental institutions and crown corporations with the responsibility of proactively eradicating discriminatory barriers (systemic or otherwise) to equitable access, equitable access being fundamental to civic engagement and, thus, to social cohesion. The arts councils were not exempt from the process of reflexively analyzing their barriers to accessibility. The Canada Council and the Ontario Arts Council—the two largest public arts funders in Canada—commissioned studies that indicated that in order to be demographically accessible and politically proactive, the arts councils needed to open funding streams to the musics practiced by many of the historically disadvantaged groups: musics that were predominantly non-Western classical, many involving elements of improvisation.[14] Since that time, the music sections of the major Canadian arts councils have gradually removed genre restrictions to their granting programs. Additionally, the peer committees that assess grant applications and make funding suggestions must now include a proportion of artists from historically disadvantaged communities.[15]

In 2016, equity—in terms of artists and art forms—continues to be a strategic priority for the Canada Council, but public engagement with the arts has become an increasingly important factor in the funding equation. The authors of the Canada Council's 2011–16 Strategic Plan, in contextualizing the importance of public engagement to the arts, articulate the link between the government and the public that influences contemporary council priorities:

> The theme of public engagement in arts and culture is increasingly on the policy agendas of governments worldwide, including concerns for cultural rights, arts education, expressive life, citizen participation, social cohesion, and cultural diversity. While the Council has had a long and deep commitment to connecting Canadians to the arts, public engagement has a greater currency today than it had in the past.[16]

Further, the 2011–16 Strategic Plan notes that "it will take a more active role in advancing a public conversation on the expressive needs and aspirations of the citizenry at large,"[17] which suggests that audiences (or prospective audiences and youth) are becoming as important a determinant of equity and arts funding, as are artists.

Meanwhile, performance departments at many postsecondary musical training institutions in Canada, another important set of gatekeepers, have not yet accepted this new reality, or if they have, then their administrators have not found a way to accommodate it into their programs. Few offer improvisation classes (outside of jazz programs) as a part of their curricula; fewer have integrated non-Western improvisatory musics into their performance (as opposed to ethnomusicology or jazz) divisions.

Time to Change the Curriculum?

Haynes describes today's early music practitioners—and arguably, the overarching Western classical world merits the same epithet—as having developed a "cover band mentality"[18]:

> Once all of the good Baroque pieces have been performed and recorded, what do we do? [...] Surely we should share the sense of freedom that musicians felt at the time. Not just in arranging their own and other people's compositions, but in writing new ones. But I know it will be something of a miracle to overcome our habitual Canonic thinking, which constrains us to play the same pieces over and over again, like cover bands.
>
> The modern cover band typically imitates one of the famous rock groups of the late 1960s. [...] The basic attribute of cover bands, however, is that they play someone else's music.
>
> [...] A cover band (Rock or Baroque) pretends to be making it up, but in fact *they* know that *we* know it has happened before.[19]

I doubt many of my Western classical music colleagues would appreciate being put into the same category as musicians who play popular rock music.

The former will defend and justify the comparative complexities of their music over rock. As someone who underwent the rigors of Western classical performance training, I sympathize with their position. My colleagues have mastered extraordinary technical skills that they creatively incorporate into their interpretations of composed repertoire. Symphony orchestra playing has its own demands and requires a very particular type of rigor and discipline.[20] Nevertheless, with the exception of conducting, no type of Western classical performance *requires* an intimate—and integrated—knowledge of the building blocks of composition.

Haynes directs his argument at baroque and early music specialists who, if they sincerely aspire to historically informed performances, should develop the facility to improvise in the same manner as the musicians whose music they are emulating. What about other Western classical musicians: those who perform repertoire from the late eighteenth century onward, or who haven't specialized in baroque performance practice? Should acquiring improvisatory skills also apply to them?

Katharine Rapoport, who teaches viola at the University of Toronto and edited the Royal Conservatory of Music's 2013 viola syllabus, believes today's performance majors should learn to improvise:

> It's important for [students] to be able to play improvisatory music and also to understand the elements of different styles. Music—for example—that involves improvisation: jazz styles and other ethnic musics that they might encounter.[21]

When I asked whether Rapoport thought it should become a compulsory part of performance studies, she replied affirmatively, but also explained why adding it to the system can be problematic:

> I think it should be highly encouraged. I think everyone should get a term of it, and then there should be a continuity. So, yes, I'd love to see it as part of the curriculum. ... The trouble with the curricula is that they are already well-filled with valid and useful subjects. Students only have twenty-four hours in a day, and they're just scrambling. I think schools make executive decisions based on what's already there and they don't always have room to put more on. Personally, I'd love to see it there.
>
> But someone who hasn't done a lot [of improvisation] doesn't necessarily see the benefit. I think it's great for their aural perception and their ear training. And it's great for accessing their emotional life. ... It benefits their interpretation of more "classical" music. It benefits their performance of it: there's more creativity happening.[22]

Rapoport also noted that younger people, including younger teachers, are more aware of improvisation generally and are interested in incorporating it into their playing and teaching: something that she hopes will change the continuing paucity of improvisation classes in the country's performance programs. Upon learning that orchestral violinist and concertmaster Stephen Sitarski had been coaching improvisation to violinists at the National Youth Orchestra of Canada (NYOC),[23] Rapoport suggests,

> If there's someone like Stephen Sitarski there who's doing some improv with them, I think we've got people in certain places who are starting to encourage even the ones who are set on that kind of [orchestral] performance career. I hope there'll be more and more people that keep working with youngsters at university and college level: ... at the playing schools. It would be great if they get exposed to [improvisation] because then they know it's there.[24]

Sitarski, who has been a regular coach with the NYOC—a five-week summer orchestral program that is a tacit prerequisite for any young Canadian aiming toward an orchestral career—introduced improvisation sessions in 2012 to a small group of violinists:

> Until three years ago, the kids would arrive on Sunday, and on Monday they would start sectionals. And that was all they had. We decided that an important element—not just for orchestral playing, but for being a musician—was playing in an ensemble. So, now they are in string quartets, woodwind quintets, brass quintets, percussion ensembles, mixed ensembles. ... But when you do the math (there are ten cellists, ten violists, and usually twenty-four to twenty-eight violins), you've got at least a quartet of violinists (the "orphans" as they are called) who don't have an ensemble. ... I thought it would be fun to make them feel that not only are they *not* being [ripped off] but they are actually involved in something more fun with more variety than the other quartets.[25]

Like Rapoport, Sitarski also mentions how improvisation benefits ear training:

> Improv is a lot about ear training: listening, responding, finding. What is the idea? Am I interested in it? Do I want to make it more interesting? Do I want to change it completely, come up with something new?[26]

Both Sitarski and Rapoport mention the sense of playing "freely" that they attribute to a musician's exposure to improvisation. Rapoport notices how her students' playing is "freer" after they have improvised. Sitarski also talks about performative freedom, recalling an experience he had with improvisation as a Masters student:

> [My friend] had a chamber orchestra on one of her recitals to accompany her on a Mozart concerto for the second half of a performance.

In the first half, she had chosen two of Stockhausen's poems, made copies, and at the concert she put the two poems on everyone's stand and explained in the dress rehearsal, "here's what's gonna happen, but it's not something we can rehearse. There's no way that we know how it's going to turn out. You just respond to the poem with your instrument, or not. Or with anything. Or if you don't feel like making any sound, be silent. Completely free." So, in the concert, she encouraged the audience to participate, too.

People started making sounds. There was imitative stuff happening, some introduced new ideas ... And I don't know when the first piece ended and the second piece started, but it was probably about half an hour of just free improv from a group of about two dozen players.

Now, that's not the whole story. ... The piece eventually finished—whenever we decided it was finished—then intermission, then the Mozart concerto. I can tell you, I *remember* to this day how *free* I felt in the Mozart after this experiment. ... I remember thinking it was so obvious: this is so much easier to play!

Was that because we were not just trying to read the notes? Or be perfect? The whole first half was 'anything goes,' be free, make whatever sound you want. And then Mozart is all of a sudden very easy, beautiful, free, uncomplicated music: joyous.

So, it was the idea of there being no right or wrong; there are notes on the page. That was a profound revelation to me. ... And Mozart! Mozart being one of the most detail-oriented: has to be in tune; has to be rhythmic; everything has to be so perfect; and yet it felt freer than I've ever felt. That remained with me my whole life and that was part of the reason I thought I'd introduce NYOC students to some of this. Because I think it helps you when you go to the notes on the page: some of the burden is lifted.[27]

Improvisers with Western Classical Training: Lori Freedman and Matt Brubeck

Lori Freedman—Montreal-based clarinetist, composer and improvisation coach—elucidates Sitarski's thoughts about how improvisation helps with playing composed music. She says it helps one understand the composer's creative mind:

One of the things that I find is very helpful for me—as the musician who reads notation instruction given to me by other composers—is that improvisation is a tremendous tool in learning other musicians' minds: their compositions. [It helps] to get around problems that I might be encountering.[28]

Yet, Freedman has a very different perspective to Rapoport and Sitarski on interpretation and creativity:

> I never looked at interpretation as creative. Interpretation is like following somebody else's creative instruction. You just do what you're told. ... Early on in my solo ventures, audiences would say, "Wow, how do you do that?" Well, I'm just playing the music! The music is great. I'm just playing what I see. Anybody who really wants to can do this. It's because the music is great—or not. So, I don't take much credit for that.[29]

Perhaps Freedman sees the performance of a musical score as fundamentally different to the creation of music (whether that creation happens through composition or improvisation) because the combination of her improvisational fluency with the technical skills she has acquired as a student of Western classical music performance have provided her with multiple frames of reference.

Freedman coached improvisation ensembles at McGill University from 2001 to 2010. She likens McGill's music faculty to the University of Toronto's and "all the big provincial universities in Canada," and describes their programs as "straight in a box."[30]

Meanwhile, Freedman's McGill ensembles, which were for-credit classes that grew in size each year, never found a home in the course syllabus. McGill teachers who, when confronted by students interested in contemporary and creative forms of music making, were either unable or unwilling to teach outside the canon, steered their students to Freedman's ensembles. But Freedman notes that those teachers—beyond acknowledging that the ensembles existed and served a purpose—were uninterested in learning about improvisation, participating in open workshops, or attending any performances the ensembles gave.[31]

Meanwhile, cellist Matt Brubeck has been teaching jazz improvisation and creative improvisation at York University, an institution that (although it offers Western classical-focused classes and private lessons) does not emphasize Western classical performance in its music faculty but offers a range of Western, non-Western, classical, and nonclassical music courses to its students. While Brubeck acknowledges that he comes from a family that valued improvisation, he also said that any sense of improvisation he received at home was restricted to the piano.

Like Rapoport, Sitarski, and Freedman, Brubeck received training in Western classical music. He began improvising while working as a freelance orchestral musician:

> I started playing cello when I was around ten. I don't remember improvising much on the cello [with the exception of] the obvious things that kids do once they figure out boogie woogie. But I didn't seriously get into it until after university; after I finished my Masters

degree. ... I think I played one piece that had some improvisation in it in my Masters recital. ... It was more jazz oriented. It took me a longer time to feel confident to "freely" improvise.[32]

In describing his transition into improvisatory work, Brubeck suggests that it is a pragmatic skill for today's students to develop:

The ability to improvise meant that ... I became the "go to guy" in the San Francisco-Bay area if they needed someone who could play off the page. So, it just meant that all sorts of strange gigs came my way. And it meant that because I was a freelance classical player at the time, I witnessed the slow transition of my career going from four, sometimes five different orchestras—their different seasons and driving all over—to more centralized work. ... My major break was playing in a Berkeley Shakespeare Company—an outdoor play big band that required a bit of improvisation. Ralph Carnie, who had done some work with Tom Waits, was also in that band; and then Tom needed a cello player for one of his records. So that's one of the things that got me on the map.

As you know, in the classical world—and this is very pragmatic— I definitely think that it can diversify people's career paths to have improvisation in the arsenal of things that they can do. ... String players have it easy compared to people who specialize in bassoon. But there are only so many orchestral gigs out there.[33]

Brubeck also notes how the "depersonalized" atmosphere at orchestral auditions—while instituted to enable fairness—can be a deterrent for even the most highly skilled Western classical musicians in the pursuit of an orchestral career.[34]

In my conversation with Freedman, we touched upon the increasingly precarious financial position of orchestras in North America, and she commented on the attachment professional Western classical teaching programs have on the orchestra:

How did we get into that orchestral focus? We were taught that it was very *professional*. We train at the conservatory, and then the university, and then we get a job and then we're professional. ... It's funny, too—just in the business of things—how that model has infiltrated the layperson's perception of musicians.

It legitimizes your existence as a classical musician to be in an orchestra?

Exactly. The final goal. ... And when you get a new student—and they're obviously keeners—you ask them, "what do you want to do with the violin in say the next five, ten years?" And they say, "get into an orchestra, play in a string quartet." What do you tell them?[35]

Likening herself to jazz musicians, Freedman continues by discussing the question of Western classically trained musicians whose interests lie outside of the orchestra:

> It's a tricky one administratively. And for the ego. As the fringe, as the alternative, as the "not in the box musician," you can get pretty bogged down. … Jazz musicians know better what they are heading for after their studies 'cause they don't have the "safe" institutions: there is no orchestra when they get out. If in the end they have to get a day job, so be it. For me too, that route would be better than being told what to play and when. For me, that would be like death![36]

Nevertheless, Freedman—like Brubeck—has maintained a full-time career as a musician. Both have carved niches and names for themselves, drawing from a combination of their instrumental foundations in Western classical technique and their improvisation-based musicking abilities.

When McGill's Faculty of Music administration changed in 2010, they cancelled Freedman's class without warning and without informing her. Freedman admitted to being disappointed, but qualified that, "it's not even an ego thing. It's that the students were deprived of learning about and developing their personal musical voice."[37] She notes that while improvisation classes struggle to find a place in training institutions, it has become a desirable identifier for today's young musicians:

> A lot of people—I'm finding that the older-young generation in their mid to late thirties and forties—all have the word improvisation on their website. But they're never out there at the improvisation venues, either listening or playing. It's the catchword. And they put it there because they've done some Cage, they've done some open scores maybe. But they're not actually practicing improvisers. … [For] the younger ones—the twenty-year olds—it's getting to be pretty standard; but not at the universities.[38]

Brubeck offers a fiscal explanation that limits the flexibility of some post-secondary music institutions to cater to the educational desires of students:

> At York, there is one pot of money for the music department, so students can study whatever they want within the music department. At another school (a school with which I'm no longer affiliated), each division within music had its own pot of money. So, performance had its own pot of money; jazz had its pot of money.[39] There were performance students at that school who wanted to study half of the term with me, and half of the term with their classical performance instructor. But because the performance division has a separate pot of money to the jazz division—and perhaps, too, because the performance

instructor's position was full time (as opposed to part-time) and may have required a certain number of teaching hours—the administration would not allow it.[40]

Thus, as Freedman points out, young musicians know that improvisation has value in the contemporary world; and as Brubeck suggests, some students actively want to enhance their performative knowledge with improvisatory skills. Yet, administrators and traditionalists—whether motivated (or paralyzed) by financial constraints or by disinterest—too often thwart the tools that professionals, like Freedman and Brubeck, have to offer students: tools that will help the next generation of Western classical musicians grow and thrive in a field with diminishing traditional opportunities.

Incorporating Improvisation Into Teaching Strategies

Brubeck and Freedman highlight using improvisation as a tool to understand and overcome technical obstacles they (and their students) encounter when playing their instruments. Their examples suggest that improvisation allows musicians to go further in learning how to use their instruments than traditional teaching does.

Freedman offers a teaching example that utilizes improvisation as a creative catalyst to overcome technical problems specific to the instrument:

> When I was growing up and studying the clarinet ever so righteously, there were certain kinds of solutions. "You have this problem? Okay, do this." And they were prescribed and pretty general. … You have a problem with a run: dot it up, play around with the rhythm a bit, play it forwards and backwards. These kinds of things seem to be fairly standard exercises to iron out problems. But I found that taking it a few steps further—in that when I located what the real problem was, what the real problems are—I make up pieces around them. I improvise pieces around them. And that brings music to a technical problem. … Technically, I was far behind understanding what to do than musically in my life. If I can't make a note speak high in the clarinet register and I get the wrong tone—the undertone—I go for the undertone. But [I'll] make a whole piece around that. And then one can't do it wrong anymore. … In going for the wrong thing, [the problem] corrects itself.
>
> For example, on the bass clarinet, it's really hard to make a clear tone around high C when you're a beginner. What I try to do is encourage the clarinetist to go for the undertone, the unwanted tone. And pretty soon, they can't get it. They can only get the pure tone. … It helps bring musical reason for doing something technically difficult.

So it becomes a teaching aid for technique?

Yeah, for me. And it gets the technical challenge out of that zone. It becomes a musical challenge. … Technical is the tool: the mechanics of playing that thing. Musical is other stuff like direction, flow, subtler things. ... [In improvising around a technique], you're exercising the thing. You're practicing *and* you're exercising the brain. You're not being a robot.[41]

In describing how improvisatory abilities benefit Western classical musicians, Brubeck also refers to the physical aspect of playing an instrument; in particular, how improvisation helps musicians know their instrument better:

> In the learning-music-off-the-page model, you're playing a note because it's written there, and therefore, you associate with the other notes written around it—like the physical gestures to get to it. But if you play a note without associating how it's written, then you are making up—for yourself as a musician—what you have to do with your hands or your breath or whatever; what you have to do to get to that note. So, getting to a note in classical music means getting there in a specific context associated with music notation. And I see improvisers pride themselves in making connections between any two notes they can think of. So, in that sense, I think it helps *any* musician understand the geography of their instrument: what is physically necessary. You may determine that some things are impossible. There are things that are really awkward across clarinet breaks, for example. You understand how to get from point A to point X, and you don't need notation to do that. I can imagine that would help *with* notation practice because you've figured out ways to do things physically.[42]

As a teacher, Brubeck feels it is his place to "provoke" students out of their "comfort zones"[43]:

> If someone came with a jazz background, I might try to provoke them to not play jazz. And someone who was classical, I might try to provoke them to do something else. ... Obviously, you work with their strengths, too. But I think in the context of taking lessons, they need to be provoked to do some things that are not normally in their improvisational practice or in their music world. Sometimes I just ask them to listen to stuff ... If a guitar player has never heard Fred Frith, I'll say, well there's [something] you should check out. They don't have to like it, but I think they should know that it's there.
>
> For classical musicians: I give them something with a very familiar progression, like a typical cyclical root motion—ii-V-I baroque music. These are chord sequences that they have in their ears; and they also have storehouses of idiomatic gestures from baroque.[44]

When I ask Brubeck about how he "provokes" Western classical musicians beyond baroque music—a style that would be within their comfort zone—he responded:

> I think modal improvisation pushes them a bit. ... I work with Lydian or Dorian: something where they actually have—even if they don't know it—a good fingering for it.
>
> *So you give them parameters?*
>
> Yes, and sometimes—maybe it's more of an ear training exercise—I like the idea of, within a mode, trying to imitate what someone else does. If that's too hard for them, trying to have them imitate the contour or shape of the melodic line; even if every little interval isn't right, getting the overall charting with the highs and lows.[45]

Sitarski uses a technique similar to modal improvising, but less restrictive. He has the students each play and sustain a long tone—"any note they want"[46]—so that each of those long tones form the notes of a chord:

> I usually start it off. I'll usually play a three or four-note pattern once. I basically say, "Look, I'm going to start it off and you don't have to repeat it. It doesn't have to be the same intervals or same rhythm, but I put an idea out there." And part of improv is being able to take an idea and create something from that idea of your own. And then someone will change it or someone else will either work with that same idea or introduce something different, but always going back to that drone. It's interesting to have some kind of completely unplanned harmonic structure because then, based on what you're listening to, you can either work with it or not.[47]

Sitarski takes care to tell the students that there is no right or wrong way to improvise in his class. To those who "flat out say, 'I can't do this,' I ask, 'What do you mean, what do you think it is? I'm not asking you to improvise a Mozart cadenza on the spot.'"[48]

Both Sitarski and Rapoport use the concept of scenarios to inspire improvisation. Rapoport said that she encourages her students who are considering working with young people to do "story and music kinds of improvisation. 'There was a strange noise. *Wham!*' I encourage them to at least bring [improvisation] into the work that they do because that's what I'm trying to pass on to my students."[49]

Sitarski describes his technique as "abstract, yet programmatic":

> I will give them very small scenarios. "Lightning strike." I'll point to someone and say, "represent what you think a lightning strike

would be on your instrument." So, they might try to rip off some scale-like thing. Then, I'll say, "dark alley at night"; "school ground, kids playing." ... And it's interesting to actually see very different and innovative approaches to representing that idea.[50]

Can we attribute some of the Western classical student's fear of improvisation to our tendency to equate improvisation with jazz? Freedman suggests that "it's a natural tendency in this day and age, in this area of the world to make that connection."[51] She qualifies her perspective, saying, "I don't even know what 'jazz' is anymore. It depends upon who you're talking to and how old they are."[52]

During my conversation with Sitarski, his comment, "I'm the first to say that I'm not an experienced improviser: you can't just put me there in front of a jazz combo and say, 'there's your solo'"[53] also indicates an equating of improvisation with jazz. When pressed, he admitted that he was referring to a specific type of improvisation: one that has its own history, technique, and rules. Jazz improvisation is tied to a way of understanding harmonic movement that is not unlike Western classical harmony, but it employs an alternate vocabulary and has a distinct emphasis on rhythm.

Has our Western classical pedagogy, which demands exactness in performance, conferred upon our students a musical mindset that assumes *all* performance must conform to strict structural parameters? Might a musician's (specifically the Western classical musician) *not* knowing these parameters intimately contribute to their fear of improvisation? Moreover, have we exacerbated this attitude by separating ear training and theory from instrumental training?

Righting Historical Disadvantage; Advantaging Improvisation

As Canadian public arts funders continue to emphasize equitable disbursement of funds—across geographic regions, genres, ethnocultural demographies, and economic demographies—all arts organizations must prove that they have not only artistic value, but also demographic value.[54] Historically advantaged organizations—such as Western classical music ensembles—have, thus, tried to create partnerships with formerly disadvantaged demographies by attempting artistic collaborations.

Musically, the disadvantage that Western classical musicians have in such collaborations (specifically those that cross genres) is that, as Brubeck points out, "the world is made of more improvised music than notated music, period, end of story. Western music is this funny little corner of the world: the idea of the *work* being the notated thing."[55] As a consequence, the composer usually defines the parameters of collaboration. But can this lead to long-term sustained collaborations?

In response to the question of whether improvisatory abilities help musicians play across genres, Brubeck said,

> Absolutely. I think it is very important for that sort of collaboration: that sort of collaboration *would* happen. It's just as much of a leap for someone from a non-notated tradition to try to get into the Western thing as the other way around. It's hard for both people to do it. I guess I'm proposing a common ground. I think the European art music model has isolated a lot of musicians away from other possibilities. And it often just seems that the people who are interested in improvisation—have some improvisatory ability—are the ones who are willing to make the leap … [like] Yehudi Menuhin.[56]

The motto on the city of Toronto's coat of arms reads, "diversity is our strength," and Torontonians (including media and politicians) pride themselves on saying they live in "the most diverse city in the world." While certain neighborhoods maintain references to the groups that first inhabited them (Greektown, Koreatown, the Gay Village, Little India, Little Portugal, Chinatown), the cast of peoples of different ethnocultural backgrounds mixes and coexists in everyday life.[57] By extension, diverse groups of music should also mix; and many do. Toronto has nurtured, for example, a number of successful Indo-jazz and Indo-rock bands since the mid-1990s, including Tasa, Autorickshaw, Induswest, Thomas Handy Trio, Rakatak, and Hot fo' Gandhi.

Ravi Naimpally, leader and tabla player of Tasa, says that improvisation was fundamental to the creation and continued development of the band. In addition to Naimpally, the band is composed of four other musicians: guitarist John Gzowski who has a background in jazz, contemporary Western (classical) music, and Arabic music; rock bassist Chris Gartner; Western classically trained percussionist Alan Hetherington, who specializes in Brazilian rhythm; and reed/flute/bansuri player Ernie Tollar, who has undertaken in-depth performance studies in jazz, Arabic, and Karnatic musics. Says Naimpally of Tasa's creative process, "the ability to improvise gives you an 'in' with other improvising traditions, without having to delve deep into that tradition."[58]

Tollar and Gzowski also belonged to the band Maza Mezé, a nine-member ensemble formed in 1995 that focused on the songs and sounds of Mediterranean traditions, specifically Arabic, Greek, and Bulgarian folk songs. At the time of their tenth anniversary, the group consisted of five singers—Maryem Hassan Tollar, Jayne Brown, Sophia Grigoriadis, Roula Said, and Jennifer Moore—percussionists Debashis Sinha and Jeff Wilson, violinist Rick Hyslop, plus Tollar and Gzowski. In addition to performing traditional songs, the group created their own songs. Individual members contributed lyrics and melodic or rhythmic material. Collectively, the rest of the ensemble created parts for the remainder of the song. The material for the songs, although always stylistically reminiscent of the Middle East or the Mediterranean, often bears the unique stamp of the individual to whom the work is credited. For example, Debashis Sinha has written lyrics in his family's mother tongue, Bengali;

Jennifer Moore in French and Esperanto; and Rick Hyslop in Swedish. The collaboratively created song "In the Heart" has lyrics in Arabic, English, and Greek, and uses musical idioms from a variety of musical traditions.

Maza Mezé was the first nonclassical and non-jazz group to have been offered a record contract with Canadian Broadcasting Corporation (CBC) Records.[59] Said describes the role of improvisation in the process of creation and performance as "magic":

> There's a certain magic in improv. It allows you to dive off the edge. ... There is the possibility for discovery, for something to come in that might not with a composer. ... There's a certain magic circle space between performers.[60]

Jason Stanyek has suggested that improvisation creates "spaces for intercultural dialogue."[61] The concept of intercultural dialogue, across all aspects of Canadian life, has been an increasingly important means of nurturing social cohesion in Canada since the early days of multiculturalism. Propelled by government initiatives, Canadian artists have also been affected by this concern; and whether artists receive government funding or seek corporate alliances, intercultural considerations—between ethnocultural groups, between advantaged and disadvantaged populations, between generations—are an important priority for funders.

Ingrid Monson has noted, "the one thing to remember about improvisation is that it's never just the relationship between notes, but between the people playing them."[62] As Brubeck points out, though, musicians coming from traditional Western classical music institutions are inadequately prepared for intercultural musical dialogue because the Western classical platform segregates performance from creation.

Where, then, do we place Western classical music and musicians in the diverse tapestry of Toronto's (and Canada's) communities of people and the musics they perform and create? Most Western classical musicians cannot enter into a musical relationship with anyone outside of their own. The experiences of Brubeck and Freedman suggest that a growing number of students want improvisatory skills and know that such abilities have value, even if the students are not aware that part of the "value" in our contemporary sociopolitical culture comes from being able to engage in musical dialogue. Is it not time, then, that we who teach and perform within the tradition of Western classical music give our students the tools to communicate with other musics and give them the option to enter the space where performers create magic?

Notes

1. Nettl, "An Art Neglected in Scholarship," 12.
2. Laudan Nooshin, "Improvisation as 'Other,'" 242–96.
3. Ibid., 246.
4. Haynes, *The End of Early Music*, 4.
5. Ibid.

6. Ibid., 5.
7. Ibid.
8. Battersby, *Gender and Genius*, 3.
9. Ibid.
10. Ibid.
11. Nooshin, "Improvisation as 'Other,'" 250.
12. As international tourism has increased peoples' awareness of non-Western cultural practices, tourists sometimes exoticize foreign peoples and their cultures. This can result in a visitor's stereotyping a people with particular aspects of their culture, thereafter desiring an essentialized representation of a culture which the ethnocultural outsider deems to be "authentic." Expressive cultural practises—particularly music and dance—are particularly prone to being essentialized not only by audiences and well-intended promoters, but also by performers who choose to perform a stereotype of their ethnoculture in their adopted (or host) country. Moreover, music and dance are often used to represent ethnocultural groups because promoters and bureaucrats consider them socially harmless cultural goods.
13. Some ethnocultural musical groups received funding specifically targeted for multicultural projects, but this funding did not come from the arts councils.
14. Reports that influenced funding equity at Canadian arts councils included the following: Gary Cristall and Valdine Ciwko, "Report of a Feasibility Study for a Folk Arts Program to the Ontario Arts Council" (Toronto: Ontario Arts Council, 1987); Paul Reynolds, "Many Songs: A Survey of Non-Classical Music in Canada: A Summary for the Jazz/Folk Advisory Committee" (Ottawa: Canada Council Touring Office, February 1993); Lillian Allen, "First Steps on the Road to Cultural and Racial Equity: From Multiculturalism to Access, a Report to the Honourable Karen Haslam, Minister of Culture and Communications" (Toronto: Ontario Ministry of Culture and Communications, March 1992).
    Artists practicing non-Western or nonclassical musics who were not from historically disadvantaged groups, by extension, also gained access to arts funding.
15. Council officers dedicated to equity (in the case of the Canada Council, the Equity Office) determine the proportion of assessors they consider equitable to a peer assessment committee. Ultimately, external government auditors must consider this proportion acceptable.
16. Canada Council for the Arts, *Strategic Plan, 2011–16*, 5.
17. Ibid., 7.
18. Haynes, *The End of Early Music*, 203.
19. Ibid., 203–4.
20. Orchestral string players are at a disadvantage in that they have a diminished degree of personal expressive license. Part of their skill lies in restraining their individual interpretive imaginations and drawing instead upon a palette of expressive devices in order to "blend" and cohere expressively with the other members of their section.
21. Katharine Rapoport, interview with author, Toronto, Ontario, September 2014.
22. Ibid.
23. Sitarski is currently concertmaster of Esprit Orchestra and the Hamilton Philharmonic Orchestra. In 2012, he stepped down after fifteen years from his position as concertmaster of the Kitchener-Waterloo Symphony Orchestra.
24. Ibid.

25. Stephen Sitarski, interview with author, Hamilton, Ontario, September 2014.
26. Ibid.
27. Ibid.
28. Lori Freedman, telephone interview with author, September 2014.
29. Ibid.
30. Ibid. Freedman noted that—in the history of the faculty syllabus—"improvisation" has appeared only once, and then, not even in the jazz division. Rather, it was one topic in a theory course.
31. Ibid.
32. Matt Brubeck, interview with author, Toronto, Ontario, October 2014.
33. Ibid.
34. Ibid.
35. Freedman, telephone interview. In addition to the increasingly tenuous nature of North American orchestral work, the studio and theatre work that once required Western classical music training has virtually evaporated as digital samples have replaced live instrumentalists.
36. Ibid.
37. Ibid.
38. Ibid.
39. Brubeck was associated with the jazz division.
40. Matt Brubeck, follow-up interview with author, Toronto, Ontario, January 2015.
41. Freedman, telephone interview, September 2014.
42. Brubeck, interview.
43. Ibid.
44. Ibid.
45. Ibid.
46. Sitarski, interview.
47. Ibid.
48. Ibid.
49. Rapoport, interview.
50. Sitarski, interview.
51. Freedman, telephone interview.
52. Ibid.
53. Sitarski, interview.
54. Canada's two largest public arts funders are the Canada Council for the Arts and the Ontario Arts Council. Both have outlined their priorities in their respective strategic plans. Canada Council for the Arts, *Strategic Plan 2011–16*; Ontario Arts Council, *Vital Arts and Public Value*.
55. Brubeck, interview.
56. Ibid. Twentieth century audiences and string players consider Baron Yehudi Menuhin (1916–99) one of the great Western classical violinists of the last century, but non-Western and nonclassical musicians also admired Menuhin for his musical openness. A child prodigy, Menuhin performed the canonic work of the Western classical violin repertoire early in his career. Later, he used his status to promote the value of other musics by multiple means, including through collaboration. In 1966, Menuhin recorded the first of three genre-crossing West Meets East albums with sitarist Ravi Shankar, inspiring Shankar's subsequent "East Meets West" endeavors. Menuhin also recorded a series of duets through the 1970s with jazz violinist Stéphane Grappelli.

57. I have written about Canadian diversity and music at length and in greater detail—including the impact that legislated multiculturalism has had, particularly in expressive practises, on maintaining cultural boundaries—elsewhere. See Attariwala, *Eh 440*.
58. Ravi Naimpally, interview with author, November 2004.
59. The nine-member group no longer performs regularly together, but since the mid-2000s, the members have been working in smaller groupings.
60. Roula Said, interview with author, November 2004.
61. Stanyek, "Transmissions of an Interculture," 89.
62. Qtd. in Gewertz, "Swinging into the University."

Works Cited

Attariwala, Parmela. *Eh 440: Tuning into the Effects of Official Multiculturalism on Publicly Funded Music in Canada*. Ph.D. diss., University of Toronto, 2013.

Battersby, Christine. *Gender and Genius: Towards a Feminist Aesthetics*. Bloomington: Indiana University Press, 1989.

Canada Council for the Arts. *Strategic Plan 2011–16*. Ottawa: Canada Council for the Arts, 2010. http://canadacouncil.ca/~/media/files/corporate-planning%20-%20en/canadacouncil_strategicplan2011_16_en.pdf.

Gewertz, Ken. "Swinging into the University: First Quincy Jones Chair Stresses Jazz's Collaboration." *The Harvard University Gazette*. February 28, 2002. http://news.harvard.edu/gazette/2002/02.28/03-monson.html.

Haynes, Bruce. *The End of Early Music*. New York: Oxford University Press, 2007.

Maza Mezé. *Brand New Threads: Songs from Middle Eastern Canada*. ROM 03. Toronto, Ontario: Maza Mezé Productions, 2000, compact disc.

———. *Hypnotika*. TRCD 3002. Toronto, Ontario: CBC Records, 2002, compact disc.

Nettl, Bruno. "An Art Neglected in Scholarship." In *In the Course of Performance: Studies in World of Musical Improvisations*, edited by Bruno Nettl and Melinda Russell, 1–23. Chicago: University of Chicago Press, 1998.

Nooshin, Laudan. "Improvisation as 'Other': Creativity, Knowledge and Power—The Case of Iranian Classical Music." *Journal of the Royal Musical Association* 128, no. 2 (2003): 242–96.

Ontario Arts Council. *Vital Arts and Public Value: A Blueprint for 2014–2020*. Ontario Arts Council, 2014. http://www.arts.on.ca/AssetFactory.aspx?did=10276.

Stanyek, Jason. "Transmissions of an Interculture: Pan-African Jazz and Intercultural Improvisation." In *The Other Side of Nowhere: Jazz, Improvisation, and Communities in Dialogue*, edited by Daniel Fischlin and Ajay Heble, 87–130. Middletown, CT: Wesleyan University Press, 2004.

Tasa. *Bhakti*. TASA001. Toronto, Ontario: Tasa, 2000, compact disc.

———. *Soma*. TASA002. Toronto, Ontario: Tasa, 2002, compact disc.

9   Back into the Classroom
Learning Music Through Historical Improvisation

Peter Schubert and Massimiliano Guido[1]

Introduction

In this chapter we will show how historical improvisation can be taught as an end in itself, used as a first step in university-level counterpoint and harmony classes, and how these two uses of improvisation can be made to reinforce each other. We look at performers' attitudes toward improvisation and consider what is to be gained from their learning to do it. In theory teaching, our approach is based on the idea that certain basics can be absorbed quickly and made intuitive in a short time. We will comment on some exercises we have developed to engage students in vocal and keyboard improvisation. All the activities have been carried out at McGill University during undergraduate and graduate courses in the academic years 2012 through 2014.[2]

Constructivism

When we began teaching improvisation in a historical way, and using improvisation to teach theory in the undergraduate classroom, we were not aware that there already existed a strong theoretical framework for this practice: constructivism.[3] Peter R. Webster offers an excellent summary of constructivism in education in general, and a survey of writings on constructivism as it is used in music teaching.[4] The tenets of constructivism can be summarized as follows:

1 Knowledge arises from active engagement with the world.
2 Knowledge is built on previous understanding.
3 Learning is largely a social activity.

What falls out of these principles is that the teacher is a facilitator, not a dictator; that the teacher must be flexible, "learning" new ways to teach from the current crop of students; that the teacher devises activities and asks open-ended questions, allowing students to repeat things in their own words, not parroting the teacher's formulations; and that students discover knowledge for themselves. These tenets are also very much in keeping with many of the key insights associated with the problem-posing critical pedagogy advocated by the renowned Brazilian educator Paulo Freire, whose work is discussed in other chapters in this volume. Webster notes that this type of engaged teaching is not widely used: "it is safe to say that the field of music education has for years been dominated by directed instruction that is top-down in nature, often with little regard for student-constructed knowledge."[5] His extensive survey shows that when constructivist principles are occasionally used, it is in teaching at the elementary and high school levels (for band, studio, and classroom), and for teacher training at the university level.

The astounding fact emerges that they are almost nonexistent in the undergraduate classroom. In the present-day undergraduate classroom, music theory is often taught like philosophy or trigonometry, subjects for which paper and pencil suffice to express understanding. Most of us were taught that way and we replicate that training in our own classrooms. The word *theory* means "contemplation" or "observation," and maybe that's a reasonable thing to do in the classroom, to think about some object, turn it over in your mind. In music, there is a long tradition of separating speculative theory from practical music making, the *musicus* looking down on the *cantor*. It is easy to sympathize with the irritation the *musicus* feels toward the poor performer who has no idea what he's singing when he just mindlessly performs. Ideas, not noise, are considered the noblest expression of music. So, typically, ear training and piano skills are taught in separate courses, a practice that widens the gulf between the music-as-noise or music-as-physical activity and the more idealistic type of theory.

It's time to turn this prejudice on its head. We should be impatient with the *musicus* who can calculate the ratios but not sing the intervals, who can recognize the harmonic paradigm but not play the progression. One day in counterpoint class students were played a little duo that arrived on a C-D dissonant suspension on the downbeat; students were asked what note they wanted to hear below. One student announced "G" (the right answer), but when asked to sing it he couldn't. His answer, a letter that stands for a note, was abstract, based on an intellectual understanding. Perhaps he had seen many examples but not heard them. His knowledge was symbolic and visually informed. Likewise, students often go to the piano to play a two-part minuet they've composed, but sing one voice in the wrong octave, so that fourths sound where there should have been fifths. They are thinking of pitch-class, not pitch, and they don't even notice the forbidden interval.

These students are good at "paper theory." Paper theory is important, but we propose that it be used in conjunction with other forms of understanding. A certain kind of intuitive singer might immediately sing the G, but have trouble figuring out what it was, and that singer would need some paper theory. The same thing is true for classical performers who dutifully read what is placed on the music stand. One could accuse them of "paper performance" since they are often unable to introduce the simplest ornament unless coached by their teacher (who writes it in, so it's more paper). Each kind of understanding complements the other. In the first of the following two sections, we consider the advantages of teaching historical improvisation as a performance practice issue; we examine how it is conceived and practiced by performers.

Why Historical Improvisation?

Webster's survey shows that when constructivism is used in music teaching, it often takes the form of composition and improvisation. We have a fairly good idea what composition is, but what do we mean by improvisation? When we presented this paper in Guelph, we heard a comment that we have heard many times: a graduate student said that what we were talking about was "not improvisation, because it is highly codified by given rules." This common misapprehension assumes that improvisation must be completely unfettered, like free jazz. But even the freest improvisation, if successful, is meaningful to the performer and intelligible to the listener, and so must obey some constraints, even if they are unrecognized by the performer and listener.

By adding the adjective "historical" to improvisation, we establish some limitations and add some features that are generally agreed upon. First, we refer to a practice that happened in a precise context, is supported by documentation, and is clear enough to be reproduced. This implies that we adhere to a precise style, and we are interested in recreating that particular process for making music. We try to obtain results analogous to what we estimate was the improvised music produced by the musicians of that time. This means that we can evaluate the result against a long-established and well-known tradition. We can ask, "Does this cadenza sound like Mozart?" or "Does this fugue sound like J.K.F. Fischer?"

We look at historical improvisation not only as an end in itself, as a kind of skills training, but as a tool for introducing students to a repertoire and style, set in a precise generative system, a shared musical syntax. This approach is something of a novelty nowadays, because we live in a time where many styles are practiced at once: a student may play Rachmaninoff one day and Bach the next. Different styles contaminate each other. Historical improvisation allows students a deep, detailed engagement with the particularities of a single style—and by extension, a musical-historical moment in time, as they move back and forth between their own improvisation and a model item from the repertoire.

In fact, for the long period we are focused on (1500–1800), improvisation was either prior to, or coexisted with, composition: choirboys often grew up to become composers, and Kapellmeisters and virtuoso instrumentalists both improvised and composed.[6] By the late nineteenth century, due in part to increased specialization (particularly of orchestral players), the cult of the genius composer, and the decline of improvised singing in the church, the only musicians left who improvised were keyboard players.[7] What happens to an improvised practice when time goes by? Depending on several factors, it might partially sediment in a fixed form—that is, to be written out and encapsulated into a composition: we have the *Well-tempered Clavier* as the fossil remains of some Bach improvisations.

Scholars have recently demonstrated that it is possible to invert the process and isolate the improvised part, helping us to understand how composition came to be, through daily practice of a shared repository of motives and techniques. Hints about extemporized music are to be found in theoretical and literary works as well. A theoretician might inform us about a particular technique, or report on a specific musician well versed in improvisation. Dealing with historical improvisation is, therefore, solving a puzzle. First, one has to collect evidence (the pieces) from different kinds of sources and interpret them. A second essential moment it is to bring them back to life, both in the classroom and on stage.[8]

Using Improvisation to Teach … Improvisation

There are many ways to reintegrate historical improvisation into the curriculum. Looking at the requirements of many schools in North America and Europe, we see that early music departments are more often offering courses in practical improvisation, both for soloists and ensembles. Until this point, organists were the only ones who managed to keep the tradition somewhat alive, especially in some geographic areas (France, Germany, U.S.) where liturgical playing still demands improvisatory skills. Continuo players are also well acquainted with improvisation, even if they are usually requested to prepare their accompaniments in advance. It is not uncommon that super stellar baroque conductors impose their own way of realizing continuo on their players with the intent of providing a refined, reliable interpretation, ready for recording, but in so doing they lose a great amount of "authenticity" or historical accuracy. Getting familiar with improvisation is not an easy and quick requirement, but it is also a much more rewarding way of approaching the repertoire.

Although essential to the training of skilled early music performers, these kinds of activities have a limited impact on the majority of students. In the framework of our research, we are more interested in offering an introduction to the comprehension of improvisatory elements within different repertoires and some tools for making the students understand how to integrate improvisation into their own experience as performers. This resulted in a graduate seminar about performance practice and improvisation in early music, mostly intended for students in a performance curriculum.

We began by asking students where improvisation fits into historical practice, and about the degrees of freedom different kinds of improvised practice allow. Many students had no idea how important improvisation was in past centuries. Students were asked to make a "concept map" of their ideas of the different kinds of improvisation and rate them on a scale. A hypothetical result is pictured in Figure 9.1.

More limited,   Freer,
less responsibility .... more responsibility

Ornament a melody	Realize a figured bass	Play a jazz standard	Play a cadenza	Play a fugue or sonata

Figure 9.1 Concept map with different ideas on improvisation.

What we call melodic ornamentation, at the leftmost extreme, offers a range of options, from vibrato or a short trill to a substantial Bellini cadenza. Such ornaments are usually determined by what note you start on and where you end, and what rhythms, skips, and steps are allowed in the style, and so on. The structure of the piece is essentially in place, and the player does not need knowledge of voice leading or harmony. Likewise, the structure of the piece is already in place for the performer realizing a figured bass or a partimento, or playing a jazz standard, but only one voice is given (the bass in the former, the melody in the latter), and the player is responsible for the rest of the textures, melodic material, voice leading, and so on. A violin or keyboard cadenza, on the other hand, demands the invention of harmonic progressions and some knowledge of voice leading. Finally, at the rightmost extreme, making a fugue or a sonata treats improvisation as "fast composition;" that is, the making of a musical object from scratch: all the chords, all the melodies, are pulled out of the air.

The course explored the relation between improvisation and performance with a particular emphasis on the late Renaissance and Baroque. We questioned the approach influenced by the Romantic vision that considers improvising music in opposition to performing the repertoire, with reference to the ancient one, that integrates improvisation, composition, and performance in a coherent musical whole. Students were solicited, starting from personal experiences and background, to assess their own learning process, especially as relates to the use of memory in music making. Our goal was to make them able to elaborate or revise their approach to historical performance practice, integrating into it improvisation, and to have a better critical appreciation of the sources.

The results of this course were encouraging. As a social constructivist experiment, it benefitted from a mixed population of students: classical wind players, a jazz pianist, a theorist, an organist, a harpsichordist, and a conductor. The students learned from each other how different the idea of improvisation can be and how it affects a musician. There was a general sense of disbelief when we started teaching note against note counterpoint. Such an activity was not contemplated under the improvisatory label. The historical approach we introduced ("do not think, play it!") was centered on the making moment. Theory tends to dissolve when you are pushing keys, since fingers move quickly and you just need some basic instruction for visualizing your path throughout notes.[9] We tried to look at repertoire not as written in stone, a work of art, perfect and untouchable. We demonstrated how, in the Renaissance and Baroque, musicians took pieces of their colleagues and reworked them, exactly as jazz musicians are used to doing.

The topics for the final paper, chosen by the students, are also representative of the variety of approaches that improvisation can liberate in the classroom. Our main goal was to make the students think about the way improvisation could affect their own learning process, improving their musicianship, and matching the topics with the student's background.

Table 9.1 Student Backgrounds and Final Project Topics

Jazz piano	Early Baroque Ostintato versus American Bebop
Organ	How to Improvise a Chopin Nocturn
Theory	Subject Diminution in Bach's WTK
Oboe	Improvising Ornaments in Style (Forgetting About the Exam!)
Conducting	Different Approaches to Dowland's Lute Music
Harpsichord	Improvising a Double for a Bach Sarabanade
Clarinet	Teaching Music by Improvisation in Elementary School and College

During the course, we asked the students to keep a learning diary, annotating their impressions and the development of their skills. To our amazement, their responses are quite similar to what we know about singers and musicians of the Renaissance. We can see a close relationship between intellectual activities, performance practice, embodiment, analysis, and music rendition, all combining mind and body processes.

#1: "Started practicing improvising on a solo instrument a melody against a CF [cantus firmus]. What I learned from this experience is that it seems obvious that when an experienced organist sits down at the bench he not only has his *head full of rules and patterns*, but of the *possible functions of each CF note sounding*. There are many different possibilities, but he *quickly understands* all the ranges of possible lines, modulation, or basic chordal sequence, *and executes one of those*, as if plucking them from the memory palace."

#2: "I found I could make a better line *once I had actually sort of analyzed the possible functions of each bass note*, something that I don't have much experience doing, so *it took a while*."

#3: "I noticed an improvement in the process of improvising on a CF. This depends on applying the rules naturally. *While improvising my fingers are producing right intervals*."

#4: "I think that *playing and transposing* Diruta's examples could enable me to *develop my muscle memory.*"

What we see from these quotes is that the students recognized that pattern memory and physical memory can replace rules, and that playing and thinking can be one, a far cry from present-day instrumental and theory teaching, each in its own "silo." At the end of the seminar, improvisation was no longer a magic word but a concrete set of possible music techniques. Creativity and imagination are still in the picture but are framed within some stylistic rules. What we learned together is that you can improvise in many ways, feeling free and fresh, even if you are singing a note against note counterpoint.

Using Improvisation to Teach Counterpoint and Harmony

In the Renaissance and Baroque periods, improvisation was the way students learned music. Young singers and keyboard players were introduced to the art of composition by learning how to recombine preexisting materials directly on the spot, internalizing the rules of counterpoint—the very word *counterpoint* referred originally to improvisation.[10] In present-day curricula, counterpoint and theory are considered part of written, abstract composition. At the same time, improvisation, in the Early Music environment is beginning to become a specialized activity for advanced students who already possess a written theoretical background.

Species counterpoint is often taught laboriously with many layers of aesthetic requirements overlaid onto the simple matter of correct voice leading. We believe that the species should be taught as quickly as possible and judged only for minimal correctness, and that the most efficient way to do this is through improvisation. A method of using classroom time has been described elsewhere.[11] In our experience, however, even having students play and sing in every class meeting does not ensure that they will do it at home, probably because this challenging activity is not fun in itself.

Improvising canons, on the other hand, is an activity that students will do out of class. This is because it is fun, and one reason it's fun is that it must be done with a partner. This exercise gives music training a social aspect that is often missing in theory courses (not to mention the practice room). As mentioned above, one of the tenets of constructivism is that learning is a social activity, and here we see that it makes the exercise more successful.

Teaching harmony in a collaborative way is also possible in the classroom.[12] If one student improvises a melodic continuation to a given two-bar basic idea, or a bass line to a given melody, then the other members of the class can sing it back (memory training), write it down (dictation), and individuals can comment on it (proto-analysis). Such "instant composition" encourages experimenting with alternative solutions in a nonjudgmental context.

Improvisation can be a low-key, fun, social activity in which each student experiences personal involvement. The experience will make the "lesson" (whether to avoid singing parallel fifths, to emulate Albinoni, or to play in invertible counterpoint at the twelfth) more memorable and more enduring than if it were the product of studying for a test.

Conclusion

As Peter Webster put it: "In music and music education, constructivism has made little headway in changing the fundamental way teachers are prepared or how in-service professionals do their jobs."[13] We hope to have suggested some ways in which to conceive and integrate improvisation, following the principles of constructivist doctrine, into the present-day classroom. We hope to have indicated how it contributes to the modern student's sense of musical style from different periods, how it impacts memory and competent musical behavior, and how it encourages students to learn from one another. To close with the words of one of our students in the performance seminar: "The more tools that I have the better I am able to make decisions as to what I will do where. Again, I have said it before, but I will say it again, *I wish I had time to really get good at this stuff.*"

Notes

1. This is a slightly altered version of a paper given during the *Summit on Improvisation Pedagogy and Community Impact*, University of Guelph, May 23–26, 2013.
2. All the activities described here were part of the research project, "Improvisation in Classical Music Education: Rethinking Our Future by Learning Our Past," generously financed by the Social Sciences and Humanities Research Council of Canada (M. Guido and P. Schubert, principal investigators) in conjunction with a Banting Postdoctoral Fellowship that supported M. Guido's research at McGill. The project outcomes and full description are available at www.mentemani.org/ Connection.
3. The authors are grateful to Kelly Symons for introducing them to this school of thought and guiding them to some useful readings on the subject.
4. Webster, "Construction of Music Learning."
5. Ibid., 45–46.
6. See Schubert, "From Improvisation to Composition," 93–130.
7. For a discussion of increased specialization in the production of music, see chapter 7 of Lydia Goehr's *The Imaginary Museum of Musical Works: An Essay in the Philosophy of Music*, "Musical Production without the Work-Concept."
8. See Guido, "Rethinking Counterpoint through Improvisation."
9. See Guido, "Counterpoint in the Fingers" and "Con questa sicura strada."
10. See Schubert, "Counterpoint Pedagogy."
11. See Schubert, "Thinking in Music."
12. See Schubert, "Teaching Music Analysis through Improvisation."
13. Webster, "Construction of Music Learning," 74.

Works Cited

Goehr, Lydia. "Musical Production without the Work-Concept." In *The Imaginary Museum of Musical Works: An Essay in the Philosophy of Music*, 176–204. Oxford: Oxford University Press, 2007.

Guido, Massimiliano. "'Con questa sicura strada:' Girolamo Diruta's and Adriano Banchieri's Instructions on How to Improvise Versets." *The Organ Yearbook* 42, (2013): 40–52.

———. "Counterpoint in the Fingers: A Practical Approach to Girolamo Diruta's *Breve et Facile Regola di Contrappunto*." *Philomusica on-line* 11, no. 2 (2011): 63–76.

———. "Rethinking Counterpoint through Improvisation: A Multidisciplinary Conversation with Edoardo Bellotti, Michele Chiarmida, Michael Dodds, Andreas Schiltknecht, Peter Schubert, and Nicola Straffelini." *Philomusica on-line* 11, no. 2 (2011): 5–9.

Schubert, Peter. "Counterpoint Pedagogy in the Renaissance." *The Cambridge History of Western Music Theory*, edited by Thomas Christensen, 503–33. Cambridge: Cambridge University Press, 2002.

———. "From Improvisation to Composition: Three 16th Century Case Studies." In *Improvising Early Music: Collected Writings of the Orpheus Institute*, edited by Dirk Moelants, 93–130. Ghent: Leuven University Press, 2014.

———. "Teaching Music Analysis through Improvisation." In *Engaging Students: Essays in Music Pedagogy, Vol. 2*. http://www.flipcamp.org/engagingstudents2/.

———. "Thinking in Music." *Journal of Music Theory Pedagogy* 25 (2011): 217–33.

Webster, Peter. "Construction of Music Learning." In *MENC Handbook of Research on Music Learning, Vol. 1*, edited by Richard Colwell and Peter R. Webster, 35–83. New York: Oxford University Press, 2011.

10 Thoroughbass as Pedagogy in the Teaching of Improvisation in Undergraduate Music Theory Courses

Vincent P. Benitez

Introduction

During a weeklong seminar on organ improvisation held in Toulouse, France, in 1993, Philippe Lefebvre, one of the titular organists at Notre Dame Cathedral in Paris, told American organist and conductor Jeffrey Brillhart that in order to improvise, *one must search* ("il faut chercher").[1] For Brillhart, who described himself at the time as an inexperienced improviser, these words changed his attitude toward not only improvisation but also music making in general. Pointing to Lefebvre's remark as signifying a defining moment in his development as a musician, Brillhart remarked that "[one] *must* search if one is to grow," and "[to] improvise is *to search*." But what exactly does one search for when improvising? Developing a technique? Expressing the artistic and immaterial?

To ponder these issues from a different vantage point, let us consider Charles Tournemire's ideas about improvisation, as reflected by his *Précis d'exécution de registration et d'improvisation à l'orgue* (1936).[2] In his approach to this spontaneous art, Tournemire (1870–1939) focused on its spiritual side. For this great organist/composer of the twentieth century, technique, although important, was only a means to an end that served as a conduit to the beyond where one could experience the divine. Affixing technical rules to improvisation was virtually impossible, although an improvisation should sound as if it were written down. Ultimately, Tournemire believed that the art of improvisation centered on the expression of beauty, emotion, poetry, and a vivid imagination. He compared it to a mysterious flame that illuminated the soul of an artist. Technique fades into the background when the improviser's thought is noble and emotion genuine. This inexplicable, enlightening force inspires the improviser to uncover beauty and consequently obtain a glimpse of God, who is the author of all beauty.

Tournemire's thoughts on improvisation suggest that he viewed the created world as bearing witness to the beauty of God.[3] As a devout Roman Catholic, he probably took his cue from Romans 1:20: "For since the creation of the world His invisible attributes are clearly seen, being understood by the things that are made, even His eternal power and Godhead" (NKJV). Thus, as a created being responding to the author of the universe via improvisation, Tournemire elicits an intangible, created beauty from a tangible technique that does not compete with it; rather, this technique helps to bring forth a beauty that reaffirms the cosmic beauty of God. In other words, created beauty, emanating frequently from arduous technical experimentation, radiates from the divinely wrought natural beauty of the world.

If improvisation is truly a search for growth as a musician, and if that growth's goal is fluency with diverse musical languages, then improvisation should be a cornerstone of any music student's training. We should encourage students to explore music through improvisation, having them engaged in a search that places them in direct contact with the art of music from compositional, tactile, and theoretical vantage points. But all of this training should ultimately be geared toward finding beauty in life through improvisation, allowing students to experience the spiritual in art as well as in themselves. Adapting the words of Jeremy S. Begbie, we can say that "creation's beauty can be brought to light precisely *in* and *through* the [...] strenuous formation and re-formation" of musical materials.[4] And for me, that energetic elaboration can be especially accomplished through the study of improvisation.

How might we approach the teaching of improvisation in undergraduate music theory curricula to facilitate such pedagogical goals? Since undergraduate music theory courses invariably center on the teaching of tonal harmony and eighteenth-century counterpoint, one obvious choice would be to teach improvisation through the use of Baroque thoroughbass. Such a pedagogical approach would be a very dynamic way to get students engaged in learning about the vertical and linear forces of music. In short, they would experience both harmony and counterpoint in an economical way while extemporizing.

In this chapter, I show how thoroughbass can be used to teach improvisation in second-year tonal harmony and upper-level eighteenth-century counterpoint classes in a conservatory setting. The exercises I propose that would help advance this goal are somewhat detached from the actual experience of the classroom. Although based in part on my practice as a teacher, they favor the more theoretical side of realizing figured basses, focusing more on principles rather than actual pedagogical situations. I encourage readers to take my suggestions and adapt them to their teaching needs. Last, I am directing my pedagogical efforts to music students who have had at least 1 to 2 years of tonal harmony, which would include exposure to figured bass, and an introduction to species counterpoint. These students, moreover, should be proficient on an instrument, possess some elementary keyboard skills, and have some familiarity with music history and style.

The practice of thoroughbass reflected the change in orientation from the tenor-based intervallic polyphony of the Medieval and Renaissance periods to the bass-driven chordal voice leading of the Baroque. During that period, thoroughbass supplied a veritable window into all forms and styles of music. Through the pedagogical approach outlined in this article, I desire to open such a window for present-day students of tonal harmony and eighteenth-century counterpoint by improving their fluency in part writing, analysis, stylistic composition, and, above all else, improvisation.

Improvising First-Species Counterpoint

Let's start with some unmeasured, two-part contrapuntal exercises in first species where a counterpoint using only consonances is supplied against a cantus firmus. We want to structure the counterpoint so that it forms a good musical line against the cantus firmus through a combination of contrary, oblique, similar, and parallel motion. Furthermore, in keeping with first species, perfect consonances most likely should open and close the exercises, with a mixture of imperfect and perfect consonances sounding in between. Finally, because we're dealing with tonal counterpoint, our beginnings and endings should be clearly key defining.

G:

Example 10.1 Unmeasured bass line in G major.

Example 10.1 provides an unmeasured bass line in G major. Let's focus on both the beginning and ending of this exercise. For the moment, try to imagine the following. We can easily place a D5 and B4 above the beginning G2 and G3 in the bass, and an F♯5 and G5 above the bass's closing notes, A2 and G2. Of course, other notes could work. In keeping with the contrapuntal axiom that stepwise motion is preferred, we can complete the exercise by connecting its beginning and ending notes with those moving predominantly by step. Our improvisation consisting of first-species counterpoint could look like Example 10.2.

G: 5   3   5   6   8   3   6   8

Example 10.2 Proposed improvised first species counterpoint to the G major bass line.

Checking for intervals, we have used only consonant ones, with a balanced mix of perfect and imperfect consonances. Moreover, we have emphasized contrary motion, the best type to use in counterpoint.

Let's try another example, this one in D major but with some figured bass (Example 10.3).[5] As a result, we're going to introduce some dissonant intervals, such as the diminished fifth and minor seventh, due to the use of two dominant seventh chords.

Example 10.3 Unmeasured bass line with figured bass in D major.

Again, let's try to imagine the following. First, let's supply beginning and ending notes to the exercise. I propose that we begin with A4, G4, and F♯4 in the counterpoint. Such melodic motion is in keeping with how the diminished fifth is approached and resolved—in this case, to a major third. Moreover, this tritone "spices up" our work.

Let's now focus on the ending of the exercise, beginning with the applied dominant seventh, V7/V, the third chord from the end. In keeping with the goal to animate this exercise with dissonant intervals, let's insert a D over the E, which introduces a minor seventh. Given this note, we will have to retain the D for the cadential 6/4 chord. This D moves down by step, of course, to the third of the dominant chord, ultimately satisfying the need of the seventh of the applied V7/V to resolve.

As we supply the rest of the counterpoint, we'll have to introduce an ascending leap into the mix to prepare the D of our V7/V. Imagine a leap to an E5 above the C♯3 in the bass figured as a first-inversion chord. Of course, our ending notes balance that leap with stepwise motion in the opposite direction. Here's the bass line with a first-species counterpoint enhanced with some dissonant intervals (Example 10.4).

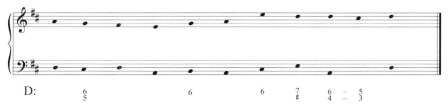

Example 10.4 Proposed improvised first species counterpoint to the D-major bass line.

Improvising over Figured Basses

Let's increase the level of difficulty by providing more harmonically oriented parts to given figured basses. We're still going to limit ourselves to two-part frameworks. Although we'll be dealing with given chord progressions that dictate our choices of notes, how those notes are employed in a given texture, and the voice leading between chords, is of paramount concern. But before we tackle such figured basses, let us provide a structural backdrop by considering how Baroque musicians harmonized scale degrees.

In his book entitled *Thorough-Bass Accompaniment according to Johann David Heinichen*, George J. Buelow summarizes how a student of thorough-bass should approach the task of accompanying properly through a paraphrase of the Gospel of John (1:1): "In the beginning was the triad."[6] Since thoroughbass was a window into harmony for musicians of the Baroque, students must know how to use triads, along with seventh chords, in order to improvise with any facility. Johann David Heinichen, composer and author of *Der Generalbass in der Composition* (Dresden, 1728), suggested that students learn triads on each scale degree and play them in different voicings.[7] And the best way to do that was through the *rule of the octave*, a term associated with stock harmonizations of ascending and descending diatonic scales.

Example 10.5 shows an ascending C-major scale with a rule-of-the-octave harmonization signified through figured bass. In this example, there are root-position tonic and dominant triads on scale degrees 1 and 5 that speak to the key-defining nature of both these scale degrees and their attendant harmonies. There are likewise first-inversion triads and seventh chords on scale degrees 2, 3, 4, 6, and 7 that attest to the more linear nature of these scale degrees and their associated chords. As a result, we have a practical tonal-harmonic framework to generate contrapuntal lines.

Example 10.5 Rule of the octave harmonization using a C-major scale.

With the "rule of the octave" as a backdrop, let's explore how we can supply an upper part composed of idiomatic keyboard figurations to a figured bass. Here we're going to focus on how to elaborate a structural counterpoint using embellishing tones—that is, nonharmonic tones as well as harmonic ones (such as consonant skips and arpeggiations). In this endeavor, we'll be incorporating certain musical-rhetorical figures, such as the *groppo*, *messanza*, *suspirans*, and *figura corta* in the lines that we develop.[8]

Example 10.6 displays a figured bass with passing tones in the key of B♭ major. Example 10.7 shows how a structural counterpoint serving as the basis for an improvisation could be placed against it. As in our previous first-species examples, we have developed a line consisting solely of consonances. As shown in Example 10.8, we can elaborate this line with nonharmonic tones and consonant skips. From the standpoint of musical-rhetorical figures, the elaborated structural counterpoint features *groppos* (a figure consisting of upper and lower neighbors decorating a principal note) and *messanzas* (a figure consisting of a mixture of stepwise motion and consonant leaps).

Example 10.6 Bass line with figured bass in B♭ major.

Example 10.7 B♭-major bass line with structural counterpoint.

Example 10.8 Final realization of the B♭-major bass line.

My focus on the improvisation of single lines above given figured basses is derived from the compositional practice of biciniums, two-part pieces used as teaching tools in Protestant Germany during the Renaissance and Baroque periods. I am employing this genre both to teach improvisation and reinforce harmony and counterpoint, a strategy sympathetic to the teaching of counterpoint historically, since the fundamentals of this art have traditionally been presented within a two-voice framework, moving to more voices after essential concepts have been mastered. In sum, the ability to supply an improvised counterpoint above a given figured bass is a valuable skill for any student to develop. Indeed, one can control two voices to a degree not possible with three or more voices.

Example 10.9 shows a more sophisticated example of a bicinium, verse 4 of "Meinen Jesum laß ich nicht" by Johann Gottfried Walther (1684–1748), Johann Sebastian Bach's cousin. In this instance, Walther enhances the hymn tune in the soprano with continuous sixteenth-note motion, while the accompanimental bass moves mainly in eighth notes. Both voices are in sync with the harmony suggested by the chorale tune. In addition to the *groppo* and *messanza* figures mentioned earlier, Walther uses three additional musical-rhetorical figures throughout this verse: (1) the *superjectio*, an upper neighbor added to each note of a descending scalar line; (2) the *suspirans*, a figure rebounding from an actual or implied rest; and (3) the *figura corta*, an anapestic or dactylic rhythmic figure.

Example 10.9 Johann Gottfried Walther, "Meinen Jesum laß ich nicht," verse 4.

Improvising over a Ground Bass

I would like to turn now to the topic of improvising a part over a ground bass. Using a basso ostinato in such a fashion not only promotes unity and coherence in an improvisation through a consistent tonal-harmonic foundation but also encourages unlimited fantasy with respect to the improvisation's musical texture. In other words, over a four- or eight-measure ground bass, with clear harmonic implications, the improviser could easily devise an endless series of creative keyboard figurations.

For an excellent example of the different types of keyboard figurations that one could devise while improvising over a ground bass, let's take a look at the theme and first six variations of Bach's Passacaglia in C minor for organ, BWV 582. To begin with, the passacaglia theme has obvious melodic interest, with arcs that balance each other through an opening ascent and subsequent descent (see Example 10.10). The theme, moreover, includes two four-measure phrases that have clear harmonic profiles, with the first one concluding with a half cadence, and the second with an authentic cadence.[9]

Example 10.10 Johann Sebastian Bach, Passacaglia in C Minor, BWV 582, Basso Ostinato and variations 1–3.

After the passacaglia theme is sounded, the first two variations emphasize chordal syncopations in the guise of an offbeat figure tied to a dotted eighth note followed by a sixteenth. Variation 3 features an imitative texture of flowing eighth notes, as a *suspirans* figure is employed motivically throughout the musical edifice. Variations 4 and 5 (see Example 10.11) increase the music's motion through the use of a sixteenth note, anapestic *figura corta* figure, again sounded in an imitative environment. Variation 6 continues the upsurge in motion with constant sixteenth notes

Example 10.11 Johann Sebastian Bach, Passacaglia in C Minor, BWV 582, variations 4–6.

set imitatively, which not only materialize via the motivic auspices of a *suspirans* figure but also attest to the music's inventive textures by way of musical-rhetorical figures.

With Bach's Passacaglia as inspiration, I supply four hypothetically improvised variations using different Baroque figurative patterns, over a realized figured bass (see Example 10.12). As shown in Example 10.13a, a simple way to improvise over a ground bass is to supply broken-chord figurations based on the line's harmonic design. Having a block-chord harmonization of the bass line in mind, it is very easy to play these sonorities as a series of broken-chord figures. Example 10.13b features scalar motives, including *groppos* and *messanzas*. Here it is probably advisable to focus on a structural counterpoint first based on the underlying chords. After that,

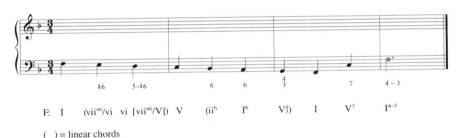

Example 10.12 Ground bass in F major used as the basis for a series of four improvisations.

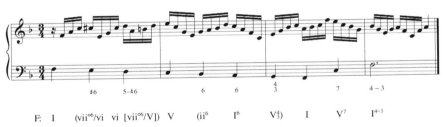

Example 10.13a Ground bass in F major: variation 1, broken-chord figurations.

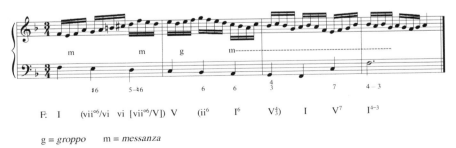

g = *groppo*   m = *messanza*

Example 10.13b Ground bass in F major: variation 2, scalar figurations.

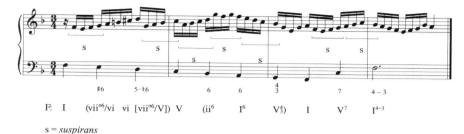

s = *suspirans*

Example 10.13c Ground bass in F major: variation 3, *suspirans*-based figurations.

f.c. = *figura corta*

Example 10.13d Ground bass in F major: variation 4, scales, repeated notes (*figura cortas*), and dotted notes.

incorporate additional chordal notes interspersed with embellishing tones. Example 10.13c uses a motivic *suspirans* figure. Again, focus on a structural counterpoint first before adding more notes. Finally, Example 10.13d includes scales, repeated notes, and dotted notes. The repeated notes, furthermore, are set as dactylic *figura cortas*.

When teaching students how to improvise over a ground bass, or within any of the musical scenarios that I have outlined in this chapter, I recommend that they write out their solutions first before they improvise them. This could initially take the form of devising a solution and then improvising one in alternation. The next stage could consist of a student writing out part of a solution and then improvising the rest. When a teacher has determined that his or her students have demonstrated an adequate grasp of the theoretical components under consideration, he or she could then direct them to improvise exclusively. At that point, the teacher should focus on developing the spontaneous creativity of his or her students through informed critiques of the lines that they improvise.

Conclusion

In this chapter, I have suggested ways to teach improvisation in eighteenth-century counterpoint and music theory classes by using thoroughbass applied to keyboard biciniums. Besides spurring their creative imagination, improvisation via thoroughbass can teach students about harmony and counterpoint from vantage points not likely encountered in traditional written instruction. Indeed, we might consider it a sort of harmonic atelier, supplying insights into the nature of tonality, divulging the secrets of a God-given art. As Lawrence Dreyfus writes in *Bach and the Patterns of Invention*, what "lay at the core of musical and human experience" for J. S. Bach was an intangible divine spark, which was attained by "arduous work and experimental discovery."[10] For me, this divine spark, a glimpse of the beautiful, is the ultimate goal of improvisation. And using thoroughbass as a means of experimental discovery is one path to experience it.

Notes

1. Jeffrey Brillhart, *Breaking Free*, 4.
2. The following information about Tournemire's approach to improvisation is taken from Charles Tournemire, *Précis d'exécution de registration et d'improvisation à l'orgue*, 102. See also Vincent P. Benitez, "Messiaen as Improviser," 131–32.
3. My reading of Tournemire's "theology of beauty" is indebted in part to Jeremy S. Begbie's "Created Beauty: The Witness of J. S. Bach," 83–108.
4. Begbie, *Resonant Witness*, 16.
5. This bass line is adapted from one contained in John R. Shannon, *Improvising in Traditional 17th- and 18th-Century Harmonic Style*, 1:14.
6. Such pronouncements are a part of musical tradition, as seen by pianist Hans von Bülow's like-minded anecdotal paraphrase of the Gospel of John, "In the beginning was rhythm." See Buelow, *Thorough-Bass Accompaniment*, 29; and Benitez, "A Creative Legacy," 129.
7. Buelow, *Thorough-Bass Accompaniment*, 29.
8. For more information on musical-rhetorical figures, see Benitez, "Musical-Rhetorical Figures in the *Orgelbüchlein* of J. S. Bach" (1985), viii–x; Benitez, "Musical-Rhetorical Figures in the *Orgelbüchlein* of J. S. Bach" (1987), 3–21; and Bartel, *Musica Poetica*, 167–457.
9. The first four measures of this theme are taken from André Raison's *Trio en passacaille* from the *Messe du deuxième ton* of his *Premier livre d'orgue* (1688).
10. Dreyfus, *Bach and the Patterns of Invention*, 57.

Works Cited

Bartel, Dietrich. *Musica Poetica: Musical-Rhetorical Figures in German Baroque Music*. Lincoln: University of Nebraska Press, 1997.

Begbie, Jeremy S. "Created Beauty: The Witness of J. S. Bach." In *Resonant Witness: Conversations between Music and Theology*, edited by Jeremy S. Begbie and Steven R. Guthrie, 83–108. Grand Rapids, MI: William B. Eerdmans Publishing, 2011.

Benitez, Vincent P. "A Creative Legacy: Messiaen as Teacher of Analysis." *College Music Symposium* 40 (2000): 117–39.

———. "Messiaen as Improviser." *Dutch Journal of Music Theory* 13, no. 2 (May 2008): 129–44.

————. "Musical-Rhetorical Figures in the *Orgelbüchlein* of J. S. Bach." DMA research paper, Arizona State University, 1985.

————. "Musical-Rhetorical Figures in the *Orgelbüchlein* of J. S. Bach." *Bach* 18, no. 1 (January 1987): 3–21.

Brillhart, Jeffrey. *Breaking Free: Finding a Personal Language for Organ Improvisation through 20th-Century French Improvisation Techniques.* Colfax, NC: Wayne Leupold Editions, 2011.

Buelow, George J. *Thorough-Bass Accompaniment According to Johann David Heinichen.* Rev. ed. Lincoln: University of Nebraska Press, 1986.

Dreyfus, Laurence. *Bach and the Patterns of Invention.* Cambridge, MA: Harvard University Press, 1996.

Shannon, John R. *Improvising in Traditional 17th- and 18th-Century Harmonic Style: A Volume Based on the Musical Language of the Mature Baroque.* 2 vols. Edited by Wayne Leupold. Colfax, NC: Wayne Leupold Editions, 2010.

Tournemire, Charles. *Précis d'exécution de registration et d'improvisation à l'orgue.* Paris: Éditions Max Eschig, 1936.

11 Improvise Globally, Strategize Locally

Institutional Structures and Ethnomusicological Agency

Scott Currie

In highly influential art and vernacular music traditions from West Africa to South Asia and throughout the Americas, as well as in contemporary popular musics worldwide, improvisation plays a vital and often essential role, yet its study and practice, as many of this volume's contributors have suggested, remain marginal at best in canonical Euro-American postsecondary music curricula, typically limited to reductive chord-scale modern-jazz methods, if taught at all. Needless to say, ethnomusicologists—whose disciplinary scope embraces the more expansive spectrum of art, vernacular, and popular traditions noted above—frequently find themselves at odds with conventional, text-centered, "great-works" paradigms of musical creativity, along with the theory/practice and town/gown dichotomies these presuppose and reinforce. Drawing upon academic experiences in a variety of university music-school contexts, I outline the manner in which ethnomusicologists' cross-cultural conceptions, collaborative pedagogical models, community-engagement orientations, and experiential discovery-oriented paradigms can offer viable, empowering means of understanding and inspiring creativity.

In so doing, I will engage two sets of research questions posed by George Lewis with regard to the critical development of improvisation pedagogy:

- How can cross-cultural models of learning and teaching extend experimental learning and teaching methods? How can new musical communities and social formations that presume the importance of improvisation be incorporated into the academy? What kinds of new social models will result from such initiatives, and what can be gained from theorizing these newer models of music making?[1]
- What kinds of new theoretical and organizational models, as well as new practices, can be developed for the creation and nurturing of itinerant-institutional partnerships for the teaching of improvisation, the development of improvisation teachers, and theories of education that embed improvisation itself as a methodology?[2]

In exploring these issues in relation to university-level music curricula, I pay particular attention to the ethical dimensions of collaborative extemporization suggested by Lewis' reference to the demand "that improvisors assume both personal and collective responsibility for the real-time articulation of form within form,"[3] as elaborated by Panagiotis Kanellopoulos, whose "understanding of improvisation [as it emerges in 'improvised music'] ... presupposes that all participants act in ways which entail shared responsibility for the creation of the music."[4]

Having sounded the theme of improvisational ethics, I should probably make clear from the outset that, while I certainly aim at "developing a robust and alternative pedagogy that reaches across cultural and social divides," I am afraid that my own curricular initiatives undertaken thus far and analyzed below offer relatively little support for Ajay Heble and Ellen Waterman's suggested characterization of "improvisatory performance practices"—without qualification—as "activist forms of insurgent knowledge production."[5] By and large, my students do not represent themselves (to me at least) as revolutionaries, but rather as aspiring professional musicians and music educators. Inasmuch as most of them arrive at my university's school of music thoroughly grounded in conventional Euro-American paradigms of text-centered music making, the improvisational practices I teach have indeed often "purposefully confounded familiar frameworks of assumption" associated with such classical training, but my main challenge in the classroom is to ensure that these extemporaneous "forms of artistic practice" *can* ultimately be "assimilated using dominant structures of understanding"[6] enshrined in our curriculum, albeit suitably problematized and modified by engaged praxis. Even the unflaggingly enthusiastic support of my school's last progressive director has not empowered me (nor any of my like-minded colleagues) to place improvisation "at the core of the music curriculum" of my institution, as Keith Sawyer recommends; instead, I have by necessity pursued the "more incremental change to music education" he discourages, keeping it "essentially as is ... while carefully introducing some improvisational practice into the current music education curriculum."[7] In short, I find myself in much the same position as many if not most of my colleagues seeking to create an engaging space for improvisational interaction within classically oriented conservatories and music schools, which generally marginalize or even discourage the practice, among students whose relatively limited experience all too often entails correspondingly limited initial interest in it as well.[8]

Some basic information regarding the school may prove helpful to an understanding of the institutional context within which the improvisational initiatives at issue took place. The University of Minnesota (UMN) School of Music serves approximately 550 majors (about 60 percent undergraduate and 40 percent graduate) and 4,350 nonmajors with a faculty of around 50 full-time members, making it mid-sized in comparison to its larger counterparts at peer institutions such as the University of Indiana or the University of Michigan. Of its most recent cohort of incoming undergraduate students, nearly three-quarters came from Minnesota and over 90 percent were

Midwesterners; by contrast, only about a third of its latest entering class of graduate students came from Minnesota and almost one quarter were international students, with the rest spread more-or-less evenly across some twenty states of origin. At the undergraduate level, the School of Music offers Bachelor of Music (B.M.) degrees in classical performance, music education and music therapy, as well as Bachelor of Arts (B.A.) degrees with applied and academic emphases. At the graduate level it offers Master of Music (M.M.) degrees in classical performance, conducting, and music education, as well as Master of Arts degrees in musicology, music theory, composition, and music therapy, in addition to Doctor of Musical Arts (D.M.A.) degrees in classical performance and conducting, along with Doctor of Philosophy degrees in musicology, music theory, composition, and music education.

Aside from the noteworthy lack of a degree-granting jazz program among these, and notwithstanding both the distinctive aspects of the institution (e.g., its unique status as the only public university in the Midwestern Big Ten located in a major metropolitan area) and the many distinctions faculty members have earned as artists, scholars, and teachers, it is hard to imagine anyone describing it as unconventional. Indeed, the sorts of institutional constraints encountered in advancing improvisation seem broadly representative of those faced in any number of conservatories and schools of music nationwide: Euro-American focused curricula, strict disciplinary specializations, academic/applied (theory/practice) divisions, town-versus-gown boundaries, and text-centered pedagogical paradigms are hardly unique to Minnesota. What has distinguished it among peer institutions with regard to the study of improvisation are a series of curricular initiatives that challenge or circumvent these constraints in order to offer students opportunities to reconceptualize their practice through hands-on engagement with global improvisational traditions.[9]

Director's Task Force on Improvisation

My involvement with these improvisation initiatives at Minnesota began when I agreed to chair the new director's task force on improvisation across the curriculum, charged with seeking and exploring new ways to provide all students in the School of Music with meaningful improvisational experiences over the course of their programs of study. Meeting regularly during the 2009–10 academic year, this faculty working group brought academics from musicology, music education, and theory/composition together with applied colleagues with instrumental, vocal, and ensemble specializations,[10] for the purposes of defining a core conception of improvisation, surveying improvisation curricula at peer institutions, articulating a rationale for its further integration into Minnesota's curriculum, and drafting recommendations to advance this curricular integration. In setting its agenda, our group quickly reached a general consensus around three main points of conceptualization: that improvisation should not be limited to jazz; that it should unite theory and practice; and that it should be understood as an essential skill not only in music making but also in fields beyond music, insofar as it represents a practice central to a wide variety of professions (e.g., business, medicine/nursing, crisis management) in which practitioners must prepare to engage the unforeseen creatively. On this basis, we elaborated the notion of composing music while performing into a field-specific definition along the following lines:

- In the music world, improvisation refers to the creative processes through which an artist's engagement with his or her immediate soundscape shapes or determines salient aspects of a musical work in the course of its performance.
- Although these processes span a broad gamut—from the personally expressive interpretation of a previously notated or memorized composition to the completely spontaneous extemporaneous conception of musical works without any discernable reliance on preexisting materials or structures—typically improvisation takes place in the context of musical situations allowing the performer significant freedom, within well-defined constraints, to create original music in real time that harmonizes the considerations of the moment with established aesthetic models and practices.
- To the extent that situations of this sort clearly and unambiguously demand that performers accept personal creative responsibility for musical outcomes, improvisational praxis can play a key role in developing the individually expressive conceptions of musical artistry that the Western classical canon shares with many of the world's other prominent musical traditions.

The first two items concerning responsive engagement and agency within structure emphasize pedagogical principles common to many improvisational traditions (including modern jazz), but the last point, regarding the sense of creative responsibility for musical outcomes that improvisation cultivates, has received comparatively little attention until quite recently.[11] This foregrounding of the ethical dimensions of improvisation represented a key underpinning of the main rationale we advanced for its further curricular integration, that of developing creative faculties essential to musical artistry, especially the speculative innovative thinking involved in visualizing and hearing beyond what is written, and the personal investment entailed by the commitment to its articulate, extemporaneous expression. Related rationales included improvisation's ability to

- Build musicianship, by reinforcing ear training and providing practical applications of music theory, and by stressing aural modes of conceiving and internalizing music.
- Hone interpretive skills, by developing the embellishment techniques and active aural skills that make scores and libretti come to life.

- Increase self-confidence and reduce performance anxiety.
- Foster collaborative communication skills for ensemble performance, specifically the ability to respond resourcefully and artfully to unexpected developments on stage.

Our final rationale sought to place these classically oriented pedagogical arguments in a broader, global context by noting the integral role that improvisation plays in a great many important Western and non-Western musical traditions, from jazz and baroque to world and popular music.

Along with fostering creative responsibility, broadening musical context became central to our recommended implementation strategies, insofar as our survey of peer-institution curricula offered relatively little in the way of models we could build upon at Minnesota. On the one hand, the vast majority of schools we examined in our (extensive but by no means exhaustive) search dealt with improvisation mainly in the context of one or another jazz degree program, which (as noted above) Minnesota did not offer, and lacked sufficient faculty to introduce in the foreseeable future. On the other hand, those schools that did place significant curricular emphasis on improvisation outside of jazz had mostly implemented non-jazz improvisation degree programs, which at best represented quite an aspirational longshot prospect for Minnesota (albeit one included in our recommendations). Accordingly, along with our more modest suggestions for integrating improvisation into existing academic courses, ensemble repertories, and studio instruction, we proposed the organization of a guest-artist series of monthly performance-based lecture-demonstrations by master improvisers representing the broadest possible cultural-historical range of traditions, and the development of an advanced seminar exploring three to four global improvisational traditions in a modular format, balancing academic study with a significant performance component.

Worlds of Improvisation and Creativity

While our improvisation task force soon enough found most of its recommendations languishing in the dusty oblivion to which reform proposals of this sort are almost inevitably consigned, the collegial discussions it engendered did effectively galvanize a core group of faculty committed to implementing any action points that could be realized with available resources and opportunities at hand. The first such initiative emerged from the convergence of task-force recommendations for a global improvisation seminar and a monthly series of improvisation master classes. Developed jointly and team-taught with my colleague Erkki Huovinen, our Worlds of Improvisation course served to advance Lewis' research agenda by demonstrating the manner in which our ethnomusicological conceptions, collaborative pedagogical models, and community-engagement orientations could foster "cross-cultural models of learning and teaching" leading to the "creation and nurturing of itinerant-institutional partnerships for the teaching of improvisation."[12]

Designed as a graduate seminar for M.M. and D.M.A. performance students satisfying a musicology requirement, as well as for M.A. and Ph.D. musicology, theory, composition, and music-education students pursuing secondary-field study, the course challenged conventional boundaries separating theory from practice by scheduling fifty-minute weekly lab sessions devoted to hands-on improvisation in addition to more traditional two-hour seminar discussions of improvisational traditions and practices. The course also sought to build bridges across the town/gown divide by incorporating into the structure of the course a series of master classes featuring representative artists from each improvisational tradition under study, a majority of whom lived and worked in the Twin Cities metropolitan area, each contributing with distinction to the vitality of its world-music scenes.[13] As an integral part of the seminar's curricular structure, the series also helped to invert standard text-centered paradigms of musical creativity by making student transcription and analysis of the guest artists' master-class performances and talks central to their final term projects and research papers.

In both its 2010 pilot offering and its subsequent 2012 reprise, we structured the seminar's cross-cultural curriculum around four to five modules: Afro-Cuban son, modern jazz, Arabic maqam, Hindustani raga, and contemporary Americana in the former; and Afro-Brazilian samba, African American gospel, Turkish makam, and Karnatak raga in the latter.[14] By scheduling master-classes in each tradition at the conclusion of the three- to four-week module devoted to its study, we were able to leverage students' personal and collective senses of creative responsibility into strong motivation to prepare for each encounter with our guest artists. In fact, both Huovinen and I found our mode of interaction with the students shifting away from an instructor-centered paradigm of top-down information delivery toward a more collaborative model of sharing relevant literature, scholarly expertise, and musical insights to facilitate students' own efforts to master the rudiments of each tradition in time for each first-hand guest-artist experience. Because many of the locally resident artists welcomed continuing interaction, and most of the visiting artists proved quite receptive to follow-up e-mail correspondence, the students' independent research projects often helped to reinforce the "itinerant-institutional partnerships" forged through this initiative, illustrating the manner in which cross-cultural community engagement can serve to incorporate "new musical communities and social formations that presume the importance of improvisation … into the academy."[15]

In between these two seminar offerings, a fortuitous administrative reorganization at Minnesota made it possible to build upon the model of Worlds of Improvisation in developing an undergraduate course for music educators. The founding of a new Creative Studies and Media (CSM) division in the spring of 2011 united academic faculty specializing in musicology, theory, and composition with applied faculty from the jazz ensemble and guitar studio—including a pair of kindred spirits who had worked with me on the improvisation task force—for the purpose of spurring collegial collaboration on curricular innovation. Almost immediately upon the announcement of the new division's launch came a request for CSM to develop a new course for the music education curriculum to address state certification requirements for music teachers in improvisation and non-Western (i.e., non-Euro-American) musical traditions, specifically including Native American music. Seizing this opportunity, jazz ensemble director Dean Sorenson and I worked together to propose and pilot a team-taught course on Improvisation and Creativity, balancing traditional lecture-style instruction with hands-on improvisational experience and featuring guest-artist lecture-demonstrations to complement cross-cultural curriculum modules on jazz improvisation and composition, Afro-Cuban son and mambo, Arab taqsim and çiftetelli, and Ojibwe powwow and round dance.[16] Not only has this (now annual) curricular offering further advanced the aspects of Lewis' research agenda discussed above, but it has also served to answer his call for "the development of improvisation teachers, and theories of education that embed improvisation itself as a methodology."[17]

New Audiences, Innovative Practice, and Improvising Ecosystems

In the summer of 2012, the active engagement of UMN School of Music Director David Myers as American consultant on the steering committee that developed the European Joint Master of Music degree program in New Audiences and Innovative Practice (NAIP), along with strategic funding he obtained from the Dean of the UMN College of Liberal Arts, made it possible for me to attend the NAIP program's Intensive Summer Institute in Sigtuna, Sweden, to explore the possibility of establishing an affiliate partnership with the consortium of northern European conservatories and music schools offering the program.[18] The central role accorded to improvisation—both as an integral part of the creative work-process throughout the activities scheduled during the course of the institute, and as one of the main elements underpinning the program's curriculum modules and specialization areas— emphasized the ethical dimensions of collaborative extemporization not only as representing a critical aspect of individual artistic development, but also as providing an important basis for reconceptualizing creative ensemble direction, interdisciplinary and transcultural practice, and community-engaged performance conception. Based on my experiences attending and presenting improvisation workshops at that 2012 NAIP summer institute and the two that followed, and my comparative analysis of the various NAIP member-institution's programs at staff development meetings, I drafted a Masters-level curriculum proposal for implementing the program at Minnesota.

Briefly summarized, the NAIP program is designed to prepare students for a rapidly changing world where careers in music demand broader international perspectives and greater professional responsiveness to diverse contexts than ever. Over the course of a two-year M.M. program, students learn to conceive and realize creative projects in diverse artistic, community, and interdisciplinary settings, and acquire the skills to attract and cultivate new audiences. NAIP's core curriculum includes compulsory modules in arts leadership, arts entrepreneurship, audience engagement, and practice-based research, and offers students opportunities to specialize in ensemble conception, collaborative practice, or community engagement. As noted above, the study and practice of improvisation represents an essential component of these curricular requirements and specialization, and plays a key role in the collaborative creative process leading to a final master's thesis lecture recital project, in which students organize, program, manage, rehearse, and direct a performance in a nontraditional venue, then critically assess the strategies employed to attract and engage a new audience for their innovative practice. The ten-day intensive summer institutes, which bring together entering students from all participating institutions for an introduction to NAIP's core principles along with its international faculty, serve as microcosms of the program as a whole, by engaging students in collaborative self-directed creative projects that engage local artists, educators, and audience members in the communities where they take place.

At Minnesota, I worked with my fellow CSM faculty member Maja Radovanlija, who attended and jointly presented a series of improvisation workshops with me at the 2013 NAIP summer institute, to develop an ongoing collaborative creative initiative that could serve as a cornerstone of the proposed NAIP curriculum I drafted for UMN. In partnership with Experimental and Media Arts faculty member Diane Willow, we conceived Improvising Ecosystems to bring interdisciplinary student-faculty teams of musicians and artists together with environmental scientists and activists for on-site dialogues about ecological issues and processes that inspire collaborative interdisciplinary performance-installations. In our pilot project, *Sounds and Visions of Cedar Creek*, which emerged from a weekend creative retreat in fall 2013 at a university ecosystem science reserve, our team of twelve improvising musicians and artists explored ecological transformations in the liminal zone between prairie and forest, in works premiered at the UMN Institute on the Environment and Regis Center for Art. Our subsequent project *Cloquet: Disturbing Eco-Tones* gathered together an interdisciplinary team of fifteen faculty, staff, and students for a weekend creative retreat in fall 2014 at a university forestry center, interacting on-site with researchers investigating environmental issues such as climate change, as well as a guest artist-activist from the Ojibwe Fond du Lac reservation within whose borders the center is located. Drawing creative inspiration from the conceptual understandings and personal experiences with climate change gained on-site, this latest collaborative project not only found expression in an interdisciplinary performance-installation at the UMN Nash Gallery in fall 2014, but also opened a wider interdisciplinary conversation among academics, artists, activists, and ecological researchers throughout the 2014–15 year at Minnesota's Institute for Advanced Study.[19] In these initiatives, our community-engaged models of organization and practice "developed for the creation and nurturing of itinerant-institutional partnerships" along the lines of Lewis' recommendations have merged with "cross-cultural models of learning and teaching" to engender new "musical communities and social formations that presume the importance of improvisation" and have incorporated them into the academy.

Future Prospects for Transformational Improvisation

As indicated at the outset, these initiatives—however promising as case studies in improvisational pedagogy—represent incremental steps at best in the direction mapped out by Lewis and Kanellopoulos,[20] and have not transformed the overall institutional curriculum in any fundamental way. That said, my recent experiences, in opening up curricular spaces for holistically conceived, community-engaged, culturally cosmopolitan forms of improvisational agency that have challenged these structural constraints, give me reason to believe that the ethical dimensions of musical praxis foregrounded by these initiatives could play a key role in supporting the development of students' artistry in the near term, and perhaps help improve their long-term prospects for fulfilling careers in a professional world that may well increasingly demand well-honed talents for dealing creatively with unforeseen challenges and opportunities.[21]

Although unfamiliar and thus often intimidating at first for some, several of my students have reported finding the improvisational experience of taking creative responsibility for what they play empowering and even transformational in some significant respects, particularly insofar as it entails a substantial personal investment in the works performed (notated or not) and focuses their attention on the dynamic interdependence that ensemble members must foster and maintain through their mutually responsive contributions. Furthermore, I have found that framing these improvisational experiences in a global context, through comparative study of various cultural traditions, encourages students to identify with the creative challenges faced by artists whose formative professional development may well have taken place outside the bounds of Western conservatory-style training, and thus to appreciate the value of community-based forms of musical knowledge seldom acknowledged institutionally. Ultimately, I have come to believe, when such empowering, empathetic paradigms of creative practice acquire a deeper sense of purpose (e.g., through shared engagement with environmental issues uniting musicians with other artists, academics, and activists), improvisation can demonstrate how music can contribute to transformative social movements and even serve as a model for collective ethical action.

Notes

1. Lewis, "Improvisation and Pedagogy."
2. Ibid.
3. Lewis, "Teaching Improvised Music," 82.
4. Kanellopoulos, "Music Improvisation as Action," 106.
5. Heble and Waterman, "Sounds of Hope."
6. Ibid.
7. Sawyer, "Improvisation and Teaching."
8. Patricia Campbell's observation that "[e]ngaged as they are in developing expertise in Western art music, music majors in universities, colleges, and conservatories are rarely required to study improvisation as a separate course" ("Learning to Improvise Music," 132) aptly sums up the fundamental challenge faced by advocates for improvisation studies within conventional academic curricula.
9. These initiatives stem in many important respects from the example, impetus, guidance, and support for curricular innovation provided by David Myers, Professor of Music Education and Director of the UMN School of Music, 2008–2014.
10. The task force's membership included Erkki Huovinen (musicology/music theory), Guerino Mazzola (music theory/composition), Eugene Rousseau (saxophone), Todd Snead (music education), Dean Sorenson (jazz ensembles), and Wendy Zaro-Mullins (vocals)—all of whom contributed significantly to the conceptualizations and recommendations summarized below.
11. See, for example, recent work by Nicholls (*An Ethics of Improvisation*) and Fischlin, Heble, and Lipsitz (*The Fierce Urgency of Now*), in addition to the above cited work by Lewis ("Teaching Improvised Music") and Kanellopoulos ("Musical Improvisation as Action").
12. Lewis, "Improvisation and Pedagogy."
13. A philosophy of community engagement informed and guided our efforts toward the cultivation of mutually enriching itinerant-institutional relationships with distinguished local artists based on shared respect and reciprocity. Showcasing in this manner musical traditions not ordinarily represented in our school's primarily Euro-American classically oriented curriculum also served to foreground issues of cultural diversity and equity, while demonstrating the parochiality of this dominant tradition's relative neglect and marginalization of improvisational forms of music making.
14. We are greatly indebted to our outstanding roster of participating guest artists, including Damian Rodriguez (Afro-Cuban son), Rex Richardson (modern jazz), Bassam Saba (Arab maqam), Pooja and Allalaghatta Pavan (Hindustani raga), Jacqueline Schwab (contemporary Americana), Eliezer Freitas Santos (Afro-Brazilian samba), Robert Robinson (African American gospel), Eyman and Denise Gürtan (Turkish makam), and Nirmala Rajasekar (Karnatak raga). We also gratefully acknowledge the support we received from the School of Music, its Community Engagement Leadership Team, and the UMN Institute for Global Studies that made these events possible.
15. Lewis, "Improvisation and Pedagogy."
16. We greatly appreciate the inspiring contributions of our talented roster of guest artist-presenters, including Maria Schneider (modern-jazz composition), Bassam Saba (Arab taqsim/çiftetelli), and Michael Sullivan (Ojibwe powwow/round dance), along with the funding from the School of Music and its Community Engagement Leadership Team that made these events possible.
17. Lewis, "Improvisation and Pedagogy."

18. At the time, NAIP's full-partner roster of participating institutions included the Iceland Academy of the Arts (Reykjavik, Iceland), the Royal Conservatory (The Hague, Netherlands), the Prince Claus Conservatory (Groningen, Netherlands), and the Royal College of Music (Stockholm, Sweden).

19. This initiative, made possible by grant funding from the UMN Institute on the Environment and Institute for Advanced Study, has benefitted greatly from the much appreciated contributions of Ojibwe musician-educator and Minnesota Public Radio artist-in-residence Lyz Jaakola, improvisational artist-educator and Association for the Advancement of Creative Musicians member Douglas Ewart, and our new UMN team member Matthew Tucker of the Department of Landscape Architecture.

20. Lewis, "Teaching Improvised Music"; Kanellopoulos, "Musical Improvisation as Action."

21. In the wake of the Minnesota Orchestra management's fifteen-month (2012–14) lockout of their unionized musicians in order to extract salary and work-rule concessions—"the longest work stoppage for any symphonic orchestra in U.S. history" (Royce, "Three-Year Minnesota Orchestra")—and the wave of orchestral bankruptcies following the 2008 financial crisis, it has become increasingly difficult for even the most optimistic UMN music students to bank on the prospects for the sort of stable salaried employment that orchestral careers once offered. The consequent paradigm shift toward the pursuit of "portfolio careers" essentially demands that young musicians strategize their professional development improvisationally, rather than merely following and reproducing established models of practice.

Works Cited

Campbell, Patricia Shehan. "Learning to Improvise Music, Improvising to Learn Music." In *Musical Improvisation: Art, Education, and Society*, edited by Gabriel Solis and Bruno Nettl, 119–42. Urbana: University of Illinois Press, 2009.

Fischlin, Daniel, Ajay Heble, and George Lipsitz. *The Fierce Urgency of Now: Improvisation, Rights, and the Ethics of Cocreation*. Durham, NC: Duke University Press. 2013.

Heble, Ajay, and Ellen Waterman. "Sounds of Hope, Sounds of Change: Improvisation, Pedagogy, Social Justice." *Critical Studies in Improvisation/Études critiques en improvisation* 3, no. 2 (2008).

Kanellopoulos, Panagiotis A. "Musical Improvisation as Action: An Arendtian Perspective." *Action, Criticism, and Theory for Music Education* 6, no. 3 (2007): 97–127.

Lewis, George E. "Teaching Improvised Music: An Ethnographic Memoir." In *Arcana: Musicians on Music*, edited by John Zorn, 78–109. New York: Granary Books/Hips Road, 2000.

———. "Improvisation and Pedagogy: Background and Focus of Inquiry." *Critical Studies in Improvisation/Études critiques en improvisation* 3, no. 2 (2008).

Nicholls, Tracey. *An Ethics of Improvisation: Aesthetic Possibilities for a Political Future*. Lanham, MD: Lexington Books/Rowman & Littlefield, 2012.

Royce, Graydon. "Three-Year Minnesota Orchestra Deal Ends 15-Month Lockout." [*Minneapolis*] *Star Tribune*. January 18, 2014. http://www.startribune.com/entertainment/music/240153421.html.

Sawyer, R. Keith. "Improvisation and Teaching." *Critical Studies in Improvisation/Études critiques en improvisation* 3, no. 2 (2008).

12 Teaching the "Compleat Musician"

Contemporary Improvisation at New England Conservatory

Tanya Kalmanovitch

> "For let us be clear about one thing: The conservatory is a very special kind of musical institution in our society."
> —Gunther Schuller, "The Compleat Musician in the Complete Conservatory"

Introduction

My encounter with the pedagogy of improvisation began eight years ago, in the fall of 2006. I was newly hired by the Contemporary Improvisation department at New England Conservatory (NEC), one of the world's great music schools and, for several decades now, one of the world's most progressive. During his tenure as president of NEC from 1967 to 1977, the musical polymath Gunther Schuller instigated a series of reforms that hung on a single, radical proposition: that a music conservatory should admit all of the world's musical languages.[1]

A school for "all musical languages" is a vast and quixotic project: it is an aspiration more than it can be an accomplishment. Yet the structures that Schuller put in place—according contemporary music equal status to the classical canon, creating programs that extended the concert stage to the surrounding communities, enhancing the place of African American music and musicians in the conservatory, and establishing two departments dedicated to improvised music—have served in subsequent decades to sustain a rich and unparalleled institutional culture. Schuller launched his presidency during NEC's Centennial with a symposium, "The Conservatory Redefined." In an address to the symposium, he outlined the dimensions of "total" or "complete musician": a musician with an expansive range and depth of musical perception, a sharp and focused instrumental capacity, a broad general intellectual horizon, and "the tools by which [the musician] can live a life in music which is rich, meaningful and rewarding—and not only monetarily rewarding—and not mere drudgery, as is so often the case."[2]

When Schuller opened the Jazz Studies department in 1969, NEC became the first major classical music school to admit Black music and musical improvisation into the academy. Three years later, he further broadened the school's musical scope by establishing the Third Stream department under the direction of pianist and improviser Ran Blake. "Third Stream" was a term that Schuller originally coined to describe the confluence of classical and jazz music. Understood as a musical process rather than as a genre, however, Third Stream was porous enough to admit any musical language.[3] The department changed its name to "Contemporary Improvisation" in the 1990s, and under later chairs Ken Schaphorst, Allan Chase, and Hankus Netsky, the department expanded its enrollment and offerings.

In this chapter, I chronicle how teaching in the particular environment of New England Conservatory came to shape my thinking about music, music education, and the model of the professional musician. I evaluate the Contemporary Improvisation program as it enters its fifth decade: How does the department realize a utopian premise of a world without musical boundaries? Finally, I discuss how my own approach to a pedagogy of improvisation evolved in relationship with discussions in my entrepreneurship classes, and assess how the NEC's model can fit an ever-changing context for professional employment.

Arriving at the Conservatory

In his 1967 address, Schuller outlined the dilemma facing the conservatory: "how to reconcile the conservatory's basically conservative, tradition-perpetuating function with its other obligation to constantly re-evaluate those traditions, lest the conservatory become merely a museum."[4] Four decades later, NEC maintains a tense balance between its status as a site of tradition and an engine of innovation. It is audible in the sounds of jazz quartets and string quartets overlapping in halls lined with practice rooms; visible in an imposing bronze statue of Beethoven at the foot of a marble staircase in Jordan Hall; and palpable in rehearsal rooms with scarred walls and strands of carpet pulled loose, as though worn from students' collective labors in sound. My first students were classical musicians enrolled in a new nonmajors' improvisation ensemble. They brought diverse influences to our group—works by Giacinto Scelsi, John Cage, Palestrina, John Zorn, and Scriabin—that we reinterpreted though improvisation. It seemed that I had arrived in a place where there were truly no musical boundaries, where the full range of my musical experiences could be put to effective use.

The effect, at first, was exhilarating. As a violist studying at the Juilliard School in the late 1980s, I encountered the scope of New York City's music scene with a similar kind of breathlessness. But my teachers at Juilliard seemed to view my interest in improvising as a kind of betrayal at worst, and at best a distraction from the real business of becoming a Serious Musician. I never felt at home in the narrow band of the viola repertoire, and I was drawn to improvisation as a natural and essential expression of my musicianship. As I explored improvisation in the coming years, I was able to build strong personal and professional relationships in multiple styles, expanding my range as performer. But within what I came to claim as my own community—musicians who identified as jazz musicians and free improvisers—I encountered still more barriers: different conceptions of what counts for "free" in improvisation, subtle markers of style and genre, barriers of gender, instrument and social class, and performance contexts that seemed to lack the minute sensitivity to context, collaboration, and nuance that I loved in classical music.

The "I-Word"

A violist entering Juilliard today would have a rather different experience to my own of twenty-five years ago. Presently, improvisation is enjoying something of a renaissance in Western art music, and this volume is evidence of a welcome expansion in the conversation about improvisation and music pedagogy. But "improvisation" is an expansive term upon which a great many things can be projected. Despite its ubiquity, the term remains largely unexamined in the context of music education. What improvisation is, and what improvisers do, is not always clearly understood.

In part, this is because language is stubbornly inadequate to the task of representing the kinds of things we can know through musical practice. Whenever I describe myself as an "improviser," or a teacher of "improvisation," I experience a twinge of uncertainty, because "improvisation" is not a neutral term. "Improvisation," when used in Western music, implies an unnecessary conflict: between the authority and substance of musical texts, on one hand, and on the other, an idealized notion of musical freedom, sometimes conflated with exoticized concepts of non-Western musical practice. (It's for these reasons, in part, that my colleague Robert Labaree playfully and seriously treats "improvisation" as a four-letter word, and substitutes the term "I-word."[5])

It's also because a renewed interest in improvisation emerges at a time when conservatories are challenged again to defend the role of professional music education in the face of changing professional models. A conservatory is a specialized training school with an explicit focus on preparing students for professional careers as performers and composers. Accordingly, conservatory curricula emphasize performance over general education. Conservatories advance a notion of music as being of central importance to the human condition, while carefully policing the boundaries of their musical environment—a condition that, over the course of my time at NEC, became a source of conflict and fascination.

Another source of conflict arises from the very definition of a "professional musician." The conservatory model of professionalism is generally a twentieth-century model: a musician is someone whose primary income is derived from rehearsing, performing, and occasionally teaching music. In the twenty-first century, this professional path seems increasingly uncertain. At a time of declining professional opportunity and sharply rising educational costs, "improvisation" joins other constructions—the musician as "entrepreneur," the "citizen musician," the "post-genre musician," the "composer/performer/improviser," and "the twenty-first-century musician"—that aim to expand the notion of what a professional musician can be and do in the world. These are welcome developments, but they contain a kernel of unspoken fear: individual fears about music's social relevance and economic impact, and institutional fears about the viability of a professional training school. An expansive concept of a Serious Musician—as a creative agent, as a force for social good, as an agent of his or her own opportunity— is without a doubt a Good Thing. But in order to speak to the kernel of fear, we need to develop a new concept of the professional musician.

Currently, these issues occupy an unsteady place in the conservatory. Consistent with its culture of innovation, NEC was among the first American conservatories to take seriously the issue of its students' professional development.[6] In 2010, my role at NEC expanded to include teaching in NEC's newly opened department of Entrepreneurial Musicianship. These classes afforded me a crucial second space from which to consider my status as an artist, teacher, and improviser. In my classes, we engaged in conversations that didn't seem to be regularly taking place elsewhere in the school. We talked openly about the value of music, and the personal values that drove us all into investment in conservatory training. These conversations rekindled feelings of wonder, possibility, and connection—the feelings that had originally brought me into the music profession. At the same time, my students posed questions that I could not easily answer: Will I have a job after I graduate? Is there an audience for the music I love? Does my music matter to anyone else but me? These questions unfolded in parallel with the questions I asked myself as I entered the middle years of my career, almost wholly dependent on the conservatory for my income.

When I joined the Contemporary Improvisation faculty, I felt as though I had arrived. As a young, female improvising musician, I had spent my professional life at various musical barricades: genre, gender, practice, and professional community. Joining the faculty at NEC—a place where great artists like Steve Lacy, Jimmy Giuffre, and Paul Bley had taught—conferred a legitimacy that my career had previously lacked. It not only gave me credibility among my peers, it allowed me access to a new set of collaborators and conversations. What felt like an arrival was, in fact, a point of departure as I began to grapple with issues that arise from improvisation's volatile relationship to professional success.

NEC's Contemporary Improvisation Program

In remarks at a 2011 preconcert discussion honoring late faculty member Joe Maneri, Gunther Schuller said, "I feel that my vision for this department has now been realized."[7] Currently, the department occupies an intentionally ambiguous place with respect to genre, process, and cultural location. Presently, the department has 48 students: among them are instrumentalists and composers from a range of classical and traditional music backgrounds, including Syrian, Korean, and Indian music. Students receive their instrumental training across the divides of instrument and department—a fiddler might take lessons from a classical musician one semester, and a sitarist the next. Ensembles explore a defined repertoire (e.g., American Roots Ensemble, World Music Ensemble, or Jewish Music Ensemble), or explore musical processes and the development of original works (e.g., my own Composition/Improvisation ensemble, the Songwriters' Workshop, or Anthony Coleman's Survivor's Breakfast).

The original concept of "Third Stream" permeates the department's program design and curricula, reflecting a set of practices that were set into play by Ran Blake during nearly four decades as the department's chair. At heart, the program is concerned with fostering the development of an individual musician's personal voice through aural transmission, and the synthesis of multiple musical styles. A premise of "all musical languages" is translated to a skills-based curriculum that inscribes "improvisation" with exceptional properties. In remarks on the CI department's website, Chair Hankus Netsky defines "Contemporary Improvisation" as a term that "liberates the idea of improvisation from any specific genre."[8] He advances the model of the "composer/performer/improviser" as a modern musician whose skills can deftly slice through musical difference to accomplish "what musicians have already been doing for years"—to negotiate musical difference and to uncover an individual voice. Expanding on Schuller's notion of a "complete musician," Netsky says, "We have entered an era when musical labels mean less and less and each individual musician draws on multiple influences to define who they are."[9]

That an artistic project of "all musical languages," "multiple influences," and "personal voice" unfolds within the context of a music conservatory poses both problems and possibilities. In the classical music conservatory setting, students' progress is evaluated through processes (auditions, juries, and course grades) that measure students' performance against a common set of artistic standards linked to instrumental repertoire or canon. In the Contemporary Improvisation department, however, the ideal is that instruments are liberated from their traditional roles, and personal processes replace musical texts. How can "all musical languages" be taught and evaluated? How can authority be measured in the general absence of musical texts? How can "personal voice" be taught, and assigned a grade? Expanding on Blake's core program, the department has evolved a number of systems that create a productive, if sometimes imperfect, environment in which to negotiate solutions to these problems.

First, the fact that the Contemporary Improvisation program takes place in the setting of a Western music conservatory introduces a degree of enclosure. Consistent with the role of jazz in the original Third Stream construction, core curricula tend to privilege Western- over non-Western musical materials, in particular those from twentieth-century African

American styles. This mandates a basic degree of aural skills (interval and pitch recognition), English-language skills, and a basic measure of literacy in Western music notation. Admitted students tend to display at least a basic level of skills in these areas that allows them to function productively in classes and ensembles.

The problem of "all musical languages" is resolved rhetorically by "liberating" improvisation from genre and privileging aural transmission over notation. This conceptual and practical move diverts the departmental focus from musical style, and establishes a core project of cultivating individual artistic voices unlimited by a single stylistic identity. A brief program description for the core course "The Development of Personal Style" outlines how individual voice is thought to emerge:

> As you master basic ear skills, the Contemporary Improvisation program of studies becomes more flexible and becomes tailored to your individual needs. You will begin to define yourself by choosing the artists or styles most germane to your musical personality then, through deep aural absorption of your chosen musical roots, a synthesis becomes possible, and a musical self-portrait will begin to emerge in your improvisations.[10]

Personal voice, then, emerges as a natural consequence of deep experience: it is a kind of musical autobiography, reflecting an individual musician's most meaningful influences. Although this formulation seems to suggest that personal voice is a fixed notion, it is a spacious enough construction to accommodate and negotiate musical difference, artistic development, and the multiple and constructed nature of musical identities.

The CI program also promotes students' reflexive self-awareness through a range of administrative features. Throughout their programs, CI students are asked to think critically about the impact of their assumptions, values, choices, processes, and actions. In auditions, students are asked to bring a recomposition of a preexisting piece that "uses an existing composition as a point of departure to express your personal musical style." Admitted students are free to choose from a wide range of studio teachers, not limited by instrumental major or department.[11] Students are required to reflect on their choices throughout the program, activating a sense of ownership over their own education and artistic development. In the year-end "promotional" (NEC's term for a performance jury), Contemporary Improvisation students are asked to submit a personal essay in which they reflect on their work in their entire program, and develop a plan for the coming year. Finally, the department's themed concerts involve a significant workshop component, an environment in which artistic choices and processes are openly supported and negotiated.

Negotiation also forms a significant part of the student evaluation process. A broad range of faculty takes part in the department's audition and jury committees. As different points of view come into contact, they are subject to a process of discussion and negotiation. Despite committee members' diverging artistic practices and personal opinions, a surprising degree of accord arises from a shared commitment to developing students' authentic voices. A tacit agreement privileges personal authenticity over instrumental proficiency or stylistic command: a successful student performance is one in which the students' intentions can be clearly "read" by its evaluators and audience.

All of this is facilitated by the fact that CI activities take place in an institutional setting that permits an unusual degree of movement between departments. Students collaborate with peers outside their departments, and movement between jazz, classical, and CI departments is surprisingly fluid: it is not uncommon for students outside the CI department to take active roles in CI concerts and ensembles. This transdepartmental movement is not unique to the CI department: NEC's classical composition department, for example, is another complex community with relationships to the jazz, CI, Liberal Arts, and classical performance departments. The fact that these different programs operate largely in isolation but in close proximity presents opportunities: even areas of friction are often productive for new understanding.

Can You Teach "Improvisation"?

By establishing "personal voice" as a central project, the Contemporary Improvisation department is successful in bringing essential questions of twenty-first-century musicianship to the fore. I have great affection and respect for the seriousness of intent with which my students approach their work—as though novitiates to a priesthood—and for the surprising generosity with which my colleagues enjoin and encourage them in this process. The culture of the conservatory is one in which students and teachers see themselves engaged in work that is somehow *more* than work: it is not a stretch to suggest that their work is more of a calling. However, over time I began to perceive an inherent tension between the conservatory's twin projects of cultivating personal voice, and cultivating professional success.

In the meritocratic context of the conservatory, the value of students' work is measured primarily through excellence in performance and external professional recognition. Yet "improvised music" comprises a broad range of musical styles and professional communities, each with different status in the marketplace and different patronage structures. In terms of pedagogy and professional development, then, it can be misleading to speak of "improvisation" as a singular noun. Can you teach "improvisation"? Can you train professional "improvisers"?

In working my way through these questions, it became necessary for me to separate several strands of the professional training project: (1) engineering music: the business of transmitting instrumental performance skills, improvisatory skills, compositional skills, stylistic vocabularies, and competencies in directing musical performance; (2) defining an individual voice: establishing a unique identity and core set of artistic concerns; (3) determining a professional path: examining the relationship of one's music to an existing market, and discovering the best options for balancing time, energy, and income to support an artistic life; and (4) defining music's inherent value: finding the language to speak about the value of one's musical work, and the impacts it can make in a community. My work in the Contemporary Improvisation department capably served these first two points, but it was through teaching entrepreneurship classes that I began to address the latter two. Over time, my work in entrepreneurship came to complement my performance pedagogy, and these twin platforms have offered a productive space in which to understand each of these threads individually and integrally.

My colleagues have their own approaches to answering these questions— as individual teachers and as participants in a constantly evolving departmental conversation that deserves more detailed treatment than the scope of this essay can allow. In place of a more substantial treatment of the department's pedagogies, I wish to offer an overview of my own approach to teaching improvising musicians. Over the course of my time at NEC, my teaching has undergone a substantial shift from a model of pedagogy rooted in professional competency (skills and stylistic competencies), toward a pedagogy rooted in personal agency. Such a pedagogy is an effortful and intentional one, not without its own vulnerabilities and hesitations: it involves a substantial shift in the frame of reference: from the student as a processor of musical styles, to the student as a musical, human being.[12]

Understanding Personal Choice

In classroom and performance teaching, I believe that the strongest contribution an educator can make is to help students understand the basic materials they're working with, and to expand their capacity to make choices about their best use.

Studio teaching and ensemble coaching is focused mainly on musical engineering: the frame of live performance introduces a sharp focus on *how* and *why* you make musical choices, and *what* the best ways are to realize your ideas. In this context, I teach improvisation by calling the deceptively simple building blocks of music into heightened awareness: expanding concepts like time, space, pitch, intervals, timbre, and articulation to introduce a sense of infinite variety and possibility. Mastering any one of these arenas requires a substantial degree of time and effort. This is demanding work because it strips music down to its fundamentals. There is little to "do" and "practice" but music itself.

In contrast to methodological or repertoire-driven approaches to teaching improvisation, I rely on comparatively little textual material. Instead, through performance and discussion, I guide students in examining these foundational materials, and understanding their own internal limitation in their use. The most difficult questions students face are also the most basic: What is the sound that only I can make? What is the music that sounds like me? What sound do I wish to make now?

In entrepreneurship classes, I use the same process to examine the basic assumptions that we bring to our musical lives. In addition to the questions listed above, I invite students to examine questions such as: What is my definition of success and failure? What tacit understandings of success have I inherited, and how can I tell the difference between what I believe and what others believe for me? What is a professional musician? What is an artist? How are these roles defined in our culture and in the professional market? How do I wish to define these roles for myself? What is my definition of a life worth living?

Cultivating Personal Agency

In teaching entrepreneurship, I see my primary role as cultivating students' sense of personal agency—their capacity to act in the world, to think for themselves, and to advocate for their own development. In class assignments, discussions, and lectures, I move students from the role of passive recipients to active agents of their musical lives.

The same orientation informs my approach to teaching performance. In teaching performance, however, cultural and institutional forces shape the relationship between student and teacher as an inherently asymmetrical one. The NEC website presents the studio teacher as "an artist who embodies a rich musical tradition" who will "challenge you to master your art through rigorous practice and performance."[13] As mentors, then, studio teachers occupy an intimate psychological space on a spectrum from kindly psychotherapist to Svengali. Students and teachers alike approach studio lessons with great expectations.

Considering the breadth of the Contemporary Improvisation program, I initially experienced my role as studio teacher as a somewhat uncomfortable one. The Contemporary Improvisation department's practice of encouraging multiple studio assignments carried a benefit of distributing the responsibility for "all musical languages" among several primary teachers, but it also limited the time available to explore the complex and lengthy processes of musical development. I came to address this by reframing my approach: from competencies-based practice, toward a layered approach of musical work and reflective practices. Over time, I came to see my work teaching improvisation not as a task conveying a specific tradition, but as introducing students to processes of self-realization. My lessons took on a holistic character: along with intensive work on improvisation, I assessed students' developing artistic direction and their progress through their programs. At times, what I asked them to practice was something musical—a specific exercise designed to cultivate a certain kind of musical awareness. Just as often, my assignments were practical in nature, as when I've asked students to actively cultivate collaborative relationships outside of their assigned ensembles, or to establish a clear set of goals for their musical, personal, and professional development over the course of a semester.

Active Listening

Active listening informs the curriculum of my entrepreneurship and performance teaching alike. Music is, in its essence, a communicative act; and communication involves both sending and receiving meaningful information.

In studio classes and ensembles, I advance active listening as a crucial musical skill, crucial to developing a shared sense of meaning—among performers, and between performers and their audiences. I often speak of listening as a form of mindfulness practice. For example, I might ask students to work on solo improvisation focusing only on one note at a time, proceeding to the note only when its intention is fully present to them. This exercise can cultivate an awareness of the impulses, doubts, and hesitations that arise around the task making one's own sound, as well as a sense of the infinite possibilities that exist in the spaces between notes.

In ensemble performance, the problems and possibilities in this exercise are compounded exponentially as students consider their own emerging voices in the context of others'. Contemporary Improvisation ensembles are by default diverse ones: students arrive with different experiences, and sometimes-conflicting aesthetic and professional goals. Any successful ensemble performance requires an almost alchemical process of forming a whole out of a set of individual parts, a process that requires a substantial investment from all involved. I inspire students to develop a sense of respect and commitment to this process by invoking a notion of the ensemble as an intentional community.

For example, the moment before beginning an improvisation is an anxious one for many students. Their collective improvisations often begin haphazardly, with one musician arbitrarily breaking the silence with his or her sound. I reframe this moment as a potent one: an entry into a ritual space that is pregnant with all possibility. I instruct students to enter this space intentionally and with great respect. I teach students to become comfortable with musical silences, moments that allow us to absorb what has happened, and that will inform what comes next. I discuss musical endings: how to become as attentive to how things end as to how they begin.

Breaking Down the Walls of the School

In all my teaching, I look for ways to expand the walls of the studio, classroom, and rehearsal room to encompass the entire school and students' own communities. My approach to teaching is shaped by a drive to relate musical performance to social issues in ways that show clear artistic, practical, and professional impact. I encourage students to see their education as continuous with their lives before and after school: reflecting on the motivations that brought them to this point, and will drive them into an expanded sense of the place of the musician as an active agent of positive change in the world.

I frequently invite other faculty members to my classes and ensembles, as auditors, as guest teachers, and as collaborators in the teaching process: in so doing, I encourage students to understand the full range of possibility in the school as a learning community. In my entrepreneurship classes, I often work one-on-one with students on individual projects that take root in class and flourish after the semester. Among these are tours and teaching residencies in the Middle East, Central Asia, and the Caribbean; a crowd-funded album of original music for electric guitar quartet inspired by histories of Japanese internment camps; and a residential farm in Massachusetts that blends music education with awareness of sustainable agriculture. With the cooperation of students and faculty at NEC, I developed a partnership with the Afghanistan National Institute of Music in Kabul (ANIM) and NEC. Over three years, this project yielded several faculty/student exchanges, a Boston residency for ANIM's orchestra, and full-time employment for several NEC alumni.

Summary

Over the past several years, my teaching and improvising alike have come to be informed by the same goal: to advance an understanding of live music as a catalyst for human development. In my entrepreneurship classes I guide students in understanding their invisible, essential qualities as persons and musicians, and I support them in building musical careers that are strongly tied to a sense of mission. What counts for success is not external recognition, after all, but the continual expression of our highest skills and deepest values. Success in improvised music, similarly, rests not on technical virtuosity, experience, or pedigree; rather, it depends on the degree to which a musician can find his or her own voice—to borrow my collaborator Mat Maneri's evocative phrase, "one's secret melody"—and share this with others in its fullest expression. In this, I see a direct connection between improvisation and human development. Improvisation is an endlessly enriching interaction, a form of play as most serious work.

When I first began working at NEC, I had the sense that the school's reputation was conferring a great value on my own career. Over the past several years, however, my work there has had an unexpected effect, that of moving my notion of success from an external location to a personal location. NEC has offered me access to an extraordinary set of cultural resources, and a broad platform from which to develop my work. Through teaching, I have reestablished a sense of music's value in immanently human, rather than distantly aesthetic, terms. My work at NEC has also cultivated a sense of the music school as an artistic community in its own right: as a potent site in which to *do* music itself. The music profession tends to assign a subsidiary role to teaching, but I have come to see teaching as continuous with performance and with my ongoing artistic development. Ultimately, I've come to see the conservatory in its essence: as an intentional community oriented, at its best, around bringing out the full human potential of all its members.

Notes

1. With a musical identity spread over multiple domains, Schuller (1925–2015) was active as a composer in both classical music and jazz, and as a musicologist, historian, and administrator. His career embodied a progressive concept of what a musician can be.
2. Schuller, "The Compleat Musician," 242.
3. "Third Stream" has often been described by jazz historians as a genre, but "streaming" might be better understood as a process by which different musical languages meet and mingle.
4. Schuller, "The Compleat Musician," 238.
5. Robert Labaree, "Living with the I-Word."
6. Under the direction of Angela Beeching, NEC's Office of Career Development set a benchmark in supporting students' engagement with their professional lives outside the conservatory.
7. New England Conservatory, "Contemporary Improvisation Program at NEC."
8. Hankus Netsky, "Contemporary Improvisation," *New England Conservatory.* Available at http://necmusic.edu/contemporary-improvisation.
9. New England Conservatory, "Contemporary Improvisation Program at NEC."
10. New England Conservatory, "Contemporary Improvisation."
11. NEC defines a studio teacher as a mentor "who guides your progression as a musician and your journey through the literature, traditions and pedagogy of your major" (New England Conservatory, "Degree Requirements"). Unlike classical majors, whose primary relationship is to their studio teacher, CI students typically work with a number of different studio teachers during the course of a degree program, including teachers from other departments.
12. In this, I am inspired by the quote attributed to cellist Pablo Casals: "I am a human being first, a musician second, and cellist third."
13. New England Conservatory, "Faculty."

Works Cited

Larabee, Robert. "Living with the I-Word: Improvisation and Its Alternates." *Critical Studies in Improvisation/Études critiques en improvisation* 9, no. 2 (2013). http://www.criticalimprov.com/article/view/2204.
New England Conservatory. "Contemporary Improvisation." 2013. http://necmusic.edu/contemporary-improvisation.
———. "Contemporary Improvisation Program at NEC." July 2013. http://necmusic.edu/pdf/aboutnec/press/Contemporary_Improvisation.pdf.
———. "Degree Requirements." 2010. http://necmusic.edu/composition/degree-requirements.
———. "Faculty." http://necmusic.edu/faculty.
Schuller, Gunther. "The Compleat Musician in the Complete Conservatory." In *Musings: The Musical World of Gunther Schuller*, 237–46. New York: Oxford University Press, 1986.

13 Becoming Music
Building Castles with Sound

William Parker

This chapter is based on Parker's talk at the Summit on Improvisation, Pedagogy, and Community Impact, presented by the Improvisation, Community, and Social Practice (ICASP) project on May 23, 2013, at Boarding House for the Arts in Guelph, Ontario, Canada. Parker here discusses his life in music, describing the process through which he learned to make music and find his voice in New York in the 1970s. Crucially, he reminds us to anchor theories of pedagogy in the language and logic of practice, observing that "improvisation" was not an operative term in the community that taught him how to "just play."

I've been involved in creative music since about 1971, that is, as a participating musician and not just as a listener. You listen and the music speaks to you. It was collecting in my heart and soul. I wanted to participate. I was black and I had a sense of spirituality. I knew inside that I could make a contribution to the world of not just music but black revolutionary fire music.

The first thing is to get an invitation from the music itself to be invited into its house. To develop a relationship with it as a living thing outside of oneself, as something you can feel, like the wind, but you can only see when it moves something. Then you can enter the rooms in this house of music. The context—the aesthetic—that music is spiritual and political, and that the desired purpose of music is to heal, uplift, and change lives, invigorates and stimulates the soul and spirit. The side effect of music is to elevate the mind from intelligence to wisdom, filling all listeners with a greater sense of compassion. Then establish the parameters of that existence. One of the first things that is established is the acknowledgement that humans did not invent music. Music existed before we got here. It is a force, a living spirit that is found in all creation. What's important is not necessarily learning *how to play* music, but rather *how to become* music. Finding one's place-ment and role in the world called music, in other words, is not about making sound on instruments. Music is the art of living. It is, I believe, the key to discovering the essence of life.

Okay, why do you play music? Can you play a tree or mountain? Can you play the wind? John Coltrane said that in 1957 he received a spiritual awakening and that he wanted to devote his life to playing music to heal and uplift people from one state to another state. So that's the purpose. That is the reason music exists. Music is the healing force of the universe. So music could be a conduit or could heal people. And that is the reason I stepped into the field of music, because I felt I couldn't do anything else. I felt that this is what I could do.

So then how do you get from A to Z? What do you do? I took some lessons. Everyone said well, you know, you studied with Richard Davis, with Jimmy Garrison, with Wilbur Ware, Milt Hinton, with Art Davis. Did you learn anything? Well I studied with these guys, whether I learned something? I don't know. In 1973 I went to Cecil Taylor's house at 96 Chamber Street. I went to 131 Prince Street in Soho where Ornette Coleman lived. It was called Artists House. Ornette would always let you in and talk. He would let you into his concerts for free. So what do you learn about improvisation from hanging out with Ornette Coleman? You learn that it's wonderful.

Then I started to write music reviews. Once I went to the public Library on 125th Street to listen to the Karl Berger Quartet. That was Karl Berger (vibes), Carlos Ward (alto sax), Horace Arnold (drums), and Charlie Haden (bass). The concert was great. Afterward I gave Charlie a first draft of my manuscript *Document Humanum*. Charlie told me certain things to do to get into bass playing, while at Cecil's loft I was invited to come to his big band rehearsals, which took place every evening. There was a concert coming up at Carnegie Hall, and at the same time I'm going daily to Studio We at 193 Eldridge Street. Many musicians were passing through there: Frank Lowe, Daniel Carter, Juma Sultan, Sonny Donaldson, Marzette Watts, Archie Shepp, Dave Burrell, and all kinds of creative beings from all over the place. Most of them will never be included in any of the history books. Musicians like Clemson Parker, Freddie J. Williams, Eugene Mohammed, Hassan Dawkins, Hasan Hakim, Ali Abuwi, and Jimmy Vass, they all were great musicians. So I was around all these musicians whose records I listened to and they weren't talking about improvisation. They were talking about, "come on and play."

In 1975 I met Don Cherry. He said "come play with me at the Five Spot," so I go and play. Okay, now did Don Cherry ever hear me play the bass? No. But he said, "You've got the vibe. Come on and play." He didn't audition me. We didn't rehearse. Billy Higgins, Ed Blackwell, Frank Lowe, and Hakim Jami were all in the band. They didn't talk improvisation either.

Okay so, in December 1980, Cecil gives me a call and says, "Come down, I want you to join the unit." So, from 1980 to 1991, I played with Cecil Taylor. Now, during that time, around 1982, through the bassist Peter Kowald, I got involved with European improvisers from Germany, England, France, Holland, and Italy. Han Bennink, Evan Parker, Peter Brötzmann, Tony Oxley, Connie Bauer, Enrico Rava, Derek Bailey, and many others. So I started going to Europe. Much of this work came through an organization called Free Music Produktion (FMP) and that was the first time I heard the word *improvisation*. You know, Americans, we didn't use the word *improvisation*, we just called it black music, or whatever you wanted to call it. But that was the first time I heard the words "improvised music." And then they started talking about Free Music and improvised music, and then I realized that a parallel music was taking place in New York. It was called new music or music associated with the downtown scene. It was all different music. Each musician had a different sensibility and aesthetic. There were as many ways to improvise as there were to speak. There were many languages of improvisation all spoken in different accents and voices. They were kind of talking about improvisation. I was lucky enough to cross paths with all kinds of musicians, the musicians from the Bronx who are totally home grown, the folk musicians from Cuba, space and experimental musicians, singers, dancers, and blues-based musicians; I even played with a composer who wrote a piece for whistling tea pots. Everyone had his or her idea of music.

You could go to Bennington College and study with Bill Dixon or Milford Graves, but the best way to really learn was to play, play, and play. No matter who you studied with you had to face the music one on one with yourself. To skip ahead, I eventually met Hamid Drake and Fred Anderson and we hit it off immediately and began to develop a very close and creative relationship. The basic difference between black musicians from Chicago and black musicians from New York is that the Chicago musicians were entrusted with the concept that they were composers and composers make more money than improvisers. What they forgot is that they were still black in music, and they were in a world that was not controlled by black people. And the part that is controlled by black people is really controlled by white people and did not want to include "Great Black Music."

What a wonderful phrase, "Great Black Music." I began to play with some of the musicians from Chicago: Henry Threadgill, Muhal Richard Abrams, Roscoe Mitchell, and Anthony Braxton. They had different ideas and ways of putting music together as indeed they should. I had also played with Joseph Jarman in 1973 at the Artists House. All the music was quite amazing. Every person I met was like a school unto itself and every gig a *class* in improvisation. Not one person had the same concept. Frank Wright was different from Daniel Carter and Daniel was different from Byard Lancaster. You know, and it was about the music, building castles with sound, that could be the description of improvisation.

These last years I was teaching a little bit over at the New School. I get all sorts of students, saxophone students, drum students, and piano students. I would ask the students, "Have you heard of Sunny Murray or Jimmy Lyons?" and their faces would be blank. Creative music is basically any music that has been personalized to fit the system of music and aesthetics: the musician who is playing that music without following popular trends. Then I found out that the information about who we are and what we do has not been properly taught or documented. So I began cataloguing what I was doing and what I had learned getting closer to the realization of my destiny.

It's good that everyone is speaking and coming together because everyone has a different idea about things. People's lives can be enhanced by learning about improvisation. And by learning about music, okay? I think it will be more enhanced than by learning about a lot of the things people learn about these days. So I think in the final analysis, no matter how you look at it, it's a plus. What it is, the mystery of it, will always be a mystery. And I don't think you can tap into that, but what I found, and I know I didn't talk about what I do when I do pedagogy, but I'll talk about that maybe next time I come or somethin', but I just thought that Coltrane, all the innovators dropped out of school. Anyone that innovated music dropped out of school, or were self-taught. And that gave me one little clue that the idea of aesthetics was more important than the techniques. You know, and that's what I base my guide on when teaching improvisation. It's more aesthetics than techniques. Technique is just how one saves the drowning child. Aesthetics is the impulse to save the child.

The bottom line is that improvisation is an integral part of our lives, and everybody is talking about it in a wonderful way because it's wonderful, you know, and we have to keep doing it. Whether we know exactly what it is or not, we have to have room for all to play. I'm rooting for the music and for the people who make it, but at the same time I feel that we are headed for the jazz reservation. And when I say we, I mean people who are in their sixties and in their seventies. We try to get our last breath of playing and doing what we do, but we're basically the same as the Indians in America, we're headed toward extinction. We've done what we've done, and we had a good little run, maybe a few more years and we pass on. What has happened to the legacy of John Coltrane, Albert Ayler, Frank Wright, David S. Ware, or Fred Anderson? Who carries the torch today and who will carry the torch tomorrow? Improvisation still fights for its life in competitions in getting funding for the musicians. It has not gotten the respect it deserves. The battle between European formalism and African conjuring rages on. I heard one musician say of what we do, "Oh you're just a lot of black guys sweating, playing their guts out. There is no intellectual process happening in the music you make." Another musician said, "There is no structure in the music." There is nothing on earth that does not have structure. No one, by mere words alone, can subtract from the existence and beauty of living people. We are not a subculture. The music of Bach does not supersede the music of the Baka people of the Congo. They both have a right to exist. You can love it or hate it, but it has the right to exist because it is alive like the wind and the trees. The mystery cannot be taught. It can be brought out of the music student, but it appears differently to each person. And no matter how much you teach it, the speciality, the mystery, will always be there. You know, that's what gives me hope. I want to see what all these students are going to do, in the future. And I'm looking forward to that because you know they already have the New School where they're teaching bebop, and that's totally fair. Or you have people just standardizing songs, and no new

Charlie Parkers out there yet. So now I want to see, in the next ten years, whether we get some new improvisers. Because now it's truly been all these great ideas coming in, and we might come up with the idea that we know something, but all the great ideas, they can't be taught. Unfortunately, they cannot be taught. The great ones will be the great ones no matter what. Mamma's on crack, daddy's on crack, kid is brilliant. Okay? Mama's an alcoholic, dad didn't finish school, kid is brilliant. Okay, why? How? Why is this kid brilliant and the other kid whose parents are both PhDs not? These are the things I'm thinking about now. Can brilliance be made? Can it be enhanced? And I just know that brilliance will live as long as people are alive.

Section III

Improvisation and Community-Engaged Pedagogy

14 The Music Is the Pedagogy

David Dove

Six musicians are in a studio at a community arts center; three are teenagers and three are adults. It is likely that they all identify as artists. They include two musicians who are undergoing formal training, with careers in classical music ahead of them. Another musician has a nonacademic yet traditional musical background, having learned to play guitar in rock bands. One participant is both a poet and a self-taught musician. The sixth has her background in the visual arts. Having never participated in any kind of group music making (or collaborative sound making) before, her medium is sound produced through the use of electronics. These six—all regular attendees of this weekly event—discovered this opportunity through various avenues: word of mouth, a social media post, a high school workshop, or in the schedule of activities offered at the center.

Ten preteens are in an after-school program at a public housing project. After issuing them very strong words (including threats) regarding the consequences of their behavior, their counselor hands their charge over to a Nameless Sound facilitator and leaves the room. The facilitator reminds the kids that they are not required to attend the session. But if they are going to stay in the room, they will be asked to participate. Two leave the session, and the emotional climate of the room begins to shift. The remaining preteens begin assembling the instruments. Though not formally trained through any other musical context, these kids have indeed developed their own affinities and approaches to the instruments that are brought to them every week. The kids and this facilitator have now all known each other for several years. They have developed their own culture within these sessions. Along with this culture, a shared, cocreated music has emerged, with its own styles and histories.

Fifteen children between the ages of five and eight years old sit in a circle. These children currently see each other every day and will all go to sleep in the very facility that they now sit in, but few of them have known each other for longer than a couple of months. Having escaped domestic abuse or homelessness, their mothers checked in to the Women and Family Emergency Center. And though their situation is transient, they are now a community with a stronger framework and more structure than these children have previously been afforded. The group music making within this temporary framework may be a wildly dynamic experience (for the participants and facilitators). It may also take a different tone, yielding opportunities for reflection and sometimes challenging self-expression. There is a wide range of possible outcomes: physical outlet, imaginative play, humor, community building, reflection, self-expression, and healing.

Forty music students playing strings, brass, winds, and percussion sit in standard orchestra formation in a public high school. If one were to view a photo of the occasion, there would be something unusual about this picture. The ubiquitous music stands have been left out of the arrangement. The students are not participating in an activity typical for them, but are being confronted with a single one-off workshop experience. Accustomed to a routine of fully composed and notated repertoire, most of the participants have only ever sounded an instrument with their eyes trained to pages of sheet music and the baton of a conductor. They did not sign up for this experience, and now they have to face something that may seem to go against everything that they have been trained to do in music. It's a one-shot introductory session, and it's likely that responses, opinions, and reactions will vary widely.

Eight four-year-olds sit and sprawl on the floor. In a day care for homeless and refugee children, they are in a community of 20 who will be together in this program for a year. The eight form a very loose and continuously shifting circle. Indeed, they are only eight for the moment. Children from the total of twenty will choose at their own will to join in and "walk-away" from the weekly activity, "music with Mr. David." The on-site councilors and Mr. David have an agreement, and it's understood that joining and leaving the group is freely elective for the children. Some will stay for the whole hour. Some will leave or join part way through the session. Some of the twenty will never join in at all.

One largely nonverbal, profoundly autistic boy enters the community center with his mother. Though it's not the case, to many he seems oblivious to his surroundings. He and his mother have come in search of an open, nonjudgmental environment where he can explore sound. He takes great pleasure in music, but his reactions to sonic stimulation can be erratic and unpredictable. This is one of his first sessions with Nameless Sound. The facilitator and his mother still have yet to determine if he'll work one-on-one with the facilitator, or in a larger group of other workshop participants. In fact, his mother is hoping that music making will provide the boy with social connections that can otherwise be difficult to forge.

A Nameless Sound creative music workshop can occur in a wide range of contexts and with a diverse range of participants. Ideally, it can happen anywhere and with anyone. Nameless Sound workshop ensembles may comprise people who identify as musicians, people who have never made music before in their life, or they may involve a spectrum of mixed experiences, abilities, and artistic identities (including actively performing musicians and people who wouldn't at all consider themselves musicians or artists). These sessions happen with children as young as three years old, they happen with adults, and they happen with people of all ages in between. They can be single events, or ongoing classes. They might be "on-location," where a Nameless Sound facilitator goes into a particular community or site as an outsider (where Nameless Sound is just one program in a larger schedule of activities), or they can be at a Nameless Sound studio or site (where participants sign themselves up and come to Nameless Sound). They can be for very large groups or for just one or two people. Though a range of practices with varying degrees of structure may take place, musical improvisation is at the core of a Nameless Sound workshop. Furthermore, free improvisation (improvisation with absolutely no score or predetermined instruction) is a key element of these sessions. The word *improvisation* implies a flexible and adaptive process. As much as anything, improvisation is about responsiveness. Given those qualities, different Nameless Sound creative music workshops should look, sound, and feel very different from one another. Further variation is found due to a range of workshop facilitators. Nameless Sound employs a staff of practicing artists as facilitators. They may lead sessions alone or in pairs, and occasionally work in groups of three. And though there are many exercises and techniques shared between them, often developed together in collaboration, each Nameless Sound workshop facilitator has his or her own individual approach. Like the improviser on stage, each should be working from her or his own unique, flexible, adaptive, and responsive practice.

Though different Nameless Sound sessions may involve seemingly disparate exercises, pieces, games, practices, conversations, and participants, all Nameless Sound workshops have a basis in particular philosophies and ideals. These philosophies were discovered and formed through years in the practice of the workshops themselves. And after years of this practice and through the collaborative efforts of Nameless Sound facilitators, the philosophies (products of the practice) have now become the foundation of the practice. This writing serves as an introduction to these principles. I abstain from offering a curriculum or specific activities. (In fact, we are opposed to the very idea of a curriculum for our workshops.) Instead, I've written this chapter in hopes that it will offer information, perspective, and encouragement for facilitators in developing their own individual approaches for creative music workshops, wherever they may be and whomever they may be with.

The *Music* Is the Pedagogy

> The senses, being explorers of the world, open the way to knowledge.
> —Maria Montessori[1]

> Deep Listening is listening in every possible way to everything possible to hear no matter what you are doing.
> —Pauline Oliveros[2]

In identifying the Nameless Sound facilitator, we resist the term *teacher*. We not only seek to avoid the limitations of this designation, we also acknowledge the restrictions and repressions that so-called "teaching" itself (as it is often understood) may have on creative and therapeutic processes. Although teaching is indeed one of the many things that might occur in a Nameless Sound session, there is a significantly broader range of activities and possible outcomes at play. As the teacher was defined by the pioneering educator Maria Montessori, a Nameless Sound facilitator is an "observer." But this practice of observing should not be assumed to be simple. To be effective, it must be honed as a skilled and experienced practice. We associate the activity of this Montessori observer in resonance with composer Pauline Oliveros' "Deep Listener" who is "listening in every possible way to everything possible to hear no matter what you are doing." In identifying the Nameless Sound facilitator, we also find resonance with the role of the dialogical "teacher-student" as defined by critical pedagogue Paulo Freire, who said "The teacher is of course an artist, but being an artist does not mean that he or she can make the profile, can shape the students. What the educator does in teaching is to make it possible for the students to become themselves."[3]

Curriculumless Sound

> The teacher is no longer merely the-one-who-teaches, but one who is himself taught in dialogue with the students, who in turn while being taught also teach. They become jointly responsible for a process in which all grow.
>
> —Paulo Freire[4]

Like the musical practice from which it was generated, a Nameless Sound workshop is itself a cocreated ensemble improvisation. And like improvised music being sounded on stage in the moment of its creation, a Nameless Sound workshop is a performance. Drawing from the collective and responsive qualities of this music, the facilitator of a workshop in musical improvisation must employ and embody the sensitivity, listening, and sense of ensemble cultivated through a practice in the music itself. As a practitioner of musical free improvisation, the Nameless Sound facilitator is positioned as a uniquely qualified dialogical "teacher-student" and an empathetic steward of a secure frame for creative work. Also like the improviser on stage, the facilitator must be open about a workshop's results and its final products. In a performance, the improvising musician may predetermine her or his first sound or gesture. But any actions beyond that cannot be strictly planned. All sounds are made in the context of the ensemble, its members, their contributions, and their reactions. Similarly in a workshop, a facilitator may prepare an initial exercise, piece, game, or question. But the exercises (pieces, games, etc.) that follow should only be offered after listening to and observing the participants, responding to their responses, and being sensitive to their presence and contributions to the session.

People often describe the improvising musician as drawing from a personal "vocabulary": sounds, gestures, phrases, ideas, stylistic elements, techniques, and tools that are spontaneously and reflexively assembled to make music in dialogue with collaborators. This individual vocabulary may become a somewhat fixed set of elements, accessed freely in performance. That being said, entirely new sounds, ideas, and gestures might also appear in the act of performance when the old ones won't do. New ideas emerge out of necessity, as solutions to the problems or situations of the moment. And these new sounds may or may not remain in the performer's vocabulary for future performances. Similarly, the workshop facilitator should have a repertoire to draw from, choosing the right exercise or question for a particular situation. And similar to the process by which new elements of a musical vocabulary are born on stage, the workshop facilitator may create new exercises or pieces (or new variations on old ideas) in response to the needs of the moment. (My own repertoire of workshop exercises is quite substantial; and almost all of these exercises have been generated in the moment, during a session, inspired as a response to the participants and the situations at hand.) These exercises that are created in the moment may or may not remain in the facilitator's vocabulary for use in future workshops. I think that many improvising musicians form much of their musical vocabulary in performance, on stage. Similarly, much of the repertoire of a workshop facilitator might be formed in response to the contributions of the participating cocreators and the needs of the moment. This vocabulary can only be cultivated through a skilled practice of observing and listening to participants. And in this activity, we find dialogical education, where all parties are both learning and teaching. None of this could happen with the rigidity of a curriculum in the way.

It is for these reasons that I am committed to this principle: experienced improvising artists are the ones who should be leading workshops in musical improvisation. In recent years, we finally see a growth of interest and advocacy for the inclusion of improvisation in formal music curriculum. Music teachers should of course become familiar with improvisation, and they should develop their own improvisational practice as musicians. They should learn exercises for musical improvisation and incorporate them into their curricula. But only an experienced practitioner can fully facilitate a workshop in musical improvisation, which is itself an improvisation, cocreated with the workshop's participants. The workshop facilitator's skill is born from the experience of the improviser's performance practice. It's an extension of what happens on stage. There is simply no substitute for a practicing artist, a performer who can embody improvisation, listening, responsiveness, and open-ness in his or her presence, intentions, and music.

That being said, I feel that it is important to offer this additional note regarding the qualifications necessary to facilitate a workshop of improvised music. Though a workshop facilitator should have a basis in the practice of the music, not all improvising musicians are suited to facilitate workshops, especially when the sessions involve children, populations who have recently experienced significant trauma, or people with special needs. During the act of performance, an effective improviser may indeed be fully attentive to the music, undistracted by all other concerns for the duration of that performance. But not all performing musicians are capable of sustaining that level of dedicated attention for the duration of a workshop or class. Total undivided attention is even more crucial in the classroom than on stage. Furthermore, the level of compassion required in a workshop session necessarily exceeds the level of communicative empathy that is needed for improvised performance on stage with one's musical colleagues. And though improvising musicians may necessarily need to be open about the end results of their on-stage performances, their own aesthetic preferences and musical dispositions might not allow them to be open about the results of their workshop sessions and the contributions of their participants.

Outcomes: Potential and Unknown

Along with the diversity of contexts that make up Nameless Sound workshops, there is a wide and unknown range of possible outcomes from these sessions. These outcomes may be clearly observable during the course of a session, or they may be happening below the surface. Some of these workshops may appear to be affairs purely concerned with "serious" music making, where self-identified artists/musicians are engaging in a creative process for which they have a strong historical and personal context. Some workshops may seem simply to be a form of play, children having fun through musical activities. Dropping in, one might think that a particular session isn't about improvisation at all, but about knowledge transfer ("teaching"!), where participants are seen learning the fundamentals of an instrument or a particular principle of music theory. Though Nameless Sound instructors are not licensed therapists (or working in that context), some workshops may look like therapy sessions, where we find that activities are engaging a participant's disability or trauma. But whether with self-identified "improvisers," pre-K children in day-care facilities, communities formed through their social marginalization or their individual or shared traumas, people with special needs in one-on-one sessions, or unsuspecting classical music students, the potential outcomes are common throughout. These may include (but are not limited to) the following general categories: creative work, play, therapy, and knowledge transfer. (There are, of course, many more potential outcomes within these and beyond these, most of which can be identified as the achievement of ideals such as empathy, tolerance, inclusiveness, self-awareness, group-awareness, sense of community, responsibility, shared leadership, imagination, development of creative voice, self-expression, self-esteem, validation, patience, creative problem solving, balance of openness with structure, spontaneity, revelation of beauty, revelation of possibility, etc.) My reemphasis on the range of contexts and outcomes is stressed to set up this point: none of these potential outcomes (creative work, play, therapy, knowledge transfer) are ever only what they appear to be. And no matter what the potential outcome, the necessary frame and the facilitator's practice that make these outcomes possible remain consistent. And though these outcomes may manifest differently in different moments and situations, all four of these general possibilities are usually occurring in all (successful) sessions, often in simultaneity. They may occur clearly in an individual or in a group. They may happen as an individual participant's internal experience, or collectively in a group below the surface, not obvious to an observer. But in a Nameless Sound session, creative work, play, therapy, and knowledge transfer are all supported by the same frame and philosophies.

The Frame: Setting the Stage

The outcomes of a session are never the result of a fixed goal, and the open possibilities include both the known and the unknown. The dynamics and exchanges within the work itself may be nuanced and complex but also powerfully affecting. The stage must be set.

The vulnerabilities and risks at play in both creative and therapeutic work must be supported and protected by a "frame." This frame includes the qualities of the physical environment, the emotional climate, the structure of the session, and the relationship of participants with each other and with the facilitators. Some considerations may seem subtle: the simple arrangement and spacing of chairs, the susceptibility of the space to outside disruption, the suitability of the instruments to the participants of the session. (Are they the right size? Are they potentially dangerous?) Some factors may be more pronounced: the presence of hostile participants, inappropriate behavior that indicates the possibility of abuse, the threats of punishment from an on-site counselor, and, of course, the presence and behavior of the Nameless Sound facilitators themselves. What the psychotherapist calls a "secure frame" necessary for creating a "safe space" for therapy, we also see as being crucial to the environment for therapy, creative work, play, and knowledge transfer. The importance of this frame in Nameless Sound sessions is consistent across the board, for all outcomes and sessions. As is the case in therapy, we feel that working without a secure frame can be harmful. The establishment of the frame (and maintenance of the safe space) in our sessions is of critical importance, but it may not be possible to predetermine exactly what it should look like in such a wide range of contexts. The achievement of the safe space might be a moving target within a single session itself. There are times when we know that we have it. And there are times when the listening, observing facilitator must be continuously looking for indicators, sensing for its presence or disappearance. What is the emotional climate of the room? What is the parity of participation? Is anyone feeling excluded? Is anyone being excluded?

Is anyone being forced to participate against her or his will? How does a Nameless Sound facilitator establish a frame and safe space in an environment where our partners in the institution force participation, threaten participants physically, belittle them by communicating low expectations and projections about them, violate their agency by drawing conclusions for them, answering questions for them, or defining their experience for them? Establishing a frame in an environment like this must be done very carefully.

In an institution exercising abuse and egregious levels of oppression, the Nameless Sound facilitator must help to cultivate a new, separate, cocreated, and shared culture with the session participants. He or she must first embody trust and respect for the group. The embodiment of this trust is a performance itself, a performance of his or her respect composed through listening, observing, and dialogue. Reliability and consistent attendance are essential in this long-term task. Eliminating the presence of hostility in the session is fundamental. This would not only include hostile participants. It would also include oppressive or abusive councilors, our partners who are authorities in the institution. This delicate business is just the start of establishing the frame in this environment. But as an outsider coming in for one hour per week, nurturing the development of a cocreated culture within a culture may take weeks, months, or even years. Again—if the safe space is not achieved, we may do more harm than good. It's also important to note that as outside visitors passing through a community for only one hour per week, we may cause harm to members of that community by undermining the existing culture (given that we leave at the end of each session, and are absent for whatever fallout may happen).

Ideally, participation in a Nameless Sound workshop is the elective choice of each individual. And each participant should have agency over his or her own contribution, involvement, and identification in the group. Elective participation and agency of all members are basics for establishing a frame. But among the sites of Nameless Sound workshops are programs held in institutions that might not agree with this ethic of elective participation and individual agency. In this case, Nameless Sound must negotiate with the site a clear understanding about our policy. Creating a secure frame within such an institution can be a great challenge. We may share with our partnering institution a goal of supporting the health and well-being of our constituents, but we may differ fundamentally on how to cultivate and protect that well-being.

What if we establish a policy of elective participation, but we only have one willing workshop participant? Then we work with that one. Our ideal is for the *workshop itself* to attract participants. Our task is to nurture that session so that it will more likely cultivate interest. Usually, it's the music itself (and the positive experience of making it) that eventually attracts those who were previously reluctant to join. Two willing participants make more vibrant music than a group of four, with half being forced against their will. When the music develops over the course of some weeks, others will likely join with a new interest and attitude. It is our conviction that when given choice and control over their activities, students learn more effectively. Furthermore, creative work and healing can only happen of one's own volition.

Some Words About the Vocabulary: Exercises/Pieces/Games/Questions

At this point, the reader may be wondering what exactly a Nameless Sound workshop actually consists of. The collective staff of Nameless Sound facilitators may have, through different variations, hundreds of activities taking the forms of exercises, pieces (whether scored verbally or otherwise), games or questions (questions to stimulate dialogue or playing). I fear that specifically outlining activities might set up a distraction in this writing. As I have previously emphasized, a tendency to choose exercises without sensitivity to an ensemble's members and the needs of the moment doesn't make any sense. At worst, it would be alienating. In the internal conversations of Nameless Sound facilitators, it's important that these elements remain less definitive. Workshop activities should be flexible, not rigidly predetermined and part of an ongoing conversation. That being said, there are some good ones, and it is hard not to share. But sharing them would be akin to offering readers a few licks to play on their horns, pretending that learning these licks will make them an improviser. So—I will abstain for now. But I'll abstain expecting that we will write a future text that will offer some of these activities. That text will not only have to be thorough enough to make it clear that these exercises, pieces, games, and questions should be part of a flexible vocabulary. That text should also be able to effectively dissuade readers from using our exercises in any kind of linear or inflexible curriculum. With all of that being said, I will continue here with some thoughts about how these activities might be employed and what their applications might be.

Among other applications, exercises might be employed to facilitate certain ideals, focus on essential dynamics of improvisation, or explore different ways of listening. They might be activities that cultivate a focus on form, developing a sense of what happens from the beginning to the middle to the end of a piece. They might lay groundwork for the development of individuals' musical styles (helping them to "find their voice"). They might emphasize different ways in which players can relate to each other, whether through vertical relationships, time-based reactions, or other strategies. These are only a few examples of the application of workshop activities.

Most importantly, activities should be chosen that allow for the participation of all who are in a given session (and are interesting to all in that session). Nameless Sound sees the medium of ensemble free improvisation as providing a unique opportunity to leverage the hierarchies of virtuosity and open up individual contribution beyond the roles prescribed to instruments in traditional idioms. Inclusivity is a priority. In early development, human language asserts identity and agency. Music making should allow for this too, without the delay of technical development or the granting of agency. Free improvisation is the musical process that most directly and immediately accesses cocreativity. Similarly, activities in our workshops (even if not free improvisation) should also allow for direct and immediate access to cocreativity and individual agency.

In addition to the exercises, pieces, games, and questions, Nameless Sound workshops might involve very concrete instruction in the playing of an instrument, music theory, or traditional musical structures. Like all workshop activities, these more traditional musical elements should be carefully chosen in response to the needs and interests of the given participants. For example, if the members of an ensemble want to learn something about improvising over chord sequences, as is typically done when performing a jazz standard, facilitators (if they are qualified to share this information and perform that music with the ensemble) should accommodate. In this instance (in the Nameless Sound workshop), a lesson in playing standard chord changes is not part of the curriculum and overall agenda of the workshop. It is seen as one of the many tools or resources available to the creative musician. But it's important that the activities in a workshop make space for all participants. If one ensemble member doesn't feel a connection to this material (or is maybe not even using an instrument or materials suitable for this activity), then it's not appropriate to the workshop.

Play It, Don't Say It

A fundamental practice when facilitating a Nameless Sound workshop is the engagement of participants through one's own playing. As a practice of the facilitator's own listening and *musical* vocabulary, it is an engagement that cannot be replaced by workshop exercises. What exactly can a facilitator do through his or her own playing in the workshop, and how does he or she do it? What can a facilitator play in response to the specific contributions of individual ensemble members to affirm that they are listening? Through the playing itself, facilitators may find ways to identify and support musical ideas put forward by participants; challenge participants toward new directions and unexplored possibilities; transfer musical knowledge (for example, introduce new rhythms or tonalities); support the emotional or expressive content being performed by participants; or simply inspire the ensemble through their own performance (whether in an improvisation or while taking a solo turn). When vulnerability is at stake or when a participant's music is expressing highly emotional content, it may be that the nonverbal practice of *only* playing ensures the safe space needed to hold that vulnerability or emotional content. In many workshop situations, it may be possible to facilitate the entire session only through one's playing, without the use of exercises. Keep in mind that the facilitator is never only a participant. His or her experience as a practicing musician, his or her charisma as a performer, and identity as the facilitator (and possibly his or her status as an outsider) will provide influence, whether the role as facilitator is spoken or unspoken. In fact, if one can facilitate a workshop only with one's playing, the facilitator may be able achieve something close to a "pure" dialogical musical exchange (without the dialogue!). This ideal, of course, reemphasizes the importance of practicing musicians being the facilitators of workshops in musical improvisation.

My inclusion of the potentially problematic term *charisma* in the previous paragraph should occasion a clarification, and some words on what role charisma might play in a creative music workshop. Investigating the term reveals origins in the designation of divinely conferred or magnetic powers. These connotations would clearly situate the concept of a facilitator's charisma in opposition to Nameless Sound's ideal of musical improvisation (and the Nameless Sound workshop) as an arena with the potential for nonhierarchical collaboration, where each and every participant can find their own voice. Though musicians today have hopefully shed residual notions of exclusive divine endowment, I would argue that the act of performance rarely escapes some quality of charisma. I would define this charisma as a quality cultivated by the performer (consciously or unconsciously) that imbues the performative moment with necessary energy and attention. So if the Nameless Sound workshop is an extension of a facilitator's performance practice, then a quality of charisma is at play. Furthermore, if curriculum and even workshop exercises are to be abandoned, the facilitator's charisma and his or her own playing may be the only resources he or she may have left. What's important is this: The Nameless Sound facilitator uses his or her charisma to help others find their own. It's a redefinition of the term that recognizes it as something that each and every individual has for him- or herself. Finding it is akin to "finding one's voice." For the Nameless Sound facilitator, there are two crucial elements that must exist alongside the recognition of a charisma at the service of our participants: the facilitator's intentions and his or her compassion. With those in place, charisma and improvisation can work together to leverage hierarchies, foster inclusion, and empower cocreation.

The Music Itself: Who's Listening to What? and the Question of Aesthetics

It may seem obvious to many that the aesthetic biases of art and music instructors are among the major inhibitors in the creative development of individuals in a class or workshop. I've heard countless personal testimonials about oppressive music teachers who, through their discouragement and biases, disheartened young musicians to the point of quitting. (This problem may have been my primary inspiration for leading creative music workshops when I began this practice in 1997.) I don't think I'm the only person who believes that we would have many more unique artists and musicians if it weren't for judgmental and biased teachers. But the question of aesthetics is a complicated one. As artists, facilitators should be aware that they indeed embody their own aesthetics, and that those aesthetics are a strength and a resource (as well as a potential limitation). Those aesthetics (like one's own voice or agency) should not be suppressed. Also, there are aesthetics that emerge collectively out of improvisations. How do we consider them? And what about the aesthetics that are implied in certain workshop exercises? There is a careful balance between checking the limits that one's own aesthetics may impose, using aesthetics as a lens to identify indicators of what might be happening in a group during an improvisation and knowing what may be the application of a particular exercise that seems to imply a certain aesthetic quality.

In a free improvisation, what does the Nameless Sound facilitator hear in the music itself? Can the aesthetics and qualities of an improvisation provide evidence of ideals being met (or not being met)? What does it mean when, over time, a group of young musicians is able to play longer and longer pieces, and come to clear endings? Are clear endings and clear musical transitions a sign of a consensus in the group? For weeks, a child has had problems with shyness. In one free improvisation, the ensemble gradually drops out, leaving this child to solo all alone. Has this child found a safe space in the music, now being supported in a potentially vulnerable moment? What does it mean when a group with frequently disruptive, restlessly uncooperative members plays music with determined, quiet delicacy? When an ensemble performs an improvisation of repetitive, simple minimalism, can we find evidence of the expansion of attention span? Do we hear evidence in some improvisations that members of an ensemble are listening closely to each other? If a particular group is exhibiting a certain type of musical dialogue, but has never done this before, do we hear that as progress, where the development of an ensemble sensibility may indicate the development of mutual respect and sense of community? What about strong physical displays of music? What emotions are being expressed in an improvisation like this? What therapy might be occurring? If we can use aesthetics as a lens, rather than a preference, we can possibly gauge some of the personal, emotional, and social dynamics at play. Indeed, an ensemble's development of its own aesthetics through musical improvisation may indicate the achievement of a safe space.

This addressing of aesthetic judgment might provide an opportune moment to make a comment about what I feel is a frequent abuse of the term *listening* among musicians and improvisers. Among the subjective responses that may follow a performance of free improvisation, a common critique is that someone "wasn't listening." But how are we to objectify the condition of someone's listening? I feel that musical improvisers can have a much more expansive and nuanced concept of this act. For facilitators of workshops in creative music, it's imperative that our understanding of listening does not fall into judgments about whether or not someone was or wasn't doing it. I would say that there is *never* a condition of "not listening." Such a thing cannot exist. The question for the Nameless Sound facilitator should not be a judgmental one about whether or not someone was listening. The question should be, "What were they listening to?" There is a range of possibilities about what one might be listening to. They include not only external aural listening (which is a continually changing, multifaceted listening that includes global, focal, textural, rhythmic, etc.). Listening can also include the internal, focused on the emotional, the corporeal, the ecstatic, the traumatic, and more. Aren't all of these possibilities at play in improvised music? One of the responsibilities of the Nameless Sound facilitator, then, is to *listen to the listening*.

Visiting Artists: The Global Community

There is a resource that the global community of free improvisers has to offer these workshops that may be more powerful than the act of improvising itself. This resource is the diversity of its practitioners and the diversity of approaches to this activity. I often feel that by keeping conversations around the subject of improvisation itself, we are missing out on another important fundamental quality of this community's practice. It's that individual creative musicians develop their own individual voices. For workshop participants (especially children, and especially children in segregated communities) to experience the range of traditions, cultures, and individual approaches possible in these collaborations may be more inspiring than the act of improvisation itself. They should hear styles clearly based on tradition, and they should hear completely nonidiomatic approaches. They should hear improvisers of different generations. They should hear both female and male improvisers. They should hear and meet creative musicians from the most diverse range of cultural and musical backgrounds. They should hear improvisers from around the world. They should hear and see that there is a global movement in music that thrives on diverse approaches and idioms (and thrives on collaborations between these diverse approaches). This is not a music that can be transmitted by one person's voice or style. The inclusion of a diverse range of visiting guest artists is an irreplaceable resource in the creative music workshop.

Never in Conclusion, but Assessed

A sound is made, and two others respond. A quick reaction produces a new sound, one never before heard by its maker. More emerge, and a slower response yields something more familiar. The music goes to both known and unknown places. The arc of this improvisation is sculpted from the collective voices, resources, desires, and responses of its participants. In turn, these individual voices are shaped from this collaborative practice. This is what happens in just a few minutes. This is what happens over many years.

The seed of Nameless Sound began with a single notion. As a creative musician, I felt that my own formal music education was too conservative. As a youth in the school music program, I was never provided a framework for creativity (an opportunity to improvise, the idea that I could compose, the notion to experiment outside the conventions of the instrument, etc.). Wanting to offer young musicians something that was missing from my own training, I volunteered to facilitate an improvisation workshop at an arts community center. As with my practice in creative music, this workshop practice took on a life of its own, frequently leading to new and unexpected places. Time and again, this practice would reveal new understandings of its applications and its possibilities. The *music* is the pedagogy. Through experiences in these sessions, I learned that this work provided a frame for more than just creative work and learning, but for a therapy as well. Over several years, invitations to bring this workshop to new contexts reemphasized its therapeutic potential. A growing understanding of a necessary framework provided a new awareness of the relationships among creativity, knowledge transfer, therapy, and play.

My performance practice was the seed. And the ideas and ideals that emerged from the work over many years were later supported by investigations into established pedagogical theories. Encounters with the workshop practices of other artists further informed and affirmed the work. Eventually, participants of the program became active musicians, artists, teachers, and even therapists in Houston and internationally. Some became my musical collaborators. Some of these musical collaborators became colleagues within the organization, facilitators who are now collaborating to develop and articulate the philosophies and ideals of the program itself. These philosophies, emerging from years of collaborative practice between the facilitators and participants, have become the foundation of Nameless Sound's current and future practice.

Always in evolution, Nameless Sound now sits at the turning point of a new phase in its development. Practice has formed ideals. Ideals and practice, together, have identified potential outcomes. And most recently, a basis for assessment has emerged. The relationship between the secure frame and the safe space (in tandem with a relationship between groundwork and outcomes) forms the basis of this assessment. The Nameless Sound facilitator does not predetermine the outcomes of a workshop (and is open to possible unknown outcomes); so while establishing a frame is fundamental groundwork to a Nameless Sound session, identifying the achievement of a safe space (which results from that frame, and from which all outcomes are possible) is the only way to identify and assess the success of our work. Though it has emerged from a practice in improvisational performance, this adaptive and flexible work has greater risks for its participants, and therefore greater responsibilities of its practitioners. The stakes are high.

Acknowledgment

Thanks are due to all current and past Nameless Sound facilitators and participants. This writing is a result of years of our collaborative work, both inside and outside of the classroom. Special acknowledgement should be given to David Feil and Jason Jackson. These ideas have formed and been cultivated under our collaborative care. These ideas are theirs as much as they are mine.

Notes

1. Montessori, *The Absorbent Mind*, 167.
2. Oliveros, "Quantum Listening," 27.
3. Qtd. in Horton and Freire, *We Make the Road*, 181.
4. Freire, *Pedagogy of the Oppressed*, 61.

Works Cited

Freire, Paulo. *Pedagogy of the Oppressed*. 3rd ed. Trans. Myra Bergman Ramos. New York: Continuum, 1994.

Horton, Myles, and Paulo Freire. "Educational Practice: Conflicts Are the Midwife of Consciousness." In *We Make the Road by Walking: Conversations on Education and Social Change*, edited by Brenda Bell, John Gaventa, and John Peters, 180–97. Philadelphia: Temple University Press, 1990.

Montessori, Maria. *The Absorbent Mind*. Oxford: Clio Press, 1988.

Oliveros, Pauline. "Quantum Listening: From Practice to Theory (To Practise Practice)." In *Culture and Humanity in the New Millenium: The Future of Human Values*, edited by Chan Sin-wai Chan and Kwok Siu Tong, 27–44. Hong Kong: The Chinese University of Hong Kong, 2002.

15 Informed by Children

Awakening Improvisatory Impulses in University Students

Matt Swanson and Patricia Shehan Campbell

Introduction

University Schools of Music at the tertiary level have long been conceived of as guardians of musical knowledge, with community engagement consisting of a one-way flow from the ivory tower to the musically impoverished masses. A long-standing common stance is of the university as the authoritative provider of musical training, with ideals of performance, scholarship, and creative expression dictated in top-down fashion in an established institutionalized curriculum. In particular, performance is a critical component within undergraduate programs of musical study, while scholarship is honed in selected academic writing courses such as music history, and composition and improvisation may be minimalized or left out altogether. The dawn of the twenty-first century has prompted a shift in the discourse, however, with many educators challenging the separation of universities from the musical lives of the communities that surround them while also applauding the integration of more expressive practices (i.e., composition and improvisation) within curricular offerings.[1] In this renewed vision, Schools of Music are no longer seen as exclusive holders of musical knowledge nor always the home and hub of the most innovative performers. Rather, they are situated as part of a broader musical community—engaging in a fluid two-way exchange while they draw from and build upon the richness of musical expertise from outside campus walls and in casual, nonformal surrounds.

With respect to improvisation, such expertise can be seen as arising long before its presence in university programs of musical study. In fact, improvisation is situated in the unlikely hands of children who, in their earliest ages and stages, embrace the possibilities for spontaneously creative musical expressions. In communities across the demographic spectrum, children might be termed "improvisational natives," with their primary musical interactions characterized by spontaneity, exploration, and invention. The improvisatory impulses of children are neither taught nor trained, but rather emanate fluidly as part of their natural, developmental assimilation of the musical material that surrounds them. Ironically, it is the formal institutions of music education that begin to erode these impulses in favor of more rigid and sequential approaches to music making, to the point that students at the tertiary level have often lost sight of the creative, playful propensities that they had known as children. Thus, the situation arises that students in music teacher preparation programs are often intimidated by, and feel unequipped to teach, the practice of improvisation. In order to overcome these barriers, this chapter posits that what is required is less a process of transmitting skills, and more of an "awakening" of existing improvisatory tendencies, and a connection to the improvisational expertise that lives and breathes in children and across an array of cultural traditions in the community.

Toward this end, this chapter casts a lens on a single School of Music at a university in the American west. Following a review of literature on improvisational practices in children's music making, this particular university "case" is considered both as an indicator of the kind of structures that have traditionally dampened spontaneous musical expression, as well as a launch point for imagining the kind of curricular shifts that would allow for a rekindling of improvisatory impulses among music students. The discussion documents successful courses and curricular initiatives and emphases that have offered university students opportunities to work through the nature of music as process-rich, holistic, and integrative. K–12 schools are next considered as the "frontlines" of the divide between childlike playfulness and adult rigidity—where university-trained teachers may "reencounter" the spontaneous musical spirit that they once knew as children. Initiatives and trends that have given rise to synergies across this divide in schools are given attention in this section. Finally, a summative section pays tribute to the musical spontaneity of children and adults alike, and will underscore the human penchant for improvisation—if only we would allow it.

Children at Musical Play

It appears that improvisation is a human trait that emerges early and often in a lifetime of expressive practices. Even in their first year, children are engaging in the improvisatory and interactive practice of musical play, beginning with the back-and-forth improvisations of "infant directed speech."[2] These early interactions between babies and their primary caregivers carry a spontaneous musicality, through which words are imbued with melody and expression, meanings are intensified, and communicative intentions are allowed to resonate to their fullest. Rather than passively absorbing this musical speech, babies respond to their caregiver's verbal and musical explorations with their own impromptu expressions and vocalizations, creating a mutual interplay that drives forward the flow of the interactions.[3]

Given the improvisatory nature of these early forays into musical communication, it is no wonder that young children continue to incorporate inventive music making into their language development and play. Young observed children aged 18 months to 3 years in a day-care setting, noting the types of vocalizations that freely emanated within the context of their play.[4] "Chanting and intoning" emerged from a 2 year-old boy who, after locating a picture of a football in a book, began to chant "pop ball!" in a dramatic and rhythmic fashion, in synchrony with the steps of his exaggerated walk. Another two-year-old boy made melodic "free-flowing vocalizations" on open vowel sounds while he manipulated the pieces of a wooden train set. A two-year-old girl sang fragments of a familiar greeting song, making lyrical substitutions based on the animal puzzle with which she was playing.[5] The impetus for this kind of spontaneous musical expression is manifold—whether it is the development of language and communication skills, self-regulation and focus, or children's desire to "relocate" known sonic material within the context of their immediate surroundings. Regardless of the function, however, improvisatory vocalizations seem to be of integral importance to young children's ability to navigate their independent play.

Beyond the realm of solitary play, improvisation has also been illustrated as a central process in the group play of preschool children. According to Sawyer, children's imaginative play is driven by an improvisatory give-and-take, making it an important arena in which to explore and refine social skills—"a context for practicing how to collectively manage an ongoing interaction."[6] The necessity of responding and adapting in the moment is characteristic across a variety of contexts of play, from nonmusical fantasy play[7] to the collective creation of spontaneous songs through social interaction.[8] Because children's social play is nonscripted and contingent upon the interactional dynamics of the group, improvisation becomes the primary vehicle for musical expression in such contexts, in a manner not unlike an improvisational theater group.[9]

As children reach school age, the improvisational foundation built in their early years continues to play a significant role in their musical lives, even as they enter the world of formal music education. Though most investigations of primary school children's musical experiences have cast an exclusive lens on the music classroom, researchers at the interface of music education and ethnomusicology have expanded the scope of investigation to include the gamut of children's daily experiences, offering a window into the musical cultures of children and the role of improvisation within these. Following John Blacking's initial recognition of children's musical activity as an autonomous entity[10] (distinguishable from that of adults and worthy of study as such), researchers have taken to playgrounds, hallways, homes, and community spaces, documenting the music therein and amassing a body of literature that is global in scope.[11]

Drawing upon these studies, we see that primary schoolchildren have engaged in a variety of forms of improvisatory music making in their day-to-day lives. They participate in myriad singing games, chants, handclaps, and jump rope games[12] that retain a spontaneous, inventive character as they are passed among groups of peers at play. Though children are often acutely aware of the "right" way to perform these songs and games, their penchant for musical creativity leads them to seek novel variations that are "spontaneously composed on the model of familiar traditional items."[13] Thus, as they draw upon a "generative matrix" of internalized patterns and structures,[14] each child or group of children places their own unique compositional stamp on the repertoire. As Marsh noted in her study of playground games across five countries, this variation is often quite intentional.[15] She documented groups of children adding new verses to existing musical structures, substituting lyrics in favor of local relevance, reorganizing musical formulae, condensing textual or melodic structures, and developing variations within movement schemes.[16] Far from the compositional imagery of a solitary composer at a desk, these innovations occurred among the laughter, cheers, and kinesthetic energy of play—emerging in the moment, and through the give-and-take of social interaction. Though an adult perspective might hold these songs and games as fixed forms to be recorded and passed between generations, children's preference for playful improvisation leads rather to dynamic and fluid forms to be shared and innovated among friends.

Beyond the obvious songs and musical games observed in these playground contexts, there exists a more subtle yet more pervasive form of musical improvisation—that is, the free form "musical doodlings"[17] that children readily emit, whether sitting at the breakfast table, waiting for class to start, or riding on the bus. These might take the form of "musical utterances," consisting of fragments, bits, and pieces that may narrate or synthesize a child's musical thinking or emotional state, or provide a melodic contour or rhythmic structure for the activity currently underway.[18] Whether singing directions in the sandbox, chanting across the monkey bars, riffing freely alongside Lego building, or rapping through a lunchroom cleanup, children are actively and creatively expressing themselves through musical vocalizations on a moment-to-moment basis. These kinds of spontaneous utterances can function to aggregate or synthesize the disparate musical ideas that float about in an individual child's head, and can be socially constructed among a group of individuals as well. As an illustration, Whiteman observed a group of five-year-old boys in New South Wales spontaneously start to throw back-and-forth melodic variations of a song they knew from their church choir, all the while attempting a style of beat boxing observed on the older children's playground, and combining this with Hip Hop dance moves reflecting their exposure to music videos.[19]

Another form of improvisatory musicking takes the form of rhythmic play, or "rhythmicking."[20] Using tables, chairs, playground equipment, floors, toys, and themselves, children readily pound out rhythmic ideas with hands, feet, sticks, and utensils. They routinely utilize their whole bodies to express the rhythmic patterns in their heads, whether gesturing with their arms, nodding their heads, shaking their hips, or stomping with their feet. Such pulse-driven behavior is pervasive across the span of children's daily flow of activity, both in and out of the classroom. Even the music classroom can provide a backdrop for freely improvised rhythms, as it did in Mrs. Bedford's class when four sixth-grade boys echoed their teacher's clave pattern with a spontaneous four-part polyrhythm.[21] This outburst was quickly quieted however (and similarly the younger author of this chapter can recall countless instances of admonishment for his own drumming on the table during class), showing how these spontaneous musicking behaviors are systematically pushed out of formal spaces and into realms where free play can flourish.

As children move into the upper elementary and adolescent years of formal music education, there is a shift toward a greater emphasis on the reproduction of musical scores in band, orchestras, and choir contexts. Yet still, there are many informal spaces they inhabit where improvisational expression may manifest in the community beyond educational institutions. At home a child or young adult might make a habit of exploring an instrument such as piano or guitar, learning familiar material by ear while also inventing original ideas and variations. She might even engage in formal lessons, but save some practice time to play "off the page" in a way that is personally relevant and expressive. She might form a musical group with friends, meeting regularly to "jam" while forging new material and a collective sound. She might also take part in the music or dance of a cultural tradition within the community, learning and performing repertoire but also inventing and sharing her own extrapolations. Unfortunately, with the transition into adulthood, the torch of musical exploration is increasingly passed to those who have self-selected for their musical propensities, leaving many with the stamp of the "nonmusician" that they will carry into adulthood. In contrast to the inventive musicality that thrives in childhood regardless of the formal institutions at play, the later years of youth relegate musical improvisation to the specialized few, while many are deemed "unfit" to express their ideas publicly, outside the shower or the driver seat of their single-occupancy vehicle.

The musical characteristics of children's improvisations are often distinct from what they encounter in a formal music classroom. Melodically, children typically utilize a small range of a fifth or less, although they might just as readily make leaps well over an octave. The tessitura of their sung ideas also tends to be lower than that prescribed by music educators (centered around, or even below, middle C), a likely outgrowth of the need to fluidly switch between spoken and sung material.[22] Rhythmically, children's improvisations can exhibit a complexity beyond what one would find in a developmentally targeted songbook[23]—the syncopated and polyrhythmic patterns that frequently occur perhaps reflecting children's exposure to groove-driven popular music. Children's independent music making also has the tendency to unify the voice and the body into one cohesive whole, seamlessly blending movement and sound.[24] Finally, the tendency to utilize and combine song fragments versus whole songs is unique to children's musical expression, and may afford children the flexibility to creatively "customize" their music to the particulars of their surroundings.[25]

Children's music making is certainly mediated by cultural context, defying any kind of tidy universal definition. For example, the Bollywood-infused play songs of children in Dehli,[26] the songs and games in the Baganda girls of Uganda,[27]and the beats and rhymes of African American boys on the streets of New York City[28] may share little in common stylistically. Rather, each child's culture interfaces in a two-way exchange with the adult culture that surrounds it, drawing upon the musical syntax of the adult culture while actively participating in cultural production of its own. The thread connecting children's musical cultures may be less about the music itself (with the exception of mass-disseminated "pop" sounds that trickle into ears worldwide), and more about the way in which children engage with the music. Improvisation represents one of the cornerstones of this unique engagement. Indeed, Marsh found improvisation to be a common element across the five countries in which she conducted her research, noting in each context children's "disposition to 'play around with' the texts, movements, melodies, and rhythms ... in a constant effort to create something new, to increase the level of amusement, and stamp their own imprimatur on the games they play."[29] Improvisation is certainly a key facet of children's "way of being" in the musical world—one that they carry from their earliest days on the planet all the way through their early years of schooling.

Improvisation Training at the University

The ubiquitous *presence* of improvisatory practices in children's lives stands in stark contrast to the notable *absence* of such practices in tertiary settings. Schools of Music frequently neglect to feature improvisation studies from the programs of most music majors, historically compartmentalizing it as the exclusive domain of students of jazz and organ performance. The large remainder of music students—in all other realms of performance, music education, and BA academic studies in music history and theory— graduate with little to no experience in the essential creative processes of improvisation and composition. Their cohorts in the visual arts will produce portfolios of paintings, drawings, sculptures, photographs, and multimedia installations, but music students historically have concentrated their efforts on re-creating masterworks (and various lesser works) without an opportunity to have their own musical voices heard alone or collaboratively with others in unique and original expressions. Systematic improvisation training could unfold for them with training in style-specific "languages" such as Jazz, Hindustani, Irish trad, and European classical, such that all music majors could then know opportunities for robust creative exploration and intensive analysis and reflection of the internal structures of music as expressive practice. In particular, music education students who will graduate to school positions—and arguably all music students who will be developing portfolio careers that may require them to sing and play "on their feet," spontaneously—could greatly benefit from an education that underscores improvisation as one of the central goals of a four-year degree.

At the university under study, the prospect for studies in improvisation and composition as foundational to music majors is a long-standing topic of "discussion and consideration," though there is little sense of any urgency in making a change. The conventional hierarchy of performance über-all is continuing, however, and the spectrum of the creative process is yet to be fully realized. Courses currently on the music major menu run the jazz-organ gamut of "Essential Skills in Jazz Improvisation" (three levels) and "Non-Traditional Improvisation/Composition Techniques for Jazz Performers" (three levels) to "Organ Improvisation and Service Playing" (three levels) and "Baroque Ornamentation and Improvisation" (a single course). These are small-enrollment courses explicitly geared to jazz and organ performance majors. No students outside these majors are advised to enroll in them, and course scheduling does not allow them to do so due to conflicts with their other program requirements. Faculty discussion has asserted the importance of a creativity-rich curriculum that will balance creative exploration and rigorous development of craft, but no allowances are offered for students to do so in specialized courses.

In the absence of courses, students have found their own avenues for free musical expression. The Improvised Music Project (IMP) is one such avenue. The IMP was formed by students in the Jazz Studies department and aims to serve as a "voice, network and source for live improvised music."[30] The group hosts regular jams at local venues, monthly concerts at a coffee shop near campus, and an annual festival that spans three days of improvised performances. By engaging with the surrounding community in this way, students are afforded myriad opportunities to play with sound, stretch the boundaries of their instrument, and engage in spontaneous ways with fellow musicians both on and off campus. Although the IMP is a natural outgrowth of the Jazz Studies program, it stands to reason that such a structure could also become core across the span of musical study. This would not only provide music students of all types with the space to sonically express their knowledge in personally relevant, inventive ways; it would also serve as a conduit to connect a greater number of students with improvisational activity in the community. Such activity would allow the playful propensities known to students in their early years to come out of the shadows—leading to a rekindling of the divergent thinking patterns once nurtured in childhood, and a revitalization of students' art forms in joyful, interactive contexts.

Beyond these spaces for wide open, student-driven improvisational activity, there are numerous potential occasions for weaving creative improvisation into music major courses, most of them not fully realized. Core musicianship and theory studies are likely locations of improvisatory exercises, in which students can be introduced to aspects of melody and mode, rhythm, texture, or form through opportunities to play spontaneously with their features. In-class explorations can deepen understandings of musical features, and out-of-class assignments to "make something in the style of" components such as Lydian mode, or additive meter such as 7/8 or 10/8, or contrapuntal texture can be thoughtfully considered and then shared in a later class. When afforded opportunities to improvise, students are in fact playing with the ideas that have been presented to them "in theory" and that are then converted to practice. Concepts and skills are believed by cognitive scientists to be best learned when the knowledge is "situated," constructed from active experiences,[31] and improvisation may be an exemplar of the real-life situated learning of music. More than any other experience, improvisation as a pedagogical strategy allows for music students to receive a more thorough-going and comprehensive musical training, where music theory, ear-training, and performance can be woven together in an information-rich context. The formats of ensemble rehearsals, from orchestras to bands to choirs, could be redesigned to correlate with real-world experiences that students will meet beyond their university studies, including the formation of small groups to allow opportunities to improvise in the style of a featured composer or piece. Such activity need not be long and laborious, nor usurping of time meant for rehearsals of larger works, but could complement the larger ensemble's aim of performance and analysis of music. Improvisation could also be integrated within the private studio lesson, or in weekly or monthly master classes when duo-pianists, or students of the oboe, violin, or voice studio, are invited to explore a theme. The incorporation of improvisation and other modes of "student voice" and musical enquiry into current conventional courses has the potential to enhance student understanding and allow participation in musical decision making.

In ethnomusicology, opportunities abound for improvisation. Particularly since many of the genres and practices of the world's cultures are improvisatory in nature, it stands to reason that playful manipulation of sonic features—within the boundaries of cultural rules—is possible. At the university under study, students are encouraged to improvise in steelband, gamelan, gospel choir, and Zimarimba ensemble. (Of course, the extent of improvisation varies according to the genre, such that, for example, Zimarimba practice is flexible and free so long as the chordal progressions are solid and strong, while improvisatory possibilities in the gamelan are limited to the elaborating instruments.) While beginning students of these traditions are learning-the-ropes and finding-their-footing, they are discovering small windows for their creative voice in short solos and simultaneous collective expressions. The length of their solo improvisations, as well as the sophistication of content, increases for students who continuously enroll in these ensembles and are given the floor to develop a theme. Visiting artists in the Ethnomusicology program have also been a significant source of improvisational experience, where artists who specialize in Hindustani vocal forms, Senegalese drumming, Wagogo song and dancing, Tejano conjunto, Afghan rabab and tabla, and Irish fiddle invite students to take a turn for four-beats, or eight-beats, or even the equivalent of a full-length stanza.

Beyond those traditions that necessitate the development by musicians of improvisatory skills as integral to their performance, there are numerous university contexts in which improvisation could be readily employed as a means of musical education. In a reflection of the natural propensity for exploration and expression they once had as children, university students can be led to a rediscovery of themselves as playfully expressive in musical ways. There are those members of the faculty who have recognized that the act of improvising offers students a way to work out an understanding of a concept (e.g., a metric aberration, a divergence from melodic expectations, an unfamiliar harmonic progress) by playing with it. They are underscoring intellectual understandings by facilitating opportunities for musical experimentation-on-a-theme (i.e., concept), giving time and space for students to explore, examine, and express in free and flexible ways or with a tilt toward multiple "rules" that invite playful improvisation with some restrictions added. Still, faculty charged with teaching many of the standard theory, aural skills, and keyboard courses are holding to conventional top-down lecture-discussion and limited occasions for the infusion of improvisation training exercises. Perhaps they do not recall their own childhoods or the playful ways in which learning transpired.

There are enthusiastic pronouncements arising from research and theory on the benefits of improvisation as a key component of the training of music students. Patricia Nardone (2002) argued from a phenomenological perspective of the life-world of musicians. She viewed improvisation as important for both its experience and context, and refers to it as comprising the elemental "lived meanings" for those entering the professional world. She described the process of improvisation as having the capacity for ensuring spontaneity while also yielding to it, exploring familiar and unfamiliar musical terrain, drawing from corporeal and incorporeal sources of musical inspirations, and having trust and confidence in oneself and others in musical risk-taking.[32] This musical spontaneity is present among children who sing because they must, dance in a full-bodied joyful manner, and play the surfaces of floors, walls, and objects they can find that are sonically responsive to their contact. It lies largely dormant, however, and requires an awakening that can come in a university's music studies. Earlier, Eric Clarke explained the contribution of improvisation to the developing musically expressive self, and claimed that courses and course experiences in improvisation were an effective counterbalance to the "arid academicism" of more conventional and long-standing courses.[33] He quite reasonably posited that improvisation could encourage students to take a questioning approach to musical performance, so that their voices are honored in musical decision making. His view was that improvisation "brings together the skills of performing, listening and creating in contrast to the deep 'division of labour' that exists within the culture of Western classical music."[34] These assertions are persuasive of the position that improvisation fully integrates the individual facets of a musician's training—synthesizing the considerable pallette of intellectual understandings and performance skills into a uniquely expressive (and artistic) voice.

Improvisation is less evident in university programs of study than would seem to be the case, given the extent of research, pedagogical papers, and policy documents that sing its praise or urge its presence.[35] The rhetoric is considerable, while the realities of applying the ideals to practice are yet limited. It is not beyond the grasp of faculty performers, theorists, historians, conductors, composers, and music educators to envelop improvisation within current or newly fashioned courses to introduce students to rhythmic and melodic motives that can be sung and played, and then performed in playfully free expressions at different pitch levels, in various textures and on various timbres. They can be encouraged in various venues and contexts to learn phrase structures and formal designs by improvising both rhythmic and melodic phrases in varied meters, within the scope of recommended durations and pitches, and with one phrase complementing and contrasting another phrase. They can internalize harmonic functions as they start from a given melody and create a bass line for it, or a harmonic progression. They can overcome their inhibitions to improvisation when faculty maneuver sessions that offer students opportunities to perform on unfamiliar instruments, to work in small groups, to express brief ideas (of four or eight beats) followed by prearranged tutti responses, and to engage in crafting musical expressions that feature preset parameters of key, length, and pitch and durational content. Improvisation may be at its best in these instructional circumstances when it is model based or integrally linked to analytical listening experiences, and when the natural processes of solo and interactive play akin to children's improvisatory music making are evident. These means of learning-by-doing assert the useful role of improvisation in ensuring that music students learn music to the fullest.

The Improvisation Weave in Music Education

True testimony of the imprint of improvisation training in university programs of music is in the ways in which it is absorbed by students as a key feature of their musical identity—on stage, in places of worship, in schools and community venues, and in other public occasions where music is made. As many music students graduate into teaching positions, they find themselves with opportunities to utilize their improvisatory impulses in ways that model and motivate such improvisation in school music settings. Some will teach children whose own capacity for musical expression is alive and well, and not yet "gone-into-hiding" (nor are they yet snuffed out by systems of learning that demand fixed music making while devaluing musical flexibility). Others will teach adolescent youth in a time of inhibitions yet also tremendous creative energy that, when tapped, may flood into musically inventive expressions of powerful proportions. The weave of improvisation in music education programs is a direct result of teachers whose university programs regularly provided them with opportunities for enlightened and spontaneous music making, particularly with a recognition (and application) of the natural elements that are evident in children's own creative musical thinking and doing.

The musical education of children and youth in schools took a decided turn toward improvisation and composition with the emergence of the National Standards for Arts Education,[36] which prompted teachers to begin to include exercises in creative music making in not only children's music classes but also ensembles, and keyboard and guitar classes. The Core Standards, issued in 2014, advocate a greater emphasis on creativity-in-action as the processes of creating, performing, and responding, and have emerged as chief artistic goals of elementary and secondary school programs in music (as well as dance, media arts, theatre, and visual arts). The Core "anchor standards" of the creating process encompass the generation of artistic ideas and works, the organization and development of these ideas, and the refinement and completion of artist work. The creating standard seems to lean in the direction of composition and songwriting, with less in the way of improvisation, although the decision to feature improvisation is within the scope of the music educator. Notably, composition and improvisation were in motion much earlier than in this time of standards, often as a balance to the performance-based curriculum that was the staple diet of North American school music programs since the mid-nineteenth century. Interest in composition led to the development of composers-in-residence in schools which, funded by the Ford Foundation, were continued through the 1960s. The highly innovative Manhattanville Music Curriculum Project, created in the late 1960s, was a curricular model for developing aural acuity, creative thought, and facility with musical sounds. Although relatively short-lived and more regional than national, its emphasis on improvisation sparked new life into a considerable number of elementary school music programs of the time.

A half-century since Manhattanville, and aside from the standards, educators are leaning toward improvisation and composition as pathways to the expression by young people in schools of a full range of emotions and deep communication. There are projects with varied media, from acoustic to electronic instruments, with percussion instruments—particularly drums—among the most commonly used in group improvisation. Creative improvisation projects for classrooms may have a specific task or a closed problem in mind, while others entail open tasks that are intended to trigger greater freedom of expression. Pedagogical methods such as the Orff-Schulwerk and Dalcroze support the presence of improvisation in elementary school classrooms, and are often aimed at children's joy and wonder in expressing themselves in song, movement/dance, and instrumental ways. Their professional organizations, the American Orff-Schulwerk Association and the Dalcroze Society of America, publish model lessons that feature techniques for the implementation of improvisational strategies for children (and for teachers of children). In middle and high school settings, improvisation figures prominently in jazz ensembles (including big band ensembles, instrumental combos, and vocal jazz groups) where students may copy the work of notable recording artists prior to coming into their own personal expressions, while guitar and keyboard classes feature experiences in which students are invited to improvise melodies over the chordal progressions they have learned. Collective and solo scale-playing are encouraged by the teacher, who typically assigns in jazz ensembles solos for standards like "C Jam Blues," "Green Dolphin Street," and "A Night in Tunisia" based on the ability of students to play their scales well. Effective educators understand that improvisation by their aspiring young musicians requires their capacity to capture a childlike interest in playful musical expression with the disciplinary rigor of instrumental performance.

Given the wide variety of ways in which improvisation can be incorporated in the K–12 music classroom, and the resonance of this activity with children's intuitive approaches to music, it is reasonable to consider the merits of a full tertiary course on "improvisation in music education." At the university under study, such a course is not in existence, though it is a topic under consideration. A quarter- or semester-long experience could offer students the time and space to freely manipulate sounds and materials in a way that a child might. For example, a class might be faced with a collection of instruments and attempt to collectively create a musical piece without speaking or planning. Or an assignment might pose the challenge of improvising a collection of pieces on "found sound" materials. In class, students could engage in a variety of improvisatory exercises—not unlike the exercises in the context of improvisatory theater—such as creating spontaneous individual pieces based on prompts such as picture cues, telling a story through on-the-spot instrumental wanderings, or accompanying an unfamiliar silent movie on a collection of instruments. Such a course could rekindle the kind of joyful discovery that for many has been tucked away in a dormant state since childhood, all the while equipping students with the comfort and skill to facilitate improvisational activities in the classrooms where they will eventually teach.

Closure

The "state of affairs" of improvisation in tertiary music education, as exemplified by the particular case in this chapter, shows just how far we have yet to go. Given the notable absence of improvisatory opportunities in the vast majority of musical study at the university level, and the extent to which improvisation is relegated into the specialized domains of organ performance and jazz studies, it is not surprising that so many university-trained music teachers feel they are swimming upstream in the pursuit of improvisatory experiences with their students. Many curricular developments at the tertiary level—as well as initiatives at the primary and secondary levels—will be crucial in addressing this issue, and it is important to bear in mind a simple reality: We (adults) do not need to be *taught* to improvise; rather we need to be *reminded*. Just as we are "born to groove,"[37] we are born to improvise. What is needed is space in the tertiary curriculum for students to develop their natural propensities: space to be playful and explore; space to invent and express themselves without suffocating parameters; and space to break rules in the process of discovering them. With a rekindling of these childlike dispositions, there exists the potential for synergies in K–12 settings—replacing the "I don't know how to improvise" rhetoric with an acknowledgement of improvisation as a primary vehicle for musically connecting with K–12 students. This is the key not only to training responsive teachers with relevant pedagogical practices, but also to cultivating musicians who are engaged, playful, thinking, and expressive.

Notes

1. Campbell et al., "Transforming Music Study."
2. Trevarthen, "Origins of Musical Identity."
3. Dissanayake, "Antecedents of the Temporal Arts."
4. Young, "Young Children's Spontaneous Vocalising."
5. Young, "Young Children's Spontaneous Vocalising," 62.
6. Sawyer, *Pretend Play as Improvisation*, xxv.
7. Corsaro, *Friendship and Peer Culture*.
8. Kartomi, "Musical Improvisations by Children at Play."
9. Sawyer, *Pretend Play as Improvisation*.
10. Blacking, *Venda Children's Songs*.
11. See, for example, Addo, "Children's Idiomatic Expressions"; Campbell, *Songs in Their Heads*; Harwood, "Music Learning"; Marsh, *The Musical Playground*.
12. Gaunt, *The Games*; Harwood, "Music Learning"; Marsh, *The Musical Playground*; Opie and Opie, *The Singing Game*.
13. McDowell, "The Transmission of Children's Folklore," 57.
14. Treitler, "Orality and Literacy," 46.
15. Marsh, *The Musical Playground*.
16. Ibid., 217.
17. Kartomi, "Musical Improvisations."
18. Campbell, *Songs in Their Heads*.
19. Whiteman, "The Complex Ecologies," 471.
20. Campbell, *Songs in Their Heads*; Lum and Campbell, "The Sonic Surrounds."
21. Campbell, *Songs in Their Heads*, 55.
22. Marsh, *The Musical Playground*.
23. Campbell, *Songs in Their Heads*.
24. Riddell, *Work*; Harwood, "Music Learning."
25. Young, "Young Children's Spontaneous Vocalising."
26. Sarrazin, "Children's Urban and Rural Musical Worlds."
27. Nannyonga-Tamusuza, "Girlhood Songs."
28. Roberts, "A Historical Look."
29. Marsh, *The Musical Playground*, 262.
30. See the IMP website, http://improvisedmusicproject.com/.
31. Merrill, "Constructivism."
32. Campbell, *Songs in Their Heads*.
33. Clarke, "Understanding the Psychology."
34. Campbell, "Learning to Improvise Music," 133.

35. Campbell et al., "Transforming Music Study"; Lum and Campbell, "The Sonic Surrounds," Sawyer, *Pretend Play*.
36. Consortium of National Arts Education Association, *National Standards*, 1994.
37. Keil and Campbell, "Born to Groove."

Works Cited

Addo, Akosua Obuo. "Children's Idiomatic Expressions of Cultural Knowledge." *International Journal of Music Education* 30, no. 1 (1997): 15–24.
Blacking, John. *Venda Children's Songs: A Study in Ethnomusicological Analysis.* Chicago, University of Chicago Press, 1995. First published 1967.
Campbell, Patricia Shehan. "Learning to Improvise Music, Improvising to Learn Music." In *Musical Improvisation: Art, Education, and Society*, edited by Gabriel Solis and Bruno Nettl, 119–42. Chicago: University of Illinois Press, 2009.
———. *Songs in Their Heads: Music and Its Meaning in Children's Lives.* New York: Oxford University Press, 2010.
Campbell, Patricia Shehan, Ed Sarath, Juan Chattah, Lee Higgins, Victoria Lindsay Levine, David Rudge, and Timothy Rice. "Transforming Music Study from Its Foundations: A Manifesto for Progressive Change in the Undergraduate Preparation of Music Majors." (Report of the Task Force on the Undergraduate Music Major.) *The College Music Society,* November 2014.
Clarke, Eric. "Understanding the Psychology of Performance." In *Musical Performance: A Guide to Understanding*, edited by John Rink, 59–72. Cambridge: Cambridge University Press, 2002.
Consortium of National Arts Education. *National Standards for Arts Education.* Reston, VA: Music Educators National Conference, 1994.
Corsaro, William A. *Friendship and Peer Culture in the Early Years.* Norwood, NJ: Ablex Pub., 1985.
Dissanayake, Ellen. "Antecedents of the Temporal Arts in Early Mother-Infant Interaction." In *The Origins of Music*, edited by Nils Wallin, Björn Merker, and Steven Brown, 389–410. Cambridge, MA: MIT Press, 2000.
Gaunt, Kyra D. *The Games Black Girls Play: Learning the Ropes from Double-Dutch to Hip-Hop.* New York: New York University Press, 2006.
Harwood, E. "Music Learning in Context: A Playground Tale." *Research Studies in Music Education* 11, no. 1 (1998): 52–60.
IMP. improvisedmusicproject.com. 2015. http://improvisedmusicproject.com/.
Kartomi, Margaret J. "Musical Improvisations by Children at Play." *World of Music* 33, no. 3 (1991): 53–65.
Keil, Charles, and Patricia Shehan Campbell. "Born to Groove." 2006. http://bornto groove.org/course/view.php?id=2.
Lum, Chee-Hoo, and Patricia Shehan Campbell. "The Sonic Surrounds of an Elementary School." *Journal of Research in Music Education* 55, no. 1 (2007): 31–47.
Marsh, Kathryn. *The Musical Playground: Global Tradition and Change in Children's Songs and Games.* New York: Oxford University Press, 2008.
McDowell, John H. "The Transmission of Children's Folklore." In *Children's Folklore: A Source Book*, edited by Brian Sutton-Smith, Jay Mechling, Thomas W. Johnson, and Felicia McMahon, 51–62. Logan: Utah State University Press, 1995.
Merrill, M. David. "Constructivism and Instructional Design." *Educational Technology* 31, no. 5 (May 1991): 45–53.

Nannyonga-Tamusuza, Sylvia. (2013). "Girlhood Songs, Musical Tales, and Musical Games as Strategies for Socialization into Womanhood among the Bahanda of Uganda." In *The Oxford Handbook of Children's Musical Cultures*, edited by Patricia Shehan Campbell and Trevor Wiggins, 114–30. New York: Oxford University Press, 2013.

Nardone, Patricia L. *The Experience of Improvisation in Music: A Phenomenological Psychological Analysis*. PhD diss., Saybrook Institute, 1996.

Opie, Iona, and Peter Opie. *The Singing Game*. New York: Oxford University Press, 1988.

Riddell, Cecilia. *Work: Traditional Singing Games of Elementary School Children in Los Angeles*. PhD diss., University of California, Los Angeles, 1990.

Roberts, J. Christopher. "A Historical Look at Three Recordings of Children's Musicking in New York City." In *The Oxford Handbook of Children's Musical Cultures*, edited by Patricia Shehan Campbell and Trevor Wiggins, 575–89. New York: Oxford University Press, 2013.

Sarrazin, Natalie. "Children's Urban and Rural Musical Worlds in North India." In *The Oxford Handbook of Children's Musical Cultures*, edited by Patricia Shehan Campbell and Trevor Wiggins, 249–65. New York: Oxford University Press, 2013.

Sawyer, R. Keith. *Pretend Play as Improvisation: Conversation in the Preschool Classroom*. Mahwah, NJ: Erlbaum Associates, 1997.

Treitler, Leo. "Orality and Literacy in the Music of the European Middle Ages." In *The Oral and Literate in Music*, edited by Yoshiko Tokumaru and Osamu Yamaguti, 38–56. Tokyo: Academia Music, 1986.

Trevarthen, Colwyn. "Origins of Musical Identity: Evidence from Infancy for Musical Social Awareness." In *Musical Identities*, edited by Raymond A.R. MacDonald, David J. Hargreaves, and Dorothy Miell, 21–38. Oxford: Oxford University Press, 2002.

Whiteman, Peter. "The Complex Ecologies of Early Childhood Musical Cultures." In *The Oxford Handbook of Children's Musical Cultures*, edited by Patricia Shehan Campbell and Trevor Wiggins, 466–78. New York: Oxford University Press, 2013.

Young, Susan. "Young Children's Spontaneous Vocalising: Insights into Play and Pathways to Singing." *International Journal of Early Childhood* 36, no. 2 (December 2004): 59–74.

16 "Things That You Hope a Human Being Will Be"

Jane Bunnett in Conversation with Ajay Heble

Ajay Heble and Jane Bunnett

On February 11, 2011, I sat down with Toronto-based soprano saxophonist, flutist, and bandleader Jane Bunnett for an interview in front of a live audience at the Guelph Public Library, Guelph, Ontario, for a session of Thinking Spaces: the Improvisation, Community, and Social Practice Reading Group. Earlier that day, Jane had participated in a series of unannounced public interventions during which she and two other musicians (Rob Wallace and Amadeo Ventura) had walked into Guelph cafés, libraries, and a downtown bookstore with their musical instruments in hand. Handing out sundry percussion instruments to passersby and encouraging participation from her (sometimes captivated, sometimes bewildered) accidental audiences, Jane and her fellow animators transformed these public spaces, which, for a few moments, unexpectedly came alive with the spirit, spark, and sense of creative community-making that so often characterizes improvised music. These interventions were the first in a series of public events to launch an exciting new community-based pedagogical initiative, and to showcase Jane Bunnett's role as our inaugural year-long Improviser-in-Residence, an initiative made possible through a partnership between the Improvisation, Community, and Social Practice (ICASP) research project, and Musagetes, an international foundation that strives to make the arts more central and meaningful in peoples' lives. In the interview, we had a wide-ranging conversation focusing on Jane Bunnett's impressive body of work, her plans for the year-long residency, the social force or improvised forms of creative practice, and the characteristics that define a good improvising musician: in Jane's words, "that the person listens when you're playing with them, the person is generous, the person is supportive. All these things that you hope a human being will be will come out in the musical activity."

Since launching in 2011, the Improviser-in-Residence program has been through a number of iterations, featuring artists from a wide range of improvising contexts: Jane Bunnett (Canada, 2011), Miya Masaoka (U.S., 2012), Scott Thomson and Susanna Hood (Canada, 2012), Rich Marsella (Canada, 2013), and, most recently, Dong-Won Kim (South Korea, 2014). The central objectives for this initiative are

- To connect the communities of Guelph (and surrounding areas) with profound direct and indirect experiences of improvised music making
- To promote the creative process, concept development, and experimentation in musical improvisation
- To track the process of the program itself through a complementary research component

From the outset, the Improviser-in-Residence initiative has been concerned to reach beyond traditional academic settings into broader communities, and, in effect, to redefine the very nature of "research" and "pedagogy" by prompting a critical reassessment of orthodox assumptions about where "knowledge" or "expertise" resides. Challenging conventional boundaries between pedagogy and performance, classroom and community, the initiative is part of a series of ongoing efforts to develop, and to build on, well-established, active, and mutually supportive partnerships in ways that highlight how community and university research and pedagogy can purposefully support one another.

By all accounts, the residencies have been successful in igniting community interaction, opening up new directions for research and pedagogy, encouraging the involvement of community members who might not otherwise be exposed to improvised or experimental music, and in engaging forms of musical and artistic dialogue across diverse communities of interest and involvement. Our artists have all been skilled educators who have facilitated community impact workshops alongside ensemble musical performances, bringing together new approaches to community building and music making. During her yearlong residency with us, for example, Jane Bunnett worked actively with a wide variety of groups in the community (by my count: she was directly engaged with some ten-plus community-based organizations), designing and facilitating workshops, doing talks, and participating in collaborative performances. She worked with students in local area high schools (including an alternative school) and at the University of Guelph, with patients at two health care centers (including people with Acquired Brain Injuries, and people suffering from post-traumatic stress disorder), as well with a social service organization, KidsAbility, that offers programs for kids with physical and developmental disabilities.

For the workshops she facilitated for KidsAbility, the culminating event was a public concert with the youth participants at The Guelph Jazz Festival (at the Festival's biggest public event, an open-air tent), where thousands of people were in attendance. Comments we continue to receive from parents, youth, staff working at social service organizations, and creative practitioners make clear that the activities associated with our residencies have played a vital role in helping to foster vibrant, cohesive communities, often within at-risk urban youth populations. Indeed, a key impact of the workshops has been a lesson for us, as researchers and educators, in learning from children and youth—in this particular case, from young people with profound physical and developmental challenges who, along with the parents and teachers who work with them every day, have taught us transformational lessons about adaptation, playfulness, and grace.

Heading now into its fifth year, the Improviser-in-Residence initiative continues to offer a resonant test-case for thinking through the ways in which improvisation can function as a dynamic model for community-engaged pedagogy. As Mark Laver's chapter in this volume on "The Share," a project that emerged from the 2012 residency, makes clear, there have, indeed, been several highlights over the first four years of the program (and these have been reinforced through the research we've conducted via interviews and observation): the participation of kids of all abilities, the facilitation of intergenerational relationships, increased self-confidence and leadership on the part of participants, and a profound recognition of the deep interconnectedness between the practices of art making and community making. In this sense, improvisation, which is, of course, at the core of the residency, is not just about the music that gets performed, but, perhaps equally importantly and more profoundly, about how people come together in difference. In the interview reprinted below, which I conducted with Jane Bunnett to launch the inaugural version of the residency, she shares her own sense of excitement in discovering the amazing opportunities, the pedagogical potential, that such an initiative has opened up both for her and for the program's many participants.[1]

—Ajay Heble

Figure 16.1 Jane Bunnett. Photograph by Thomas King.

AH: And now I'll be talking to Jane [Bunnett]. Jane is our inaugural Improviser-in-Residence, which is part of a collaborative partnership between the ICASP project—Improvisation, Community, and Social Practice—and Musagetes. When we were searching for candidates for this inaugural residency, Jane quickly rose to the top of our wish list. She is, of course, no stranger to the Guelph community. She's gifted us with several remarkable and memorable performances here over the years at the Guelph Jazz Festival. She also comes to us with significant experience working with at-risk and inner-city populations, and with a profound commitment to intercultural music making. She's a multiple Juno award winner, a recipient of the Order of Canada, a Grammy Award nominee, and an artist whose recordings and performances have allowed her to move impressively across many dimensions of musical experience. Working in and working across different contexts of music-makings—Cuban musics, post-Monk and post-Mingus, avant-garde, free jazz, new music, gospels, spirituals, and the list goes on—she's worked with Don Pullen, Steve Lacy, Sheila Jordan, Jeanne Lee, Charlie Haden, Andrew Cyrille, the Penderecki String Quartet, Slim Gaillard, Henry Grimes, Hilario Durán, Paul Bley, the Cuban piano masters, Billy Hart, Stanley Cowell, Dewey Redman, and the list goes on and on and on. It's a veritable who's who of creative music. Indeed, her work represents an exceptional trajectory through the entire history of contemporary jazz and improvised music. It really is an honor to have you here as part of our residency program.

JB: Thanks. It's an honor to be given this great opportunity. It's a challenge, but every time I'm coming into town I just think that it's a gift also for me because for me there will be a lot of self-discovery, being aware of things that I take for granted. So, this is an interesting facet, to have a different learning curve with this.

AH: Perhaps we could start by talking about the work you're going to be doing as part of your residency here. This is, of course, a brand new initiative for us and for you—and it's really one I've dreamed about for a long time—having an Improviser-in-Residence position. We've all heard about Composers-in-Residence, Artists-in-Residence … but I've always thought, wow, wouldn't it be great to have an Improviser-in-Residence position. And from the start it's been about something that's a little bit different from the standard academic residency. For me, this is first and foremost a *community* residency, that is, we want to bring artists and community partners together to create these sustained projects in the community. It certainly means a lot to have you here. Can you talk about what it means for you to be the very first Improviser-in-Residence here in Guelph?

JB: As I mentioned, there's already been some sort of discovery, things that, like I've said, I've taken for granted. My observations that I've taken, even from [the unannounced public interventions] today, is that people ultimately do have rhythm. We white people have rhythm! But it was interesting because if in the library you could see that people were joining in, that some of them were sort of halfway there because of the commitment to just totally engage ... if they were among friends, there was a little part of them that didn't totally want to take the hand off the laptop. I don't know if they were half pretending they were doing something—I couldn't do that—half doing the rhythm thing and then typing. But generally people looked quite happy when they engaged in the musical activity.

AH: The first thing I noticed was just the smiles.

JB: Mmhmm.

AH: At the library, and the Bookshelf, and the café, you went in unannounced and provided them with the gift of music and people were lighting up.

JB: It's an incredible opportunity we as musicians have, like you said, to engage the community and draw people out and hopefully be conduits—is that the right word—to be able to get different groups to ... this is a new thing, and for me, you can't sort of walk in and say "I'm going to do this, I'm going to do this." These ideas are sort of moving around, and as I get to know people and get to know the personality of a certain group, and of course the facilitator that you're working with, I see that there will be tie-ins. At first, when we talked about doing that, I thought, "this is contrived, I don't see how this is possible," when you've got people with all sorts of different issues. But I think it will be possible to put some groups together that people maybe wouldn't have thought could work together. For example, we've just done a couple of sessions at Homewood [Health Centre], and both of them have been totally different. The first one was quite remarkable because there was one woman who came in, and she definitely did not want to be there. She came in and she looked very, very unhappy. She's from Nunavut, and I had been told that she hated white people, so prepare for that, and I don't blame her. ... She was sitting there, and right away when someone has their arms like this it's going to be hard to pry those arms away and put an instrument in there. Gradually, we were able to connect and she was able to connect with the group. At one point, it was so funny ... it was either that day or the day before, working with KidsAbility, which is another group, I guess you are all familiar with KidsAbility. We worked with them the year before and we were doing this potato chip song and it turned into peanut butter, and I mentioned this to the group at the Homewood. Taking a word and how words have rhythm, like peanut butter. She picked up on it right away, this woman. Peanut butter. Oh, I should backtrack a bit. Just before that we were all sitting down drumming and I got up and I started to move with the drum. I started to actually dance a bit with the drum as I was playing. And she got up and all of a sudden she was dancing around the room, hitting the drum, and she had heard me talk about peanut butter and she starting going "peanut butter, peanut butter," and she's hitting the drum and really getting into it. "Peanut butter!" and everyone started joining in. The doors were open and I thought, "If anybody walks by, if any of these doctors walk by, they're probably going to close us down." But we were all singing and everyone hitting the drum, going, "peanut butter, peanut butter," and she was having the time of her life. And at the end, we just sort of talked as we were packing up and I asked her, "How do you feel?" And she said, "I have never been so happy in my entire life!"

AH: So what do you think accounts for that change?

JB: Well, I think the fact that she was connecting with people that she's probably been sitting around with in group therapy and been probably very intense. A lot of people in that place are going through something at that time, and I think that in so many ways, that music, in a million different ways, and one of the things is that it takes you out of ... that it's not just you ... that you're part of something bigger, and also that you do have some control. I think with music there's something that is bigger than you, but you're still a part of it and you still feel like you have some power to control what's happening. You're a part of something, you're a part of the piece, you're a part of what is happening at that moment. I think it's abstract, but at the same time it's such a grounded thing. You know, we've had music in our culture since way before the language, we had words, so if it was banging rhythms, that existed before. And I think it's just such a strong instinct. And in our culture, in North American cultures, because in so many others it's not a problem, and in Cuban culture I've seen it first hand, that everybody is a participant in Cuban music. You don't sit back and watch other people perform. You may have other people that are better musicians or more equipped, or technically they're advanced, but still there's a participation. The audiences are very important participators in musical activity in other cultures, and in our culture it's been cut off. Even in East Coast culture there's more, Newfoundland and P.E.I. [Prince Edward Island] and those places, there are kitchen parties and music. People are banging on something. So they're engaged in the activity; whereas here, we have sort of left it for ... it's a specialty.

AH: So these interventions that you've just done today, of course, were an attempt to encourage people to engage in that act of participation?

JB: Yeah. I think even if it just makes somebody think for a moment about music, then that, in itself, is even an important thing: "Oh, there was some musical activity that sort of passed by me today." And I think anything that you do as a group, and in the reading I've been doing lately, that's why even those rock songs, "We will rock you," look at the phenomenon, stadiums of people going [Jane demonstrates] stomp, stomp, clap, stomp, stomp, clap. All these people that are just engaged in something, and it's so powerful!

AH: I know you've spent a lot of time and energy in preparing for the work you're doing here.

[To audience] While Jane is here, she's going to be working with several different groups in the community, ranging from students in high school to patients at health care centers to people who have acquired brain injuries, people suffering from trauma, kids with physical and developmental disabilities.

[To Jane] And I know that you've spent quite a bit of time thinking about each of these groups you're working with and designing projects specific to those groups. I'm wondering if you find yourself following the plans that you've prepared, or are there situations where you find yourself having to reinvent your methods? I'm thinking by way of a context for this question about a comment you made to me in a previous interview. You were talking about that wonderful record you made with Paul Bley, *Double Time*, about how you really prepared for that recording by working on all this music, and when you sat down to do the record with Paul he resisted your efforts. You said to me, "He didn't really let me prepare." You told me in that earlier interview that Larry Cramer, your musical and life-partner, told you, "This is what you do best. This is what you practice for. This is why you spend all those hours working on things—so you can jump into a situation like this and just play. And not play the licks that you've been working on." And I wonder if there is something similar going on in the work for this residency. I know you've been talking about these plans you're putting into place. Are those plans being resisted when you find yourself in the moment in those situations?

JB: Well, I'm sort of formulating things, formulating projects that I would like to see happen, but there will ultimately be a lot of shifting because I know some of the stuff is not totally formulated. And I think that it's really important for me to get a sense, like I said, of the dynamic of the group. Like especially, for example, [when working with students at the alternative high school] Give Yourself Credit. These kids must have an incredible amount of courage to be doing what they're doing. It's really hard for them. A few of them have kids too, and here they are they're working toward a high school credit. So my idea may not be their idea. I might get in there and they might totally resist. What I think is so cool is not so cool. And then I'm going to have to do some shifting because ultimately I want them to be engaged in something they are really excited about. You have to go with the group and work with them and what they want. I can't just go in and impose some idea that I think is so cool. So I'm hoping that they are going to think that the idea is cool, and that we'll be able to do something that's going to give them a face. I'm very project driven. Being the sort of person that I am, I need to have a goal at the end when I do something. So with each group I've tried to think of something that will showcase the work in the end to the community and will maybe bridge a gap. In the case of Give Yourself Credit, that these kids will be able to vent if they need to vent on what their situation is, that somehow they can get some respect. And that the community will respect the organization and what these kids are trying to achieve, and they'll get a credit for it, too.

AH: Let's talk about improvisation, which is, of course, the central focus for this residency. What attracts you to improvised music and do you think there's something, in particular, about improvised music making that speaks to and resonates with these communities that you're working with, many of which are marginalized?

JB: Well, I guess the first thing is that you can never duplicate. Every performance, every activity is unique in itself and that's what makes it special. We're trying to develop something, and if, by improvising, we improve on an idea … that doesn't mean that we're always going to do something totally, totally different; but we're going to embellish something, make it bigger, go one direction, go a different direction than expected but still on a course. That's the exciting thing for me: just starting with a blank wall, nothing's there, and then creating something, something that has meaning not only to the people doing it, but the activity at that moment, the pleasure that you get when you actually are playing. Like with musicians, when you're playing with like-minded musicians, that feeling is one of the most wonderful feelings in the world. Time stops. Everything stops. You kind of lose sense of yourself. I mean, I always find for me no matter how terrible I feel … there was one day when I walked into the Homewood, and I just really felt like I was the last person who should be in here with these folks because I feel terrible myself today. And I felt great afterward. I mean after the activity, working with them, and just improvising, I felt so much better. That connecting, there's no language, it's the music that's happening. It's a very powerful and very remarkable thing to do.

AH: This comment that there's no language except for music puts me in mind of something else you said in that previous interview we did, which is perhaps worth repeating here. We were talking then about an ad hoc grouping of musicians, improvising musicians, I'd brought together at the Guelph Jazz Festival. You were playing with Getatchew Mekuria from Ethiopia and Jah Youssouf from Mali and Alain Derbez from Mexico and Hamid Drake from the U.S.: musicians from all around the world. And the amazing thing about that event is that many of you were meeting for the very first time and doing so onstage in front of an audience, and that you were performing with no prearranged musical direction and there was no language in common. There was literally no language in common onstage, and yet you created absolutely wondrous music. In thinking about that event, we started talking in that interview about the extent to which musical improvisation might be linked with these broader social issues: communication, human rights, social justice, building community. And you said to me: "When you sit down and you're in a collective like that it entails all the things that we as human beings should just be, and in that way, it can teach something to the listener to carry forth too. Just dealing with all the things that life entails." Now it's clear to me that, in speaking with you, and indeed in speaking with so many of the artists who play at the Guelph Jazz Festival, that there is something profoundly important going on in that moment, when musicians improvise together, especially improvising across these global communities. Something profoundly important is going on in terms of the kinds of broader social issues we were talking about there. Now in your case, you've done a whole lot of work, not only in intercultural contexts ... your work with and commitment to Cuban music and Cuban musicians certainly comes to mind. ... but you've also done a lot of work in Toronto and now in Guelph with at-risk and inner-city kids and populations. I'm wondering if you can say a bit more about how some of your previous experiences have shaped your understanding of the social importance of improvised music? And are there particular instances? You've already begun to talk about these in terms of some of the work you've done in the residency, but are there other particular instances you can talk about where you really felt that you were making a difference, having an impact with your music, a particular kind of social impact? You mentioned some of the examples from Homewood. I know certainly from talking to the parents and the staff and the kids at KidsAbility about the work you did there a few years ago, it's tremendously inspiring for those people. But I'd be interested in hearing from you if there are particular moments that stand out as having an impact.

JB: Gosh, there are lots. It's more so down the road where people will come up to you and say, "Four years ago I heard you. I just was going through something, or something or another was happening, and I heard a performance with you, and did this thing and it just helped me so much." That kind of stuff, I do hear that a lot. Because I feel like the music that I do comes from a very spiritual place. I'm not a religious person in the context of going to church and that kind of thing—as much as I like churches—but I find for me when I play music I try to do it from a very deep place. Musicians that I like to work with and hope to work with are the kind of people that, as human beings, even if they weren't musicians, they would still be the kind of people I would want to be around. The fact that they play music is great. Those kind of personality traits in the music are very important, that the person listens when you're playing with them, the person is generous, the person is supportive. All these things that you hope a human being will be will come out in the musical activity. I think when the situation is right like that, you mentioned Dewey Redman and Don Pullen, many of the musicians that I've worked with have been from that place. Even Paul Bley, who's crazy, crazy! He's brilliant crazy, but he's still, as a musician, incredibly … I've never had quite an experience such as playing with Paul Bley, and what he gives as a musician. It's unexplainable, really. I think that translates to people, like the people that like what I do, and then you get that nice feedback. Because sometimes you just feel like chucking it, which I have. Three years ago I was ready to quit music. I hit the wall and had enough. I made 17 records. I can't do it anymore. I'm tired. I'm tired of making records and I'm tired of touring. I'm tired of feeling like, "Oh she just put out another record … great." But it was a very interesting transition to get myself out of that, and get back into music. So now I feel like with working at Homewood and working with some people, I know what that feeling is to feel disengaged from music, too. I'm not the kind of musician … I think there are a lot of musicians out there who were, at seven years old, protégés, and by the time they were seventeen or eighteen they were terrific musicians. I haven't been an academic, and I started playing when I was twenty-two. So I started quite late. But I feel musically because of certain things that have happened that I can connect with people musically. I have a different way of working, and I think certain people pick up on that.

AH: In terms of the impact of your music, as I said earlier, one example that certainly comes to mind for me has to do with those workshops you did with KidsAbility here a few years ago.

JB: Rob [Wallace] was with us, too.

AH: Rob and Larry [Cramer] were part of that. This [KidsAbility Centre for Child Development] is an organization that works with kids who have physical and developmental disabilities here in Guelph, and they're all very excited to have you back working with the kids there again this year as part of your residency. Now, when you were here a couple of years ago, those workshops that you did with the youth culminated in a brilliant performance that you did at the Jazz Festival tent, which is the largest outdoor venue at the Jazz Festival, where there are literally thousands of people. Those workshops were hugely inspiring I think for all of us, and anyone who was participating and watching. Many people in the audience were moved to tears. And the interviews that we conducted afterward with the participants and with the staff from KidsAbility made it clear just what a significant impact you had on those kids. And I remember remarking to you right after that final concert with the kids how … I think you only had three or four workshops with them … imagine if we had a whole year. Well, now we do! That's the amazing thing. I thought you were able to accomplish so much just in that short period of time. So, now we have a whole year, and I'm wondering what this opportunity for extended contact might enable you to do that you couldn't do the first time around?

JB: I think fine-tune things a bit more. I think some of the regulars that are back, they are more comfortable with me. They know me a little bit. And probably we'll increase the repertoire. We have a songbook together now. Thanks to Slim [Gaillard], he's given me some material to work with. There's a couple of new kids in there. One who's really dynamite actually. We just have to make sure he doesn't steal the show, because he's a bit of a ham. He's a great kid. I think we'll just be able to have more pieces of music, and be able to present them. Maybe give more kids more cameos than we had before.

AH: One of the things you did last time was you had each of the kids bring a photograph and create a kind of composition or story around the photo.

JB: Yes, we're doing that again too.

AH: I thought that was very successful.

JB: We've got a few things up our sleeve. It's gonna be fun.

AH: In addition to being a performer, improviser, composer, educator, and bandleader, you're also an organizer. Indeed, you're one of the driving forces behind the Art of Jazz Festival, and I know that the Art of Jazz has an educational mandate, that it does a lot of outreach work in the community as well. I'm wondering if you see connections between your work as a festival organizer with The Art of Jazz and the work you're doing with the residency.

JB: Yeah! It's just giving me more opportunity to develop my skills, number one. Well, number one, let me take my hat off to you because this kind of thing could never happen in Toronto, I don't think, what you've done. I mean maybe it could, but we're a long way from … because of the kind of community Guelph is. It's very rootsy, and partly because it's a university town, there's a great sort of feeling of teamwork here. I mean, just doing what we were doing today, I'm sure I would have got my soprano [saxophone] shoved down my … [grabs throat, laughs] if I did that at the reference library! I think there's a lot to learn by working in a smaller community … how to go out and then work in a larger community. It think some of the things we're doing … it would be very difficult. The Art of Jazz, we worked up in the Jane and Finch area with about 350 kids that were bussed in from all the schools up there up to one of the schools, C.W. Jefferys. We were working with Jon Hendricks, and that was, how do you say it, just an overwhelming project because of the amount of kids and the organization of trying to bus kids in. And the biggest thing is that, unlike here in Guelph, the family thing is so rough now in Toronto. There are so many moms and no fathers in the situation, so the family structure is so disheveled, and so when you're working with young people it's difficult—very, very difficult! It's difficult here, but not as difficult. I think I've been given an opportunity to do what I like to do and, maybe at some point, help in Toronto. Or actually, possibly going down into the Regent Park area. Next year they're building a whole new complex down there. So I think the Art of Jazz will be having an office down there, and we will be working with youth in music down there.

AH: So even though the festival is moving its location, you're going to continue to work in Toronto.

JB: Yes. The next couple of years we'll be working in Brampton, and they're sure we'll be there forever, and who knows, you know? But I'd like to get back into Toronto, too, but for us in the Distillery [district] the place is just too rich for our blood [laughs]. In the sense—you all know the Distillery, right—they're about boutiques and the high-end. We're talking about the real estate people. What do you call them ... the Corp. The corporation that's down there that owns everything in the Distillery, they're really not ... I shouldn't be, I'll get in big trouble for this but, anyway ... that it's not their agenda, really. So, that's why. They're building condos and two of the stages are gone that we were working in. Condos are going up and that's going to be two, three years of condo building. Yah. We need more condos. So, that's one of the reasons we moved [the Festival] to Brampton, and they're thrilled to have us. But still I'd like to be back in Toronto, too. It's keeping your chops going, you know. Just keeping the momentum ... you know what it's like, if you take a year off, it's tricky to get back in the saddle.

AH: That's true.

JB: That was the choice, but this is an amazing opportunity. Like I said, self-discovery, going to the Homewood and KidsAbility, and Give Yourself Credit. That's the group I like most ... teenagers. I was a very, very rebellious teenager, and so fortunate that I ended up okay. Because, you know, I had some real brushes in my teenage life. So I like to work with at-risk kids. I think the potential is HUGE for them. And just a lot of them have been dealt really crappy circumstances. They're not in the position where they want to be.

AH: What do you think the greatest challenges are going to be during this year that you're with us at Guelph?

JB: Take a guess?! Doing it all! It's a hell of a lot, right Kim!

KIM THORNE: You can do it.

JB: Just keep breathing.

AH: Making it all happen.

JB: Making it all happen. But I've got great people working with me, so ...

AH: Shifting focus a little bit, can you talk about what it's like to be a woman improviser in what is largely a male-dominated field?

JB: Sometimes good, sometimes bad. Sometimes it's great! Let me put it this way, if it's a women's festival, it's great if they hire me. I love the women's festivals, and if they don't hire me, I hate them! Generally, it's great. I've been fortunate, partly because my partner is a trumpet player so he often can be in the picture. But I've had a couple of pretty bad experiences, when I didn't choose my adversaries, I guess is the word. A very bad experience in the North Sea at a jam session. I'll tell you that story another time. ... But it was actually a musician that was in Wynton Marsalis' big band, at the North Sea Jazz Festival Jam Session.

I almost got in a fist fight on the stage because he told me I had to get off the stage, and that I shouldn't be playing, and to go home and practice. He pulled this ... in front of a huge room of people, and I could have handled it better myself, but being feisty I decided to make a real scene out of it. But ultimately, I got him fired ... because his display was really uncalled for. It was a whole group of young women that were overseas. It was one of these IAJE [International Association for Jazz Education] all-women groups. They were all up front just watching this thing happen. So I kinda felt like ... I just had it out with the guy. And then I wrote a letter and put it under his door and that went over well, but ... [laughter] So, there's been a few things but not a lot. The reason being because a lot of the time I've chosen, I've been careful to not put myself in a situation where I will be really vulnerable and possibly get my feelings hurt. I haven't gone into situations trying to prove something: "I'm going to walk into the situation because I want to play," or something like that. The musicians that I've worked with have all been really supportive and great people, and so if you keep those kinds of things in mind then, you sort of buff yourself to what people are saying about you.

AH: What about the industry, more broadly?

JB: Well, to tell you the truth, I try and manipulate that. To be perfectly honest! I really do. I mean, my mother always said to me, "You get more bees with honey." I don't mean it the way that just came out. Oh, my god! But I mean, there's no reason to walk into a situation and be a certain way. You try to be up front and respectful and treat me ... there have been a couple of things that have happened, that I've lost ... you know what's been more of a problem, to tell you the truth, and I seriously mean this, being Canadian.

AH: I was just going to say ...

JB: Being Canadian. Not being white, not being a woman, but being Canadian, and not having a New York address. People have told me, the critics, U.S. journalists, say stuff: "She doesn't live in the States." This is a New Yorky thing too. I've played in New York: "Well, she doesn't live here. Where's she from? Canada?" You can't be any good if you're from Canada. In fact, Paul Bley was one of the musicians. He saw my bio when we were doing *Double Time* and he said, "Take it out that you're Canadian." He said, "Take it out of your bio. Don't say you're Canadian." I said, "Really? But I'm proud to be Canadian." He said, "No, that doesn't work," and he told me, "Get a New York address." He told me, "It doesn't even matter if it's just a box. Just get a New York address." And I was like, "God!"

AH: So have you done those things?

JB: No, I haven't. I haven't. I haven't. Maybe I should. I should listen to Uncle Paul.

AH: I just have one more question.

JB: Well, they're good questions. They're hard questions.

AH: Earlier today you were involved in a number of unannounced public interventions, and I think they went off really well, and I was just wondering if you could tell us about your response to what went down.

JB: It was fun because I think most of the people were really nice. Don't you think, guys? They were nice. There wasn't one nasty ... I know in Toronto, for sure, if we'd done it in Toronto there would have been ten that would have been, "Get out of my face!" definitely. But everybody was smiling. "Okay, I'll shake this. I don't really want to but I will."

AH: But by then they wanted to, right?

JB: Yes, some of them were sort of like ...

AH: Those people in the library, on campus, they were totally into it!

JB: They were like, "I won't do it. I won't do it." But next time you see them, finally they got into it. And it was interesting because most people were sort of halfway there. They weren't totally (gesturing with a hand shaking up and down). There were a few that got totally into it, but there were some that were like, "I'm talking to my friend and I'm shaking the banana, and I'm doing my computer, too." So they were wanting to hide a little bit behind something, and not totally look like they were getting into it. And I thought it was interesting too ... I tried to make a point about looking into people's eyes ... 'cause I tend to close my eyes sometimes when I play, but I tried to look people in the faces as they were playing because that's an important thing when you're playing too ... to have eye contact with the musicians. Because it's not ... I mean I do close my eyes when I'm concentrating, but there still should be a certain amount of eye connection ... because you get a sense of body language and where the music is going to go. Is this person really digging what I'm doing? Are they following? So it was interesting because everybody really looked me in the face. Nobody turned away when I looked at them.

AH: How did today's experience compare to the stint you did at St. Lawrence Market [in Toronto], where you were busking.

JB: Oh, that was painful. So for those who don't know, the [Toronto] *Star* did a ... it was around Juno time and they wanted to see how people respond to their Canadian ... a Canadian artist. So luckily they put me in the St. Lawrence Market, which was better than [what they did with] Joshua Bell. They put Joshua Bell in the Wall Street subway. Poor guy. So this was a copycat thing. Some people would push their kids up: "Put some money in the hat. I'm not gonna do it, but you're gonna do it." So that was kind of interesting. Generally, people were quite nice, but nobody did come up and speak to me. The *Star* reporters were running after them and asking them questions afterward. But Joshua Bell, his experiences were terrible. Now mind you, it was work time. This was 8:30 in the morning. They actually had it on camera where the parents would have their kid and they would be taking them out of the subway, and the kid would be like, "What is he doing?" Trying to see the violinist, and the parents were standing in front of the kid's view so they couldn't see Joshua even playing. "We're not going to stop for the music." And you see these kids, "I want to stay," and the parent pulling the kid. I made more money than he did [laughing]. I made forty-six dollars and he made twenty-five. It was very interesting. This was Wall Street, and I'm in a market. Much more the kind of person who wants to meet the sausage guy and wants to talk sausages and stuff, whereas on Wall Street no one's talking sausages. But it was a different environment. Still, the guy makes $30,000 to $40,000 a concert, and one woman put in $20 because she'd seen him three weeks ago. But nobody recognized him. Nobody stopped a second to hear him. So, it was a pretty good experience, but this was better. We didn't give instruments out either. They probably would have run.

AH: Well, you brought some music …

JB: Well, you suggested I bring some …

AH: Do you want to play something?

JB: Well … what do you think? I don't know …

AH: What did you bring?

JB: I brought this one that has a bunch of stuff. It's got some Paul Bley, and this is sort of my own bootleg. I make the bootleg 'cause I owe the record company like $8,000 [laughs]. I can't buy any more CDs. So, I did this. Well maybe … this hasn't been released. I'm trying to think of what to do. … Maybe I'll play you this. This is something I did with all nature sounds in Algonquin Park. And it's just a short piece. I was actually commissioned by the CBC to do it. And it was interesting. There were six people commissioned to write music for their favorite park in Canada. So, I think Bruce Cockburn did one, and what's-her-name from out east. And everybody's piece was eight minutes, four seconds, eight minutes, six seconds, everybody's piece. Isn't that weird?

AH: It is weird.

JB: So this was done. … [working with CD player] Oh, Miss Techie … with bata drums, which are the hourglass Cuban drums and myself on piano and playing flutes. And it's a song cycle. In the Afro-Cuban music you have all these different saints, which are connected to the elements of nature. So it can be fire, water, trees, green—they're connected to colors. They're called the Orishas. And this is a song cycle of all the different particular … because each saint has a particular rhythm. This is called "bata mata chango." So it's all the whole cycle of all the Orishas compacted into this eight minutes. And you can hear all these nature sounds. So I'm trying to think what I'm going to do with this. I would like somebody to actually animate something for it.

[Music plays.]

JB: Summer's only how many months? [laughs]

AH: That's beautiful.

JB: Thanks. That was kind of a different departure for me. I like playing that for Cubans because there is so much space in there. They're like, "I don't get it." That was Pancho [Quinto] playing there.

AH: Oh, was it?

JB: Yeah. That was fun playing with Pancho. Afterward, I took it back and played it for his family. It was cool and unusual.

AH: Maybe we can see if people from the audience have questions for Jane.

AUDIENCE MEMBER: We all have that slightly blissed out expression of having meditated through that beautiful piece.

JB: It is. ... I haven't listened to it in a while, but I like the zone it put me in when I was working on it. I would love to ... I have this idea. ... I just haven't met the person to do it, but an animation. Do you remember Norman McLaren?

AH: I do.

JB: Do you remember the one where the drop of water hits the ... it takes place in a canoe. Does it take place in a canoe or something and then there was a fly on his skin? ... Anyway, I'd like something that would start with a drop of water, and then the ripples come out and then all these things start to happen with the ripples ... animals ...

AH: I have someone in mind for you ...

JB: Do you? Really? I'd like to do that. I don't know what I'd do with it after I do it, but ... get it shown on an airplane or something. [laughing] Maybe, I don't know.

AUDIENCE MEMBER: I want to ask a question about that really touching incident you brought up in the Homewood, with the indigenous woman who was so angry.

JB: Mmmhmm.

AUDIENCE MEMBER: ... and then so happy. Where are you going to go from there?

JB: Well, it was interesting. So, so, so ... I was so pumped on Wednesday to see her, right? So this is how life goes, right? I'm pumped and I told Larry about her. I called that night and I was pumped because I was really nervous about going into Homewood. Anyway, I'm all excited to see her and I'm waiting in the hall. Guys are waiting outside to load the stuff in and she's coming out to have a smoke, and I say, "Hey, how are you doing? We're going to play today." She said, "No, I'm not coming today." "Oh." I'm taking it totally personally, of course. "Ohh." "No," she said, "I'm having a caribou roast. And I've been waiting for the caribou roast. And, and, and." I said, "Oh. It's only from three to four thirty. Can't you come and do the music and then go do the caribou roast?" She was going to a friend's house because someone had brought some caribou. And she said, "Nope. I've been waiting for this for a long time. And I'm taking him, and I'm taking her, and I'm taking ...," and she ran down. ... You're taking the whole class! So finally when

Calvin [Clinical Social Worker at Homewood] came up, "Oh I've got an incident." "Well, don't worry. I've heard. I ran into her, and she told me." I don't know how she sabotaged the class. He said, "Maybe we'll just cancel because I don't see the point." But you know she was nice about it. I said, "I'm sorry. I'm gonna be so disappointed. You were so great last week. Oh, and I had some ideas about this week." "Nope. I'm not coming to class this week. You'll see me again but not today." So off she went. So Calvin said when we got in there, "I don't know. We'll see. I don't know what's going to happen. We'll see." So we went in there and there's two totally brand new people sitting on the stage. And I said, "Well, we can still do something with two people," and one other enthusiast: this one guy who's very enthusiastic. He's got one rhythm that he really does well and he does it a lot. He said, "Well, do I have enough time? Do you want me to go out and round up a few people?" "Sure, if you think you can." So he comes back in five minutes. No, he doesn't come back. … All of a sudden these women start coming in the door … five … and then four more … and then he came and stuck his head in to make sure they got in and then he went out again. So he was out there hustling people in for the session. So how many did we have? Quite a few.

AUDIENCE MEMBER: Ten or eleven.

JB: No, didn't we have more than that? It was way more than the first one. So, anyway, all these folks came in and they were pretty enthusiastic. And all first-timers except for a couple. And then one of the guys decided not to go to the caribou roast and came to the class. So, anyway, I hope she'll be here next week, because she really did say she had a good time. Food won. Food and music, it's a tough call, right?

AUDIENCE MEMBER: But maybe a similar collaborative community experience, right?

JB: Yeah, yeah, absolutely! Well, something like that is a part of somebody's culture. I don't blame her. Can I come? Is there really caribou?

AH: Any other questions from the audience?

AUDIENCE MEMBER: I just was wondering when you were talking about the interventions today … because a lot of site-specific work that isn't in theaters, there are negotiations of the space and the people in the space and sometimes it's really complicated. And you were saying that in Toronto they would have been really annoyed and not into it. But I wonder if they would have been, because I was worried about that here too because it's a library and people are supposed to be quiet.

JB: Yes.

AUDIENCE MEMBER: I mean, upstairs I knew there would be kids that would be interested, but I wasn't sure about downstairs. I wonder if it is about the way you set that up. There was such a warmth and there was such a connection with everybody. I think that possibly that was why people were willing to go with it. But I wonder how the kind of spaces and the people in the spaces affect the kind of music you make, because obviously you've just done this beautiful site-specific park piece which is from Algonquin, which is totally different ...

JB: Well, definitely. If you get a bad reception you don't feel exactly welcome to be like, "I'm going to play for you ... if you like it or not." ... The Red Brick [Café] was especially easy to play because people were joining in. When you walk into a bigger space, like the big library, it's a little bit trickier because there is so much space. But in the smaller areas where you are contained, it's kind of like everybody ends up, when you have a party, in your kitchen. Why is that? When people are tight together, it's like people sitting in a circle playing. It was interesting, for example, with KidsAbility I'm now sitting on the floor which actually gives me some issues with my back, but it seems to be much better to be on the floor with them, playing with us all at the same eyesight. I don't know how we came about figuring that all out, but when I sit at the piano it's really [points]—maybe that's why we get you to play the piano! I'd like to do both, but we'll figure out ... It's good because with the kids we're more connected, instead of being on chairs and people are all at different levels.

AUDIENCE MEMBER: I was just thinking of the meat counter at the St. Lawrence Market saying it's too loud for my business and you feeling really ...

JB: Oh I felt just terrible afterward, like, "Okay, I'll just pack up and go ..."

AUDIENCE MEMBER: And the kind of conversation you had to have, right, of how to then think about playing your own music?

JB: No, I really didn't feel like playing afterward. But if the guy's trying to make a living, you know, and he can't hear ... gives her pork sausages and she wanted lamb, it's not good for business, so ...

AUDIENCE MEMBER: These negotiations in space are complicated ...

JB: But you know what, I guess music is also its own negotiation, in a way. It's interesting because I've always just gone out and played music and now I'm having to think about things. Really hard!! (laughter). We musicians just want to play, eh? Give me a bottle of beer and I'll play. That's it. But now I have to think heady stuff. You're making me think, Ajay!

AH: Anybody else want to make Jane think?

AUDIENCE MEMBER: Can I ask you a question about you and music? You say you were late coming to music. You were twenty-two. And in sort of the same breath you said you were really profoundly affected by the power of connection through music. Is that what drew you to music?

JB: Yes. Absolutely. And I have to say there was one really pivotal experience. Everyone does have a pivotal experience. Ballet dancers ... they say, when they went to see the Nutcracker. And everything was [Jane gestures with dancing fingers] ... and that moment they decided that they wanted to do it. There's always something, and for me it was really hearing Mingus, Charles Mingus in San Francisco. It so blew my mind, because I thought they were all classical musicians. And later I told Don Pullen that and he just thought it was hilarious that I thought that. Here's a guy who started out playing organ in trios, you know, strip clubs and stuff. First church, but his early gigs were … Anyway, but I thought that they were all classical musicians because their technique was so … they had such command of their instruments. But then there was this dialogue that they were having together. I looked at that and thought, "This is one of the most beautiful things I've ever seen. Look how these guys are communicating with each other." And that's what really made me think I want to become … I want to be in, up there, in that kind of environment where everybody is communicating like that. And I was playing classical piano at the time, so when I came back from that trip it was "finish up my piano studies, and I want to play jazz." I knew at that point.

AH: And here you are.

JB: And here I am. Here I am.

Interview Transcription by Elizabeth Johnstone

Note

1. An earlier version of this interview appeared on the Improvisation, Community, and Social Practice (ICASP) website (improvcommunity.com), and in the limited-edition book, *Things That You Hope a Human Being Will Be: 2011 Improviser-in-Residence Jane Bunnett*, edited by Ajay Heble and Alissa Firth-Eagland. We'd like to acknowledge the original publishers, ICASP and the Musagetes Foundation. The version that appears here includes an expanded preface.

17 The Share

Improvisation and Community in the Neoliberal University

Mark Laver

On October 13, 2012, Guelph's Exhibition Park was host to a "dynamic and uncommon dance and music event."[1] Anyone who passed through the area on that chilly, damp afternoon saw a host of local and Toronto-based professional and amateur musicians and dancers playing together under the trees of the park, and on the verandas, driveways, and lawns of the homes that immediately surround it.

Figure 17.1 Promotional image for "The Share."

Devised by 2012 Improvisation, Community, and Social Practice (ICASP) Improvisers-in-Residence[2] Scott Thomson and Susanna Hood, *The Share* (as the event was called) purposefully disrupted boundaries between professional and amateur, between public and private, between performance and play, and between the presentational and the participatory.[3] With this event, Thomson, Hood, and their numerous collaborators cocreated a processual pedagogical and aesthetic model that can serve as a sharp critique *of* and an inspiring alternative *to* current structural and pedagogical trends in the university that co-hosted the event—and, more broadly, to the frighteningly rapid encroachment of neoliberal ideology in institutional education around the world.

Thomson and Hood were the third "Improvisers-in-Residence," following internationally renowned saxophonist and flautist, Jane Bunnett, and New York–based sound artist Miya Masaoka. Conceived by ICASP project director Ajay Heble, hosted by the ICASP project at the University of Guelph, and co-presented by the international philanthropic arts organization Musagetes, the "Improviser-in-Residence" program "brings improvising musicians into meaningful contact with the local community."[4] This "contact" has taken a number of different forms since the inception of the program, from Bunnett's wide-ranging work with the KidsAbility Centre for Child Development and the Homewood Health Centre, to Masaoka's workshops with local high school students, to Rich Marsella's community performance of Rimsky-Korsakov's *Scheherazade,* scheduled as part of the 2013 Guelph Jazz Festival. While Thomson and Hood did work extensively with KidsAbility and other local organizations, their energies were directed primarily toward *The Share.*

Figure 17.2 Susanna Hood and Scott Thomson. Photograph by Joane Hétu.

Like many of Thomson's previous projects, *The Share* is what he calls a "cartographic composition": a site-specific piece for mobile musicians playing (mostly) loosely structured musical material. As with Thomson's previous work, Thomson and Hood's plan for *The Share* deployed musicians such that they were able to explore all of the nooks and crannies of the site, while at the same time inviting listeners to move freely from point to point in the park, granting them an improvisatory agency that is largely absent from a conventionally staged performance paradigm. *The Share* differed conceptually from Thomson's previous cartographic compositions in a number of crucial ways, however. In the first place, whereas most of Thomson's earlier pieces were created for professional performers like the Toronto-based Radiant Brass Ensemble, for this project Thomson and Hood sought out amateur musicians from the Guelph community to collaborate with a small number of professionals. Moreover, Thomson and Hood almost entirely relinquished compositional and choreographic control of the piece. Having recruited musicians and dancers, Thomson and Hood organized them into small groups and appointed a professional musician or dancer to manage each group. Therefore, their influence did not extend much farther than conception and recruitment: they instructed each group to collectively develop its own material with some mindfulness to the overarching themes of the project, but offered little or no other specific oversight.

Figure 17.3 Judy Gill, Roy Bateman, and Tania Gill. Image capture from video by Nicholas Loess.

Thematically, the project reflected the proximity of the October 13 event to Thanksgiving. Each of the small groups of musicians and dancers was deliberately intergenerational. Some were family groups, such as hurdy-gurdyist Ben Grossman's duet with his saxophonist son Eden (although I ended up subbing for Ben on saxophone), and Toronto pianist Tania Gill's trio with her mother, Judy, and son, Roy (pictured here). The musicians and dancers in other groups had previously been unacquainted—as was the case with the dance group I worked with, facilitated by Lynette Segal—but nevertheless maintained the intergenerational emphasis, with participants usually ranging from preschool-aged children to grandparent-aged adults. As Thomson told me, "The intergenerational piece came about when we started talking about the themes, the thematics of a park in fall. [...] [W]e thought about Thanksgiving as one of the times in the year when different generations in the same family, and sometimes in different families actually get together and spend a lot of time together ... for better or for worse."[5]

The Thanksgiving scenario was meant to structure the way that each group developed its own musical or movement content as well. Originally, Thomson and Hood proposed that the oldest and youngest members of the intergenerational groups would *share* with each other their favorite songs and dances—hence the title of the project. Thomson explained,

> [M]usic creates its own generation gaps, so that the musical experience of a young person is very different from the musical experiences of an older person, but that hasn't always been the case in musical history. If you go not too many generations back, the majority of humans would have sung the same songs their grandparents did, probably with them as part of community festivals or as types of rituals or religious ceremonies or whatever. So we thought of *The Share* as a way to bridge some of those gaps, and primarily so people could have fun working together, and maybe meet some new people, and perform in a way that hopefully emphasizes participation and deemphasizes performance values that might lend themselves to performance anxiety or stress or nerves.[6]

Although not every group stuck to the letter of this vision, in the weeks leading up to the event, all of the groups were thoroughly collaborative in developing their material. In my dance group with Lynette Segal, Ben Grossman's daughter, Isabelle, was a major creative force, while Hood told me that in one of the small groups she danced with, the primary (albeit, not always purposeful) creator was Asa, an 18-month-old boy. Consistently, the appointed professional group facilitators played a minimal role in the creative process apart from scheduling meetings in advance of the event.

Where Thomson and Hood did play a critical structural role, however, was in ensuring that the participatory framework that undergirded the creative process extended to the audience as well. They scheduled all of the small group episodes around the park so that they would overlap, and so that consecutive events were positioned at fairly distant points in the park. This made it largely impossible for any single listener to experience every entire musical or dance episode, meaning that each listener was empowered to choose which group she or he wanted to visit, but also that listeners would almost invariably arrive at a music or dance site in the middle of a performance. Thomson described the rationale for obfuscating beginnings and endings:

> If an audience member enters into the middle of something they're more likely to … feel a sense of active agency in relation to the thing. The beginning of a piece tells people to shut-up and listen, the ending of a piece tells people to clap. Those are the jobs of the passive listener: to shut-up and listen, and to clap. […] If you enter into the middle of something, it doesn't have those subtle or not-so-subtle cues, and so people might join in, they might walk away, they might talk to their friends, their relationship to the music is different because the performance conventions are different. […] I'm interested in creating unfolding experiences, not ones that are dictated by beginnings and endings.[7]

Thomson's thinking on these issues has been influenced by ethnomusicologist Thomas Turino's theorization of participatory music making, set out in his book, *Music as Social Life: The Politics of Participation*. Like Thomson, Turino situates the processual orientation of community music making in what he calls the "participatory frame." Turino posits, "In fully participatory occasions there are no artist-audience distinctions, only participants and potential participants. […] In participatory music making one's primary attention is on the activity, on *the doing*, and on the other participants, rather than on an end product that results from the activity."[8] "The result," Turino concludes, "is that participatory music making leads to a special kind of concentration on the other people one is interacting with through sound and motion and on the activity in itself and for itself. This heightened concentration on the other participants is one reason that participatory music-dance is such a strong force for social bonding."[9]

In this way, the collaborative creative efforts of the groups in *The Share* are best understood not as some kind of artistic creation directed toward a singular, definitive performance, but rather as a kind of reciprocal pedagogy—in a word, sharing. Indeed, in Thomson's view, the process of sharing *was* the purpose of the entire project; the October 13 event was simply a public stage in an otherwise private, intimate procedure. For instance, Thomson was reluctant to refer to the meetings that preceded October 13 as "rehearsals," because that word implies a degree of instrumentality: "Well, in my view there have been no rehearsals. Nothing is preparation for *The Share*. *The Share* is just an unfolding of stuff that's already happening. So, the work starts in relative privacy, and then it ends with relative publicity, but it's the same work."[10] I asked Thomson about the pedagogical valence of sharing: "Well, I mean, 'share' is […] a kittens and rainbows kind of word, but, if you peel away some of the culturally-coded cheesiness to the word, it's kind of a perfect pedagogical model as I see it. By sharing, it implies an exchange that is not informed by hierarchies. […] It's a very intimate kind of pedagogy when it takes place out of necessity."[11]

Campus Neoliberalism and the Program Prioritization Process (PPP)

At roughly the same moment that Thomson, Hood, and their collaborators were facilitating *The Share* in Exhibition Park, up the hill on the University of Guelph campus, university administration was making plans to announce a dramatic, new review process to be overseen by American consultancy firm, Academic Strategy Partners (ASP), under the direction of Dr. Robert C. Dickeson. Based on his 1999 study, *Prioritizing Academic Programs and Services*, "Program Prioritization" (as Dickeson terms it) entails an extensive review of all university programs—academic and nonacademic, from languages to parking services—with a view to reallocating resources from programs that are perceived to be unsuccessful to those that are seen to be more successful. Success is measured according to a ten-point rubric that takes into account factors such as size, scope, productivity, internal and external demand, cost, impact, justification, and "overall essentiality."[12] Underlying all of these factors, of course, is an operative understanding that universities are faced with an economic crisis. At the time that they retained ASP's services, the University of Guelph, for instance, was grappling with a $32.4-million budget shortfall—a significant problem, to be sure.[13]

Rather than cutting equally from all programs in order to make up the deficit—a common administrative tactic—Dickeson proposes that universities tackle what he calls "program bloat." As Dickeson explained in one of his 2010 workshops "Academic Impressions," universities across North America have historically sought to add new programs with a view to attracting new students, thus leaving them with a glut of programs that have had inconsistent results. "As we keep adding and adding and adding, without chopping along the way, resources are getting scarcer," Dickeson told his audience. "The price of program bloat for all is impoverishment for each."[14]

Dickeson is a very busy man. His "Program Prioritization" consultancy has been taken up at over a hundred schools across the U.S. In Canada, so far only Guelph, the University of Regina, and Wilfrid Laurier University in Waterloo have initiated the review process, but according to James Bradshaw of *The Globe and Mail*, many other universities are watching these three pilot projects with great interest—if also great trepidation.[15] The sheer popularity of Dickeson's program reflects not only the reality of the economic crisis in higher education, but also the systemic understanding that economic crisis can only be resolved through neoliberal management intervention.

Indeed, the proposed response to crisis—and the framing of the "economic crisis" itself—are reflective of the broader neoliberal sociocultural climate from which they emerged. When we encounter the term *neoliberalism* in mainstream media and academic discourses, it is commonly in the context of discussions of economic policy: corporate tax cuts, market deregulation, the enactment of "right to work" legislation (or other policy levers that hinder the formation and activity of trade unions), the dismantling of state social welfare networks, and the facilitation of globalized flows of capital are common policy moves that have been in evidence in neoliberal governments around the world, especially since the late 1970s. As historian and philosopher Philip Mirowski reminds us, however, although neoliberalism is most obviously manifest in economics, it is most importantly, a set of epistemological concerns.[16]

Paramount in the neoliberal episteme is the virtual infallibility of markets. According to neoliberal commentators from Friedrich Hayek and Milton Babbitt[17] to Ronald Reagan and Margaret Thatcher to Stephen Harper and the Koch Brothers, whereas other kinds of social institutions and structures—like national governments, for instance—ultimately constrain human development and fulfillment, the market stands as the only real potential locus of meaningful human achievement, and concomitantly as an unfailing corrective to any manner of social challenge. Whether the inequitable treatment of First Nations peoples in Canada, global social problems like human trafficking, imminent ecological catastrophes like climate change and global warming, or issues in education like those the *PPP* was meant to address, virtually any problem, adherents to neoliberal ideology would have us believe, has a market-based solution if only we think creatively enough.

If the market is understood to be the exclusive source of effective solutions to social problems, however—and indeed, the predominant force around which a society is structured—it is because social problems and solutions have become difficult to imagine outside of their market implications. Lack of social equity with respect to minoritized communities is attributed to that group's unequal access to the market as a producer or as a consumer; joblessness and poverty are routinely blamed on overregulation or excessive taxation by the state that deters corporate investment and job creation; climate change is blamed on the lack of a financial incentive that would encourage corporations to stop engaging in the behaviors that lead to global warming; and the perceived crisis in education is blamed on a bloated public sector and its individual agents who are seen to be inefficient, unaccountable, and out of touch (more on this later).

And of course, if (and when) the market fails to solve the social problem, or if an individual actor fails to succeed in the form or manner to which he or she aspired, the market is never to blame; the fault inevitably lies with the would-be manipulators of the market for *not* thinking creatively enough. In this way, the infallibility of the market remains sacrosanct, even in the face of abundant evidence to the contrary. The market, according to neoliberal logic, becomes a thing apart. As if by magic or divine intervention,[18] it is lifted out of the everyday institutions and legislative structures that comprise its material and intellectual architecture—it transcends and eclipses the fact of its human construction—to become something quasi-natural. We are meant to interact with it as we do with the ocean. If we sink and drown, it's because we navigated poorly or neglected to account for bad weather coming in. It's never the ocean's fault.

This central epistemic concern regarding a "naturalized" market entails a similarly "naturalized" set of social relations. Every individual's relationship to core social institutions and other members of society is suffused with market logic. If neoliberal "common sense" dictates that all incentives and punitive measures must be economic, then virtually all public interactions are reimagined as services performed in exchange for capital—whether that capital investment comes in the form of consumer purchase or tax dollars. In turn, contracts (or contractual logic) become the lynchpin upon which all public social relationships are predicated. Contractualism—in a purely economic guise—binds not only employees to employers, but producers to consumers, "taxpayers" to governments, and citizens to one another. Crucially, it is this form of contractualism from which central neoliberal buzzwords like "accountability," "efficiency," "benchmarks," and "outputs" emerge. As managerial tactics that were previously the province of private corporations begin to encroach on the operations of public institutions, institutions of all stripes are increasingly obliged to explicitly and quantifiably justify the degree to which they are fulfilling their end of the economic contract. Evidently, accountability and efficiency are not in and of themselves problematic institutional qualities; certainly they are vitally important for private corporations, and highly desirable for public institutions. The problem, however, lies in the neoliberal fetishization of "hard" metrics as the only appropriate means to evaluate those and other qualities. The *PPP* audit, for instance, largely evaluated programs with explicitly quantifiable measures like enrollment, numbers of patents and publications (with less weight placed on quality), revenue (in terms of a combination of grant dollars, fundraising success, and sales), and operating cost.[19] Such metrics reframe qualities that are soft and unstable—like learning, citizenship, community, and justice—as *outputs* that must be quantifiable. And because of the market logic that undergirds neoliberal ideology, the principal quantifiable unit of measurement for nearly every metric is (or is reducible to) the dollar.[20]

In this way, public trust in public institutions is tautologically eroded. Capital profit is unquestionably the central purpose of private corporations, so dollars make sense as a metrical unit to measure achievement, and by extension as a premise for contracts. Consumers and investors justifiably have an expectation that their capital will be restored to them in equal measure—either in dollars or commodities or services. Hence, dollars are an easy and a reasonably accurate way to gauge value. In a classical understanding of social democracy, however, dollars and value are not so readily proportional. Democratic citizenship entails compromise; the purpose of taxation is to contribute to a broader public good from which all citizens benefit, regardless of how much or how little they are able to pay into it. Whether the value that you as an individual extract from your government in terms of services is precisely commensurate with the value that you as an individual invest in it through your tax dollars is irrelevant. The prosperity (broadly defined) of the citizenry as a whole is the aim, and while this by no means precludes the possibility of individual accumulation of capital, it does constrain it inasmuch as individual wealth takes second place to overall social well-being articulated through the obligations of citizenship.[21]

Dollars are therefore an ineffective and inaccurate way of measuring the health of a democracy (at least in its classical and—I and many others would argue—more desirable formulation), simply because the dollars that an individual puts in specifically shouldn't match the dollars or dollar value that an individual gets out. As Martha Nussbaum suggests,

> Achievements in health and education, for example, are very poorly correlated with economic growth. Nor does political liberty track growth, as we can see from the stunning success of China. So producing economic growth does not mean producing democracy. Nor does it mean producing a healthy, engaged, educated population in which opportunities for a good life are available to all social classes.[22]

By contrast, neoliberal ideology dictates a radically delimited concept of citizenship and a purely monetaristic species of social contract, wherein taxation should—almost in a moral sense—precisely align with the dollar value of services, exactly as they are supposed to do in the private sector, with no regard for the eroded bonds of citizenship.[23] In effect, taxes are reframed as capital, tax-funded public services are reframed as capital-funded consumer services, and the moral centrality of the public good is eclipsed by the moral centrality of the open market. Moreover, because public institutions are chiefly predicated on an older democratic concept, burdened by expensive social problems and obligations, they are ontologically uncompetitive, incapable of paying out the kind of dividends that a private corporation can. Under this regime, public institutions—from government departments to transportation infrastructure to schools—are made to engage in a ruthless pursuit of corporate "efficiency." In this quixotic enterprise, public institutions are typically expected either to adopt corporate management practices, or to turn key aspects of their operations and governance over to private businesses (through divestiture and privatization), or—as in the case of *Program Prioritization* at the University of Guelph—a mixture of both. And when public institutions inevitably fail, even after borrowing the best and brightest corporate organizational paradigms and management procedures, the ontological primacy of markets and corporations is confirmed.

Robert Dickeson's review system is therefore neoliberal through and through. It establishes external, primarily financial metrics to evaluate all programs, and applies those metrics regardless of the academic and cultural contingencies of the program. It frames the relationship between students and academic departments according to the capitalist logic of supply and demand. It systematically deemphasizes the value of research—especially research that lacks external funding through government or private philanthropic resources, or that isn't readily monetizable in the market. And it puts departments into "free market" competition with one another for scant resources. In response to a workshop question about how to encourage faculty buy-in to his program (a pervasive problem for schools that retain ASP's services, as one might imagine), Dickeson reminded his audience that the highest-ranked departments could in fact see an increase in their resources, albeit one achieved by bleeding out the lowest-ranked departments.[24]

Almost invariably, the lowest-ranked departments are those that are commonly regarded to have the most tangential relationship to the job market. At the University of Guelph, for instance, humanistic disciplines like languages, fine arts, philosophy, and music—where job options are either less obvious or perhaps merely less lucrative—tended to rate among the less successful programs according to Dickeson's rubric, while the various STEM (science, technology, economics, and mathematics) divisions tended to rank much higher.[25] Indeed, in a rather bitter irony, the highest-ranked divisions across the university were administrative, with the office that manages the parking lots and the Canadian coffee chain Tim Horton's included among the most productive and profitable programs.[26] Much in the same way that neoliberalism systematically undermines faith in public institutions and in the very notion of a public good, Dickeson's system affirms *avant la lettre* a growing public devaluing of the humanities by measuring their worth according to a series of metrics that privilege the sciences, social sciences (especially economics), and bizarrely, noninstructional administrative or service divisions. If enrollment, "revenue streams," "patents," and cost-efficiency are among the key metrics of success,[27] humanities classes—where optimal class sizes are small, where student tuition covers a smaller percentage of operational expenses, and where external revenue streams and research patents are virtually unheard of—inevitably and necessarily struggle to measure up.[28]

Such noncompetitive programs are under particular threat to be merged with larger, more quantifiably successful programs, or to be cut entirely. While Dickeson's team frames the proposed evisceration of the humanities as a progressive and productive development by rhetorically emphasizing words like "opportunity" and "collaboration" to offer productive solutions for seemingly troubled programs, the logic that undergirds this language is wholly market based, wherein "opportunity" and "collaboration" effectively serve as fluffy metaphorical stand-ins for "mergers" and "acquisitions." After all, any "collaboration" initiated under the kind of external duress that *Program Prioritization* represents under the kind of egregiously inaccurate metrics that Dickeson's system imposes is, I would suggest, much closer to a "hostile takeover."

The real "problem" uncovered by the *PPP*, however—the real source of the budgetary crisis that the *PPP* was brought in to solve—is teachers. According to the *PPP*'s conclusions, faculty salaries are a key reason for the budgetary shortfall. As University of Guelph provost Maureen Mancuso put it in her summary remarks upon the release of the report in October 2013, "[budgetary] planning assumptions show a continuous annual gap between expected new revenues and expense increases [that is] mainly due to compensation costs."[29] Consequently, in addition to pressuring underperforming departments to merge or dissolve, another central recommendation of the report is to extract more labor from its principal workforce by increasing the teaching load for full-time faculty.

Significantly, according to the Council of Ontario Universities, the actual culprit in all this is static government funding. Since 2009 in Ontario, the Ministry of Training, Colleges, and Universities has failed to index its budgetary appropriations for postsecondary schools in the province either to inflation, or to operational and infrastructure costs that have risen dramatically as a negative consequence of increased enrollment. Of course, state divestiture of public universities is by no means unique to Ontario; in the United States, according to Jeffrey Selingo, "by some measures, state taxpayer support for higher education hasn't been this low since 1965, when there were some sixteen million fewer students in the system."[30] These factors, however, are not directly counted in the *Program Priotization* evaluatory scheme. Hence, according to Dickeson and his team, at least, faculty are left holding the bag for the university's financial problems, while the neoliberal government policy that likely led to the budget crunch in the first place largely escapes scrutiny. In Guelph (as has been the case elsewhere), it does not seem a coincidence that the people held chiefly accountable by the *PPP* for budget shortfalls are the very same people—university faculty—who are most likely to be motivated to hold the *PPP* to account for its dubious math and violently austere disciplinary conclusions. In so doing, Dickeson and his consultants preemptively depict those who would question their methods or recommendations as out-of-touch and self-interested. In sum, neoliberal government policy downloads costs onto students, while private neoliberal advocates download the blame for rising costs onto their teachers.

All of these factors speak to a new modality in the relationship between schools, faculty, and students. Students, in the neoliberal regime, are fundamentally reimagined as consumers (indeed, following Dickeson's example, the University of Guelph authors of the *PPP* use the words "student," "client," and "consumer" more or less interchangeably); departments become ancillary brands that target particular student demographics; and universities are transmuted into large-scale holding corporations that oversee the operations of those subsidiary brands. Lopping off a department, then, is as easy and logical as General Motors shutting down its Buick operations, or Pepsi stopping the manufacture of its vanilla cola. Students, moreover, like any consumer, are essentially reducible to their tuition dollars. In the parlance of "Program Prioritization," each student is a financial unit, and program efficiency is evaluated according to a "cost per unit" model.

Additionally, students are increasingly funneled into programs and departments that directly—and exclusively—position them to fill ready-made niches in a postindustrial labor force. This is by no means to cast aspersions on the value (nor on the utility) of the STEM disciplines, or on the students or faculty who are implicated therein. On the other hand, a pervasive deemphasis on a robust education in the humanistic disciplines—where students are invited and required to critically engage with systemic social issues in terms of culture and ideology—risks yielding generations of university graduates who are optimally skilled as useful as agents of capitalist labor and consumption, but who have only minimally developed faculties of critical thought and cultural analysis that they might otherwise direct toward a trenchantly critical assessment of the systems and processes in which their labor and consumption is broadly implicated. As John Dewey noted in his formative 1916 book, *Democracy and Education* (and as countless other teachers and scholars have echoed since), schools are not only places where students go to learn skills that will serve them in the workforce; crucially, schools are places where students go to learn how to be *citizens*. Hence, a pedagogy that amplifies instrumental skills and deemphasizes creative and critical thought impacts not only graduating students; it impacts the contours of *democracy*.

Teachers, meanwhile—especially those who do speak out against the sweeping onslaught of neoliberal epistemology—are routinely classed as effete intellectuals, invested only in protecting an outmoded university system that has heretofore enabled their purportedly elite lifestyles. We can certainly see this in the *PPP*—and in cognate institutional auditing procedures like the *IPRM* at Wilfrid Laurier University in Waterloo, Ontario—but it's a phenomenon that extends across institutional, provincial, national, even continental boundaries. We see it in the present moment (March 2015) at the University of Toronto, where University Provost Cheryl Regehr essentially characterized striking graduate student teaching assistants (who are campaigning for greater job security, and to have their stipend increased to meet or exceed poverty-level wages as indexed to the cost of living in the city of Toronto) as entitled millennials who are blind to financial reality.[31] We see it in the rampant anti-intellectualism that pervades the public discourse of the Harper Conservative government in Canada, where academic critics of the government have been accused of everything from "siding with child pornographers"[32] to "siding with terrorists."[33] We see it in Wisconsin, where in February 2015, Governor Scott Walker and other state legislators proposed to revise the state-mandated mission of public universities, excising language that enshrines public education as a public good, dedicated to improving the "human condition" through a tenacious "search for truth," and replacing it with a mission to fulfill "the state's workforce needs" "in recognition of the constitutional obligation to provide by law for the establishment of a state university."[34] We see it in North Carolina, where forty-six degree programs were cut in the spring of 2015 in response to "market pressure." State university board member Steve Long's explanation justifying the cuts is indicative of the political climate: "We're capitalists, and we have to look at what the demand is, and we have to respond to the demand."[35] We see it perhaps most nakedly in the rhetoric of the U.S. Tea Party movement, wherein—as Henry Giroux (drawing on Frank Rich) has written—"the war against literacy and informed judgment is made abundantly clear in the populist rage sweeping the country in the form of [...] a massive collective anger that 'is aimed at the educated, not the wealthy.'"[36] In an episteme that reduces every intellectual position to market logic, it becomes difficult or impossible to imagine that any opinion would have at its core anything other than financial self-interest.

So this is indeed a crisis, but not in the way that Program Prioritization makes it out to be. It's not a crisis of finances, but a crisis of conscience. What is the place of public education in the neoliberal paradigm? What is the place of the public good? Most urgently, what is the place of *citizenship*? And of course, where do music and improvisation fit in?

Resisting Neoliberalism, Teaching for Democracy

Evidently, as an endeavor that was developed under university auspices, *The Share* fits uncomfortably in this neoliberal regime. In the first place, recall that the architects of the event, Scott Thomson and Susanna Hood, were emphatic that the quality of the performance "product" was largely irrelevant to the perceived "success" of the project; rather, the fundamental reward consisted in the joys and pleasures that emerged from the process of dancing and making music together. Indeed, Turino suggests that this is a hallmark of the participatory performative frame: "Quality is gauged by how participants *feel* during the activity, with little thought to how the music and dance might sound or look apart from the act of doing and those involved."[37] The quality of community "feeling" is obviously a tricky one for a neoliberal rubric like Dickeson's to quantify.

Furthermore, there could be no cost-per-unit measurement of the event, because it was free to all participants—listeners, dancers, and music-makers alike. What's more, the vast majority of participants not only had no affiliation with the university, but there was no real prospect that any of them would ever become University of Guelph students or patrons. In a climate where many so-called community outreach activities are chiefly marketing enterprises directed toward attracting potential new students or donors, *The Share* was more or less a community-directed event that happened to have a conceptual affiliation with a university department. As an instrumentalized neoliberal university marketing enterprise, therefore, *The Share* was an utter failure.

On the contrary, even though Thomson and Hood were not specifically aware of Dickeson or Program Prioritization, *The Share* posed a sharp rejoinder—and an inspiring alternative—to the pedagogical and political implications of the *PPP* and the many cognate institutional auditing procedures that have become so ubiquitous around the world. At a time when the value of public education—indeed, the value of the public good as a foundational principle of democratic citizenship—is under fire, *The Share* fostered a vital space for participants to make art, of course, but also to *play at democracy*.

For John Dewey, democracy is more than merely a polity, more than simply a set of rules for governance:

> A democracy is more than a form of government; it is primarily a mode of associated living, of conjoint communicated experience. The extension in space of the number of individuals who participate in an interest so that each has to refer his own action to that of others, and to consider the action of others to give point and direction to his own, is equivalent to the breaking down of those barriers of class, race, and national territory which kept men from perceiving the full import of their activity.[38]

Note the centrality and interdependency of critical thought and dialogue in Dewey's formulation: democracy is a "conjoint *communicated* experience" that is premised upon a *consideration* of "the action of others to give point and direction to [one's] own."[39] As Dewey envisions it, democratic citizenship must strike a fine balance between empowerment and empathy, with rich critical dialogue as its fulcrum. Citizens must feel empowered to *think* and to *speak*—to continually critically examine the circumstances of their "conjoint experience," and to give voice to their respective, emergent conclusions. At the same time, they must feel impelled to *listen*—to meaningfully and earnestly engage with the thoughts and voices of others. In this way, metaphorically at least,[40] democracy is radically heterophonic and profoundly improvisatory.

The Share's processual creative paradigm was unquestionably an artistic, aesthetic pursuit, but it was equally a practice of democracy. In the first place, the structures of pedagogical power developed by Thomson and Hood were purposefully unstable. Recall that Thomson and Hood played only a minimal role in the development of each group's own series of pieces; that the individual facilitators appointed by Thomson and Hood actively fostered dialogue and collaboration; and that *children* were consistently among the most present, impactful voices in every group. Every member of every group was able to contribute to the heterophony, and virtually every participant saw something of *herself or himself* in the "dynamic and uncommon music and dance event" that the groups created *together*.

At the same time, *The Share* was also an exercise in confronting individual vulnerability. For many of the participants, the event marked their first encounter with public music making or dancing. I vividly recall the anxiety of the eldest member of one of the multigenerational groups, a retired real estate agent from Victoria, British Columbia, as she prepared to sing in public for the first time with her daughter (a professional pianist) and grandson, and how worried a nine-year-old accordionist was about playing her instrument in front of other people. Indeed, I can still feel my own physical and emotional discomfort as I prepared to dance with a group of children (along with a couple of other grown-ups) whose brimming confidence, ease, and grace stood in stark contrast (in my own mind, at least) to my awkward, lurching attempts at movement. As a musician and as a teacher, I seldom lack for confidence; as a dancer, though, I lack for confidence, experience, and skill in equal measure.

And yet, even as I felt anxious and vulnerable, I was very conscious that many or most of the participants shared my anxieties. There's a critical distinction between individual vulnerability and shared, distributed vulnerability—as a feeling, as a pedagogical strategy, and as an aspect of the emotional register of democratic citizenship. Confronting (and potentially overcoming) shared vulnerability creates a sense of deep intimacy and empathy among a collective. When we recognize vulnerability in others, that recognition lightens the individual burden to a degree; we cease to be isolated and alienated by our anxiety when we see that others share it. Moreover, by taking the crucial step of recognizing and empathizing with the vulnerability of another person, we begin to disrupt the ontological boundaries between subject and object, self and other that are the most durable impediments to human relationships and democratic citizenship. Indeed, for Martha Nussbaum, vulnerability is a foundational *condition* for democracy—"Democratic equality brings vulnerability."[41] Nussbaum elaborates,

> When we meet in society, if we have not learned to see both self and other in that way, imagining in one another inner faculties of thought and emotion, democracy is bound to fail, because democracy is built upon respect and concern, and these in turn are built upon the ability to see other people as human beings, not simply objects.[42]

Of course, sharing vulnerability isn't easy or natural; vigilant and assiduous management is required to ensure that we feel safe enough to feel vulnerable together and to empathize with vulnerability in others. It also requires continual, intentional cultivation. *This* is the kind of cultural work that *The Share* did—indeed, that music education can do, especially when it is oriented around improvisation. With their event, Thomson and Hood carefully developed a safe space for *play* and experimentation; a space that was purposefully free of any kind of instrumentality, be it the prospect of a future performance (in the conventional sense, at least) or some less immediate but no less daunting financial stake. The purpose of *The Share*—insofar as a singular purpose was ever in evidence—lay in the encounter among individuals ("meeting in society," as it were), the spontaneous negotiation of difference, and the process of engaging in and building something together. By inviting us to engage with one another in these ways, *The Share* effectively asked participants to *play at democracy*—to experiment and improvise with the valences of democratic citizenship in a space where the stakes were lower and less apparent, but no less important or impactful. As Dewey explains, "Education has no more serious responsibility than making adequate provision for enjoyment of [play]; not only for the sake of immediate health, but still more if possible for the sake of its lasting effect upon habits of mind. Art is again the answer to this demand."[43] If improvisation is a useful metaphor for democratic social practice, then play gives life to that metaphor, suturing the play-space to the real-life scenario by actively and intentionally cultivating structures of empathetic thought and feeling that will enrich a kind of interior citizenship that is predicated on dialogue and empathy: a *citizenship of the heart.*

The kinds of difference that participants were obliged to negotiate were especially important. Many university classes tend to be dominated by a particular ethnic and socioeconomic constituency: in Guelph in southwestern Ontario, at least, most students tend to be white and middle class. Because the event had a fairly loose connection with the University of Guelph, however, those students and faculty who did participate were obliged to work across generational (making music and dancing with children and the elderly), class, ethnic, and physical differences in ways that would seldom be called for in a classroom setting.[44] Hence, the physical and epistemological frameworks of the classroom encounter—so familiar to students and faculty alike as to be virtually invisible—were fundamentally disrupted. In this way, *The Share* activated a kind of social citizenship that was predicated not on unity or singularity (in the way that national citizenship under neoliberalism has increasingly come to be understood as a system of exchange of individual tax dollars for state services), but on empathy and difference.

The kind of citizenship that Nussbaum, Dewey, and others advocate—and the kind that *The Share* contributed to teaching—plainly doesn't fit in the institutional structures or ideological underpinnings of *Program Prioritization.* Unlike in Dickeson's approach, "incentives" to participate in this community spirit are not reducible to capital. Instead, communities are knitted together by empathy and love. These qualities are too expansive (and perhaps too beautiful) to be quantified by dollar-based metrics in institutional audits. Nussbaum, Dewey, Thomson, and Hood imagine a spirit of community belonging that starts in the heart, and draws together the mind and the voice. Moreover, they insist on a kind of pedagogy that fosters that spirit, and on educational institutions that actively contribute to it, bridging the classroom and the community. Finally, they require a recognition that a precisely, ontologically *immeasurable instability* remains at the core of any community—a quality that thwarts the quest for quantifiable fixity that undergirds Dickeson's project. As Henry Giroux writes,

> Central to such an educational project is the continual struggle by teachers to connect their pedagogical practices to the building of an inclusive and just democracy, which should be open to many forms, offers no political guarantees, and provides an important normative dimension to politics as an ongoing process that never ends. Such a project is based on the realization that a democracy open to exchange, question, and self-criticism never reaches the limits of justice; it is never just enough and never finished.[45]

Any vibrant, democratic community must be vigilantly self-critical, perpetually *emergent*, and avowedly *improvisatory*, lest the relations that structure a community ossify into hierarchies of power, for power necessarily breeds its opposite.

Paying the Bills

Despite the clear antithesis between *The Share* and the neoliberal administrative regime, in a sense, the event—and the Improviser-in-Residence project more generally—has emerged in part as a result of the neoliberalization at the University of Guelph. In their 2000 study of university management practices in Australia, Simon Marginson and Mark Considine pointed to the emergence of "limited life *areas* of research or research *centres*, sponsored from above for research funding purposes"[46] (like the Improvisation, Community, and Social Practice project) as evidence of growing neoliberalization. Indeed, the *PPP* itself offers some evidence for the extent to which the ICASP funding model (though certainly not the research itself) is symptomatic of neoliberalism in the academy. After all, the intra-institutional support for ICASP—and for the School of English and Theatre Studies (SETS), more broadly—reflects the extent of the extra-institutional revenue those programs have generated, both in the form of government grants and philanthropic support. Indeed, the express purpose of the *PPP* was to more effectively incentivize individual faculty, departments, and other programs by rewarding internally the programs that manifest the greatest external financial success. This is by no means to discount the generous support that the University of Guelph and its many peer institutions have offered to worthy projects and programs; nor is it to discredit the crucial work that state funding organizations like SSHRC undertake. Evidently, the point of this chapter is to argue for the enormous value of the programming and research that has emerged from ICASP, none of which would be possible without the university's and SSHRC's continued support. Moreover, ICASP is only one of a number of large- and small-scale SSHRC-funded initiatives to have an explicitly activist agenda. Nevertheless, it's worth considering the economic and ideological circumstances that undergird both the fact and the contours of that support.

In particular, following Marginson and Considine, it's important to remember that ICASP is, as currently constituted, by definition a *temporary* project,[47] and to this point the university's support has remained contingent on the government funding. Whereas a university department carries with it a sense of permanence and stability (notwithstanding the threat of "collaboration" posed by the *PPP*), a temporary project like ICASP necessarily remains contingent and precarious, reflecting the wider precarity that Luc Boltanski and Eve Chiapello have suggested is a pervasive aspect of neoliberalism, both structurally and epistemologically.[48]

Moreover, where appeals for government funding have failed or fallen short, and at a time where departments are competing for increasingly scarce university resources that are often being allocated based on success in attracting external resources, many departments—and many universities—are motivated to look to the corporate sector for financial help. Many schools have made lucrative contacts with various corporations—the Scotiabank Information Commons at Brock University in St. Catharines, Ontario, and at the University of Toronto, the Telus Centre for the Performing Arts at the Royal Conservatory of Music in Toronto, Ontario, and the Irving Centre at Acadia University in Wolfville, Nova Scotia, are a few among the many examples of this phenomenon.

As with any sponsorship initiative, of course, from the perspective of the corporate partner these relationships are mobilized chiefly to fulfill marketing goals. At Brock and at the University of Toronto, Scotiabank connects its brand with knowledge, information, and research, all while integrating itself into the day-to-day experience of many thousands of young students who are about to embark on lives full of mortgages, lines of credit, RRSPs, and myriad other banking services. Or at least, students will begin thinking about such matters once they have paid down enough of their bank-owned student debt (itself a consequence of ubiquitous state divestiture in public education that led universities to seek out these kinds of corporate partnerships with banks and other entities in the first place) to qualify for these new, more glamorous kinds of debt. Likewise, Telus—operator of Canada's largest mobile phone network—connects its brand with one of Canada's finest new concert venues, while also connecting their products with the eighteen- to twenty-three-year-old Canadians who comprise the demographic most likely to purchase stylish, bandwidth-guzzling smartphones. Meanwhile, through its sponsorship of the KC Irving Environmental Science Centre at Acadia University, the Irving Oil corporation is able to present a public image that glosses to some extent its involvement with the less palatable aspects of the oil industry—Irving's involvement, for instance, with a proposed fracking project near the Elsipogtog First Nation reserve in Kent Country, New Brunswick.[49]

Of course, marketing enterprises like these are harmless in comparison to the catastrophic sponsorship or ostensibly philanthropic relationships that a number of universities have entered into with corporate and individual entities like the Koch brothers. The Wichita-based oil barons have donated upward of $12.7 million to 163 colleges and universities.[50] While the influence that those donations have purchased isn't always clear, in at least four cases documented by Greenpeace, the Kochs have made their sizable donations contingent on university acquiescence to Koch influence in many aspects of university administration, including new faculty hires and curriculum development. At Utah State University, West Virginia University, Clemson University, and (most notoriously) Florida State University, Koch dollars were explicitly, contractually linked to the school's willingness to hire faculty who will "support the research into the causes, measurements, impact, and appreciation of economic freedom" (as in the language of the Clemson contract).[51] In the 2007 case at FSU, according to an internal memo, Economics Department chair Bruce Benson advised his colleagues, "They [the Koch brothers] want to expose students to what they believe are vital concepts about the benefits of the market and the dangers of government failure, and they want to support and mentor students who share their views. Therefore, they are trying to convince us to hire faculty who will provide exposure and mentoring. If we are not willing to hire such faculty, they are not willing to fund us."[52] Moreover, lest readers imagine that this kind of malevolence is the sole domain of the widely demonized Koch brothers, it is worth noting that at numerous other universities, trustees and big-ticket corporate and private donors have exerted undue influence on administration, teaching, and research—from the dubious revocation of a job offer to Steven G. Salaita at the University of Illinois Urbana-Champaign,[53] to the indelible impact Cargill, Monsanto, and other large-scale agribusinesses have had on research into food and agriculture, as exhaustively detailed by advocacy organization Food & Water Watch in their 2012 report, *Public Research, Private Gain: Corporate Influence Over University Agriculture Research*.[54] Clearly, as state funding has waned and corporations have stepped in to fill the financial void, those donors have worked behind the scenes to gradually transform many institutions of higher education from a public good into instrumental entities that will serve the labor and knowledge needs of private capital interests as they make their way through the market.

The city of Guelph is lucky to be home to the headquarters of the Musagetes Foundation. While Musagetes is certainly not as deep-pocketed as the Irving family or Scotiabank let alone the Koch brothers, the organization shares with ICASP a vision and a passion for the advocacy and support of community art. With additional programs in Lecce (Italy), Rijeka (Croatia), Lethbridge (Alberta, Canada), and Sudbury (Ontario, Canada), Musagetes is an international foundation that (according to their mission statement) "makes the arts more central and meaningful in people's lives, in our communities, and in our societies."[55] Musagetes is certainly not untouched by corporate influence (nor, for that matter, is any philanthropic organization): its cofounders, Michael Barnstijn and Louise MacCallum, have both been connected with Research In Motion, Barnstijn as a co-founder and executive of that organization, and MacCallum as a software engineer. RIM is best known as the creator of the Blackberry, and its head offices are in Waterloo, Ontario, just thirty minutes down the highway from Guelph. Nevertheless, unlike corporate sponsors like Scotiabank, Telus, or Irving, or higher-profile, influence-seeking donors like the Koch brothers, neither Barnstijn nor Blackberry has any degree of visibility whatsoever in the projects Musagetes funds. Branding and marketing are entirely immaterial to their philanthropy. In this way, Musagetes represents an incredibly rare species of donor: one that is genuinely, unerringly invested in its own stated mission, and in the artistic activities that it chooses to support. The collaboration between ICASP at the University of Guelph and Musagetes has proved to be a remarkably fruitful one over the years, particularly in its facilitation of the Improviser-in-Residence project that yielded *The Share*, among a host of other initiatives (some of which are detailed by Ajay Heble in his chapter in this volume).

Conclusion: Public Intellectuals Resisting Neoliberalism

Indeed, simply because such collaborative partners are rare does not mean that we as academics should not seek them out. In a climate when the very language of collaboration has been rhetorically co-opted by Dickeson and other such operators, it has become increasingly imperative that academics work with focused determination to recuperate the word in all of its constructive, positive connotations. Where university funding lacks— and where corporate capital lurks as a tantalizing lure—we must strive to work across departments and offices to pool resources that are untainted by undue corporate influence. We must strive to develop new kinds of community partnerships in unexpected places. Philanthropic foundations like Musagetes are an obvious (if disappointingly uncommon) choice, but other kinds of organizations—small businesses, public service organizations, trade unions, other levels or other offices of government, and secondary and elementary schools—all represent potential partners in much more broadly based collaborative endeavors than those so dubiously tendered by Scotiabank and the Koch brothers. We must ask ourselves, what is at stake in a world overrun with the ideologies and ideologues of neoliberalism? Everything. So who are the potential stakeholders—the potential partners and collaborators—that might work together to resist this toxic, cataclysmic worldview? Virtually everyone, everywhere.

With this in mind, we must consider how to collectively raise the volume of our resistance by making our voices heard loudly and clearly across a whole tapestry of global constituencies. This means that we must increasingly embrace our potential role as *public intellectuals*. We must seek out places where we're mostly likely to be read or heard—community forums, newspapers, social media—and we must consider communicating in terms that are broadly approachable, albeit without patronizing, pandering, or diluting the content of the message. Evidently this kind of "output" doesn't fit easily into the evaluative mechanisms attached to academic tenure and promotion. Mass-mediated publications are seldom peer reviewed, and there's rarely a ready niche for community outreach work in a teaching dossier. But public intellectualism can work—it has worked. While there is no clear evidence of causality, there is a clear correlation between the strong faculty pushback against the *PPP* at the University of Guelph (as documented in both internal meeting minutes and a small number of faculty-authored editorials published in local and national newspapers) and a change in the tenor of the administrative rhetoric. Whereas in the early days of the *PPP* in 2012, provost Maureen Mancuso regularly decried the budgetary crisis and posited

PPP-grounded austerity as a necessary solution, in the weeks following the release of the final report in the fall of 2013, anxious faculty were gently reminded in meetings that the *PPP* had never been intended as a cure-all, or as the only solution: it was meant to "inform" broader integrated strategic planning, but was "not [the] sole determinant of any program's future."[56] Consistent with this softened rhetoric, while the *PPP* did play a role in budget allocations for 2014–15—the budget for the first fiscal year following its release, and the only data so far on the specific impact that Program Prioritization has had anywhere in Canada—according to the administration, each department's score that emerged from the *PPP* played a comparatively minimal role (18 percent, to be precise) in final budget determinations.[57] If this outcome was less catastrophic than many faculty expected, the strident, publicly visible opposition to Program Prioritization that came from many corners of the University of Guelph surely played some role. After all, if neoliberalism demands that we focus inward on our individual needs, protect our own resources, preserve our own careers, and pursue our own achievements, what better way to resist than to look outward, and to speak, write, and think generously and expansively? *The Share* took place in a city park, not in the campus on the hill. We must follow that example.

Most urgently, we must reconfigure out classrooms as sites of resistance—if we have not done so already. We must speak out critically and fearlessly on issues that impact our students—even where, especially where, they may implicate our hometowns, our home countries, or our home institutions. We must foster spaces for critical debate: as much as we must impress upon our students the desperate urgency of the situation in which we find ourselves, we must also *listen* to our students and other interlocutors, even when we don't necessarily like or agree with what we hear. If conservative "think tanks" like the Alberta-based Fraser Institute and the North Carolina–based Civitas Institute are, respectively, prepared to use their resources and networks to advocate for pedagogies that are grounded in "the principles of economic freedom and its relation to global prosperity,"[58] or to class educators as disconnected intellectuals who use their lecterns to brainwash students with leftist rhetoric on behalf of a "vast shadowy network [...] [of] the organizations, the people, and the funders that make up the radical liberal left,"[59] we must develop *connections* with our students so that the resistance we help to foment is one built on consensus—albeit a consensus that is messy, multilayered, and determinedly indeterminate. If democracy is to survive the neoliberal onslaught, like Thomson and Hood, we must make our classrooms into safe spaces where our students can experiment and play with citizenship.

Obviously this puts immense, perhaps unfair pressure on academics. With our teaching, service, and research responsibilities, we are perpetually short of time. And with so many of us ensconced in sessional or adjunct positions, we are increasingly short of money as well. But it is crucial to remember that we are in these vexed positions because we are among the principal targets of the ideological assault of neoliberalism. Where our social contributions are undervalued and our labor is underpaid, or where our lives lack for comfort and security, it is precisely because of the neoliberal assault on who we are, what we do, and what we believe in. The consequence of these day-to-day burdens that we face is a further burden, but also a tremendous opportunity: leadership in this global struggle. For if the world is in crisis, and if the official, corporate- and state-sanctioned responses to that crisis effectively serve to extract capital profit from it rather than to resolve it, then it is incumbent on us to imagine new, unheard of, impossible responses. So let us sing and dance on balconies and in parks, let us come together as communities, and let us improvise a new-old kind of citizenship that grows from empathy, love, and beauty.

If neoliberal capitalism constrains and directs epistemology, then the first site of resistance must be the imagination. As educators, we must recuperate the capacity to dream—in ourselves, in our students, in our institutions, and in our communities. *The Share* may indeed only have been transformational for those who experienced it, and its power may not have lasted much beyond the moment of the experience. But this speaks not to the inefficacy or evanescence of our goals; on the contrary, it speaks to how urgently we need to foster spaces like *The Share* if we are in fact committed to resisting neoliberalism. As a play-space, as an improvisatory paradigm, as a patently noninstrumentalized undertaking, and as an initiative that linked the campus and the community, *The Share* was not only an art project; it was an experiment in fomenting an *epistemology of resistance*. It was a concatenation of physical spaces and a series of moments in time where participants could recognize and cultivate the playful and empathetic registers of democratic citizenship. And it was a resonant reminder that even in the darkest hours of institutional neoliberalism, despite all of the deeply destructive symptoms of the ongoing neoliberalization of university management (which, we should remember, flow directly into the catastrophic impact of neoliberalism as it has been practiced by governments around the world), there *is* beauty, there *is* joy, and there *is* community to be found in this new terrain if only we look hard enough together to find it.

Notes

1. Hood and Thomson, "The Share."
2. You can read more about the Improviser-in-Residence program in Heble's contribution to this volume, "'Things That You Hope a Human Being Will Be': Jane Bunnett in Conversation with Ajay Heble."
3. Turino, *Music as Social Life*.
4. Improvisation, Community, and Social Practice, "Improviser-in-Residence."
5. Scott Thomson, interview with author, October 12, 2012.
6. Ibid.
7. Ibid.
8. Turino, *Music as Social Life*, 28.
9. Ibid., 29.

10. Thomson, interview with author, October 12, 2012.
11. Ibid.
12. Lederman, "The Pressure."
13. University of Guelph, "PPP Task Force Report."
14. Qtd. in Lederman, "The Pressure."
15. Bradshaw, "No Department is Safe."
16. Mirowski, "Postface," 417.
17. cf. Plehwe, "Introduction."
18. It's worth noting, if only as an intriguing metaphor, that in the U.S. context in particular, faith in the market is often contiguous to—if not inextricably bound up with—religious faith, particularly for the huge numbers of evangelical Christians who are active in populist neoliberal movements like the Tea Party.
19. Sullivan et al., *Program Prioritization*.
20. See Olssen and Peters, "Neoliberalism."
21. There is an element of contractualism at play here too, of course, but it is a broadly *social* and *human* contract rather than a narrowly economic one.
22. Nussbaum, *Not for Profit*, 15.
23. Mirowski, "Postface," 436.
24. Lederman, "The Pressure."
25. Sullivan et al., *Program Prioritization*.
26. Sullivan et al., *Program Prioritization*, 13.
27. Sullivan et al., *Program Prioritization*, 34.
28. It's worth noting that the School of English and Theatre Studies (SETS)—the division that houses the Improvisation, Community, and Social Practice Project—was actually one of the more highly ranked research programs at the university. While the high ranking of SETS was largely anomalous with the humanities disciplines, it is an anomaly that is worth remarking upon, particularly since SETS faculty have been uncommonly successful in attracting external funding for their research, teaching, and artistic initiatives through government and other sources. I will speak to the character of this anomaly in my closing section.
29. University of Guelph, "PPP Task Force Released."
30. Selingo, *College (Un)bound*, xiv.
31. Regehr and Hildyard, "Open Letter."
32. Chartrand, "Vic Toews."
33. Kerr, "Worried?"
34. Mayer, "The University of Wisconsin."
35. Schaefer, "Board of Governors."
36. Giroux, *Neoliberalism's War*, 18.
37. Turino, *Music as Social Life*, 29.
38. Dewey, *Democracy and Education*.
39. Ibid.
40. I wish to be careful here not to recapitulate the facile equation between jazz improvisation and democracy that so regularly emerges from powerful institutions like the U.S. government and Jazz at Lincoln Center. As I have argued elsewhere, this equation is chiefly directed toward territorializing improvisation, positioning jazz as *a priori* evidence of American exceptionalism, and increasing its utility as a propaganda tool for the U.S. government, or as an aspect of

a brand identity for would-be corporate stakeholders like Time Warner or Starwood Hotels (see Laver, "Freedom of Choice").
41. Nussbaum, *Not for Profit*, 100.
42. Ibid., 6.
43. Dewey, *Democracy and Education*.
44. At least one participant was paraplegic, and many dancers in particular were physically equipped to contribute in a wide variety of dimensions.
45. Giroux, *Neoliberalism's War*, 40.
46. Qtd. in Olssen and Peters, "Neoliberalism," 327.
47. Indeed, ICASP no longer exists per se, having been eclipsed in 2014 by the International Institute for Critical Studies in Improvisation when one seven-year Social Sciences and Humanities Research Council grant was succeeded by another.
48. Boltanski and Chiapello, *The New Spirit*.
49. Howe, "Fracked-Up Business."
50. Of course, $12.7 million is a tiny fraction of the $900 million the Koch brothers anticipate spending during the 2016 U.S. elections (Confessore, "Koch Brothers"), another aspect of the public, democratic sphere in which they use their virtually unlimited, effectively unbridled capital resources to shape ostensibly democratic discourses and institutions.
51. Gibson, "Koch on Campus."
52. Pilkington, "Koch Brothers."
53. Jaschik, "Out of A Job."
54. Food and Water Watch, *Public Research*.
55. Musagetes, "Home."
56. University of Guelph, "Update on Integrated Planning."
57. University of Guelph Board of Governors, "Integrated Plan."
58. Fraser, "Lesson Plans."
59. Myrick, "Mapping the Left."

Works Cited

Boltanski, Luc, and Eve Chiapello. *The New Spirit of Capitalism*. Translated by Gregory Elliott. New York: Verso, 2007.

Bradshaw, James. "No Department Is Safe as Universities Employ U.S. Cost-Cutting Strategy." *The Globe and Mail*. December 25, 2012. http://www.theglobeandmail.com/news/national/education/no-department-is-safe-as-universities-employ-us-cost-cutting-strategy/article6711261/.

Chartrand, Fred. "Vic Toews Accuses Bill's Opponents of Siding with Child Pornographers." *Toronto Star*. February 13, 2012. http://www.thestar.com/news/canada/2012/02/13/vic_toews_accuses_bills_opponents_of_siding_with_child_pornographers.html.

Confessore, Nicholas. "Koch Brothers' Budget of $889 Million for 2016 is on Par with both Parties' Spending." *New York Times*. January 26, 2015. http://www.nytimes.com/2015/01/27/us/politics/kochs-plan-to-spend-900-million-on-2016-campaign.html?_r=0.

Dewey, John. *Democracy and Education: An Introduction to the Philosophy of Education*. Project Gutenberg, 2008 [updated 2015]. http://www.gutenberg.org/files/852/852-h/852-h.htm.

Dickeson, Robert C. *Prioritizing Academica Programs and Services: Reallocating Resources to Achieve Strategic Balance.* San Francisco, CA: John Wiley & Sons, 1999.

Food and Water Watch. *Public Research, Private Gain: Corporate Influence Over University Agriculture Research.* Washington, DC: Food and Water Watch, 2012. http://www.foodandwaterwatch.org/insight/public-research-private-gain.

Fraser Institute. "Lesson Plans." Accessed 4 December 2015. https://www.fraserinstitute. org/education-programs/teachers/classroom-resources/lesson-plans.

Gibson, Connor. "Koch on Campus: Polluting Higher Education." *greenpeace.org.* Accessed 5 March 2015. http://www.greenpeace.org/usa/en/campaigns/global-warming-and-energy/polluterwatch/koch-industries/KOCH-POLLUTION-ON-CAMPUS-Academic-Freedom-Under-Assault-from-Charles-Kochs-50-million-Campaign-to-Infiltrate-Higher-Education/.

Giroux, Henry. *Neoliberalism's War on Higher Education.* Chicago: Haymarket Books, 2014.

Hood, Susanna. Interview with the Author. October 22, 2012.

Hood, Susanna, and Scott Thomson. "The Share: A Family-Friendly Music and Dance Event." Improvisation, Community, and Social Practice. http://www.improvcommunity.ca/news/share-family-friendly-music-and-dance-event.

Howe, Miles. "The Fracked-Up Business of LNG on Canada's East Coast," *Vice Media.* March 6, 2015. http://www.vice.com/en_ca/read/the-fracked-up-business-of-lng-on-canadas-east-coast-687.

Improvisation, Community, and Social Practice. "Improviser-in-Residence," *improvcommunity.ca.* Accessed August 1, 2011. http://www.improvcommunity. ca/projects/improviser-residence.

Jaschik, Scott. "Out of a Job." *Inside Higher Ed.* August 6, 2014. http://www. insidehighered.com/news/2014/08/06/u-illinois-apparently-revokes-job-offer-controversial-scholar.

Kerr, Joanna. "Worried about C-51? You're Probably a Terrorist." iPOLITICS. March 17, 2015. http://www.ipolitics.ca/2015/03/17/worried-about-c-51-youre-probably-a-terrorist/.

Laver, Mark. "Freedom of Choice: Jazz, Neoliberalism, and the Lincoln Center." *Popular Music & Society* 37 (July 2015): 538–56.

Lederman, Doug. "The Pressure to Prioritize." *Inside Higher Ed.* November 11, 2010. https://www.insidehighered.com/news/2010/11/11/priorities.

Mayer, Greg. "The University of Wisconsin: Now with Less Truth Seeking, More 'Workforce Needs.'" *Why Evolution Is True.* February 5, 2015. https://why-evolutionistrue.wordpress.com/2015/02/05/the-university-of-wisconsin-now-with-less-truth-seeking-more-workforce-needs/.

Mirowski, Philip. "Postface: Defining Neoliberalism." In *The Road from Mont Pelerin: The Making of the Neoliberal Thought Collective,* edited by Philip Mirowski and Dieter Plehwe, 417–56. Cambridge, MA: Harvard University Press, 2009.

Musagetes. "About: Founders, Board, Advisers." *Musagetes.ca.* http://musagetes.ca/ about/board-of-directors-staff/.

Musagetes. "Home." Accessed 16 March 2015. http://musagetes.ca.

Myrick, Susan. "Mapping the Left: An Introduction." Accessed 22 January 2015. https://www.nccivitas.org/2015/mapping-left-introduction/.

Nussbaum, Martha. *Not For Profit: Why Democracy Needs the Humanities.* Princeton, NJ: Princeton University Press, 2010.

Olssen, Mark, and Michael A. Peters. "Neoliberalism, Higher Education and the Knowledge Economy: From the Free Market to Knowledge Capitalism." *Journal of Education Policy* 20 (May 2005): 313–45.

Pilkington, Ed. "Koch Brothers Sought Say in Academic Hiring in Return for University Donation." *The Guardian.* September 12, 2014. http://www.theguardian.com/world/2014/sep/12/koch-brothers-sought-say-academic-hiring-university-donation?CMP=twt_gu.

Plehwe, Dieter. "Introduction." In *The Road from Mont Pelerin: The Making of the Neoliberal Thought Collective*, edited by Philip Mirowski and Dieter Plehwe, 1–44. Cambridge, MA: Harvard University Press, 2009.

Regehr, Cheryl, and Angela Hildyard. "Open Letter to the University of Toronto Community." March 5, 2015. http://www.provost.utoronto.ca/Assets/Provost+Digital+Assets/Openletter.pdf.

Schaefer, Sam. "Board of Governors Discontinues 46 Degree Programs across UNC System." *Daily Tarheel.* May 23, 2015. http://www.dailytarheel.com/article/2015/05/board-of-governors-eliminates-46-degree-programs-across-unc-system.

Selingo, Jeffrey J. *College (Un)bound: The Future of Higher Education and What It Means for Students.* New York: Houghton Mifflin Harcourt, 2013.

Sullivan, J. Alan, Michelle Fach, and PPP Task Force. *Program Prioritization Process Task Force Report.* September 9, 2013. University of Guelph.

Turino, Thomas. *Music as Social Life: The Politics of Participation.* Chicago: University of Chicago Press, 2008.

University of Guelph. "PPP Task Force Report Released," *uoguelph.ca.* October 2, 2013. http://www.uoguelph.ca/news/2013/10/ppp_task_force.html.

University of Guelph. "Update on Integrated Planning and the PPP." October 9, 2013.

University of Guelph Board of Governors. "Integrated Plan, Multi Year Plan (MYP2) and Preliminary 2014/2015 MTCU Operating Fund Budget. Guelph: University of Guelph, 2014. https://www.uoguelph.ca/finance/sites/default/files/public/Integrated%20Plan,%20Multi%20Year%20Plan%20(MYP2)%20and%20Preliminary%202014%202015%20MTCU%20Operating%20Fund%20Budget%202.pdf.

18 *Control This!* Digital Improvisation and Pedagogy[1]

Mark V. Campbell

Control This! was a community outreach project that brought together newcomers to Canada and music production stations (MPCs) to explore controllerism and improvisatory digital music making. According to Producer and MPC Performer Fresh Kils, "controllerism is the innovation and utilization of new interfaces,"[2] a way to control and manipulate digital samples of music. As a partnership between the University of Guelph led Improvisation, Community, and Social Practice (ICASP) project and Immigrant Family Services Guelph, *Control This!* was a five-workshop series that took place in September 2012. The goal was to explore all creative aspects of the MPC and to provide an avenue for newcomer youth to acclimatize to Canada. The project utilized a well-known community space and I rented MPCs, which were available on a first-come, first-served basis to participants. Without sheet music or preconceived ideas of the genres of music to be explored in the program, the inherent improvisatory nature of our inquisitiveness set in motion several crucial learning moments.

I conceived of the *Control This!* Project, relying on my background as an educator and DJ, in an effort to trouble some of the linear notions of educator and learner that have long underpinned theories of pedagogy. Not only did the project's digital engagements make knowledge fluid, but it also pushed us to ask what is at stake in new formulations of improvisation pedagogy in digital culture. Further, how might digital technologies and music making culture illuminate the importance of facilitation and collaboration in a learning setting outside of the classroom? To best understand my observations and reflections, I begin by first positioning myself, taking seriously the way in which my power and privilege made possible specific scenarios and opportunities. Following, I detail three critical learning moments that provide a snapshot of scenarios that have fueled many of my ideas around improvisation and digital culture. These moments are best captured in an analysis that makes central power, knowledge, and discursivity—the unsaid and invisible structures that made possible the *Control This!* project.

In taking critical pedagogy seriously, I begin from my social location and positioning. As a straight, able-bodied male from within the academy, I had the privilege to attend and graduate from a postsecondary institution. I have been actively DJing for twenty years and have strong social networks that provide me with access to numerous sites within hip-hop culture. I was born in Canada and speak the nation's dominant language. The project participants were all young people under twenty-five and newcomers to Canada. Their social location amplified my relative ease of movement and acclimation in and to Canadian society. I chose to do a community outreach project around controllerism, cognizant that my familiarity with analogue turntables would not likely appeal to a digital generation. I also knew that for my own growth and development a community project would be a purposeful way to explore something new, something that might concurrently appeal to young people in Guelph.

Pedagogically, I knew that my years of experience using analogue turntables and my years of formal teaching experiences would be assets. I knew some of my skills could be transferred from DJing to the MPC, but I knew in this new context I could not demonstrate mastery over controllerism techniques. Thus, I recruited a renowned Producer and Controllerist, Fresh Kils, to come by for the final project session. Instead of providing a step-by-step instructional guide to making the perfect beat, I thought it pedagogically interesting to encourage participants to explore and experiment on the machines. Not only would this deepen their interest by allowing them to control their learning pace; it also created a space in which the participants were empowered to navigate their own experience, fostering a sense of agency.

My role was clearly a facilitator as I assured participants that no evaluation existed, and I sought out learning opportunities right alongside them. I purposely thought it ideal for participants not to follow a set order of engagement and to only consult the MPC manual when they could not accomplish the sounds they sought to create. As part of our learning process, we held discussion circles to talk about what kinds of music the participants were listening to and interested in. We researched the elements of a good beat, explored specific techniques around sample augmentation, and utilized YouTube to watch performances by other Controllerists.

In what follows, I first elaborate my rationale for choosing controllerism and then detail significant learning moments that best express the layers and potentials of digital improvisation in the *Control This!* project. By spending time reflecting on improvisation using MPCs, part of the work here is to help us cull our pedagogical practices to determine what might work within a digital environment.

Why Controllerism?

At our contemporary moment, controllerism has emerged as a new performance practice within digital culture. Controllerism as the use and performance of digital controllers to perform live or make prerecorded music[3] allows individuals to manage and manipulate digital sound files. This instantly allows users access to a vast amount of sound banks and prerecorded sounds. Controllerism as a performance practice makes transparent some of the creative practices and processes within the sphere of music production.

Although controllerism is not immensely popular, it is an "emerging form of tactile performativity" and a subversive and potentially fun activity.[4] Well-known Producers such as Araab Muzik and Fresh Kils have taken to performing live using music production stations and other controllers to design innovative and visually stimulating musical creations. In terms of musical lineage, one can link controllerism to hip-hop's turntablism that became popular in the late 1980s with the competitions such as the Disco Music Championship (DMCs). Controllerism, in its performative and idiomatic stylings, is best understood as related to and partially evolving from jazz, bebop, hip-hop, and turntablism as a subversive form of musical creativity. I brought this form of emergent digital music to the community of Guelph, Ontario, as a way to engage young people in a futuristic musical practice related to jazz improvisation yet still in its infancy. Controllerism lacks the kinds of canonization we find in jazz education, allowing for a more malleable and flexible exploratory process. Without a central figure, song, or genre of music dominating controllerism, the young learners in the *Control This!* project were able to explore and engage without the weight of specific expectations.

Learning Moment #1: Empowerment Beyond the "Expert"

After an hour of working on sequencing an arrangement of digital samples, one participant's saved files were incorrectly named. We searched all the files on the flash memory card and could not locate the newly created sequence. The young learner was deflated, and I, as instructor/convener, was defeated. My inability to locate the saved sequence was incongruent with the immediacy of the young person's digital life. Digital technology did not produce immediate results or pleasure. At that moment, my previous experience and memories of working with the MPC 1000 were met with the young person's last sixty minutes of diligent exploration. We both were caught in a moment of not-knowing, a moment in which I became a learner and nonexpert who worked alongside the now-distraught young person.

According to my social location as a university researcher, specialist, and program facilitator, my work was to be focused on problem solving, path clearing, and opportunity creation. The fields of power I meant to disrupt were the classroom as the dominant and most widely accepted locus of learning, as well as the expert knower, the source of all answers. At this moment of potential loss, the unknown future of one's improvisatory digital creations created immense feelings of guilt, for, despite my role of educator/facilitator, I could not recover the missing files. Simultaneously, the impact on the improvising youth could be read through body language. The participant's shoulders began to slump, and excited and animated inquiries turned to whispers directed at the floor signaled both my failure as a facilitator as well as the intense pleasure brought on by their experiments with MPCs.

The young man, after a brief slumping period at his workstation, returned to work and diligently and swiftly rebuilt the sequence. The mode of reversal was clear and accidentally positioned to empower the young learner. My unwillingness to perform the role of "expert" and the all-knowing source of educational power partially encouraged the young learner to retrace his footsteps and reproduce the sequence he created. As a medium, the MPC may have also played a role in encouraging this learner to attempt to reconstruct his sequence; the erasability of the hard drive also meant the impermanence of one's mistakes and thus infinite (re)creative possibilities. In this scenario, the reverse can also happen as participants, and learners in general, become comfortably invested in the notion of an all-knowing dominant teacher-figure. Often an individual's comfort with his or her abilities and level of self-confidence play a significant role in desire for a sense of security teachers can provide by knowing all the answers.

Learning Moment #2: The Absence of Gender Amplifies the Importance of Gender

In the planning of the program, gender was not an overt consideration. Although gender stereotypes attempt to assign the field of technology to the domain of men, no specific strategies were developed in advance. Of the five participants in the project, three were absent from one session on the same day, reducing the need to share workstations. The remaining two participants, both female, were able to work on their own workstations. My normal circling the room, offering of assistance, and listening to works in progress were not needed to help participants stay on task. In near silence for more than an hour, the two female participants worked diligently, explored furiously, and designed short pieces of music. While they did not complete entire sixteen bar sequences, what was accomplished was done quietly, without my assistance or my distraction. This stands in sharp contrast to experiences with some male project participants for whom playing their latest creation or sample discovery was meant to be a participatory activity inclusive of the entire room. For these male participants, an outward performance of their emerging mastery, or at least improvisational discoveries, provided an arena to test out their notions of masculinity that clearly had something to do with public sphere performance.

Without the direct attention from the project facilitator (me), the female participants on this day worked extremely quietly and excelled in their improvisatory explorations. It may have been that the women participants were more familiar with one another and less familiar with the male participants and thus felt less a need to outwardly share their discoveries. I had never considered the difference in work environment that may be attributed to different gendered experiences. Regardless of the reason for these young women's work habits, the moment of learning here was about the impact of technology on gender identities. Clearly, male and female participants reacted differently to their machines, which meant the environment conducive to improvising on the MPCs, to be most effective, need not be monolithic or homogeneous. For the three males in this project, an outward performance of their trials and tribulation accompanied their work on the MPCs. Rather than generalizing, my point here is to highlight the need for different kinds of learning environments, especially when the participants embody different approaches to learning: not all were auditory or tactile learners. In this scenario, my impact on the learning environment as racialized male facilitator is important, possibly making male participants feel more comfortable with me and perhaps an obstacle for female participants to openly seek assistance or ask questions. Without knowing very much about the personalities of the participants prior to the workshop, I found that there could be a variety of possibilities that impacted the learning environment.

Pedagogically, differences should be planned for, and I realized that this was something of an oversight in the planning of the *Control This!* collaboration. One could plan to have different learning environments within the same seminar with quiet workstations equipped with headphones and multiuse or collaborative workstations without headphones. Similarly, staggering the entry of participants into the program could also create differentiated learning contexts with introverts beginning the class earlier than extroverts or team learners. With my different experiences with male and female participants, it became clear that within a critical pedagogy frame, facilitation of a project is equal parts managing power relations in learning contexts and conveying the material to be learned.

Learning Moment #3: Instant Improvisation? Not Quite

The final day of the program arrived, and I invited a special guest into the workspace. Producer and performer Fresh Kils happily came to Guelph to check out our program. We spent the entire time working on producing one complete beat, with significant assistance from our special guest. One of the young women who had attended every session produced an interesting beat that she shared with the class and our guest. Fresh Kils spent considerable time helping to troubleshoot issues as they arose, allowing for a greater concentration on the completion and presentation of her work.

During the previous four sessions, participants had reviewed recorded video performances of Fresh Kils prior to his arrival in Guelph. We had also spent significant time saving, troubleshooting, and losing our beats. Since the MPCs were available on a first-come, first-served basis, they were available to be used in between sessions as the machines were left in the workspace. The result was that there were many opportunities to begin making music, but there was no guarantee one could use the same machine again. There was also no further guarantee that one could find the saved sound files.

Since the MPC 1000 and 500 run on flash memory cards, it was extremely difficult to find extra cards in downtown Guelph in 2012. Moreover, participants could not take home their work since we only had as many flash memory cards as we had machines.

In a follow-up interview I did with Fresh Kils, he provided a useful perspective that helps us think through improvisation with MPCs. He proclaimed: "Once you can internalize the gear, and master your interface, then it becomes jazz. The freedom of improvisation only comes from a mastery of your instrument."[5]

One major difference between working with analogue and digital instruments and machines is the complexity of the software and the informational architecture of the digital device. Particularly if the item is new or obscure, significant troubleshooting skills are crucial to the successful use of the digital device. What this means is that improvisation using MPCs requires a pedagogy that focuses not just on the mastery of playing the device, but also on being able to repair and troubleshoot the internal components of the device. The limited number of workshops in the project attempted to consider the beginning of school in September and the desire of students to do afterschool activities. This eventually limited the aspects of performative improvisation on the MPCs, originally envisioned as taking up about fifty percent of the workshop time. Rather than emerging from the workshop series with a completed or polished piece of performative music, participants made significant strides in processual improvisation as the project's emphasis was more focused on exploration than on a completed musical script.

Future Considerations

The learning moments briefly relayed here are by no means exhaustive, but are meant to help us think through what might be at stake in new formulations of pedagogy for digital improvisation. By and large, controllerism is a creative subversion of music production centers and related aspects of digital culture. By utilizing these machines as performative tools and as ways to improvise, the art of controllerism interrupts relations of power, and revamps the relationship between consumption and music making. What might have been imagined as a linear manufacturer to consumer relationship now involves consumers acting as creative agents that find new uses for controllers.

Yet, while we might be excited by the new sets of relations put in play by controllerism, undesirable sociocultural hierarchies and prejudices do not necessarily also undergo a similar transformation of relations. As my workshop demonstrated, gender plays a role in how we imagine our engagements with technology. The modes of creativity we might envision for something new like controllerism are still filtered through many of the prisms that shape contemporary society. Undoubtedly though, it is the encouragement of a sense of agency that pushed engagements with controllerism into improvisatory explorations. Thinking through the new sets of relations controllerism fosters or disallows illuminates the hegemonic grasp of jazz standards and other canonical works. Although the jazz canon does not necessarily constrain or encourage improvisatory relations, it is the digital music stations as a medium—their changing features and constantly updated software—that might actually encourage improvisation while impeding standardization or making difficult canonization. Since there are not standards in controllerism, there lies the potential to avoid what appears to be stunningly little variation in how young jazz students engage in improvisation. The various prerecorded video performances of Fresh Kils that I showed the participants in the *Control This!* project were deeply complex innovations that relied on hip-hop's culture of sampling, popular nostalgia, and the visual dominance of videos via YouTube. These circumstances do not lend themselves to the classroom and hopefully will be open and participatory in a way that encourages future controllerists to innovate.

In terms of developing a pedagogical approach to controllerism, alongside the centrality of the mastery of one's controller is an equally important emphasis on troubleshooting and problem solving. Unlike a brass or percussive instrument, the majority of the controller's mechanics are internal and thus less tactile and accessible for a diagnostic assessment. The rapidly changing nature of a technologically driven Western society, where manufactured obsolescence is commonplace, dramatically shapes how, when, and for how long we engage forms of digital technology. Depending on how resistant future controllerists might become to the dominant prescriptive uses of the MPCs, we may continue to see how digital musicians develop skills in experimental and improvisatory ways. If the performances of Fresh Kils are any indication, with his use of samples from popular cartoons and video games, controllerists currently have a diverse palette of source samples and an unprescribed method to guide (or hamper) artistic exploration. The rapid rate of innovation by companies like Serato, maker of the digital DJ interface, significantly influence what we can imagine and create on our machines. The annual introduction of new controllers as well as quarterly and biannual software updates means any possible prescriptive uses of the MPCs that are developed are likely to be quickly challenged or enhanced by new technological possibilities. A combination of eager, young controllerists and rapid technological innovation suggests an interesting dynamic ahead, one in which what becomes "standard" or prescriptive precariously rests upon how emergent controllerists innovatively deal with technological change.

Notes

1. I'd like to acknowledge that the *Control This!* project was made possible by the Social Sciences and Humanities Research Council as I was a Postdoctoral Research Fellow at ICASP from 2011 to 2012. My reflections in this paper are made possible by Canada's Banting Postdoctoral Fellows program for which I am a fellow from 2013 to 2015.

2. Andrew "Fresh Kils" Kilgour, personal interview, September 2012.
3. Katz, *Groove Music.*
4. Attias and van Veen, "Off the Record."
5. Andrew "Fresh Kils" Kilgour, personal interview, September 2012.

Works Cited

Attias, Bernardo Alexander, and Tobias C. van Veen. "Off the Record: Turntable and Controllerism in the 21st Century (Part 2)." *Dancecult: Journal of Electronic Dance Music Culture* 4, no. 1 (2012).
Katz, Mark. *Groove Music: The Art and Culture of the Hip-hop DJ.* New York: Oxford University Press, 2012.
Kilgour, Andrew "Fresh Kils." Personal Interview. September 2012.

19 Education for Liberation, Not Mainstream Socialization

The Improvisation Pedagogy of Students at the Center in New Orleans

George Lipsitz

[I]mprovisation ... operates as a kind of foreshadowing or prophetic, description.

—Fred Moten[1]

The fundamental nature and meaning of music lie not in objects, not in musical works at all, but in action, in what people do.

—Christopher Small[2]

The quotidian practices of music education and music criticism reflect the priorities, hierarchies, and values of post-Enlightenment Western art culture. Privileging the created object over the creative act, teachers and critics generally focus attention on the constituent properties of individual musical works rather than on the collaborative and social practices that create them. Under this regime, improvisation becomes valued largely as a mechanism for producing novel, complex, and interesting musical pieces.

In the Afro-diasporic tradition, however, a musical work has other work to do. As folk singer, musicologist, and political activist Bernice Johnson Reagon explains, songs in this tradition are not ends in themselves, but devices to get people singing. Songs survive because the entire culture teaches people that running particular sounds through the body develops and cultivates a part of themselves they would not otherwise know. "You cannot sing a song," she observes, "and not change your condition."[3] In this tradition, musical performances call communities into being. Musical practices become repositories of collective memory that serve as sites of moral instruction. Musical processes function as alternative academies that generate new ways of knowing and new ways of being. Music becomes important not so much for what it is, as for what it does. Improvisation in this context is expected to create new relationships and new realities. It is not so much an objective as a vehicle, not an end but a means. In the Western art tradition, expressive culture seeks to decorate the world that already exists. In the Afro-diasporic tradition, expressive culture aims to decorate the way to other worlds.[4]

The activities that coalescence inside music do not originate only in music, nor are they confined to it. Christopher Small substitutes the neologism "musicking" for the noun "music" to emphasize the active roles played by listeners, dancers, instrument makers, stage technicians, ticket collectors, security guards, and janitors in musical performances.[5] Band leader Johnny Otis relates that he never had to instruct his horn players how to play a passage or suggest to his singers how a song should be handled because the music they played emerged from "the ways Black folks lived in their homes," from "the way Mama cooked, from the Black English grandmother and grandfather spoke, the way Daddy disciplined the kids—the emphasis on spiritual values, the way Reverend Jones preached, the way Sister Williams sang in the choir, the way the old brother down the street played the slide guitar and crooned the blues, the very special way the people danced, walked, laughed, cried, joked, got happy, shouted in church."[6]

Malcolm X argued that musical practices contained ways of knowing and ways of being that could form the basis of collective community struggle in his speech at the founding rally of the Organization of Afro-American Unity at the Audubon Ballroom in Harlem on June 28, 1964. Minister Malcolm claimed a fundamental difference between white and Black jazz musicians. The white musician, he argued, could play with the aid of sheet music, duplicating and imitating phrases and figures previously heard. The Black musician, however, plays something completely new by improvising and creating from within. Malcolm proposed that the militant organization being founded that day could draw its guiding logic from jazz improvisation, that it could come up with a "philosophy nobody has heard of yet," and "invent a society, a social system, an economic system, a political system, that is different from anything else that exists or has ever existed anywhere on this earth."[7] The new way could not simply be found, it had to be forged from within and brought into existence through improvisation.

The improvisational work of decorating the way to other worlds that Malcolm X envisioned guides the activities of Students at The Center in New Orleans, an innovative educational program that connects classroom learning to the everyday needs and long-term aspirations of the aggrieved Black community that its students come from and return to daily. The program derives its practices, processes, and perspectives from the Black resistance culture of the Crescent City, a culture in which music is a node in a network of activities that blend expressive culture and struggles for social justice.

Every weekday morning and afternoon, eleventh and twelfth grade students in two New Orleans high schools interrupt their normal school routines to meet in small classes organized by Students at the Center (SAC). Deeply rooted in the Black resistance culture of New Orleans, these classes cultivate students' capacities for mutual respect and recognition, for democratic deliberation and decision making, and for leadership inside their own neighborhoods, networks, and communities. On entering the classroom, the students rearrange the chairs so they can sit in a circle, a configuration that emphasizes their links with one another. At first, they banter casually with each other and with the class's two instructors—veteran teacher and union activist Don Randels and the renowned Ninth Ward poet, film maker, journalist, and music producer Kalamu ya Salaam. Soon, the class gets down to work and participates in an intensive discussion-based workshop that takes twice as long as one of the school's regular class periods. These classes emphasize participation and peer interaction, deploying a pedagogy derived from the story circles that the Free Southern Theater developed in the 1960s in conjunction with the Student Nonviolent Coordinating Committee's (SNCC) efforts to promote popular education and political participation among disenfranchised Black people in southern cities and towns.

The curriculum of SAC classes requires students to read challenging works of fiction and nonfiction, and then to relate what they have read to their personal experiences. A sample of the readings assigned to them includes novels, short stories, and essays by writers such as Edwidge Danticat, Mark Twain, and Virginia Woolf, and nonfiction accounts of the war in Vietnam, labor-management battles during the 1940s, and the *Plessy v. Ferguson* Supreme Court decision that made segregation the law of the land in the 1890s. The students write responses to these readings that link events and ideas that come from far away and long ago to their own immediate everyday realities. The exercises they engage in follow the trajectory described by Paulo Freire that encompasses a linked chain of activities progressing through reading, thinking, writing, speaking, listening, sharing, re-reading, and thinking anew.[8] This student-centered, interactive, and collective pedagogy requires participants to locate themselves in history and in society, to position themselves as knowing and active subjects comparing and contrasting their personal experiences with what they read in the texts. This pedagogy does not assume that a finite quantity of knowledge resides in a text and that the student's job is to find it and passively record it. Instead, it assumes that knowledge resides in an active knowing and thinking subject's encounter with the text. As Doris Sommer teaches in the public humanities projects that she organizes, "books are not sacred objects; they are invitations to play."[9] In SAC classes, reading Virginia Woolf's 1940 discussion of "Hitlerism in the hearts of men" provokes one student to think about misogyny in her family and in her city. Exploring the history of the Vietnam War leads another to wonder if the judicial system in the U.S. is at war with Black people. Exposure to the ridicule directed at Jim for being superstitious in *The Adventures of Huckleberry Finn* incites a group discussion about the relative values of family folk knowledge and scientific rationality.[10] Jim Randels finds this pedagogy effective in reaching the whole student, in bridging the gap between the culture of the home and the culture of the school. "Optimum learning occurs," he maintains, "when the immediate concerns of community and family are addressed in academic course content."[11]

The learning that takes place in Students at the Center classes can stimulate new perceptions about the students' prior educational experiences. For example, reading about the 1811 New Orleans slave revolt reminds Adrinda Kelly that she attends a school named after John McDonogh, a white slave owner. This leads her to reflect on how her school experience has encouraged her to be ashamed of being Black. She recalls her feelings of humiliation on learning "how easily and efficiently a race of people was carried across ocean depths to a 'land of liberty' that would hate them." She surmises that the man after whom her school is named must be "laughing heartily in his cold closet inching to hell," secure in the knowledge that "miseducation is the greatest divider—and oppressor."[12] Yet reading about the rebellion shows her another side of the story: that the slaves did not merely endure oppression, they resisted it. "There is no need for me to be ashamed," Kelly concludes. "Slavery was not a passive institution, and mine is not a race of domesticated animals."[13]

The SAC pedagogy requires each student to come to class prepared to read his or her writing. Everyone must speak and everyone must listen. The instructors designate individual students to read aloud, but then the reader must "pick two," which means identifying two other students in the class to respond. The responders can paraphrase the argument and add to it, make suggestions for revision, or open up a new area for general discussion in the class based on their classmate's text. Through the presentations and responses, and especially through the cross-talk that inevitably follows, students teach each other how to ask and answer questions. They come to appreciate their commonalities and their differences. They learn that they know much more together than they can possibly know individually. As they improvise a collective story, they author and authorize new social relations and new social possibilities. They also master the subject matter in a way that is radically different from the rote memorization and "drill and kill" testing that prevails in much of K–12 education today. By thinking along with the texts and relating them to their own lives, the students learn empathy, discernment, appreciation, and judgment. They come to resist what Doris Sommer calls "authoritarian single-mindedness" by recognizing that there are multiple ways to organize evidence and many disagreements about the meanings of facts.[14]

The improvisational pedagogy of the story circle that guides Students at the Center classes emanates from the freedom struggles of Black communities during the 1960s. The Free Southern Theater (FST) developed the concept of the story circle as a mechanism for promoting "creative and reflective thought" among southern Blacks in response to the troupe's dramatic performances. Similar to the search for "decolonial options" propelling indigenous struggles for autonomy, dignity, and self-determination around the world today, activists in the Black freedom movement of the 1960s recognized that domination was psychological as well as physical, mental as well material. People can be imprisoned just as surely and just as securely by ideas and concepts as they can be imprisoned by stone walls and iron bars. Sometimes ideas and concepts can be even *more* powerful technologies of domination because stone walls and iron bars can at least be seen. Activists in the Black freedom movement recognized that it would not be enough simply to remove negative racist obstacles from their paths; they had to make new paths by envisioning and enacting new democratic practices, policies, identities, and institutions. It would not be enough to merely desegregate the ranks of the pain inflictors of this world, to place dark faces in high places.[15] It was necessary to imagine, invent, and authorize new ways of thinking and new ways of being. The movement suffered many political defeats, but it succeeded in constituting the Black community as an aggrieved and insurgent polity joined together by a linked fate and common aspirations for justice. The movement created cultural practices, processes, and products that outlived its organized institutional history that continue to serve as parts of an alternative academy where the capacity to improvise endures as a basic survival mechanism. The classes conducted in New Orleans high schools under the aegis of Students at the Center evidence a present-day manifestation of this long history of struggle. Like their ancestors in the 1960s social movements, and in the centuries of struggle that preceded them, the students learn to improvise, to invert and subvert dominant ways of knowing and ways of being. SAC classes *teach* improvisation, but they also *are* improvisation. They transform the classroom, one of the places where suppression often takes place, into a site of potential and possibility. In an educational system devoted to competitive high-stakes testing, punishment-based learning, and disciplinary subordination, Black students routinely encounter the classroom as a space focused on their alleged shortcomings. SAC classes flip the script. They explore the students' assets rather than their liabilities. They revolve around the things they know and the things they want. The classroom thus becomes a site of mutuality, sociality, and possibility. SAC classes turn poison into medicine, replacing radical negativity with radical possibility. They turn the classroom space of containment into a space of creativity.

The educational philosophy of SAC conflicts radically with the dominant educational regime that systematically abandons the needs of Black and Latino children. Neoliberal "reforms" that promote vouchers, high-stakes testing, and racially targeted disciplinary suspensions work to divide Black students into two groups: the exceptional and the disposable. The education system and the society at large seem willing to offer a modicum of upward mobility to those who can be considered exceptional—those minority students who perform well in school and on high-stakes tests–but only with the proviso that they assimilate into the dominant values of a white supremacist society and leave the disposable people behind. The consequence of this approach is that the success of the exceptional is used to justify the abandonment of the disposable. Students at the Center inverts this perverse practice. It encourages talented young people to identify with their communities rather than to flee from them, to become those who lead rather than those who leave. In defending "education for liberation rather than mainstream socialization," ya Salaam explains,

> Some people have developed theories about teaching inner-city youth, and most of those theories are predicated on preparing these youths to participate in the mainstream. Such theories never question the sanity of joining a system that has systematically oppressed and exploited the very youth we are teaching. If preparing them to simply be "productive citizens" of the status quo is the bottom line of what we do, then we might as well be teaching courses in suicide.[16]

The young people in SAC classes have been handed virtually the worst of everything by this society. They know from the dwellings where they live, the schools they attend, the public transportation vehicles they ride, the meals they eat, and the media images they consume that their welfare is this society's lowest priority. They come from a community suffering from continuing racial discrimination in employment, education, and housing, from police brutality and mass incarceration, from pollution and poverty. They see every day how resignation and despair lead members of their community to turn on each other: in its later stages, genocide can look very much like suicide. In addition, the dominant cultural and political discourses the students encounter hold them responsible for their own victimization. Endless rounds of blaming and shaming tell them that there no longer is any racism. If they suffer, they are told, it is because their parents, relatives, and friends are losers who choose not to better their condition. As ya Salaam notes, "we control nothing, but we are blamed for everything."[17]

Well before the destruction that took place in the wake of Hurricane Katrina in 2005, Black people in New Orleans had long experienced brutal repression and systematic political suppression. Neoliberal policies implemented in response to the damage, displacement, dispossession, and deaths that came with the flood waters have made matters worse. Municipal, parish, state, and federal policies have given preferential treatment to the return of white residents, to policies that rebuild and reinvest in white neighborhoods. Many Black neighborhoods look just as devastated today as they did the day after the hurricane hit. Other formerly Black neighborhoods are being gentrified, filled with young white newcomers to the city who receive favored treatment from lenders and insurers along with augmented protection by the police as they usurp some of the limited housing stock that used to be available to Blacks. Policies supported by both Democrats and Republicans have achieved the goal announced by George Bush's Secretary of Housing and Urban Development in 2005 that "New Orleans is not going to be as black as it was for a long time, if ever again."[18]

In the face of this calculated cruelty and the organized abandonment of the Black working class, an improvisational pedagogy might seem like a luxury. Yet people can only fight with the tools they have in the arenas that are open to them. The curriculum and pedagogy of SAC strategically counters the neoliberal program of radical dehumanization with a praxis of radical rehumanization. This approach flows from the knowledge that the conditions that students confront today have a long history, but it is a history that also includes a legacy of successful struggle. In a poignant essay published twenty years ago, Kalamu ya Salaam explained, "I come from a people who have survived chattel slavery—the most stringent stripping away of humanity ever imaginable—and yet did not lose hope."[19] Practical work in the world grounded in improvisation enabled that hope to survive. Slaves who were forced to cut sugar cane on Louisiana plantations discovered previously untapped possibilities in the stems of the cane plants. They drilled holes in the reeds in an ordered pattern that transformed discarded stems of sugar cane into useful reed instruments capable of making music to accompany dancing at secret late night revels. The dances they did at those gatherings were themselves acts of inversion, turning the exploited work body valued by slave owners only for its labor into an expressive form of personal virtuosity on the dance floor.[20] During and after the time of slavery, quilt makers took patches of worn out garments and sacks, stitching them into patterned bed covers that served practical purposes as sources of warmth, but which also functioned as a material inventory of images recording individual and collective experiences.[21] Conjure doctors helped heal people denied access to health care by efficaciously mixing roots and herbs that transformed the toxic into the tonic.[22] This tradition cultivates talents for surprise, disguise, inversion, and improvisation. It teaches people to find value in undervalued objects, undervalued practices, and undervalued people.

Subordinated people need to create insubordinate spaces. SAC's transformation of the competitive classroom into a crucible for community follows a long tradition of Afro-diasporic place making. Jerome Smith, one of the most revered and respected figures in the Black resistance tradition of New Orleans, notes how white supremacy and segregation worked historically to deny Blacks participation in the public sphere. Yet improvisation enabled the community to turn disadvantage into advantage, to transform humiliation into honor.[23] Street parades offered opportunities for Blacks to assemble in public, to savor a sense of the collective power that came from marching, moving, playing, dancing, and singing together, to venture out onto streets in neighborhoods normally closed to them, to display their imagination, ingenuity, virtuosity, style, and skill.[24] The parade expanded the sphere of politics into the streets. People prohibited from entering the voting both could "vote" with their feet as they marched along. In subsequent years in New Orleans (as in other cities), a succession of insubordinate spaces were carved away in churches, union halls, taverns, and cultural centers. People who were exploited as workers and denied the ability to accumulate assets that appreciate in value could not pass on significant monetary inheritances to their descendants, but they have bequeathed to them a legacy of imagination, invention, and improvisation that today informs the practices of Students at the Center.

When Students at the Center classes convene, they continue this long legacy of insubordinate place making. Their use of the story circle enables them to walk in the footsteps of the Free Southern Theater, founded in 1963 at Tougaloo College in Mississippi by John O'Neal, Doris Derby, and Gilbert Moses. At the time, O'Neal and Derby were field directors of SNCC organizing drives in Jackson. O'Neal conceived of theater as a practice that could help turn negative ascription into positive affirmation. "As long as the victims of racism accept the judgments of their oppressors and rely on the approbation of that society," he argued, "they are locked in. If they do not recognize the presence of positive standards and values in the Black community then they love unwisely and will be devoured in their own flames."[25] The founders of the FST envisioned a theater that would be "free" in both senses of the word: a theater that did not charge admission to its performances, but also a theater that would be created for, from, and by Black people, free of the constraints and constrictions of "legitimate" white theater. Despite the irrepressible and ferocious theatricality of vernacular Black culture and notwithstanding the long history of efforts to stage Black-authored plays for Black audiences, African Americans have never secured control of the kinds of theater spaces and apparatuses of production that have been routinely available to whites.[26] FST's founders envisioned that this could change through the creation of theatrical forms and styles "as unique to the Negro people as the origin of blues and jazz."[27] Like blues and jazz, the new theater would use imagination, innovation, and improvisation to create theatrical events rather than mere performances. The creative act would be valorized over the created object. Plays would provoke concrete social interactions and help create new social relations. Recognizing that the theatrical texts that Black audiences needed and wanted had for the most part not yet been written, the FST sought to encourage Black playwrights by performing their works. But the group also put on other plays in new ways. They brought Samuel Beckett's *Waiting for Godot* to new performance places: to Black churches, classrooms, and meeting halls, promoting critical engagement, reflection, and discussion about its relevance to the Black community. The audience discussions that followed the performances did not have to stay centered on the plays themselves, but instead often revolved around ideas provoked by the performances that were significant to the lives of the group. After one performance of *Waiting for Godot*, for example, activist and organizer Fannie Lou Hamer commented:

> Every day we see men dressed just like these, sitting around the bars, pool halls and on the street corners waiting for something! They must be waiting for Godot. But you can't sit around waiting. Ain't nobody going to bring you nothing. You got to get up and fight for what you

want. Some people are sitting around waiting for somebody to bring in Freedom just like these men are sitting here. Waiting for Godot.[28]

As the FST turned to productions of plays by Amiri Baraka, Ossie Davis, and plays that they wrote themselves, they came to see that Black theater could provoke powerful responses. The story circle evolved out of audience discussions staged after FST performances. "Hearing is a creative act," declared John O'Neal, adding "the listening is what gives definition to the story."[29]

FST story circles followed the physical contours of that staple of Black sacred and secular culture: the ring shout.[30] Participants would sit in a circle and create a collective story as each person spoke in turn in a way that was grounded in personal experience. When not speaking, it was necessary to listen and to not interrupt the story. Each successive participant added something to the collective narrative, amplifying or elaborating on the words of the previous speaker. Once the circle had been completed, all participants engaged in cross-talk. They asked and answered questions, and discussed creative ways of representing the story to new audiences.

When the troupe moved its headquarters to New Orleans in 1966, Kalamu ya Salaam joined forces with FST Associate Director Tom Dent to create BLKARTSOUTH, a community-based acting and writing workshop that augmented the work of the FST. The story circle continued to inform the production, performance, and reception of the work of the FST, and it became a recognized and respected part of the Black resistance culture of New Orleans. It informed the original pedagogy of the Students at the Center classes as they emerged first in Frederick Douglass High School in the Ninth Ward, and persisted as they spread to other schools. An improvisational jazz aesthetic remains at the heart of this classroom practice. As ya Salaam tells the students in the classes that he and Don Randels teach, "when it's your turn to take a solo, you can't say 'Well, wait, that's not the song I wanted to play.' [No] it's *your* turn."[31]

The SAC classrooms connect students to a wider world. While clearly grounded in the Black Radical tradition, they reject any narrow racialism. They are always Black, but never only Black. Like Anna Julia Cooper who insisted that the cause of Black people was righting every as yet unredressed wrong, like Martin Luther King who declared that an injustice anywhere is an injustice everywhere, the Students at the Center embrace a world transcending citizenship. One of the instructors in SAC classes is Black and one is white. At McMain High School, SAC classes include African American and Vietnamese American students whose similar yet different experiences with the U.S. racial order provide fertile ground for productive interaction. The group of principled and dedicated New Orleans public school teachers, staff personnel, and community members working in support of SAC includes Blacks and whites. As an organization, SAC has stood side by side with Latino and Vietnamese activist groups in efforts to place student voices at the center of conversations about improving local schools.[32]

The pieces the students write in SAC classes appear in a series of books that the group has published. These texts are available online, and they circulate publicly. They provide visible and tangible evidence of the work the students have done. In a society that routinely condemns young people as unthinking sources of social problems, these books allow them to present themselves as critical thinkers and capable problem solvers. Young people whose words have been published in books acquire a new sense of responsibility to communicate with readers across lines of race, place, gender, generation, community, and class. Published writers learn to anticipate doubt and disagreement, to take care with the words that they send out into the world attached to their names. "We believe in the student as author," insists Kalamu ya Salaam, "i.e. an active thinking person who observes and questions their own existence and the whys and wherefores of the world in which the author lives."[33]

The first book by Students at the Center addressed the *New Orleans Slave Revolt of 1811*. It was followed by *Men We Love, Men We Hate*, which coalesces around competing notions of manhood and masculinity in the Black community. *The Long Ride* presents student responses to the mobilization against segregation that led to the *Plessy v. Ferguson* case, a struggle that started with an act of civil disobedience in the Ninth Ward neighborhood where many of them live. *Pedagogy, Policy and the Privatized City* intersperses student writings about "dispossession and defiance" in New Orleans with pieces by distinguished scholars that connect the students' concerns to critiques of neoliberal privatization policies. *Go to Jail* (which has not yet been published) offers a compilation of essays about the effects of the mass incarceration of Blacks in Louisiana on the students' lives. Each of these books is a kind of story circle, a chorus of many voices, a crossroads for different perceptions and perspectives.

In SAC books, and in the student activism in social movements that they reflect and shape, young people become public observers and public actors. They come to see themselves as citizens rather than spectators. Their classroom exercises are not merely rehearsals for future roles, but instead activities that have current consequences. SAC connects ideas to actions by encouraging students to participate in social change organizations. *Go to Jail* delineates this work brilliantly, detailing student involvement with the Innocence Project and other organized efforts to free wrongly convicted inmates.

The conversation among students and scholars in *Pedagogy, Policy and the Privatized City* makes an especially important and timely political intervention because New Orleans has become a laboratory for neoliberal assaults on public education. In the wake of the destruction that accompanied Hurricane Katrina in 2005, the state of Louisiana and the federal government joined forces to fire 7,500 school employees (most of whom were Black union members), to close many public schools, to subsidize the opening of new private charter schools, and to replace responsibility for public education by local residents in New Orleans with control wielded by state officials and private entrepreneurs. These changes are consistent with nationwide trends. In cities across the country, public funds subsidize private education entrepreneurs. A two-tiered public education system creates privileged access to well-funded and well-equipped schools for whites while relegating nonwhite students to underfunded and ill-equipped schools of last resort. In New Orleans, these changes led to the closing of Frederick Douglass High School in the Ninth Ward, which at the time was a key site for SAC classes, a school where the classroom could be connected easily with the nearby community. Today, SAC classes take place only in McMain High School and McDonogh #35, but it remains to be seen how long they will be allowed to continue. Aware of the always precarious institutional status of the program in a school system that is now largely run by and for outside educational entrepreneurs, ya Salaam argues that SAC's uncertain future makes its present activities all that much more important. "We have to tell the story," he explains. "I don't believe we're gonna win this one. I really do not believe we're going to win this one. But I believe the story is important. We have to tell our story."[34] He explains that if W.E.B. Du Bois had not researched and written down what happened to Black people in the reconstruction era between 1863 and 1880, we would not be able today to draw on the legacy of self-activity that he documented. Similarly, even if white supremacy and neoliberalism triumph in present-day New Orleans, SAC's writings will preserve the testimony of eyewitnesses for future generations.[35]

The improvisational pedagogy of Students at the Center has deep roots in the Black Resistance Culture of New Orleans. Its tools and techniques testify to a long lineage of art-based community making by generations of quilters and conjurors, singers and sculptors, poets and painters, and dancers and dramatists. These artists were members of oppressed communities and they often had every reason to lose hope, to give in to despair. Yet the traditions of their West African ancestors taught them that every problem has a solution, that if they were not given freedom they had to conjure it and create it. Working with the tools available to them in the arenas that were open to them, they treated as sacred any crossroads where paths collided, where decisions had to be made. In the words of a famous Funkadelic song, they realized that the linked fate that brought them so much suffering also made them "one nation under a groove" equipped with the chance to dance away from all constrictions.[36] Improvisation enabled inversion. As Nicole Mitchell, president of the Association for the Advancement of Creative Musicians explained in response to a poem written about her by Kalamu ya Salaam, improvisation "is a practice that allows you not to be focused on the smallness of who you are and your reality, but to actually experience the greatness of possibility and surprise and spontaneity."[37]

Yet while rooted in the Black Radical Tradition, the work of SAC envisions and enacts a kind of public humanities work of importance to everyone. Doris Sommer argues that because "aesthetic experience rekindles love for a world gone gray from habit" public humanities projects cultivate popular capacities for democratic and egalitarian social relations.[38] Through story circles and other improvisation-based pedagogies, people learn empathy and appreciation, discernment and judgment, consideration and co-creation. Students at the Center engages students in a process that transforms them from subjects of power into powerful subjects. The processes set in motion by these classes turn spectators into witnesses, and invite bystanders to become upstanders.[39] In SAC classes, students see that there is important work to be done in the world and that improvisation is an important way to do it.

Notes

1. Moten, *In the Break*, 63.
2. Small, *Musicking*, 8.
3. Bernice Johnson Reagon, qtd. in Jones, *Wade in the Water*, 22.
4. The phrase decorating the way to other worlds appears in Thompson, *Flash of the Spirit*, 158.
5. Small, *Musicking*, 19.
6. Johnny Otis, *Upside Your Head!*, 117.
7. Malcolm X, "Speech at the Founding Rally," 63–64.
8. Sommer, *The Work of Art*, 112.
9. Ibid., 113.
10. Author's notes from Students at the Center classes at McMain High School and McDonogh #35 High School, March 24, 2014, New Orleans, Louisiana.
11. Quoted in DeCuir, "Placing Social Justice," 171.
12. Kelly, "Resistance," 48.
13. Ibid., 50.
14. Sommer, *The Work of Art*, 104.
15. Harding, "Responsibilities," 281. The limits of "dark faces in high places" were explored in the 1940s by Charlotte Bass.
16. Salaam, "We Stand by Our Students," 66.
17. Kalamu ya Salaam, qtd. in Woods et al., "Poetic Visions."
18. Rodriguez and Minaya, "New Orleans' Racial Makeup," 1.
19. Salaam, *What is Life*, 71.
20. Camp, *Closer to Freedom*, 73–74.
21. Turner, *Crafted Lives*.
22. Smith, *Conjuring Culture*; Thompson, *Flash of the Spirit*.
23. Michna, "Stories at the Center," 547.
24. Brothers, *Louis Armstrong's New Orleans*, 17.
25. O'Neal, "Some Political Dimensions," 73.
26. See Nathan Irvin Huggins, *Harlem Renaissance* and Paula Seniors, *Beyond Lift Every Voice and Sing*.
27. John O'Neal, Doris Derby, and Gilbert Moses, qtd. in Amistad Research Center, "Free Southern Theater."

28. O'Neal, "Some Political Dimensions," 76.
29. Michna, "Stories at the Center," 539.
30. Stuckey, *Slave Culture*.
31. Michna "Stories at the Center," 550.
32. Vietnamese American Young Leaders of New Orleans, *Raise Your Hand Campaign*, available online at http://thelensnola.org/wp-content/uploads/2011/09/vayla-report.pdf.
33. Salaam, "The Student Learns," 64.
34. Buras, "'We Have to Tell Our Story,'" 39.
35. Author's conversation with ya Salaam, March 24, 2014. New Orleans, Louisiana.
36. Funkadelic, "One Nation."
37. Fischlin, Heble, and Lipsitz, *The Fierce Urgency of Now*, 37.
38. Sommer, *The Work of Art*, 89.
39. Thanks to the organization Facing History and Ourselves for the phrase and the idea of turning bystanders into upstanders.

Works Cited

Amistad Research Center. "Free Southern Theatre (1963–1978)." http://www.amistadresearchcenter.org/archon/?p=creators/creator&id=109.

Brothers, Thomas. *Louis Armstrong's New Orleans*. New York: W.W. Norton, 2007.

Buras, Kristen L. "'We Have to Tell Our Story': Neo-Griots, Schooling, and the Legacy of Racial Resistance in the Other South." In *Pedagogy, Policy, and the Privatized City: Stories of Dispossession and Defiance from New Orleans*, edited by Kristen L. Buras with Jim Randels, Kalamu ya Salaam, and Students at the Center, 17–45. New York: Teachers College Press, 2010.

Camp, Stephanie M. H. *Closer to Freedom: Enslaved Women and Everyday Resistance in the Plantation South*. Chapel Hill: University of North Carolina Press, 2004.

DeCuir, Erica. "Placing Social Justice at the Center of Standards-Based Reform: Race and Social Studies at McDonogh #35 Senior High, New Orleans, 1980–2000." In *Histories of Social Studies and Race: 1865–2000*, edited by Christie Woyshner and Chara Haeussler Bohan, 159–78. Basingstoke, UK: Palgrave, 2012.

Fischlin, Daniel, Ajay Heble, and George Lipsitz. *The Fierce Urgency of Now: Improvisation, Rights, and the Ethics of Cocreation*. Durham, NC: Duke University Press, 2013.

Funkadelic. "One Nation, Under a Groove." *One Nation, Under a Groove*. Warner Bros. Records, 1978.

Harding, Vincent. "Responsibilities of the Black Scholar to the Community." In *The State of Afro-American History: Past, Present, and Future*, edited by Darlene Clark Hine, 277–84. Baton Rouge: Louisiana State University Press, 1986.

Huggins, Nathan Irvin. *Harlem Renaissance*. New York: Oxford University Press, 2007.

Jones, Arthur. *Wade in the Water: The Wisdom of the Spirituals*. Maryknoll, NY: Orbis Books, 1993.

Kelly, Adrinda. "Resistance." In *The Long Ride: A Collection of Student Writings Based on the Events That Are Part of the Long Struggle for Civil Rights and Social Justice in New Orleans*, 2nd ed, 48–50. New Orleans: Students at the Center, 2013.

Malcolm X. "Speech at the Founding Rally of the Organization of Afro-American Unity." In *By Any Means Necessary: Speeches, Interviews, and a Letter by Malcolm X*, 33–67. New York: Pathfinder Press, 1992.

Michna, Catherine. "Stories at the Center: Story Circles, Educational Organizing, and Fate of Neighbourhood Public Schools in New Orleans." *American Quarterly* 61, no. 3 (2009): 529–55.

Moten, Fred. *In the Break: The Aesthetics of the Black Radical Tradition.* Minneapolis: University of Minnesota Press, 2003.

O'Neal, John. "Some Political Dimensions of the Free Southern Theater." *The Drama Review* 12, no. 4 (Summer 1968): 70–77.

Otis, Johnny. *Upside Your Head! Rhythm and Blues on Central Avenue.* London: Wesleyan/University Press of New England, 1993.

Rodriguez, Lori, and Zeke Minaya. "New Orleans' Racial Makeup in the Air." *Houston Chronicle.* September 29, 2005.

Salaam, Kalamu ya. "The Student Learns, The Student Teaches." In *The Long Ride: A Collection of Student Writings Based on the Events That Are Part of the Long Struggle for Civil Rights and Social Justice in New Orleans*, 64–65. New Orleans: Students at the Center, 2013.

———. "We Stand By Our Students." In *Pedagogy, Policy, and the Privatized City: Stories of Dispossession and Defiance from New Orleans*, edited by Kristen L. Buras with Jim Randels, Kalamu ya Salaam, and Students at the Center, 65–72. New York: Teachers College Press, 2010.

———. *What is Life? Reclaiming the Black Blues Self.* Chicago: Third World Press, 1994.

Seniors, Paula. *Beyond Lift Every Voice and Sing: The Culture of Uplift, Identity and Politics in Black Musical Theater.* Columbus: Ohio State University Press, 2009.

Small, Christopher. *Musicking: The Meanings of Performing and Listening.* London: Wesleyan University Press, 1998.

Smith, Theophus. *Conjuring Culture: Biblical Formations of Black America.* New York: Oxford University Press, 1995.

Sommer, Doris. *The Work of Art in the World: Civic Agency and Public Humanities.* Durham, NC: Duke University Press, 2014.

Stuckey, Sterling. *Slave Culture: Nationalist Theory and the Foundations of Black America.* New York: Oxford University Press, 1987.

Thompson, Robert Farris. *Flash of the Spirit: African & African American Art and Philosophy.* New York: Vintage, 1984.

Turner, Patricia A. *Crafted Lives: Stories and Studies of African American Quilters.* Jackson: University Press of Mississippi, 2009.

Vietnamese American Young Leaders Association of New Orleans (VAYLA-NO). *Raise Your Hand Campaign: Full Report.* New Orleans, LA: Vietnamese American Young Leaders Association of New Orleans, 2011.

Woods, Clyde (Chair), Jordan Thomas Camp, Shana Griffin, Brenda Marie Osbey, and Kalamu ya Salaam. "Poetic Visions in the Wake of Katrina." Panel discussion at the American Studies Association Annual Meeting. Washington, DC. November 5, 2009.

List of Contributors

David Ake, Professor and Chair of the Department of Musicology at the University of Miami's Frost School of Music, is an award-winning scholar and educator in the fields of jazz and popular music. His publications include the books *Jazz Cultures; Jazz Matters: Sound, Place, and Time since Bebop*; and the collection *Jazz/Not Jazz: The Music and Its Boundaries* (coedited with Charles Hiroshi Garrett and Daniel Goldmark), all for the University of California Press, as well as chapters or articles in the *Cambridge Companion to Jazz, American Music, Jazz Perspectives*, and other publications. Also active as a jazz pianist and composer, his most recent recordings as a leader are *Bridges,* which appeared on multiple Best-of-2013 lists, and *Lake Effect* (2015), both for the Posi-Tone label. Prior to joining the Frost School, Ake chaired the Department of Music at Case Western Reserve University, and was a long-time faculty member at the University of Nevada, Reno, where he served as director of the School of the Arts, as well as held other leadership positions.

Parmela Attariwala, violinist, composer, and ethnomusicologist has been active in genre-bending music and performance since moving to Toronto in 1994. She has toured and recorded with an array of musicians that includes Carla Bley, Ravi Naimpally, James Campbell, Anthony Braxton, Ernst Reijseger, and John Taylor. She has also worked extensively—as composer, musician, and movement artist—with choreographers from a range of disciplines including contact, butoh, and bharata-natyam. In addition to specializing in the performance of contemporary composed music, Attariwala is an ardent improviser and proponent of improvisational pedagogy as a tool for cross-genre musical communication. In 1995, Attariwala created the Attar Project as a vehicle to integrate the eclectic strands of her own musical background and to engage artists across musical genres and artistic practices in virtuosic collaborations that maintain the essence of each while challenging the boundaries between them. She has released three critically acclaimed Attar Project recordings. Attariwala received her formal violin training at Indiana University and the Bern Conservatory in Switzerland. She holds a master's degree in Ethnomusicology from SOAS (focusing on the history and performance of medieval North Indian devotional poetry and song), and completed her

PhD at the University of Toronto. Her doctoral work concerns the effects of official multiculturalism on contemporary Canadian music making, with a particular focus on public policy, arts funding, identity politics, notions of culture within multiculturalism, and conflicting definitions of authenticity.

Vincent P. Benitez is an Associate Professor of Music at the Pennsylvania State University. He holds a PhD in music theory from Indiana University and the DMA degree in organ performance from Arizona State University. Benitez is the author of *Olivier Messiaen: A Research and Information Guide* (Routledge). He has published articles on Messiaen in *Music Analysis, Messiaen the Theologian* (Ashgate*), the Dutch Journal of Music Theory, the Journal of Musicological Research, the Poznan Studies on Opera, Music Theory Online*, and *the College Music Symposium*, as well as reviews of books devoted to Messiaen in *Music Theory Spectrum, Performance Practice Review, NOTES*, and *the Indiana Theory Review*. Benitez has additional research interests in the analysis of Baroque music, the history of music theory, and popular music, with published articles and reviews on these topics in *The American Organist, BACH, Diapason, GAMUT, Indiana Theory Review*, and *the Rivista di Analisi e Teoria Musicale*. He is also the author of *The Words and Music of Paul McCartney: The Solo Years* (Praeger) and book chapters on *Ram* and *Band on the Run* in Praeger Publishers's four-volume series entitled *The Album.*

Jane Bunnett has turned her bands into showcases for the finest talent from Canada, the United States, and Cuba. She has been nominated for Grammy Awards, received numerous Juno Awards, and most recently, was honored with an appointment to the Order of Canada. An internationally acclaimed musician, Jane Bunnett is known for her creative integrity, improvisational daring, and courageous artistry. Her exploration of Afro-Cuban melodies expresses the universality of music, and her ability to embrace and showcase the rhythms and culture of Cuba has been groundbreaking. She has toured the world bringing her own special sound to numerous jazz festivals, displaying her versatility as a flutist, saxophone player, and composer. As an educator, spokesperson, and social activist, she remains unafraid to explore uncharted territory in her quest for excellence. In 2011, she was the inaugural Improviser-in-Residence with the Improvisation, Community, and Social Practice project at the University of Guelph.

Mark V. Campbell is a Banting Postdoctoral Fellow at the University of Regina investigating the impact of digital hip-hop programming among racialized young people in Canada. As a DJ and educator, Mark's research interests include afrosonic theory, hip-hop cultures in Canada, digital archiving, critical digital pedagogies, and DJ cultures. Mark's recent publications appear in the *Southern Journal of Canadian Studies, Antipode Online*, and the *Journal of the Canadian Association for*

Curriculum Studies. Mark's passions lie in both research and community development, and he is the founder of the Northsidehiphop.ca, an archive of Canadian hip-hop.

Patricia Shehan Campbell is Donald E. Peterson Professor of Music at the University of Washington, where she teaches courses at the interface of education and ethnomusicology. She is the author of *Songs in Their Heads* (1998; 2010, second edition); *Musician and Teacher: Orientation to Music Education* (2008); *Tunes and Grooves in Music Education* (2008); *Teaching Music Globally* (2004); coeditor with Bonnie Wade, of Oxford's *Global Music Series, Lessons from the World* (1991/2001); *Music in Cultural Context* (1996); coauthor of *Music in Childhood* (2013, 4th edition) and *Free to Be Musical: Group Improvisation in Music* (2010); and coeditor of the *Oxford Handbook on Children's Musical Cultures* (2013). She has lectured on the pedagogy of world music and children's musical culture throughout the United States, in much of Europe and Asia, in Australia, New Zealand, South America, and South Africa. Her training includes Dalcroze Eurhythmics, piano and vocal performance, and specialized study in Bulgarian choral song, Indian (Karnatic) vocal repertoire, and Thai mahori. Campbell serves as advisory board chair for Smithsonian Folkways, and is a consultant and an active player in the repatriation of Lomax recordings to families of musicians in the southern United States.

Scott Currie's ethnomusicological research to date has focused on participant-observer studies of avant-garde jazz practice in New York City and Berlin, as well as historical/ethnographic studies of Ornette Coleman's collaborations with the Master Musicians of Jajouka, Morocco. He has received grants from the German Marshall Fund, the German Academic Exchange Service (DAAD), and New York University, and published articles and reviews in the *Glendora Review, Ethnomusicology, Jazz Research Journal*, and *Studies in Symbolic Interaction*. A charter member of the Creative Studies faculty at the University of Minnesota School of Music, he has taught courses in cross-cultural improvisation, world music, American music, African American music, Afro-Caribbean music, Afropop, jazz, and rock. In addition, he has served as associate director of New York City's Vision Festival, founded the Sound Vision Orchestra, and performed on saxophones with such artists as Cecil Taylor, Bill Dixon, Alan Silva, Marty Ehrlich, J. D. Parran, and the Other Dimensions in Music collective.

David Dove, a trombone player, composer, improviser, and educator, has given performances and facilitated workshops across North America and internationally. As founding director of Nameless Sound (a nonprofit organization in Houston, Texas), he curates a concert series of international contemporary creative music, and has developed an approach, philosophy, and practice of music workshops based on creativity and improvisation. In more than fifteen weekly sessions led by a staff of artist-facilitators, Nameless Sound reaches over 1,500 young people every year in Houston public schools, community centers, homeless shelters, and refugee communities. Nameless Sound's Youth Ensemble has been the breeding ground for a generation of creative musicians from Houston, many of whom are gaining national and international recognition for their own work. Dove's early musical background ranged from studies in jazz and symphonic music, to punk rock bands. Free improvisation has been his primary (but not exclusive) approach to performance and collaboration.

Massimiliano Guido is a Lecturer at the Musicology Department of Pavia University, Italy, and has previously been a Banting Postdoctoral Fellow at McGill University. His research focuses on improvisation and counterpoint at the keyboard. He has published articles and organized international conferences on this subject.

Ajay Heble is Director of the International Institute for Critical Studies in Improvisation, and Professor of English in the School of English and Theatre Studies at the University of Guelph. He is the author or editor of several books, and a founding coeditor of the journal *Critical Studies in Improvisation/Études critiques en improvisation* (http://www. criticalimprov.com). He is also Project Director for Improvisation, Community, and Social Practice (ICASP), a large-scale Major Collaborative Research Initiative, funded by the Social Sciences and Humanities Research Council of Canada. As the Founder and Artistic Director of the Guelph Jazz Festival, Heble has jolted the citizens of Guelph into an appreciation of improvised and avant-garde music and delighted aficionados from around the world with his innovative and daring programming. Under his visionary leadership, the Festival—winner of the prestigious Premier's Award for Excellence in the Arts (2010), and a three-time recipient of the Lieutenant Governor's Award of the Arts (1997, 2000, 2001)—has achieved a rock-solid international reputation as one of the world's most inspired and provocative musical events. Recent projects include *The Improvisation Studies Reader: Spontaneous Acts* (coedited with Rebecca Caines and published by Routledge). As a pianist, he has released four CDs: *Different Windows*, a live recording of improvised music with percussionist Jesse Stewart (on the Intrepid Ear label) and three recordings with his improvising quartet The Vertical Squirrels: *Hold True/Accroche-toi* and *Time of the Sign* (both on Ambiances Magnétiques) and *Winter's Gate* (on Barcode Free).

Tanya Kalmanovitch is a musician, writer, and ethnomusicologist based in New York City. Trained at the Juilliard School, her work as a violist bridges classical, jazz, and experimental improvised music and has been profiled in *Jazz Times, Down Beat, the Globe and Mail,* and the *New York Times.* She performs and teaches regularly in North America,

Europe, the Middle East, and Central Asia, and is a faculty member at the New England Conservatory in Boston and Mannes College The New School for Music in New York. Kalmanovitch's research in theoretical psychology and ethnomusicology has explored the history of science, postcolonial identities, and musical globalization, and has been published in *The American Psychologist, World of Music,* and *New Sound.* She is currently working on a book examining the role of music and the professional musician in contemporary societies scored by war, religious extremism, and economic crisis.

Kathryn Ladano is a specialist in contemporary music and free improvisation and has performed as a soloist and chamber musician across Canada and abroad on the bass clarinet. Heavily involved in both educational and creative work, Ladano is currently the artistic director of NUMUS concerts, the director of ICE (Improvisation Concerts Ensemble) and Improvisation Studio instructor at Wilfrid Laurier University, and professor of bass clarinet performance at the University of Waterloo. She is currently pursuing her PhD at York University in Toronto under the direction of Casey Sokol, and her research interests include improvisation pedagogy, and the relationship between different types of anxieties and the practice of free improvisation.

Mark Laver, ethnomusicologist and saxophonist, is an Assistant Professor of Music at Grinnell College and a research associate with the International Institute for Critical Studies in Improvisation. His current research focuses on the intersections between jazz, improvisation, and neoliberal capitalism. His first book, *Jazz Sells: Music, Marketing, and Meaning* (Routledge), explores the use of jazz music in advertising, marketing, and branding. Other work has been published in *Popular Music and Society, Popular Music, Black Music Research Journal,* and *Critical Studies in Improvisation/Études critiques en improvisation.* Laver is also a busy saxophonist who has performed with Lee Konitz, William Parker, Eddie Prévost, and Dong-Won Kim, among many other leading international artists.

George Lipsitz is Professor of Black Studies and Sociology at the University of California, Santa Barbara. His publications include *The Fierce Urgency of Now: Improvisation, Rights, and the Ethics of Cocreation* (coauthored with Daniel Fischlin and Ajay Heble); *How Racism Takes Place;* and *Midnight at the Barrelhouse: The Johnny Otis Story.* He serves as President of the Board of Directors of the African American Policy Forum and chairs the Advisory Board of the University of California, Santa Barbara Center for Black Studies Research, which is an institutional partner of the International Institute for Critical Studies in Improvisation.

William Parker is a master musician, improviser, and composer. He plays the bass, shakuhachi, double reeds, tuba, donsongoni, and gembri. He was born in 1952 in the Bronx, New York. He studied bass with Richard Davis, Art Davis, Milt Hinton, Wilber Ware, and Jimmy Garrison. He entered the music scene in 1971 playing at Studio We, Studio Rivbea, Hilly's on The Bowery, and The Baby Grand, playing with many avant-garde musicians such as Bill Dixon, Sunny Murray, Charles Tyler, Billy Higgins, Charles Brackeen, Alan Silva, Frank Wright, Frank Lowe, Rashied Ali, Donald Ayler, Don Cherry, Cecil Taylor, Jimmy Lyons, Milford Graves, Roscoe Mitchell, Anthony Braxton, David S. Ware, Matthew Shipp, and with traditionalists like Walter Bishop, Sr., and Maxine Sullivan. Early projects with dancer and choreographer Patricia Nicholson created a huge repertoire of composed music for multiple ensembles ranging from solo works to big band projects. Parker played in the Cecil Taylor unit from 1980 through 1991. He also developed a strong relationship with the European Improvised Music scene playing with musicians such as Peter Kowald, Peter Brotzmann, Han Bennink, Tony Oxley, Derek Bailey, Louis Sclavis, and Louis Moholo. He began recording in 1994 and leading his own bands on a regular basis founding two ensembles, In Order To Survive, and The Little Huey Creative Music Orchestra. In 2001, Parker released *O'Neal's Porch*, which marked a turn toward a more universal sound, working with drummer Hamid Drake. The Raining on the Moon Quintet followed, adding vocalist Leena Conquest and the Quartet from *O'Neal's Porch*. Most notable among many recent projects is *The Inside Songs of Curtis Mayfield* and *The Essence of Ellington*. He has taught at Bennington College, New York University, The New England Conservatory of Music, Cal Arts, The New School, and Rotterdam Conservatory of Music. He has also taught music workshops throughout the world including in Paris, Berlin, and Tokyo, and the Lower East Side. Parker is also a theorist and author of several books including the *Sound Journal, Document Humanum, Music and the Shadow People, The Mayor of Punkville, Voices In the Third Person, Conversations* (Vols. 1 and 2), and *Who Owns Music?* He is also coeditor of *Giving Birth to Sound: Women in Creative Music.*

Peter Schubert teaches theory at McGill University. He has published textbooks on counterpoint, videos on improvisation, and articles on Renaissance music. He conducts VivaVoce, a professional vocal ensemble in Montreal.

Gabriel Solis is Professor of Music, African American Studies, and Anthropology at the University of Illinois, Urbana-Champaign. He is a scholar of jazz, blues, rock, and pop and of music in Australia and highland Papua New Guinea. He is the author of *Monk's Music: Thelonious Monk and Jazz History in the Making* (California) and *Thelonious Monk Quartet with John Coltrane at Carnegie Hall* (Oxford); coeditor with Bruno Nettl of *Musical Improvisation: Art, Education, and Society* (Illinois); and his articles have appeared in *The Musical Quarterly, Ethnomusicology,*

Journal of Popular Music Studies, Popular Music and Society, and *Critical Sociology,* among others.

Howard Spring is an ethnomusicologist, jazz historian, and jazz guitarist who teaches at the University of Guelph. He has published on the improvisational style of jazz guitarist Charlie Christian, the beginning of Swing, the relationship between jazz and social dance, and swing as a performance practice. He has also performed as a jazz guitarist in various clubs in the Toronto area.

Jesse Stewart is an award-winning percussionist, composer, researcher, visual artist, and educator. His music has been performed at festivals throughout Canada, the United States, and Europe. He has collaborated with such diverse musical luminaries as Pauline Oliveros, William Parker, David Mott, Hamid Drake, Ernst Reijseger, and many others. In 2012, his trio known as Stretch Orchestra (with Matt Brubeck and Kevin Breit) was honored with a Juno award for "Instrumental Album of the Year." His writings on jazz, improvisation, hip-hop, experimental music, and music pedagogy have appeared in numerous anthologies and in journals including *American Music, Black Music Research Journal, Interdisciplinary Humanities, Contemporary Music Review,* and many others. He is a Coinvestigator with the Improvisation, Community and Social Practice Project (ICASP) and the International Institute for Critical Studies in Improvisation (IICSI), both of which received seven-year, $2.5 million SSHRC grants in 2007 and 2014, respectively. He is an Associate Professor in the School for Studies in Art and Culture at Carleton University in Ottawa and an Adjunct Faculty member in the Visual Art department at the University of Ottawa. In 2014, he was named to the Order of Ottawa, one of the city's highest civic honors.

Chris Stover is an Assistant Professor at The New School, where he teaches Music Theory, Composition, and World Music and coordinates the Music Theory curriculum. He received his PhD in Music Theory and DMA in Trombone Performance from the University of Washington, and holds an MA in Music Theory from the Eastman School of Music. His work has been published by *Analytical Approaches to World Music, Journal of Jazz Studies, Journal of Music Theory Pedagogy, Latin American Music Review, Music Theory Online, Music Theory Spectrum, The Open Space Magazine,* and more, including in edited volumes for Cambridge Scholars Press and Praeger Press. Chris is an editor for the online journal *Analytical Approaches to World Music,* is on the editorial board for *Music Theory Online* and *Kronoscope,* and formerly served as managing editor of *Perspectives of New Music.* In 2015 he spent four months as a Fulbright fellow in Brazil, studying improvisation and micro-rhythmic processes in Afro-Brazilian music. He is also highly active as performer and composer in New York City and internationally.

Matt Swanson is a doctoral candidate in Music Education at the University of Washington, and teaches general music at University Child Development School. His research interests include musical creativity and song-writing, syncopation and groove, world music pedagogy, and musical identity. His current dissertation research is focusing on the process of group composition at the elementary level. A multi-instrumentalist, he has performed extensively with a number of groups, in genres ranging from bluegrass to Indian electronica. He holds an MA in curriculum and instruction from the University of Washington.

Index